THE INTERTEXTUAL JESUS

THE INTERTEXTUAL JESUS

Scripture in Q

DALE C. ALLISON, JR.

TRINITY PRESS INTERNATIONAL
Harrisburg, Pennsylvania

Unless otherwise indicated biblical quotations are usually from the New Revised Standard Version Bible copyright © 1989, Division of Christian Education of the National Council of Churches of Christ in the United States of America.

Trinity Press International, P.O. Box 1321, Harrisburg, PA 17105
Trinity Press International is a division of the Morehouse Group.

Cover design: Trude Brummer

Library of Congress Cataloging-in-Publication Data
Allison, Dale C.
    The intertextual Jesus : scripture in Q / Dale C. Allison, Jr.
        p. cm.
    Includes bibliographical references and indexes.
    ISBN 1-56338-329-2 (pbk. : alk. paper)
    1. Intertextuality in the Bible. 2. Q hypothesis (Synoptics criticism) 3. Bible.
N.T. – Relation to the Old Testament.   I. Title.
    BS1171.2 .A44 2000
    226'.066 – dc21
                                                                        00-030281

Printed in the United States of America

00   01   02   03   04   05   06   10   9   8   7   6   5   4   3   2   1

For Andrew William

ὁ υἱός μου ὁ ἀγαπητός, ἐν ᾧ εὐδόκησα

Contents

Preface

All texts depend upon and interact with preceding texts. It follows that Q, the hypothetical document used by Matthew and Luke,[1] must likewise depend upon and interact with preceding texts. The present investigation undertakes to unfold some of the ways in which this is so.

The term "intertextuality" is now often associated with this sort of undertaking. But different writers use the word differently.[2] In its broadest sense, "intertextuality" refers to all of the potential relationships between texts. The present work, however, concerns itself primarily with only one species of intertextuality, namely, deliberate literary borrowing, the sort of borrowing that a text encourages its audience to discover, and recognition of which enlarges meaning.[3] The focus, then, is upon Q's marked and unmarked quotations, its explicit references to predecessor texts, and its allusions.[4]

Because different writers also give different senses to "quotation," "reference," and "allusion," a few preliminary definitions are in order. Herein

---

1. For reasons that the hypothesis of Q deservedly enjoys the confidence of so many, see Charles E. Carlston and D. Norlan, "Once More — Statistics and Q," *HTR* 64 (1971), pp. 59–78; Joseph A. Fitzmyer, "The Priority of Mark and the 'Q' Source in Luke," in *To Advance the Gospel: New Testament Studies* (New York: Crossroad, 1981), pp. 3–40; David R. Catchpole, *The Quest for Q* (Edinburgh: T. & T. Clark, 1993), pp. 1–59; Christopher M. Tuckett, *Q and the History of Early Christianity: Studies on Q* (Edinburgh: T. & T. Clark, 1996), pp. 1–39; and Petros Vassiliadis, ΛΟΓΟΙ ΙΗΣΟΥ: *Studies in Q* (Atlanta: Scholars Press, 1999), pp. 1–38.

2. For a helpful overview, see Thaïs E. Morgan, "Is There an Intertext in This Text? Literary and Interdisciplinary Approaches to Intertextuality," *American Journal of Semiotics* 3/4 (1985), pp. 1–40.

3. Many use "intertextuality," understood as a synchronic concept, only within a post-structuralist framework and contrast it with "influence," a diachronic concept. See T. R. Hatina, "Intertextuality and Historical Criticism in New Testament Studies: Is There a Relationship?," *BibInt* 7 (1999), pp. 28–43. Although he himself regards influence and intertextuality as "mutually antagonistic," Hatina reviews the opinions of many who think otherwise and would happily classify influence as one type of intertextuality, as I have done. Note that Gérard Genette, *Palimpsests: Literature in the Second Degree* (Lincoln/London: University of Nebraska Press, 1997), even offers a definition of "intertextuality" that is exhausted by quotation, plagiarism, and allusion.

4. Herein I shall ignore the important issue of indirect scriptural influence, such as how Q might depend upon Jewish moral teaching that was inspired by Scripture. Q studies would no doubt profit by the sort of work Roy E. Ciampa has done on Galatians 1–2: *The Presence and Function of Scripture in Galatians 1 and 2* (WUNT 2/102; Tübingen: Mohr Siebeck, 1998). On p. 34 Ciampa explains that he is interested not only in scriptural citations, allusions, and echoes but also in "the scriptural background behind the words, concepts, idioms, topics, structures and concerns" of Galatians.

a "quotation" is taken to be the reproduction of several consecutive words from another text. A quotation is "marked" if acknowledgment of this circumstance is made (as in Q 4:4, which introduces part of Deut 8:3 with γέγραπται, "it is written"); it is unmarked if such an acknowledgment is not made (as in Q 12:51–53, which loosely quotes Mic 7:6 without saying so). An "explicit reference," by contrast, directs individuals to a text in their portable mental library, not by quoting from it, but by mentioning it or some episode in it outright. (Q 11:31 explicitly refers to 1 Kgs 10:1–13 = 2 Chr 9:1–12 by speaking of "the queen of the South" who "came from the ends of the earth to listen to the wisdom of Solomon"). An "allusion" exists when one text shares enough with another text, even without reproducing several consecutive words from it, to establish the latter as a subtext to which an audience is being implicitly directed. (For instance, Jesus' declaration in Q 11:20, "If I by the finger of God cast out demons, the kingdom of God has come upon you," evokes Exod 8:19, where Moses' miracles move the Egyptian magicians to exclaim: "This is the finger of God.") An allusion is a metamorphosis which, in Seneca's words, "stamps its own form upon all the features which it has drawn from what we may call the original" (*Ep.* 84.8–9): it dismantles a subtext, retains and/or reconfigures a few of its pieces, and then gives them a new home; but enough of the original remains so that one can, in accord with the text's telos, recognize what has happened. Because allusion shades insensibly into quotation, the differentiation between the two is, admittedly, not always distinct, but then we find "yellow" and "green" serviceable even though they too insensibly shade into each other.

I write as a historian. My chief goal is to recover some of the ways in which a Jewish Christian audience of the first century, an audience for whom the Jewish Scriptures were the authoritative code for deciphering religious meaning, might have related Q to that code. My hope, moreover, is that I am recovering ways in which the Sayings Source was designed by its contributors to function. If I am instead drawing lines between texts that were never drawn by those contributors and their real audiences, then in my own mind I have labored in vain. I am in this book trying, as a good detective, to recognize connections, not invent them. Creating new connections is certainly needful for homileticians, theologians, and all of us who aspire to apply ancient texts to contemporary life, but I am not seeking to do such within the covers of the present book.

I trust that those who regard the Q hypothesis as a doubtsome matter or even beset with insuperable difficulties may yet find my tracing the threads of allusion profitable. For the reconstructed Q is made up exclusively of bricks from Matthew and Luke, and this means that allusions in the Sayings Source must appear also in those canonical descendants, which should accordingly be illuminated by an exploration of Q's intertextuality.

It remains to thank my wife, Kristine Allison, John Burgess, my colleague at Pittsburgh Theological Seminary, W. D. Davies, Professor Emeritus of Duke University, Amy-Jill Levine of Vanderbilt (who suggested the title), and Michael Neth of Middle Tennessee State University for kindly commenting on portions of the manuscript, as well as Joel Marcus of Boston University, who carefully read through its entirety.

Chapter 1

Allusions and Aural Memories

Martin Luther King's famous "I Have a Dream" speech greatly enlarges its meaning through tacit references to famous predecessors. It opens with "Five score years ago," a manifest allusion to Abraham Lincoln's first words in his Gettysburg Address ("Four score and seven years ago"). There follow numerous examples of unacknowledged but obvious borrowing, among which are these:

- "This sweltering summer of the Negro's legitimate discontent will not pass until there is an invigorating autumn of freedom and equality" echoes "Now is the winter of our discontent made glorious summer by the son of York," the opening line from Shakespeare's *Richard III* (I.1.i–ii);

- "No, we are not satisfied, and we will not be satisfied until justice rolls down like waters and righteousness like a mighty stream" draws upon Amos 5:24;

- "It is a dream deeply rooted in the American dream that one day this nation will rise up and live out the true meaning of its creed — we hold these truths to be self-evident, that all men are created equal" contains a quotation from the Declaration of Independence;

- "I have a dream that one day every valley shall be exalted, every hill and mountain shall be made low, the rough places shall be made plain, and the crooked places shall be made straight and the glory of the Lord will be revealed and all flesh shall see it together" borrows from Isa 40:4–5;

- "So let freedom ring from the prodigious hilltops of New Hampshire. Let freedom ring from the mighty mountains of New York. Let freedom ring from the heightening Alleghenies of Pennsylvania" takes up the language of the old Protestant hymn composed by Samuel Francis Smith "My Country, 'Tis of Thee" ("America").

King's transformation of traditional texts was much more than ornamentation: it was rather a studied means of persuading hearts and minds. His echo of the Gettysburg Address was a way of claiming that his cause was the completion of what Lincoln began. When King alluded to Shakespeare, he was telling the whites in his audience: You cannot ignore me, I know your European tradition as well as you do. When he quoted from the Bible, an authority for both the white and African American communities, he was in effect asserting: God is on my side. And King's embedded quotations

1

from the Declaration of Independence and from Smith's nationalistic hymn announced that he was a patriot — some had slandered him for not being such — whose dream for his people in particular was the fulfillment of the American dream in general. All this he was saying indirectly, through allusion.

What we find in so many of King's speeches, namely, the expansion of meaning through allusion, is a common feature of traditional Western rhetoric.[1] The generalization includes ancient Jewish and Christian literature, whose authors were just as adept as King at adding force and augmenting sense through implicit interaction with authoritative predecessors. Examples are, for practical purposes, endless. The Hebrew Bible, which is itself increasingly recognized to be a collection of interacting texts,[2] is constantly quoted and alluded to in the Dead Sea Scrolls,[3] in the Apocrypha and Pseudepigrapha,[4] in the New Testament,[5] and in rabbinic sources.[6] The Tanak was trailed by Jewish and Christian writers who, as members of a text-based religion, incessantly occupied themselves with it. And the chief thesis of this book is that Q in its entirety belongs in the company of those writers. The Sayings Source nowhere pretends to be a linguistic island or an isolated revelation. It instead reveals in line after line that it has parental texts, and these it seeks to honor through consistent reference and emulation.

---

1. See the introduction to Udo J. Hebel, *Intertextuality, Allusion, and Quotation: An International Bibliography of Critical Studies* (New York: Greenwood, 1989), pp. 1–19.

2. See the overview in Michael Fishbane, *Biblical Interpretation in Ancient Israel* (Oxford: Clarendon, 1985).

3. There is as yet no adequate, comprehensive review of the use of Scripture at Qumran. But Michael Fishbane, "Use, Authority, and Interpretation of Mikra at Qumran," in *Mikra: Text, Translation, Reading, and Interpretation of the Hebrew Bible in Ancient Judaism and Early Christianity* (ed. Martin Jan Mulder; CRINT 2/1; Assen/Maastricht/Philadelphia: Van Gorcum/Fortress, 1988), pp. 339–77; and Phil Johann Maier, "Early Jewish Biblical Interpretation in the Qumran Literature," in *Hebrew Bible/Old Testament: The History of Its Interpretation*, vol. 1, *From the Beginnings to the Middle Ages (until 1300). Part I, Antiquity* (ed. Magne Sæbø; Göttingen: Vandenhoeck & Ruprecht, 1996), pp. 108–29, may serve as introductions.

4. See Devorah Dimant, "Use and Interpretation of Mikra in the Apocrypha and Pseudepigrapha," in Mulder, *Mikra*, pp. 379–419; Robert A. Kraft, "Scripture and Canon in Jewish Apocrypha and Pseudepigrapha," in Sæbø, *Hebrew Bible/Old Testament*, pp. 199–216; Folker Siegert, "Early Jewish Interpretation in a Hellenistic Style," in ibid., pp. 130–98.

5. Surveys include Eugen Hühn, *Die messianischen Weissagungen des israelitisch-jüdischen Volkes bis zu den Targumim, II. Teil: Die alttestamentlichen Citate und Reminiscenzen im Neuen Testamente* (Tübingen: Mohr Siebeck, 1900); Wilhelm Dittmar, *Vetus Testamentum in Novo: Die alttestamentlichen Parallelen des Neuen Testaments im Wortlaut der Urtexte und der Septuaginta* (Göttingen: Vandenhoeck & Ruprecht, 1903); M. Shires, *Finding the Old Testament in the New* (Philadelphia: Westminster, 1974); D. A. Carson and H. G. M. Williamson, eds., *It Is Written: Scripture Citing Scripture* (Cambridge: Cambridge University Press, 1988); and Hans Hübner, *Vetus Testamentum in Novo*, vol. 2, *Corpus Paulinum* (Göttingen: Vandenhoeck & Ruprecht, 1997).

6. See Daniel Boyarin, *Intertextuality and the Reading of Midrash* (Bloomington: Indiana University Press, 1990).

Previous research on Q has paid insufficient attention to this issue. Scholars have indeed discussed Q's attitude toward the Jewish law.[7] They have also observed rightly that portions of Q reflect a Deuteronomistic worldview and terminology.[8] But studies on scriptural intertextuality in Q have been either modest in scope[9] or so cursory in their treatment of proposed intertexts as to be inadequate.[10] Of course, because Q must be reconstructed from Matthew and Luke, and because the possible scriptural background of every line in those two Gospels has been explored in detail again and again, the relevant passages, the building blocks for the reconstruction of Q, have all been repeatedly examined. No study known to me, however, has yet attempted to evaluate in comprehensive fashion all of the plausible intertexts beneath Q and their interpretive implications or to discover if such evaluation reveals larger patterns across the document. This book, then, is an attempt to fill a gap in the secondary literature.

The lacuna exists partly because of the understandable preoccupation of students of Q with source-critical questions, with the document's place in our reconstructions of early Christianity, and with its meaning for the quest of the historical Jesus. But it is also true, more simply, that some have just failed to perceive many of Q's allusions. Maybe nowadays some do not know the Bible with the immediacy that, say, Tertullian, Albert the Great, and Hugo Grotius did, so that they perceive allusions less readily than did those exegetical giants. Maybe, too, the excesses of those hunting for intertexts have fostered cynicism. The knowledge that "at one time or another a H[ebrew] B[ible] text has been postulated to underlie almost every verse of the N[ew] T[estament]"[11] cannot but make one wary. One recalls that Justin Martyr discovered resemblances between the Pentateuch and Plato and took them to show the literary dependence of the latter upon the former. Parallels can be phantoms.[12]

---

7. See Daniel Kosch, *Die eschatologische Tora des Menschensohnes: Untersuchungen zur Rezeption der Stellung Jesu zur Tora in Q* (NTOA 12; Göttingen: Vandenhoeck & Ruprecht, 1989); and William R. G. Loader, *Jesus' Attitude towards the Law: A Study of the Gospels* (WUNT 2/97; Tübingen: Mohr Siebeck, 1997), pp. 390–431.

8. E.g., Otto H. Steck, *Israel und das gewaltsame Geschick der Propheten* (WMANT 23; Neukirchen-Vluyn: Neukirchener, 1967); and Arland D. Jacobson, "The Literary Unity of Q," *JBL* 101 (1982), pp. 365–89.

9. E.g., Jacques Schlosser, "L'utilisation des Écritures dans la source Q," in *L'Évangile exploré: Mélanges offerts à Simon Légasse* (ed. Alain Marchadour; LD 166; Paris: Cerf, 1996), pp. 123–46; and C. M. Tuckett, "Scripture in Q," in *The Scriptures in the Gospels* (ed. C. M. Tuckett; BETL 131; Louvain: Louvain University Press/Peeters, 1997), pp. 3–26.

10. E.g., R. Hodgson, "On the Gattung of Q: A Dialogue with James M. Robinson," *Bib* 66 (1985), pp. 73–95.

11. Todd C. Penner, "Inner-Biblical Interpretation, New Testament," in *Dictionary of Biblical Interpretation A-J* (ed. John H. Hayes; Nashville: Abingdon, 1999), p. 542.

12. See the entertaining essay of Umberto Eco, "Between Author and Text," in *Interpretation and Overinterpretation* (ed. Stefan Collini; Cambridge: Cambridge University Press, 1992), pp. 67–88; also Samuel Sandmel, "Parallelomania," *JBL* 81 (1962), pp. 1–13.

It is, moreover, a peculiar fact that even heavily allusive documents can often be understood without their intertexts, so that uninformed readers may see but not understand.[13] As Michael Riffaterre puts it, a richly allusive text is a little like a doughnut: it is centered around what is not there.[14] Although today's undergraduates find the words of "I Have a Dream" intelligible, disconcerting experience teaches that they typically fail to perceive many if not most of its allusions. The allusive function of "Five score years ago" has to be explained: "The Gettysburg Address was delivered by Abraham Lincoln on the occasion of.... Its opening words are.... " One presumes it was different in 1963, when the speech was delivered. Surely King was not intentionally casting esoteric allusions before the uncomprehending.

Covert references do not, so to speak, insist on their own way. They are only potentially transparent; hearers or readers must live and move and have their being in the right precursor texts. For those who live elsewhere, outside the right tradition, much can be missed. When Heb 13:2 enjoins, "Do not neglect to show hospitality to strangers, for by doing so some have entertained angels unawares," nothing is said about Abraham, so only those who know well the story in Genesis 18–19 will catch the allusion. Everything depends upon "the productive capacity of the reader."[15] What is manifest to some can be nonexistent to others. When those of us who grew up in the 1950s and 1960s heard Don McLean's popular song "American Pie," we did not need a commentator to tell us that the "sergeants" who "played a marching tune" were the Beatles in their late phase or that "Jack Flash" had something to do with the Rolling Stones. But those without the requisite musical knowledge could only have heard nonsense.

I recently read John Buchan's novel *Greenmantle*.[16] The explanatory notes at the end clarify the following: "left out at Pentecost," "spoiling the Egyptians," "string up like Haman," "What came you forth to seek?" "By the waters of Babylon, we sat down and wept," "Nimrod," "ephod," and "Passover Feast." But when the book was written, over eighty years ago, surely few of these expressions needed explanation; Buchan could assume a certain amount of biblical literacy among his intended public, which is why the notes are not in the earlier editions. Today, however, biblical literacy has declined sufficiently that readers require commentary. Ours is the age of the

---

13. This is because an "alluding marker has at least a double referent: it signifies unallusively, within the possible world of the literary text" as well as "allusively, to one or more texts outside its context." So Carmela Perri, "On Alluding," *Poetics* 7 (1978), p. 295. The whole article (pp. 289–307) is quite instructive.

14. Michael Riffaterre, *Semiotics of Poetry* (Bloomington: Indiana University Press, 1978), p. 13.

15. Herman Meyer, *The Poetics of Quotation in the European Novel* (Princeton: Princeton University Press, 1968), p. 5. On p. 4 he quotes Goethe: "Everyone sees the subject matter immediately before him; the substance is detected only by the man who has something to add to it."

16. John Buchan, *Greenmantle* (Oxford/New York: Oxford University Press, 1993).

annotated Bible, when people need a footnote in order to learn that when Jer 20:16 speaks in passing of "the cities that the Lord overthrew without pity," the oblique reference is to Sodom and Gomorrah. The lesson is that time deletes. Things that were obvious can, as a text's audience changes, evaporate.

Even the experts may miss things. Sherwood Anderson's short story "The Egg" is clearly a new, secular version of Genesis 1–3.[17] It tells the tragic tale of a man who is quite happy until he meets his wife, who tempts him with the American dream (in this case represented not by an apple but by an egg, that is, an egg business). When he succumbs to her bogus promise and is overcome by the ambition to be what he cannot be, unmitigated disaster follows. Not only does the plot recapitulate Genesis, but the narrator plainly borrows from Genesis, as when he speaks of "the sweat of your father's brow" (cf. Gen 3:19) and of literature "intended to be read by the gods who have just eaten of the tree of the knowledge of good and evil" (cf. Gen 3:1–5).[18] But in the secondary literature of a generation that knows not Joseph, biblical allusions have become just part of the accumulated debris of culture, so the parallels, which have largely determined the structure of the story, are either ignored[19] or viewed as nothing more than "evocative rather than informative."[20]

Q's intertextuality and its significance have in like fashion often been underestimated. This fact does not, I hasten to add, give one license to proffer numerous novel readings, and it is not the purpose of this book to find in Q heretofore unsuspected parallels. I have rather concentrated upon those allusions that have entered the minds of at least some readers of the relevant texts of Matthew and Luke down through the centuries. My presumption is that if a text has sent some to a particular scripture, then maybe it was designed to do so, and investigation is in any case in order. By the same token, if a unit has not sent any back to a particular text, then there is a strong initial inclination against its having been intended to do this.

That there is at least a fair amount of intertextuality in Q must be obvious to all. Not only are there some explicit quotations (Q 4:4, 8, 10–12; 7:27), but when one runs across names such as Abel and Zechariah (11:51), "the claims of an approach of intertextuality are self-evident: the language of the Q text requires a network of other texts for its meaning to be understood."[21] These names, moreover, tell us where Q's intertextuality is above all to be sought — in the Jewish Bible. This is confirmed again and again

---

17. Sherwood Anderson, "The Egg," in *Certain Things Last: The Selected Short Stories of Sherwood Anderson* (ed. Charles E. Modlin; New York: Four Walls Eight Windows, 1992), pp. 26–38.

18. Ibid., pp. 28, 29.

19. E.g., Gerald Joseph, "The American Triumph of the Egg: Anderson's 'The Egg' and Fitzgerald's *The Great Gatsby*," *Criticism* 7 (1965), pp. 131–40.

20. Michael D. West, "Sherwood Anderson's Triumph: 'The Egg,'" *American Quarterly* 20 (1968), p. 682.

21. Tuckett, "Scripture in Q," p. 15.

by its scriptural terms and idioms, by its cryptic or fleeting quotations, and by its many references to heroes, places, and supernatural characters of the Tanak — all of which it fails to explain. Obviously the text assumes familiarity with them, with the corporate memory of Judaism as conveyed through the Bible.[22] Consider the following lists:

Scriptural personages in Q

Abraham: 3:8; 13:28
the prophets: 6:23; 11:47, 49, 50; 13:34; 16:16
prophets and kings: 10:24
Jonah: 11:29, 30, 32
the Ninevites: 11:30, 32
Solomon: 11:31; 12:27
queen of the South (= queen of Sheba): 11:31
Abel: 11:51
Zechariah: 11:51
Isaac: 13:28
Jacob: 13:28
Noah: 17:26, 27
(Lot: 17:28)
(Lot's wife: 17:31)

Scriptural places in Q

the wilderness: 4:1; 7:24
Jerusalem: 4:9; 13:34
the temple: 4:9
Sodom: 10:12 (17:29)
Hades: 10:15
synagogues: 11:43; 12:11
between the altar and the sanctuary: 11:51
Gehenna: 12:5
heaven: 6:23; 10:15, 21; 11:13, 16; 12:33; 16:17
your house (= temple and/or Jerusalem): 13:35

Supernatural characters from Scripture

(Lord) God: 3:8; 4:8, 9, 12; 11:20; 12:6; 16:13; etc.
(Holy) Spirit: 3:16; 4:1; 12:10, 11(?)
the devil: 4:2, 3, 5, 13
angels (of God): 4:10; 12:8–9
father (= God): 6:36; 10:21, 22; 11:2, 13; 12:30
Wisdom: 7:35; 11:49
demon: 7:33; 11:14, 15, 19, 20
Beelzebul: 11:15, 19
Satan: 11:18

---

22. For what follows I cite the LXX; but we shall see from time to time herein that Q seems to reflect knowledge of other textual traditions.

Scriptural terms and idioms in Q

ὀργή/(eschatological) wrath (of God): 3:7
cf. Isa 13:9; 26:20; Zeph 2:2; etc.

μετανοέω, μετάνοια/repent(ance): 3:8; 10:13; 11:32; 17:3–4
cf. Joel 2:13–14; Jon 3:9, 10; etc.

Ἀβραάμ + πατήρ/father…Abraham: 3:8
cf. Josh 24:3; Isa 51:2; Tob 4:12

πυρὶ ἀσβέστῳ/with unquenchable (eschatological) fire: 3:17
cf. Isa 34:9–10; 66:24; Jer 7:20

ἡμέρας τεσσεράκοντα/forty days: 4:2
cf. Gen 7:4, 12, 17; 8:6; Exod 24:18; 1 Kgs 19:8

πειράζω/tempt: 4:2; 11:16
cf. Gen 22:1; Deut 8:2; 13:3; etc.

γέγραπται/it is written: 4:4, 6, 8; 7:27
cf. 1 Kgs 2:11; Dan 9:13

κύριος ὁ θεός σου/the Lord your God: 4:8, 12
cf. Lev 19:14; Deut 6:5; Hos 14:2; etc.

πτωχός/(the) poor: 6:20; 7:22
cf. Ps 9:18; 69:32; 140:12; Isa 41:17; 61:1; etc.

βασιλεία (τοῦ θεοῦ)/kingdom (of God): 6:20; 7:28; (9:62;) 10:9, 11; 11:2, 20; 12:31; 13:18, 20, 29; 16:16
cf. Ps 22:28; 103:19; 145:11; Dan 4:3; Obad 21; etc.

ὁ υἱὸς τοῦ ἀνθρώπου/Son of man: 6:22; 7:34; 9:58; 11:30; 12:8–9, 10, 20, 40; 17:24, 26, 30
cf. Ps 8:4; Ezek 2:1; Dan 7:13; etc.

προφήτης/prophet: 6:23; 7:26; 10:24; 11:47, 49; 13:34; 16:16
cf. Num 11:29; 1 Kgs 18:4; etc.

ἔθνη/Gentiles (= non-Jews): 6:33; 12:30
cf. Josh 4:24; 1 Kgs 8:5; Ps 2:8; Zech 14:19; etc.

πίστις/(religious) faith or trust: 7:9; 12:28; 17:6
cf. Deut 32:20; 1 Sam 26:23; Hab 2:4; etc.

Ἰσραήλ/Israel: 7:9; 22:30
cf. Exod 1:1; Josh 1:2; Ps 14:7; etc.

νεκροὶ ἐγείρονται/dead are raised up: 7:22
cf. Isa 26:19

πτωχοὶ εὐαγγελίζονται/the poor have good news preached to them: 7:23
cf. Isa 29:19; 61:1

γεννητοῖς γυναικῶν/born of woman: 7:28
cf. Job 11:12; Ecclus 10:18

ἡ γενεὰ ταύτη/this generation: 7:31; 11:29, 31, 32, 51
cf. Gen 7:1; Deut 1:35; Ps 12:7; 95:10

τὰ πετεινὰ τοῦ οὐρανοῦ/the birds of heaven: 9:58; 13:19
cf. 2 Sam 21:10; Jer 4:25

βλέπων εἰς τὰ ὀπίσω/looking at the things behind: 9:61
cf. Gen 19:17, 26; 8:20; 1 Sam 24:9; 2 Sam 2:20

εἰρήνη τῷ οἴκῳ τούτῳ/Peace to this house: 10:5
cf. 1 Sam 25:6

ἐν τῇ ἡμέρᾳ ἐκείνῃ/in that day (of divine judgment): 10:12
cf. Obad 8; Zeph 1:8; Zech 12:3; etc.

σάκκῳ καὶ σποδῷ/sackcloth and ashes: 10:13
cf. Neh 9:1; Ezra 4:1, 3; Isa 58:5; Jer 6:26; Dan 9:3; Jon 3:6

κύριε τοῦ οὐρανοῦ καὶ τῆς γῆς/lord of heaven and earth: 10:21
cf. Tob 7:17; also Jdt 9:12

δακτύλῳ θεοῦ/finger of God: 11:20
cf. Exod 8:19; 29:12; 31:18

γενεὰ πονηρά/evil generation: 11:29
cf. Deut 1:35

ἡ σοφία Σολομῶνος/the wisdom of Solomon: 11:31
cf. 1 Kgs 10:4, 6, 8, 24; 2 Chr 9:3, 5–7, 23

ἐκ τῶν περάτων τῆς γῆς/from the ends of the earth: 11:31
cf. LXX Dan 4:18; Theod. Dan 4:8, 19; Tob S 13:11; Wisd 6:1; the expression occurs over ten times in LXX Psalms (e.g., 60:2: ἀπὸ τῶν περάτων τῆς γῆς, for MT's מקצה הארץ)

οὐαὶ ὑμῖν ὅτι/woe to you because: 11:39, 42, 43, 44, 46, 47, 52

cf. LXX Num 21:29 (οὐαί σοι); Eccles 10:16 (οὐαί σοι); Jer 13:27 (οὐαί σοι); Ecclus 2:14 (οὐαὶ ὑμῖν); and 41:8 (οὐαὶ ὑμῖν); "woe" + dative pronoun + ὅτι (cf. אוֹי + לְ + כִּי) is a formula used on eight occasions (half in Jeremiah);[23] the Hebrew Bible contains several series of woes: Isa 5:8–23 (six woes); 5:28–33 (six woes); Amos 5:6–6:4 (five woes); and Hab 2:6–19 (five woes).[24]

ἀποδεκατόω/tithe: 11:42

cf. Lev 27:30; Deut 12:17; Neh 10:38; etc.

πατέρες ὑμῶν + rejection of προφῆται/ "your fathers" rejected "the prophets," 11:47–48

cf. Jer 7:25–26; Zech 1:4, 5

προφῆται + ἀποκτείνω/killing the prophets, 11:47–48

cf. 1 Kgs 18:4, 13; 19:10, 14; Neh 9:26

ἀποστέλλω (with God as subject) + προφῆται (who are rejected)/God sends prophets who are rejected, 11:49; 13:34

cf. 2 Chr 24:19; 36:15–16; Jer 7:24–28; 25:4

ἐν ἀγρῷ τὸν χόρτον/the grass in the field: 12:28

cf. Gen 2:5; 3:18; Num 22:4; 2 Kgs 19:26

αἱ ὀσφύες περιεζωσμέναι/loins girded: 12:35

cf. Exod 12:11; 2 Kgs 1:8; Dan 10:5

τὰ πετεινὰ τοῦ οὐρανοῦ κατεσκήνωσεν ἐν τοῖς κλάδοις αὐτοῦ/the birds of heaven nested in its branches: 13:19

cf. Ezek 17:23; 31:6; Dan 4:12

ἀποχωρεῖτε/ἀπόστητε ἀπ᾽ ἐμου (πάντες) οἱ ἐργαζόμενοι τὴν ἀνομίαν/Away from me all those working lawlessness: 13:27

cf. Ps 6:9

Ἀβραὰμ καὶ Ἰσαὰκ καὶ Ἰακώβ/Abraham, Isaac, and Jacob: 13:28

cf. Exod 3:6; 4:5; Deut 1:8; Jer 33:26; etc.

ὁ βρυγμὸς τῶν ὀδόντων/the gnashing of teeth: 13:29

cf. Job 16:9; Ps 34:16; 36:12; 112:10; Lam 2:16

ἀφίεται ὑμῖν ὁ οἶκος/your house (= temple) is forsaken: 13:35

cf. 2 Chr 24:18; Jer 12:7

ἐν ὀνόματι κυρίου/"in the name of the Lord," 13:35

cf. Josh 9:9; 1 Sam 17:45; Ps 118:26; Mic 4:5; etc.

ὁ νόμος/the (Mosaic) law: 16:16, 17

cf. Exod 24:12; Deut 1:5; 1 Kgs 2:3; etc.

αἱ ἡμέραι Νῶε/the days of Noah: 17:26

cf. Isa 54:9

ἡ κιβωτός/the ark (of Noah): 17:27

cf. Genesis 6–9

ὁ κατακλυσμός/the flood: 17:27

cf. Genesis 6–10

ἔβρεξεν πῦρ καὶ θεῖον/rained fire and sulfur: 17:29

cf. Gen 19:24

τὰς δώδεκα φυλὰς τοῦ Ἰσραήλ/the twelve tribes of Israel: 22:30

cf. Gen 49:28; Exod 24:4; Ezek 47:13

Q's words and phrases manifestly place the book within a specific linguistic tradition and a particular community of texts. Throughout it reverberates with the Tanak, whose expressions are its idioms and whose stories are its

---

23. 1 Βασ 4:7; Jer 4:13; 6:4; 13:27; 27:27; Lam 5:16; Hos 7:13; Tob 10:5.

24. Discussion in Migaku Sato, *Q und Prophetie: Studien zur Gattungs- und Traditionsgeschichte der Quelle Q* (WUNT 2/29; Tübingen: Mohr Siebeck, 1988), pp. 183–201. οὐαί was not common in either classical or Koine Greek; this makes its biblical reverberations all the louder.

memory. The prophetic spirit of the Sayings Source does not create ex nihilo but inscribes preexisting materials. It indeed does this to such an extent that one might even be tempted to ask whether the contributors to Q were not as much interpreting the Jesus tradition from the viewpoint of the Tanak as they were interpreting the Tanak from the viewpoint of the Jesus tradition. However that may be, it bears repeating that by its failure to explain all this material, Q assumes that its hearers know all about the submerged scriptural island supporting Q's coral reef, that their imaginations dwell where Q's Jesus does, namely, within the religious world of ancient Judaism and its Scriptures.

The conclusion is reinforced by Q's architectonics. As is well known, Q in turn resembles, in both its micro- and macro-Gattungs, prophetic texts and Wisdom literature.[25] So the Tanak gives Q its form as well as its vocabulary. In every way Q reflects a biblical literary legacy.

The issue concerning Q's intertextuality, then, is neither its existence nor its main source but its extent, and in particular how often it implicitly refers to scriptural texts. But how does one determine whether one text really alludes to another? The problem is that near meaningless parallels between two texts can always be uncovered if one puts in the effort.[26] And much effort has indeed been put in: "Learned and meticulous essays have been written to demonstrate the influence of everything on anything."[27] Our theological libraries are accordingly filled with learned books and journal articles promoting illusory parallels between biblical passages, parallels that were rightly never invited into subsequent publications. So in this matter we must advance warily. When is an allusion an allusion and when is it an illusion? Happily the issue has been much discussed of late,[28] and the following

---

25. John S. Kloppenborg, *The Formation of Q: Trajectories in Ancient Christian Wisdom Collections* (Studies in Antiquity and Christianity; Philadelphia: Fortress, 1987); Sato, *Q und Prophetie*; Alan Kirk, *The Composition of the Sayings Source: Genre, Synchrony, and Wisdom Redaction in Q* (NovTSup 91; Leiden/Boston/Cologne: Brill, 1998).

26. The oft-forgotten converse, of course, is that dissimilitude also always exists between two things, so in and of itself it does not disprove a meaningful relationship.

27. Ihab H. Hassan, "The Problem of Influence in Literary History: Notes towards a Definition," in *Influx: Essays on Literary Influence* (ed. Ronald Primeau; Port Washington, N.Y./London: Kennikat, 1977), p. 35.

28. See, e.g., Jon Paulien, *Decoding Revelation's Trumpets: Literary Allusions and the Interpretation of Revelation 8:7–12* (Andrews University Seminary Doctoral Dissertation Series 11; Berrien Springs, Mich.: Andrews University Press, 1987), esp. pp. 100–194; Richard B. Hays, *Echoes of Scripture in the Letters of Paul* (New Haven: Yale University Press, 1989), pp. 29–32; Michael Thompson, *Clothed with Christ: The Example and Teaching of Jesus in Romans 12.1–15.13* (JSNTSS 59; Sheffield: JSOT Press, 1991), esp. pp. 28–36; Dale C. Allison Jr., *The New Moses: A Matthean Typology* (Minneapolis: Fortress, 1993), pp. 19–23; Patricia Tull Willey, *Remember the Former Things: The Recollection of Previous Texts in Second Isaiah* (SBLDS 161; Atlanta: Scholars Press, 1997), pp. 76–84; Benjamin D. Sommer, *A Prophet Reads Scripture: Allusion in Isaiah 40–66* (Contraversions: Jews and Other Differences; Stanford: Stanford University Press, 1999); Richard L. Schultz, *The Search for Quotation: Verbal Parallels in the Prophets* (JSOTSup 180; Sheffield: Sheffield Academic Press, 1999).

suggestions, which are kept in mind throughout this work, seem the most helpful:[29]

(1) As already indicated, the history of interpretation either enhances or diminishes the plausibility of a proposed allusion. If text A has reminded commentators of text B, the odds that it was designed to do so are increased. Conversely, if commentators have uniformly missed an allusion, doubt may be appropriate.[30]

One must, however, not be unimaginative here. For Q's original audience consisted of Jewish Christians who did not yet have anything like our New Testament, whatever other traditions they might have had. Their Bible was solely what Christians today call the Old Testament. All ecclesiastical commentaries, by contrast, have been written by people who have known much more than the Tanak, who have come to the Gospels with a larger and different canon. Already by the time of the apostolic fathers, Christian books that were later to be considered canonical were being cited proportionately more often than the Hebrew Bible.[31] So from nearly the beginning most readers of the Synoptics have looked first for illustrations from the rest of the New Testament. Thus Lk (= Q) 10:21–22 ("No one knows the Son except the Father, or the Father except the Son") has most often been linked with verses from John (e.g., Jn 1:18; 10:14–15; 17:25) whereas the text most commonly called upon to elucidate Lk (= Q) 17:34 ("one will be taken and the other left") has been 1 Thess 4:17 ("Then we who are alive, who are left, will be caught up in the clouds"). But Q's first audience did not have the New Testament to think about. In other words, the earlier intertextual universe was smaller and different than the later one. This is one reason why allusions should be investigated from both ends, so to speak. Sometimes Christian readers of a New Testament hypertext may not be reminded of its scriptural hypotext, but it may work the other way around: in my reading Isa 61:1 sends a higher percentage of ecclesiastical exegetes to Mt 11:5 and Lk 7:22 than Mt 11:5 or Lk 7:22 sends to Isa 61:1. For this reason, then, an adequate survey of whether an alleged allusion has been

---

29. It should be emphasized that the point here is to uncover allusions, not dependence. One can and often does have the latter without the former, for unconscious borrowing is ubiquitous. Similarly, I shall be little concerned with indirect influence, such as the scriptural influence through Jewish moral teaching that one sees in Paul; cf. Brian S. Rosner, *Paul, Scripture, and Ethics: A Study of 1 Corinthians 5–7* (AGAJU 22; Leiden/New York/Cologne: Brill, 1994), pp. 26–58.

30. Here I am closer to Paulien, *Decoding Revelation's Trumpets*, than to Hays, *Echoes*. Hays, p. 31, finds the history of interpretation less than reliable "because Gentile Christian readers at a very early date lost Paul's sense of urgency about relating the gospel to God's dealings with Israel and, slightly later, began reading Paul's letters within the matrix of the New Testament canon." But it is also true that later circumstances — such as opposition to Marcion — encouraged the search for First Testament parallels and that many Christian exegetes have known the Jewish Scriptures inside out.

31. Franz Stuhlhofer, *Der Gebrauch der Bibel von Jesus bis Euseb: Eine statistische Untersuchung zur Kanonsgeschichte* (TVG Monographien und Studienbücher; Wuppertal: Brockhaus, 1988).

seen in the past will remember that the tracks run in both directions and that one should accordingly review not just commentaries on the allegedly allusive text but also commentaries on the text purportedly alluded to.

(ii) In the absence of explicit citation or undeniable tacit borrowing, an allusion will not be credible unless text and intertext share some combination of the following: common vocabulary, common word order, common theme(s), similar imagery, similar structure, similar circumstance(s). One of these alone will not suffice, and the greater the number of parallels, the more probable the allusion and the easier it will be to discern. To illustrate: Rev 9:2 recounts that an angel opened the shaft of the bottomless pit, "and from the shaft rose smoke like the smoke of a great furnace." The line is reminiscent of Gen 19:28, where Abraham looks down on Sodom and Gomorrah and sees "the smoke of the land going up like the smoke of a furnace":

| Rev 9:2 | ἀνέβη | καπνὸς | ἐκ τοῦ φρέατος | ὡς | καπνὸς | καμίνου |
| LXX Gen 19:28 | ἀνέβαινεν | φλὸξ[32] | (v.l. ἐκ) τῆς γῆς | ὡσεὶ | ἀτμὶς | καμίνου |

Not only are there three or (if ἐκ is included) four Greek words in common, but they occur in the same order: ἀναβαίνω (+ ἐκ) + ὡσεί/ὡς + καμίνου. Moreover, the image in both texts is the same, as is the theme: Rev 9:2 and Gen 19:8 depict the smoke that rises after God's judgment upon the ungodly. It is not any one thing shared by Rev 9:2 and Gen 19:28 that clinches the allusion but rather the evidence in the aggregate — similar vocabulary, similar word order, similar imagery, similar theme. (A coincidence of theme can be all important. When people singing "I've got to walk that lonesome valley, I've got to walk it for myself" have recalled the Twenty-third Psalm, it is only because "walk" and "valley" are connected with the theme of death [cf. Ps 23:4: "even though I walk through the valley of the shadow of death"].)

(iii) Common vocabulary, word order, theme(s), imagery, structure, and circumstance(s) are only corroborative when not commonplace. "Thus says the Lord" and collections of woes are recognizably biblical, but they appear too often to call to mind any particular passage. Stalkers of allusions must not forget that an image or phrase may begin its life attached to a particular text but, with time and use, become in itself a topos, just as a quotation can become a free-floating proverb. Many people who speak of "the separation of church and state" have no idea that Thomas Jefferson coined the phrase or that he first used it in a speech to a Baptist church in Danbury, Connecticut; and their ignorance in this matter does not prevent them from using the phrase effectively. Similarly, one wonders how many of the references to eschatological destruction coming from the mouth of an eschatological deliverer are allusions either to Isa 11:4 ("he shall strike the earth with the

---

32. While this word means "flame," the MT has קיטֹר = "smoke," which it repeats two words later (cf. Revelation's καπνός...καπνός).

rod of his mouth") or to 49:2 ("He made my mouth like a sharp sword").[33]
Some later oracles do clearly allude to one or both of those texts, but others
may not. In the latter case we would have to do with a stereotypical way of
speaking. So in order to determine that we are looking at an allusion rather
than a topos, it will help if a text and intertext share something out of the
ordinary, such as unusual imagery, uncommon motifs, or rare vocabulary.
Martin Luther King Jr.'s "Five score years ago" recalls Lincoln's "Four score
and seven years ago" not only because both phrases open their respective
speeches but because, in 1963, "X score years ago" sounded archaic and
so unusual; hence its appearance was a signal. In like manner, Dan 12:2
("Many of those who sleep in the dust of the earth will awake, some to
everlasting life, and some to shame and everlasting abhorrence") is sometimes said to allude to Isa 66:24 ("they will be an abhorrence to all flesh"),
in part because nowhere else in the Tanak do we find דראון, "abhorrence."

   (iv) The probability that one text intentionally recalls another is increased
if the latter is prominent in the tradition of the former, and especially if
it is cited or alluded to in other related texts. Suggested allusions to the
foundational stories in Genesis and Exodus accordingly have more initial
appeal than proposed allusions to obscure verses in Nehemiah. Certainly it
has always been easier to call to mind Gen 1:1 ("In the beginning . . . ") than,
say, Neh 11:6 ("All the descendants of Perez who lived in Jerusalem were
four hundred sixty-eight valiant warriors"). In line with this, my impression
is that ecclesiastical commentators, when reviewing the story of the feeding
of the five thousand in the canonical Gospels, have more often been put in
mind of Moses and the manna than the tale about Elisha in 2 Kgs 4:42–44,
despite the fact that the parallels with the latter are closer. The reason must
be that stories in Exodus have been more readily pulled out of Christian
memories than items from the cycle concerning Elisha.

   (v) The probability of an allusion is enhanced if a suggested intertext
belongs to a source that the author otherwise shows interest in. In Jon 1:5,
for example, the fleeing Jonah lies down and falls fast asleep (וישכב וירדם).
In 1 Kgs 19:5 another prophet, Elijah, who is also fleeing, lies down and
falls asleep (וישכב ויישן). One would have to be dubious that, in this passing
similarity, Jonah is recalling the story of Elijah — except that three chapters
later Jonah contains lines that strongly recall 1 Kgs 19:4:

---

33. *Ps. Sol.* 17:24 ("to destroy the unlawful nations with the word of his mouth"), 35
("he will strike the earth with the word of his mouth forever"); *1 En.* 62:2 ("the word of his
mouth will do the sinners in"); 1QS[b] 5:25 ("bring death to the ungodly with the breath of
your lips"); 2 Thess 2:8 ("will destroy with the breath of his mouth"); Rev 1:16 ("and from
his mouth came a sharp, two-edged sword"); 2:16 ("make war against them with the sword
of my mouth"); 19:15 ("from his mouth comes a sharp, two-edged sword with which to strike
down the nations"), 21 ("killed . . . by the sword that came from his mouth"); *4 Ezra* 13:9–11
("he sent forth from his lips as it were a flame of fire, and from his lips a flaming breath, and
from his tongue he shot forth a storm of sparks"). Isa 49:2 itself draws upon Jer 1:9; see Willey,
Remember the Former Things, pp. 195–96.

1 Kgs 19:4: Elijah "went a day's journey into the wilderness, and came and sat down under a solitary broom tree. He asked that he might die saying (וישאל את־נפשו למות ויאמר), 'It is enough; now, O Lord, take away my life, for (עתה יהוה קח נפשי כי) I am no better than my ancestors'"

Jon 4:3: "And now, O Lord, please take my life from me, for (ועתה יהוה קח־נא את־נפשי ממני כי) it is better for me to die than to live"

Jon 4:8: Jonah "asked that he might die. He said (וישאל את־נפשו למות ויאמר), 'It is better for me to die than to live'"

Moreover, the circumstantial parallel between Jonah and Elijah is plain: both are dejected, disillusioned prophets who, while sitting beneath a plant, ask to die and then have a dialogue with God. There is even a coincidence of numbers. Elijah first takes a day's journey into the wilderness (1 Kgs 19:4) and then a forty-days' journey (1 Kgs 19:8), whereas Jonah foretells Nineveh's destruction forty days after his day's journey into the city (Jon 3:4).

(vi) One more readily recognizes an allusion if such recognition enhances meaning in a manner congruent with a book's arguments or themes. A particularly striking example of this occurs in Jonah. If one examines the original context of the apparent quotations from Exodus, Deuteronomy, Jeremiah, and the Psalms, one discovers a pattern: Jonah consistently puts into the mouth of pagan characters phrases that are elsewhere used of Israel's relationship to God.[34] The ironic result is more than consistent with the overall theme of Jonah, which fights against a narrow nationalism. But the irony is missed if one does not know the subterranean source whence the subtexts have been mined.

When all is said and done, the preceding indices, however helpful, can only be suggestive, not determinative: subjectivity cannot be avoided. There is no "scientific method of determining allusions."[35] The best reader is, not one who mechanically or dogmatically observes indices, but one who has gained an instinct of artistry, who can delve below a text with a delicate and mature judgment bred of familiarity with the tradition to which it belongs: the truth must be divined, groped for by "taste, tact, and intuition rather than a controlling method."[36] So there will often be room for doubt and debate about the spectral things that allusions are.

To allude is by definition to suggest, not to state plainly. The allusion is like the parable: it does not dictate but rather teases the mind into active thought.[37] So the burden of recognition is on the audience, whence it follows

34. Jonathan Magonet, *Form and Meaning: Studies in Literary Techniques in the Book of Jonah* (Bible and Literature Series; Sheffield: Almond, 1983), pp. 70–72.

35. Against Paulien, *Decoding Revelation's Trumpets*, p. 106. His use of "certain" on p. 165 is also out of place.

36. M. H. Abrams, "Rationality and Imagination in Cultural History," in Wayne C. Booth, *Critical Understanding: The Powers and Limits of Pluralism* (Chicago: University of Chicago Press, 1979), p. 176.

37. Cf. C. H. Dodd, *The Parables of the Kingdom* (rev. ed.; London: Fontana, 1961), p. 16.

that to allude is to risk being missed. Nothing guarantees that the reader of Mark 15 is going to catch all the allusions to Psalms 22 and 69. The text only works its full effect upon those with the requisite textual memories.

This can be a problem for modern critics, who sometimes dismiss proposed allusions out of a bias against the implicit and the subtle: our confidence is, for obvious reasons, in the explicit and the obvious. But, as readers of Michael Fishbane's work on inner-biblical exegesis know, significant textual meaning can be, like the foundations of buildings, out of sight. Further, ancient audiences, with their much smaller textual world, may very well have been more accustomed to paying keener attention to linguistic details than most of us, who live in an age of verbal inflation and speed reading, an age in which people take in texts with their eyes, not their ears, and often do so not by concentrating on them but merely by scanning them. That the rabbis regularly associated two texts because they shared a single word (גזירה שוה) is suggestive, and it has been said more generally that "it was natural, given the acceptance of intertextuality in the ancient world, to suppose that coincidence of word or phrase was significant."[38]

Before turning to a detailed examination of Q, it may help the reader if a couple of presuppositions are here made plain. The first is that ancients who attended religious services and who heard the same sacred texts read or chanted throughout their lifetimes probably had little difficulty catching some allusions that modern readers, who are acquainted with many more books and not intimately familiar with the texts in their original languages, have often missed. Their ways were not our ways. Perhaps closer to the situation when Q circulated was that which obtained after the publication of the Authorized or King James Version:

> For three centuries the Bible was so well known that hardly any word or phrase, except those which it shared with all English books whatever, could be borrowed without recognition. If you echoed the Bible everyone knew that you were echoing the Bible. And certain associations were called up in every reader's mind — sacred associations. All your readers had heard it read, as a ritual or almost ritual act, at home, at school, and in church. . . . There could be a pious use and a profane use: but there could be no ordinary use.[39]

Like Timothy, who from childhood was acquainted with the sacred writings (2 Tim 3:15), many Jews must have been "generally well educated in the

---

38. Frances M. Young, *Biblical Exegesis and the Formation of Christian Culture* (Cambridge: Cambridge University Press, 1997), p. 133.

39. C. S. Lewis, *The Literary Impact of the Authorized Version* (FBBS 4; Philadelphia: Fortress, 1963), p. 28. The works of most of the great English writers up through the early twentieth century reverberate with the language of the Authorized Version. The generalization includes even the works of those who, like Byron and Shelley, professed unbelief. They all knew the Authorized Version; most knew it by heart.

Bible,"[40] which was presumably the centerpiece of whatever elementary education they may have had.[41] Josephus, while no doubt being a bit rhetorical, surely had some basis for claiming that first-century Jews had a "thorough and accurate knowledge" of the Scriptures and that "should anyone of our nation be questioned about the laws, he would repeat them all more readily than his own name. The result, then, of our thorough grounding in the laws from the first dawn of intelligence is that we have them, as it were, engraven on our souls."[42] Already 2 Chr 17:7–9 wants to leave the impression of an informed laity: Jehoshaphat, the Chronicler reports, sent readers around the country to teach the book of the law to the people.[43] Consider Acts 17:11 (the Jewish converts of Beroea "examined the Scriptures every day to see whether these things were so"); *1 Clem.* 53:1 ("For you [the Corinthian Christians] have understanding, you have a good understanding of the sacred Scripture, beloved, and you have studied the oracles of God"); and Polycarp, *Ep.* 12.1 ("For I am confident that you [the Philippian Christians] are well versed in the Scriptures"). These Christian sources point us in the same direction: many followers of Jesus had laid up the Scriptures in their hearts. One recalls, from a later time, the story passed on by Augustine about how, when a new translation for the "gourd" of Jon 4:6 was read, a translation different from "that which had been of old familiar to the senses and memory of all the worshippers, and had been chanted for so many generations in the church," there arose a "tumult" in a congregation: people — not the priests and teachers but the laity — corrected and denounced what had been read.[44]

Literacy may have been restricted in the first century (although less so among Jews than others),[45] but those who grew up going on the sabbath

---

40. So E. P. Sanders, *Judaism: Practice and Belief 63 BCE–66 CE* (London/Philadelphia: SCM/Trinity Press International, 1992), p. 197.

41. Cf. 4 Macc 18:10: the father of the seven martyred brothers taught them the Law and the Prophets. On Jewish schools, see Martin Hengel, *Judaism and Hellenism: Studies in Their Encounter in Palestine during the Early Hellenistic Period* (Philadelphia: Fortress, 1974), vol. 1, pp. 78–83 (Hengel establishes that Jewish schools were common by the first century C.E.); James L. Crenshaw, "Education in Ancient Israel," *JBL* 104 (1985), pp. 601–15; idem, *Education in Ancient Israel* (New York: Doubleday, 1998), pp. 85–113 (Crenshaw establishes the ambiguity of the evidence in the Tanak).

42. *C. Ap.* 2.175, 178. Cf. *Ant.* 4.211; also Philo, *Ad Gai.* 210; *Hypoth.* 7.12. For the pertinent rabbinic evidence, see S. Safrai, "Education and the Study of the Torah," in *The Jewish People in the First Century: Historical Geography, Political History, Social, Cultural, and Religious Life and Institutions* (ed. S. Safrai and M. Stern in cooperation with D. Flusser and W. C. van Unnik; Assen/Philadelphia: Van Gorcum/Fortress, 1976), vol. 2, pp. 945–70; and Birger Gerhardsson, *Memory and Manuscript: Oral Tradition and Written Transmission in Rabbinic Judaism and Early Christianity* (Lund/Copenhagen: Gleerup/Ejnar Munksgaard, 1961), pp. 56–66.

43. Cf. Deut 31:12–13; Neh 8:3, 8–9.

44. *Ep.* 75.21–22; cf. 82.35 (CSEL 34/2, ed. A. Goldbacher, pp. 320–24, 386–87). For a modern parallel from a Middle Eastern village, see Kenneth E. Bailey, "Informal Controlled Oral Tradition and the Synoptic Gospels," *Asian JT* 5 (1991), p. 43.

45. See Harry Y. Gamble, *Books and Readers in the Early Church: A History of Early*

to synagogues (Philo could call them διδασκαλεία, "schools")[46] or who fre-
quented Jewish-Christian gatherings probably knew Scripture well enough,
whether they read or not: they had learned it through their ears. We should
not equate literacy with visual literacy. There is also oral literacy,[47] and
within the context of formative Judaism and early Christianity, an inability
to read Scripture cannot be equated with an ignorance of Scripture. In this
connection it is probably relevant that "the 'Egyptian' myth which Plato
makes Socrates tell to Phaedrus is generally thought to correspond to the
truth: writing brings not improved memory but forgetfulness, by providing
the literate with an external device to rely on."[48] In any event, and as Harry
Gamble has written, limited visual literacy "had little effect on the ability of
Christians generally to gain a close acquaintance with Christian literature.
The illiterate Christian found in the public reading of Christian texts at least
as large and probably a more consistent opportunity than his pagan counterpart to participate in literacy and become familiar with texts."[49] It required,
not a scribal elite, but only ordinary memories to catch scriptural allusions,
and so it is altogether reasonable to surmise that Q's allusions — like those in
so much of the intertestamental literature — were there to be recognized.[50]
In other words, one need not posit a radical disjunction between those who
could read Q for themselves and auditors who could not.

(As an aside, it is equally true that neither Q nor what we know of
the history of early Christianity gives us much reason to posit a significant disjunction between Q's first real audiences and its implied or model
audience, that is, one able to perceive the old in the new and read the text
as it was designed to be read.[51] This is one reason why I am sympathetic
when Richard Hays, in his admirable book on Scripture in Paul, presumes
continuity among the five possible locales of the hermeneutical event — in

---

Christian Texts (New Haven/London: Yale University Press, 1995), p. 7. Relevant texts include
Philo, *Ad Gai.* 115; Josephus, *C. Ap.* 2.204; *T. Levi* 13:2; *m. Ketub.* 8:8.

46. E.g., *Mos.* 1.216; *Spec. leg.* 2.62.

47. William A. Graham, *Beyond the Written Word: Oral Aspects of Scripture in the History
of Religion* (Cambridge: Cambridge University Press, 1987), p. 31. See further Walter J. Ong,
Orality and Literacy: The Technology of the Word (London: Methuen, 1982).

48. William V. Harris, *Ancient Literacy* (Cambridge, Mass./London: Harvard University
Press, 1989), p. 30. See also pp. 31–33, 301.

49. Gamble, *Books and Readers*, pp. 8–9.

50. Cf. Devorah Dimant, "Literary Typologies and Biblical Interpretation in the Hellenistic-
Roman Period," in *Jewish Civilization in the Hellenistic-Roman Period* (ed. Shemaryahu
Talmon; Philadelphia: Trinity Press International, 1991), p. 74: when Scripture is "integrated
into the structure" of a work and "introduced without any formal marker," then "this non-
explicit use of the biblical elements relies, for achieving the desired effect, on the understanding
and participation of the reader, who is assumed to have the necessary background of knowledge
to detect the allusion."

51. Peter J. Rabinowitz, "'What's Hecuba to Us?' The Audience's Experience of Literary
Borrowing," in *The Reader in the Text: Essays on Audience and Interpretation* (ed. Susan R.
Suleiman and Inge Crosman; Princeton: Princeton University Press, 1980), pp. 241–63, after
distinguishing between the authorial audience (the hypothetical projected audience of the
author) and the real audience, shows how the distinction can be elided.

authors, in original audiences, in texts themselves, in modern readers, and in communities of interpretation.[52] Herein, however, more weight will be laid on the *intentio operis* and the *intentio lectoris* [the ancient readers as well as subsequent readers in so far as the latter show us possibilities for the former] rather than the *intentio auctoris*. This is so not only for theoretical reasons which cannot be recounted here[53] but also because of historical compulsion: with the exception of Jesus, whose contribution to Q is the subject of keen debate, the contributors to and editors of Q are unknown to us.)

We should keep in mind that Scripture was performed orally and that the voice of public reading was, as it still is among Orthodox Jews to-day, halfway between singing and conversation.[54] Now since Q itself, like Paul's epistles and the canonical Gospels, was presumably also read aloud again and again at religious gatherings,[55] its allusions — like those in Martin Luther King's speeches — must have been intended for the ears, not the eyes. This matters so much because we all know how greatly sound aids memory and recognition. It is certainly much easier to learn the words of a song from the radio than from silently reading the sheet music. Furthermore, given the intertextual density of the Bible itself, a Jewish audience must have been accustomed to catching allusions. If Q's Jewish Christian audiences had heard in their years of synagogue-going the Moses typologies of the Hebrew Bible and the Tanak's other recurrent textual exchanges, its frequent conversations with itself, then they were well prepared to listen for allusions in Q. The inner-biblical allusion was a cultural convention in Judaism.

One might retort that "the Bible knowledge of a man who took up the pen to write books would naturally be far in advance of that of the great majority of his brethren."[56] But these words of Harnack, which seem to reflect common sense, are an exaggeration. In the Roman world, unlike the Middle Ages, "there is no sign of a culture-gap between the highly literate aristocracy and the masses," and "ordinary townspeople . . . will have had plenty of opportunities to 'consume' in oral form the cultural products emanating from above."[57] Paul seemingly assumed a good deal on the part of his

---

52. Hays, *Echoes*, pp. 25–29.

53. See Eco, "Between Author and Text."

54. E. Norden, *Die Antike Kunstprosa* (Stuttgart: Teubner, 1958), vol. 1, pp. 55–57. Cf. Gerhardsson, *Memory and Manuscript*, pp. 166–68; Gamble, *Books and Readers*, pp. 225–29.

55. On orality in early Christianity, see Paul J. Achtemeier, "*Omne verbum sonat:* The New Testament and the Oral Environment of Late Western Antiquity," *JBL* 109 (1990), pp. 3–27; Werner H. Kelber, "Jesus and Tradition: Words in Time, Words in Space," *Semeia* 65 (1995), pp. 139–67; idem, "Modalities of Communication, Cognition, and Physiology of Perception: Orality, Rhetoric, Scribality," ibid., pp. 193–215. One assumes that Q functioned like Paul's letters, which were to be read aloud to congregations: Col 4:16; 1 Thess 5:27. See now Richard A. Horsley and Jonathan A. Draper, *Whoever Hears You Hears Me: Prophets, Performance, and Tradition in Q* (Harrisburg, Pa.: Trinity Press International, 1999).

56. Adolf Harnack, *Bible Reading in the Early Church* (New York/London: G. P. Putnam's Sons/William & Norgate, 1912), p. 34.

57. F. Gerald Downing, "A bas les aristos. The Relevance of Higher Literature for the

Christian hearers, not many of whom were wise by worldly standards (1 Cor 1:26). Does not 1 Cor 10:1ff., for instance, presuppose that the Corinthians could recall for themselves the Pentateuchal narrative of the exodus? In the words of Gamble, "the frequency, variety, and subtlety of Paul's recourse to Scripture presumes not only that the communities he addressed acknowledged the authority of Jewish Scripture, but also that they were sufficiently familiar with it to understand and appreciate his appeals to it, subtle and diverse as they were."[58] There is no reason to suppose that those who heard Q were any less sophisticated. Indeed, they were probably more so. Most of Paul's hearers were Gentiles, whereas most of Q's hearers were Jews who had long lived within "the intertextual space of Judaism."[59] It is suggestive that Matthew and Luke, two of Q's readers who valued it sufficiently to use it as a source, had an undeniable fondness for borrowing subtly from the Bible, and surely they expected most of their hearers — who had probably listened to Q before the later Gospels came to be — to understand and enjoy what they were doing.[60] They knew, we need not doubt, that "you must not go beyond your public. This is the main law of Literary Reminiscence: do not, except with due precautions, remind your readers of what they do not remember."[61]

This is not to say that all those who heard Q were equally sophisticated or informed listeners. Early Christian gatherings, like all other human conglomerates, will have contained some who were more learned and some who were less learned as well as some who had superior memories and some who had inferior memories. One may thus surmise that some of the more subtle allusions in ancient Christian literature would not have been picked up by everyone. Just as sometimes only the experts can espy and read the animal tracks, likewise surely some of the subtle echoes that Hays has taught us to listen for in the letters of Paul would have been heard more readily by the apostle and his scripturally literate conversation partners in mission — Barnabas, Luke, Silas, Timothy, Titus — than by the new Gentile converts in Corinth or Galatia.[62] Acts 18:24 tells us that Apollos was "well-versed

---

Understanding of the Earliest Christian Writings," *NovT* 30 (1988), pp. 212–30. Cf. Gamble, *Books and Readers*, pp. 4–5, 8–9.

58. Gamble, *Books and Readers*, pp. 212–13.

59. The expression is that of Sylvia C. Keesmaat, "Exodus and the Intertextual Transformation of Tradition in Romans 8.14–30," *JSNT* 54 (1994), p. 49.

60. On the pleasure that recognition of an allusion gives, see E. E. Kellett, *Literary Quotation and Allusion* (Port Washington, N.Y./London: Kennikat, 1933), pp. 17–20; also Perri, "On Alluding," pp. 301–3, where the allusion is instructively compared with the joke as analyzed by Freud.

61. Kellett, *Quotation and Allusion*, p. 9.

62. Hays himself, in "On the Rebound: A Response to Critiques of *Echoes of Scripture in the Letters of Paul*," in *Paul and the Scriptures of Israel* (ed. Craig A. Evans and James A. Sanders; JSNTSS 83; Sheffield: JSOT Press, 1993), p. 86, has raised a related possibility: maybe Paul "was trying, with mixed results, to resocialize his converts into a new symbolic world that was still in process of formation even in his own mind. There were some successes, some failures.

(δυνατός) in the Scriptures," which must be a virtue in which he exceeds others. Nonetheless, Paul probably taught his charges as much of the LXX as he could in the time he was with them.[63] And whatever the practice of the apostle, most of the allusions discussed in this work on Q are not so cunningly concealed that they would have been missed by Jewish Christians who had repeatedly heard the Bible recited and expounded. Q does not belong to the tradition of what Umberto Eco has called "Hermetic semiosis,"[64] nor were its compilers kin of Milton and Ben Jonson, two massively learned authors who knew that only a scant few could really appreciate what they were doing.

My other prefatory point is that ancient writers did not typically borrow in order to show off or to add surface ornamentation. It may be that the Roman orator Pollio was criticized for ostentatious quoting, but most ancient authors were, again like Martin Luther King in our own day, accustomed to borrowing from the well-known classics in order to add meaning.[65] Hence identification of their precursors is part of the task of interpretation.

It also will not do to say that the ancients took up scriptural language simply because they lacked the rhetorical resources or desire to mint fresh expressions, as though that was just the way they unreflectively spoke and wrote, and nothing more need be said. For although we all necessarily speak within our own linguistic traditions, and while it is true that every text is unavoidably a permutation and reconfiguration of a prior body of discourse, a mosaic of shorter and longer quotations (intertextuality in the broad sense),[66] it is equally true that one can be more or less consciously emulous, more or less deliberate about the sources of one's mosaic.

One does, admittedly, often run across the comment that this or that writer was just borrowing biblical language without concern for its link with any particular precursor text.[67] One needs, however, to distinguish between unconscious borrowing, coincidences, and stock expressions on the

---

Often it appears that his readers found him baffling. One reason for their incomprehension may have been that he was not able to fill in all the gaps left for his hearers by his allusive references to Scripture; he may have been consistently presupposing knowledge that he ought not to have presupposed."

63. Cf. Origen, *Hom. Exod.* 5.1 (SC 321, ed. M. Borret, p. 148).

64. Eco, "Overinterpreting Texts," in Collini, *Interpretation*, pp. 45–66.

65. Young, *Biblical Exegesis*, pp. 97–116. Contrast J. Christiaan Beker, "Echoes and Intertextuality: On the Role of Scripture in Paul's Theology," in Evans and Sanders, eds., *Paul and the Scriptures of Israel*, p. 65: Paul "may simply use Scripture to impress his audience with his profundity, while the contours and contexts of a specific fragment of the Old Testament passage are in fact not the necessary presupposition for the validity of his argument."

66. Julia Kristeva, "Word, Dialogue, and Novel," in *Desire in Language: A Semiotic Approach to Literature and Art* (ed. Léon S. Roudiez; New York: Columbia University Press, 1980), pp. 64–91.

67. See, e.g., W. Rudolph, *Jona* (Tübingen: Mohr Siebeck, 1970), p. 352 (on the psalm language of Jonah 2); and George B. Caird, *The Revelation of St. John the Divine* (BNTC; 2d ed.; London: A. & C. Black, 1984), p. 74.

one hand and allusions — deliberate prompts — on the other.[68] The existence of the former does not exclude the presence of the latter, and whether we are dealing with one or the other must be determined on a case-by-case basis.[69]

To offer a concrete illustration: Michael Fishbane has written of the Damascus Document that "little would be gained by dismissing" its biblical texture "as so much linguistic archaizing or stylistic conceit. For to separate verbal form from ideological content would be unnecessarily artificial."[70] Jonathan Campbell's analysis of CD confirms the point:

> Although CD 1–8 and 19–20, like some other Second Temple texts, may at times employ biblical language simply because of the generally pervasive, but unconscious and hence largely insignificant, saturation of the author's mind with the vocabulary of the scriptures, most of the quotations, virtual citations, and allusions we have considered do not fall into this category.... We found ourselves returning to a distinct corpus of scriptural passages.[71]

Indeed, "the writer of CD 1–8 and 19–20 employs the Bible ... by regularly incorporating into his work reminiscences of language from scriptural contexts which recount a series of Israelite and, occasionally, pre-Israelite crises, in which the 'sheep' are separated from the 'goats.' "[72] In other words, the biblical language of CD 1–8 and 19–20 creates an integrating pattern when the scriptural phrases are interpreted, not as artificial embellishment or thoughtless convention, but as allusive subtexts.

While those who heard Q probably did not have the same daily, intensive exposure to Scripture as did the Qumran sectaries, what reason is there for imagining that Q's audiences were like ill-informed moderns who run across a line from Shakespeare and know only that it is from the Bard, not from what play, so that the connotations for them are minimal? If Jewish Christians had grown up hearing Scripture recited in the synagogue, then they must have been able to construe Q's biblical allusions just as modern educated Americans construe the words and phrases of E. D. Hirsch's *Cultural Literacy*.[73] "In the days of Noah" and "Lot's wife" were, for the followers of Jesus, what "the father of his country" and "Rosa Parks" are for us, namely, abbreviations, shorthand for well-known stories. Even if Q's first audiences knew nothing like chapter and verse, and even if most of them had no formal education, surely they were yet sufficiently familiar with biblical lines and stories, with plots and segments of Scripture, to catch allusions to them.[74] That Sodom needs no introduction in Q 10:12 implies a

---

68. I here leave to one side another cause of similarity: plagiarism.

69. See point (v) on p. 12.

70. Fishbane, "Mikra at Qumran," p. 357.

71. Jonathan G. Campbell, *The Use of Scripture in the Damascus Document 1–8, 19–20* (BZAW 228; Berlin/New York: de Gruyter, 1995), p. 206.

72. Ibid., p. 208.

73. E. D. Hirsch, *Cultural Literacy* (Boston: Houghton Mifflin, 1987).

74. It should go without saying that familiarity with a tradition need not require any critical

communal norm: Q's receptors should be able to draw imaginatively upon the textual encyclopedia of their Jewish culture.

Q, as we shall see, contains many more allusions than formal quotations, and the former as opposed to the latter work only when they direct informed readers beyond themselves. An allusion is no end in itself but a suggestive element, a clue, an implied link to another text; it is a piece whose purpose is to summon what it has been subtracted from (cf. synecdoche).[75] And it is up to readers to do the summoning. The mention of Abel in Q 11:51 serves no purpose unless one carries around the tale of Genesis 4 in one's head. Q is in this instance, as regularly, not narrating an old story but referring to it on the assumption that it is known. The text contributes the allusion but not the text alluded to. Like the moral imperative, the allusion does not bring with it the power of its own fulfillment but becomes realized only with the hearer's right response.

How exactly all this works is a bit mysterious, and the errors of misinterpretation and overinterpretation always hover above the text. A fragment from a precursor can beckon that fragment's first immediate context, the entire work to which it belongs, that work's author, its genre, and/or its literary period.[76] Indeed, the intertextual possibilities are endless. Yet in practice the fragment's new home and its own textual coherence will suggest to the competent reader which one or more of various possibilities, of various deeper meanings, should be pursued. Because King's "I Have a Dream" is about the condition of African Americans, not the Civil War, "Five score years ago" is designed to recall, not the Battle of Gettysburg, but Abraham Lincoln and what he stood for. To repeat, however, the chief point in all this is simply that an alluding text is a presuming text: it posits a certain sort of audience, one capable of decoding allusions by perceiving allusionally activated texts, instructed readers who can sound on their own syllables implied but left unspoken.

---

sense or great sophistication, just a decent memory. The fact is well illustrated by the intertextuality of modern movies; see on this Umberto Eco, "Interpreting Serials," in *The Limits of Interpretation* (Bloomington/Indianapolis: Indiana University Press, 1990), pp. 83–100. One recalls that although Bonaventure's writings are full of Scripture, he thought Mary the Mother of Jesus had written the Psalms! And we all know firsthand that it does not take higher education or brilliance to sprinkle one's speech with allusions to popular music, movies, and TV shows.

75. Cf. Hays's use of John Hollander's term "metalepsis": "When a literary echo links the text in which it occurs to an earlier text, the figurative effect of the echo can lie in the unstated or suppressed (transmuted) points of resonance between the two texts.... Allusive echo functions to suggest to the reader that text B should be understood in light of a broad interplay with text A, encompassing aspects of A beyond those explicitly echoed" (*Echoes*, p. 20). Cf. also the formulation of Meyer, *Poetics of Quotation*, p. 6: "the charm of the quotation emanates from a unique tension between assimilation and dissimilation: it links itself closely with its new environment, but at the same time detaches itself from it, thus permitting another world to radiate into the self-contained world of the novel."

76. Ziva Ben-Porat, "The Poetics of Literary Allusion," *PTL: A Journal for Descriptive Poetics and Theory of Literature* 1 (1976), pp. 105–28.

Such an approach to Q seemingly puts me near the camp of those who, over the past decades, have urged that the NT writers paid some attention to the original contexts of their subtexts.[77] The debate has, however, often been guided by an apologetical desire to defend the hermeneutical moves of NT authors, to vindicate them against the charge of being arbitrary, and such an impulse does not animate the present investigation. The important question is not whether an "author respected the Old Testament context," but "how does the Old Testament context interact with the New Testament context?"[78] I am arguing only that Q arose in a social setting where Scripture was well enough known that phrases pulled from it frequently carried specific associations — associations often related to the site of extraction. This is a question, not of legitimate interpretation or illegitimate interpretation, but of the cultural connotations of conventional words and phrases.

My position is consistent with Jan Fekkes' careful work on Revelation, which has led to this result:

> When John wants to emphasize his own prophetic status and authority or illustrate his throne-room vision, he draws on the well-known experiences and examples of earlier prophets. And when he comes to describe the New Jerusalem, he builds on a biblical substructure of OT prophecies relating to the future glorified Jerusalem. Political oracles correspond to political oracles; prophecies of judgment to prophecies of judgment; and promises of salvation serve as the basis for promises of salvation. Furthermore, John employs corporate models for corporate subjects and individual models for individual subjects. Therefore we do not find Daniel being used in the portrayal of Harlot-Babylon, nor is Isaiah ever used to describe the eschatological enemy. All this challenges the common assumption that John is not consciously interpreting the OT, but simply using it as a language and image base.[79]

The implications of these observations are large. Revelation's scriptural borrowings are not neat cuttings but transplants with roots and some of the old soil.

What we find in Revelation we find elsewhere as well. 1QM 12:9–10 ("like rain clouds [(כ)עננים]and the mist clouds covering the earth [לכסות ארץ], like a rainstorm") transfers the language used of Gog in Ezek 38:9, 16 ("coming on like a storm, like a cloud covering the earth," כענן לכסות

---

77. See P. Grech, "The 'Testimonia' and Modern Hermeneutics," *NTS* 19 (1973), pp. 318–24. There are similar debates concerning the allusive extent of allusions in other literature. For an instructive example, see Earl R. Wasserman, "The Limits of Allusion in *The Rape of the Lock*," *Journal of English and Germanic Philology* 65 (1966), pp. 425–44. (With regard to Pope, his conclusion is this: "The reader is not only to appreciate the poet's invention in finding appropriate allusions but is actively invited by them to exercise, within poetic reason, his own invention by contemplating the relevance of the entire allusive context and its received interpretation.")

78. Steve Moyise, *The Old Testament in the Book of Revelation* (JSNTSS 115; Sheffield: Sheffield Academic Press, 1995), p. 19.

79. Jan Fekkes III, *Isaiah and Prophetic Traditions in the Book of Revelation: Visionary Antecedents and Their Development* (JSNTSS 93; Sheffield: JSOT Press, 1992), p. 102.

הָאָרֶץ) to the army of the saints. The seemingly ill-adapted reapplication is surprising, and one might infer that here we have proof of neglect of the original context. But this is not so at all, for both texts depict an army in the midst of the great eschatological battle. So even if the relocation, the overlaying of the saints with a description of Gog, is unexpected and from one point of view a violation of the original context, that is, erroneous exegesis, an awareness of the setting within Ezekiel 38 is nonetheless undeniable.

Consider another example. When Paul, in 1 Cor 14:25, has the unbeliever visiting a Christian assembly declare, "God is among you" (ὁ θεὸς ἐν ὑμῖν ἐστιν), he is borrowing from LXX Isa 45:14–15: "And they will bow down before you and pray to you, because God is among you (ἐν σοι ὁ θεὸς ἐστιν), and they will say, 'There is no God besides you; for you are God, and we did not know it, the God of Israel, the savior.'" The correlation goes beyond mere words. In both Paul and Isaiah the subject is the conversion of outsiders, and the context is worship.[80] Paul was evidently led to use the phrase from Isa 45:14–15 because the subject of its context was the subject of 1 Corinthians 14. Further, if readers are informed enough to know whence ὁ θεὸς ἐν ὑμῖν ἐστιν comes, surely they will also recognize the thematic congruence. In other words, for those who can invest 1 Cor 14:25 with its heritage and fill in the blanks with a knowledge of Isaiah, the snippet from there does more than echo the Bible and add a sacred ambience: Paul's words carry the amplitude of two interfering waves in phase with each other.

One last illustration. 1 Cor 1:26–31 ends with, "As it is written, 'Let the one who boasts, boast in the Lord.'" This is a loose quotation of Jer 9:23 (cf. 1 βασ 2:10). Now Jer 9:23 opens with this triadic imperative: "Do not let the wise boast in their wisdom, do not let the mighty boast in their might, do not let the wealthy boast in their wealth." It cannot be coincidence that 1 Cor 1:26–31 commences with Paul imploring the Corinthians to consider their calling with these words: "Not many of you were wise according to the flesh, not many were mighty, not many were of noble birth." The explicit quotation in v. 31 turns out to be only part of a larger borrowing. The influence of Jer 9:23 spills out beyond Paul's formal citation, to such an extent that 1 Cor 1:26 merits being labeled an allusion.[81] In other words, 1 Cor 1:26–31 interacts with Jer 9:23 in congenial ways not explicitly signaled by the text but nonetheless real: implicit borrowing introduces "As it is written...."

This investigation will venture to show that much of Q uses the Bible

---

80. Richard B. Hays, "The Conversion of the Imagination: Scripture and Eschatology in 1 Corinthians," *NTS* 45 (1999), pp. 391–94.

81. See further Gail R. O'Day, "Jeremiah 9:22–23 and 1 Corinthians 1:26–31: A Study in Intertextuality," *JBL* 109 (1990), pp. 259–67 — although her punctuation of v. 26 as a question is uncertain.

as does Paul: its scriptural speech often carries contextual associations. Q's contributors typically incorporated biblical items because they were writing to memories. They wanted to allude, to prod imaginations into juxtaposing the words of Q with this story or that pericope in Q's authoritative precursor, the Tanak.

Chapter 2

Pentateuch I

Exodus, Leviticus, Deuteronomy

I. Texts and Analysis

Q 4:1–13 // Deut 6:13, 16; 8:3; 34:1–4.[1] In doing battle with the devil, Jesus cites, in Q 4:4, the second half of LXX Deut 8:3: "And he afflicted you, and he made you famished, and he fed you with manna, which your fathers knew not, in order to teach you that one will not live by bread alone, but that one will live by everything that proceeds from the mouth of God."[2] In Q 4:10–11, Satan challenges Jesus by quoting most of LXX Ps 90:11–12: "He will command his angels concerning you . . . on their hands they will bear you up, so that you will not strike your foot against a stone."[3] In Q 4:12 Jesus responds by reciting LXX Deut 6:16a: "You will not tempt the Lord your God as you tempted him in the temptation [at Massah]."[4] And in Q 4:8, which is the concluding declaration in Matthew's version (Mt 4:10), as probably in Q,[5] Jesus, upon being solicited to worship the devil, makes rebuttal by quoting LXX Deut 6:13: "You will fear the Lord your God, and him only will you serve."[6]

---

1. There are no references to Numbers in Q. This may be due simply to the book's being less popular than the other four Pentateuchal works. In the Dead Sea Scrolls, for instance, there are more copies of Genesis, Exodus, Leviticus, and Deuteronomy than Numbers.

2. Both LXX and Q have οὐκ ἐπ' ἄρτῳ μόνῳ ζήσεται ὁ ἄνθρωπος. Matthew adds, ἀλλ' ἐπὶ παντὶ ῥήματι ἐκπορευομένῳ διὰ στόματος θεοῦ, which agrees with LXX A. (LXX B has τῷ after ῥήματι.) MT: ויענך וירעבך ויאכלך את־המן אשר לא־ידעת ולא ידעון אבתיך למען הודעך כי לא על־הלחם לבדו יחיה האדם כי על־כל־מוצא פי־יהוה יחיה האדם.

3. Q here agrees with the LXX: τοῖς ἀγγέλοις αὐτοῦ ἐντελεῖται περὶ σοῦ...ἐπὶ χειρῶν ἀροῦσίν σε, μήποτε προσκόψῃς πρὸς λίθον τὸν πόδα σου. MT: כי מלאכיו יצוה־לך... על־כפים ישאונך פן־תגף באבן רגלך. On the possible association with the exodus, see pp. 38–40 herein.

4. Q: οὐκ ἐκπειράσεις κύριον τὸν θεόν σου. So too the LXX. MT: לא תנסו את־יהוה אלהיכם.

5. So the International Q Project (IQP). Luke's interest in the temple could have moved him to turn the scene in the holy place into the climax, and Matthew's order, where the most blatant temptation ("worship me") comes at the end, is the more fitting dramatic conclusion.

6. Q   κύριον τὸν θεόν σου προσκυνήσεις καὶ αὐτῷ μόνῳ λατρεύσεις
  LXX B κύριον τὸν θεόν σου φοβηθήσῃ   καὶ αὐτῷ   λατρεύσεις
  LXX A κύριον τὸν θεόν σου προσκυνήσεις καὶ αὐτῷ μόνῳ λατρεύσεις
  MT   את־יהוה אלהיך תירא ואתו תעבד

If hearers of Q 4:1–13 know that the three citations of Deuteronomy have to do, in their original contexts, with the wilderness temptations of Israel, and if they further remember, what has never been esoteric knowledge, that Israel wandered for forty years, then they can hardly avoid thinking, as did Tertullian, *De bapt.* 20, that Jesus is here repeating Israel's history in the desert.[7] That is, Q recounts a new exodus. If Israel was in the wilderness for forty years (Deut 8:2), Jesus is there for forty days (Q 4:2; forty days symbolizes forty years in Num 14:34 and Ezek 4:56). If Israel was tempted by hunger and fed upon manna (Exod 16:2–8), so is the hungry Jesus tempted to turn stones into bread (Q 4:2–3; manna, one should recall, was spoken of as bread).[8] If Israel was tempted to put God to the test, the same thing happens to Jesus (Exod 17:1–3; Q 4:9–12).[9] And if Israel was lured to idolatry (Exodus 32), the devil confronts Jesus with the same temptation to worship something other than Israel's God (Q 4:5–8). The last parallel is all the closer when one remembers that idolatry was sometimes conceived of as demon worship (Deut 32:17; Ps 106:37–38; *1 En.* 99:7) or even worship of the devil (*Asc. Isa* 2:1–7; *Pirqe R. El.* 45 can say that Samma'el was in the golden calf, and *Exod Rab.* 43:1 has Satan accusing Israel during the episode including that object).

Q 4:4 quotes Deut 8:3, and the context of the latter verse is worth noting:

Whether Q's μόνῳ (cf. 1 Sam 7:3; Jdt 3:8) represents a Greek text known to Q (cf. LXX A; this seems the opinion of most) or whether LXX A's μόνῳ is assimilation to the Gospels is not known.

For caution about what conclusions may be drawn from the agreements of Q 4 with the LXX, see C. M. Tuckett, "The Temptation Narrative in Q," in *The Four Gospels 1992: Festschrift Frans Neirynck* (ed. F. Van Segbroeck et al.; BETL 100; Louvain: Louvain University Press/Peeters), vol. 1, pp. 479–507.

7. Tertullian, *De bapt.* 20 (CSEL 20, ed. A. Reifferscheid and G. Wissowa, pp. 217–18). Cf. Theophylact, *Comm. Mt* ad loc. (PG 123.181); Richard Chenevix Trench, *Studies in the Gospels* (2d ed.; London: Macmillan, 1867), pp. 15–16; David Friedrich Strauss, *The Life of Jesus Critically Examined* (Philadelphia: Fortress, 1972), pp. 259–63; Birger Gerhardsson, *The Testing of God's Son (Matt 4:1–11 & Par.)* (CB,NT 2/1; Lund: Gleerup, 1966); Austin Farrer, *The Triple Victory: Christ's Temptation according to St. Matthew* (Cambridge, Mass.: Cowley, 1990); Charles A. Kimball, *Jesus' Exposition of the Old Testament in Luke's Gospel* (JSNTSup 94; Sheffield: JSOT Press, 1994), pp. 80–97; Robert L. Brawley, *Text to Text Pours Forth Speech: Voices of Scripture in Luke-Acts* (Bloomington/Indianapolis: Indiana University Press, 1995), pp. 16–26; William Richard Stegner, "The Use of Scripture in Two Narratives of Early Jewish Christianity (Matthew 4.1–11; Mark 9.2–8)," in *Early Christian Interpretation of the Scriptures of Israel* (ed. Craig A. Evans and James A. Sanders; JSNTSS 148; Sheffield: Sheffield Academic Press, 1997), pp. 98–120; and Craig S. Keener, *Commentary on the Gospel of Matthew* (Grand Rapids/Cambridge, U.K.: Eerdmans, 1999), pp. 136–37.

8. Exod 16:4; Deut 8:3; Neh 9:15; Ps 78:25; 105:40; Wisd 16:20; Jn 6:31–34; *LAB* 10:7; *5 Ezra* 1:19; *b.* Yoma 75b; etc.

9. Cf. Bar-Hebraeus, *Commentary on the Gospels from the Horreum Mysterium* (trans. and ed. Wilmot Eardley W. Carr; London: SPCK, 1925), p. 15: "Thou shalt not tempt the Lord thy God — N. like those who tempted Him in the wilderness and were not esteemed worthy to enter into the promised land."

2. Remember the long way that the Lord your God has led you these forty years[10] in the wilderness, in order to humble you, testing you to know what was in your heart, whether or not you would keep his commandments. 3. He humbled you by letting you hunger, then by feeding you with manna, with which neither you nor your ancestors were acquainted, in order to make you understand that one does not live by bread alone, but by every word that comes from the mouth of the Lord.... 4. The clothes on your back did not wear out and your feet did not swell these forty years. 5. Know then in your heart that as a parent disciplines his son so the Lord your God disciplines you.

Here we have not only the verse cited in Q 4:4 but several additional elements of our story, and mostly in the same order: being led, the wilderness, the number forty,[11] temptation, hunger,[12] and sonship:

Matthew	Luke	LXX Deuteronomy	MT Deuteronomy
ἀνήχθη	ἤγετο	ἤγαγεν	הליכך
εἰς τὴν ἔρημον	ἐν τῇ ἐρήμῳ	ἐν τῇ ἐρήμῳ	ארבעים
πειρασθῆναι	τεσσεράκοντα	ἐκπειράσῃ	במדבר
τεσσεράκοντα	πειραζόμενος	τεσσεράκοντα	לנסתך
ἐπείνασεν	ἐπείνασεν	τὸν υἱὸν αὐτοῦ	ירעבך
υἱὸς τοῦ θεοῦ	υἱὸς τοῦ θεοῦ		בנו

Clearly those who know Deut 8:1ff. will come away from Q 4:1–13 with, as it has been called, *deja lu*.[13]

In addition to replaying the exodus, Q 4:1–13 appears to present Jesus as one like Moses. In Q 4:5–7, the devil takes Jesus up to a mountain and shows him all the kingdoms of the world, and this, like *2 Baruch* 76 and 84,[14] seems to be a reminiscence of the story that Moses went to the top of Pisgah, looked in all directions, and saw the land he would not enter (Num 27:12–14; Deut 3:27; 32:48–52; 34:1–4).[15] In both cases a supernatural

---

10. The LXX does not have "these forty years."

11. The MT mentions forty years in vv. 2 and 4, the LXX only in the latter.

12. While πεινάω is not used in Deuteronomy 8, it is used of the exodus in LXX Deut 25:18; cf. also Ps 107:5, 9; Isa 49:10.

13. David R. Catchpole, *The Quest for Q* (Edinburgh: T. & T. Clark, 1993), p. 230, observes that the Deuteronomistic quotations occur in reverse order (at least if Matthew here preserves the arrangement of Q) — Q 4:4 = Deut 8:3, Q 4:7 = Deut 6:16, Q 4:10 = Deut 6:13. But one fails to see that this generates meaning or that it is anything more than coincidence.

14. See Allison, *New Moses*, pp. 65–68. According to John R. Levenson, *Theology of the Program of Restoration of Ezekiel 40–48* (HSM 10; Missoula, Mont.: Scholars Press, 1976), pp. 42–44, Nebo is also used typologically in Ezekiel 40–48.

15. Exegetes of Matthew or Luke who have thought this include August Friedrich Gfrörer, *Das Jahrhundert des Heils* (Stuttgart: C. Schweizerbart, 1838), pp. 385–86; Barnabas Lindars, "The Image of Moses in the Synoptic Gospels," *Theology* 58 (1955), p. 130; Howard M. Teeple, *The Mosaic Eschatological Prophet* (JBLMS 10; Philadelphia: Society of Biblical Literature, 1957), p. 77; Robert H. Gundry, *Matthew: A Commentary on His Literary and Theological Art* (Grand Rapids: Eerdmans, 1982), p. 57; W. Wilkens, "Die Versuchung Jesu nach Matthäus," *NTS* 28 (1982), p. 485; and Terrence L. Donaldson, *Jesus on the Mountain: A*

figure (God or Satan) shows to a hero (Moses or Jesus) the entirety of a realm (all the land of Israel or all the kingdoms of the world), but the hero does not then enter or inherit that realm. In Matthew, moreover, all this takes place upon a very high mountain, which augments the parallelism. Whether or not the First Evangelist found the mountain in Q,[16] or whether he observed the parallel with Deut 34:1–4 and added to it, the upshot is pretty much the same: someone was construing the story in Q 4:1–13 as analogous to the tale of Moses on Nebo. Further, there are verbal parallels between Q 4:5–7 and LXX Deut 34:1–4:

Deut	καὶ ἔδειξεν	αὐτῷ πᾶσαν τὴν γῆν	...δώσω
Luke	ἔδειξεν	αὐτῷ πάσας τὰς βασιλείας	...δώσω
Matthew	καὶ δείκνυοιν	αὐτῷ πάσας τὰς βασιλείας	...δώσω

The similarity is all the greater because if, in Deuteronomy, God shows Moses "all the land, Gilead as far as Dan, all Naphtali, the land of Ephraim and Manasseh, all the land of Judah as far as the Western Sea, the Negeb, and the Plain, that is, the valley of Jericho the city of palm trees, as far as Zoar," the haggada greatly expanded this vision. *Sifre Deut* 357 on 34:1–9 tells us that Moses was granted a vision of "all the world," and *LAB* 19:10 also makes Moses' vision a universal one, which is what we have in Q (cf. also *Mek.* on 17:14–16).[17]

Q's new exodus typology, which, if Matthew's order be followed, agrees with the order of the temptations in Exodus, appears only to the scripturally informed, so too Jesus' likeness to Moses on Nebo. If one fails to bring to Q 4:1–13 the relevant intertextual knowledge, that is, knowledge of Israel's wilderness wanderings and Deuteronomy's account of Moses' farewell, then all the parallelism will, despite the explicit citations, be missed, for it remains altogether implicit. One will also miss the implicit contrast: Jesus succeeded where ancient Israel failed.

Two final points. First, Jesus is in our narrative called the Son of God. The content of this title for Q is difficult to specify. But one possibility is that it presents Jesus as the embodiment of true Israel, for in the Hebrew Bible Israel is spoken of as God's son,[18] and here in Q Jesus relives the foundational experiences of Israel. Moreover, sometimes Israel is called God's son precisely with reference to the exodus from Egypt, as in Exod 4:22–23 ("Then you [Moses] will say to Pharaoh, 'Thus says the Lord: Israel is my

---

Study in Matthean Theology (JSNTSS 8; Sheffield: JSOT Press, 1985), p. 93. This a reading that may be confined to relatively modern commentaries. On the parallel in *Apocalypse of Abraham* 12, which contains Sinai and Nebo motifs in the context of temptation, see Allison, *New Moses*, pp. 170–71.

16. The issue is disputed; see Donaldson, *Mountain*, pp. 87–88.

17. Also many of the texts cited in n. 108 on p. 47 belong here.

18. Texts in H. Haag, "בֵּן," *TDOT* 2 (1975), p. 155. Note Deut 32:4–6; also Keesmaat, "Exodus and the Intertextual Transformation," pp. 38–41.

firstborn son' "); Deut 8:5 (quoted above); and Hos 11:1 ("When Israel was a child I loved him, and out of Egypt I called my son").

Second, by virtue of its position, the temptation narrative functions as a sort of prologue to the rest of Q;[19] and since what comes at the beginning of a work often sets the tone for the remainder, the explicit use of Scripture in Q 4:1–13 may be reckoned programmatic.[20] Jesus' recurrent recourse to the Pentateuch in his scriptural debate with the devil displays the importance and authority of the Mosaic books as well as the need to know them by heart. Jesus can instantly cite at will a fitting word that "has been written" (γέγραπται, 4:4, 8, 12). Surely it is implied not only that it would be wise for those who follow Jesus to possess the same ability — a point made incessantly in homilies and ecclesiastical commentaries on our passage — but further that the rest of Jesus' words may well be sprinkled with the sacred oracles that he has committed to memory. Are not the hearers of Q set up to anticipate a document with significant scriptural intertextuality?

Q 6:27–45 // Leviticus 19. Vengeance, love, and judging others are the three major themes of this section of Q. They are likewise themes classically associated with Leviticus 19, part of the so-called holiness code. This chapter of the Pentateuch teaches that "vindictiveness is diametrically opposed to holy living within the covenant community,"[21] it contains instruction for reproof and judging one's neighbor (v. 15), and it famously declares, "you will love your neighbor as yourself" (v. 18). The overlap in subject matter is not fortuitous. Leviticus 19 is rather, as David Catchpole has observed, the chief intertext for Q 6:27–45.[22] This appears from the following:

(i) Q 6:36 commands disciples to "be merciful" just as "your father is merciful."[23] Joseph Fitzmyer, like other commentators, thinks this is "a take-off from Lev 19:2,"[24] a verse in which God says, "You will be holy, for I

---

19. I am here concerned only with Q as Matthew and Luke knew it, not with hypothetical earlier stages.

20. Cf. Schlosser, "L'utilisation des Écritures," pp. 142–46.

21. So H. G. L. Peels, *The Vengeance of God: The Meaning of the Root NQM and the Function of the NQM-Texts in the Context of Divine Revelation in the Old Testament* (OTS 31; Leiden/New York/Cologne: Brill, 1995), p. 51.

22. Catchpole, *Quest for Q*, pp. 101–34; cf. Richard A. Horsley, *Jesus and the Spiral of Violence: Popular Jewish Resistance in Roman Palestine* (San Francisco: Harper & Row, 1987), p. 271; Tuckett, "Scripture in Q," p. 25; idem, *Q*, pp. 431–34. Although Catchpole rightly sees that Lev 19:18 is "the unseen influence throughout the section 6:27–35" and that Q 6:36–45 interprets Lev 19:17, he has failed to perceive all of the connections between Q 6 and Leviticus 19.

23. Matthew's "Be perfect" (τέλειοι) is secondary; cf. the redactional insertion of τέλειος in Mt 19:21 diff. Mk 10:21.

24. Joseph Fitzmyer, *The Gospel according to Luke I–IX* (AB 28A; Garden City, N.Y.: Doubleday, 1981), p. 641. Lev 19:2 is in the margin of Matthew Poole, *A Commentary on the Holy Bible* (McLean, Va.: MacDonald Publishing Co., 1962), vol. 3, p. 26. Cf. Robert Horton Gundry, *The Use of the Old Testament in St. Matthew's Gospel, with Special Reference to the Messianic Hope* (NovTSup 18; Leiden: Brill, 1967), p. 73; John S. Kloppenborg, *Q Parallels: Synopsis, Critical Notes, and Concordance* (Sonoma, Calif.: Polebridge, 1988),

the Lord your God am holy."[25] There is indeed a structural parallel. In both cases a second person imperative (LXX: ἔσεσθε; MT: תהיו; Q: ἔσεσθε [so Mt 5:48] or γίνεσθε [so Lk 6:36]) precedes a justification through appeal to the *imitatio Dei* (LXX: θεὸς ὑμῶν, "your God"; יהוה אלהיכם, "the Lord your God"; Q: ὁ πατήρ ὑμῶν, "your Father"): the quality demanded of persons is a quality exhibited by God. So one may regard Q 6:36 as analogous to *Lev Rab.* 308 on 24:4, where a quotation of Lev 19:2 is prefaced by, "My children, as I am pure, so you will be pure."[26] Here too the form of Lev 19:2 is retained while another virtue is substituted for holiness, in this case purity.[27]

If Q 6:36 is indeed a reformulation of Lev 19:2, then one might infer that whoever composed our text quite consciously placed mercy above holiness. This is the view of Marcus Borg, who writes that the connection between Lev 19:2 and Q 6:36 "is apparent, and thus the replacement of holiness with mercy as the content of the *imitatio dei* was deliberate."[28] It is equally possible, however, that Q is not replacing one concept with another but rather explicating holiness in terms of mercy: mercy is the true meaning of holiness. In either case, Lev 19:2 is being reconstructed.

(ii) If we consider Q 6:36 within its Q context, there is a second pointer to Leviticus 19, namely, the earlier imperative, ἀγαπᾶτε τοὺς ἐχθροὺς ὑμῶν ("Love your enemies," 6:27). This command is parallel to the famous Lev 19:18, "Love your neighbor" (LXX: ἀγαπήσεις τὸν πλησίον σου; MT: אהבת לרעך).[29] Both use a second person imperative of ἀγαπάω + definite article + object + second person pronoun. There can be no doubt that Matthew at least thought of Lev 19:18 when editing Q's word about the enemy, for he redactionally introduced Jesus' command to love the enemy with these words, "You have heard that it was said, 'Love your neighbor and hate your enemy, but I say to you . . .'" (5:43).[30] This encourages us to surmise that the central part of the Sermon on the Plain, with "Love your enemies" at the beginning and "Be merciful as your father is merciful" at the end, may be intended to offer some sort of expansion of or contrast with the holiness

---

p. 33; François Bovon, *Das Evangelium nach Lukas (Lk 1,1–9,50)* (EKKNT 3/1; Zurich and Düsseldorf/Neukirchen-Vluyn: Benziger/Neukirchener, 1989), p. 322; and those cited in n. 28.

25. Cf. 11:44, 45; 20:7, 26. We have here a levitical refrain.

26. For additional rewritings of Lev 19:2, see point (vii) below.

27. Cf. also *b. Šabb.* 133b: "Just as he [God] is gracious and compassionate, so you be gracious and compassionate."

28. Marcus J. Borg, *Conflict, Holiness, and Politics in the Teaching of Jesus* (Lewiston, N.Y.: Edwin Mellen, 1984), p. 128. He cites in agreement H. Branscomb, H. J. Schoeps, K. Stendahl, R. S. McConnell, S. Schulz, and A. Wilder.

29. Cf. Horsley, *Jesus and the Spiral of Violence*, p. 217. Albertus Magnus, *Enarrationes in primam partem Evangelium Lucae (I–IX)* ad loc. (Opera Omnia 22, ed. A. Borgnet, p. 429), cites the first half of Lev 19:18 when commenting on Lk 6:27: "You will not take vengeance or bear a grudge against any of your people."

30. See further J. W. Doeve, *Jewish Hermeneutics in the Synoptic Gospels and Acts* (Assen: Van Gorcum, 1954), pp. 193–95.

code. Jesus follows Leviticus 19 in countering vengeance and encouraging love, but if the Pentateuchal chapter demands holiness because God is holy and then enjoins love of neighbor, Jesus demands mercy because God is merciful and then enjoins love of enemy.

Interestingly enough, the three elements of Lev 19:18b ("You will love // your neighbor // as yourself") can be related directly to all 6:27–36.[31] "You will love" is echoed in Q 6:27 ("Love your enemies") and 32 ("if you love those who love you"). The identity of "your neighbor" is addressed in 6:32–33, which demands that the disciples do more than toll collectors and Gentiles, who love only their own. And "as yourself" is related to 6:31, the golden rule, where what the self wants is the standard for determining how one should behave toward others.

(iii) If the so-called golden rule (Q 6:31) appears right in the middle of the section framed by Q 6:27 and 36, Targum Pseudo-Jonathan not only places that rule near the end of Leviticus 19 (in v. 34: "The stranger who sojourns with you will be to you as the native among you; you will love him as yourself, so that what you hate for yourself you will not do to him") but also combines it with the command to love one's neighbor in v. 18: "You will not take revenge nor harbor enmity against your kinsmen. You will love your neighbor, so that what is hateful to you, you will not to do him." That the connection between the golden rule and Lev 19:18 was an old one is proven by their joint appearance in *Did.* 1:2 and other early Christian sources.[32] It may also be pertinent that, in *Ep. Arist.* 207, the golden rule is attached both to the *imitatio Dei* (cf. Lev 19:2) and to the imperative to rebuke mildly (which depends upon Lev 19:17–18; see below), and further that when the golden rule appears in Tobit, it follows immediately a rewriting of another verse from Leviticus 19:

> Lev 19:13: You will not oppress or rob your neighbor. The wages of a hired servant will not remain with you all night until the morning.

> Tob 4:14–15: Do not keep over until the next day the wages of those who work for you, but pay them at once [cf. Lev 19:13]. . . . And what you hate, do not do to anyone.

The evidence that the golden rule was associated with Leviticus 19 is substantial.[33]

---

31. For a related analysis, see Catchpole, *Quest for Q*, p. 115.

32. E.g., Irenaeus, *Adv. haer.* 4.16.3 (SC 100, ed. A. Rousseau, pp. 564–66: "Do no injury to their neighbor" is a free rendering of Lev 19:18 influenced by a negative form of the "golden rule"); cf. idem, *Epideixis* 87 (TU 31, ed. K. Ter-Měkěrttschian and E. Ter-Minassiantz, p. 60: "The love of neighbor adds no evil to a neighbor"); *Ps.-Clem. Hom.* 12.32 (GCS 41, ed. B. Rehm, pp. 190–91); Cyprian, *De dom. orat.* 28 (CSEL 3/1, ed. G. Hartel, p. 288); Augustine, *De serm. mont.* 2.22.75 (CCSL 35, ed. A. Mutzenbecher, p. 173). Matthew could tag both the golden rule and Lev 19:18 as the sum of the Law and the Prophets; see Mt 7:12 and 22:39.

33. Q's version of the golden rule and its context align it especially with *Ep. Arist.* 207, which contains this advice for a king: "As you wish that no evil should befall you, but to

(iv) Jesus' words about the speck and the log in 6:41–42 serve to qualify the earlier injunction, "Judge not, and you will not be judged" (6:37), for in 6:41–42 the point is that reproof is a legitimate activity if it is devoid of hypocrisy: "First take the log out of your own eye, and then you will see clearly to take out the speck that is in your brother's eye" (6:42). Now the subject of reproof in and of itself takes us to Lev 19:17, Judaism's classic text on the subject, a text much expounded in antiquity.[34] Furthermore, we find this in *b. 'Arak.* 16b:

> Our Rabbis taught: You will not hate your brother in your heart (Lev 19:17). One might have believed one may only not smite him, slap him, curse him, therefore the text states, "In your heart." Scripture speaks of "hatred in the heart." Whence do we know that if a man sees something unseemly in his

share in every good thing, so you should act on the same principle towards your subjects, including the wrongdoers [ἁμαρτάνοντας], and admonish the good and upright also mercifully [ἐπιεικέστερον]. For God guides all in kindness [ἐπιεικείᾳ]." One can see the parallels at a glance:

Golden rule

Q 6:31: "As you wish that people would do to you, do so to them."

Ep. Arist. 207: "As you wish that no evil should befall you, but to share in every good thing, so you should act on the same principle towards your subjects."

Mercy/kindness

Q 6:36: "Be merciful"

Ep. Arist. 207: "admonished the good and upright also mercifully"

God as model of universal mercy/kindness

Q 6:35: God raises the sun on the evil as well as the good

Ep. Arist. 207: "God guides all in kindness"

No restriction on human mercy/kindness

Q 6:32–34: "If you love those who love you...?"

Ep. Arist. 207: "act on the same principle towards your subjects, including the wrong-doers"

Command to reprove

Q 6:42: "Remove first from your eye the log, and then you will see clearly to cast out the speck from the eye of your brother."

Ep. Arist. 207: "admonish the good and upright also kindly"

Do we have here a natural coalescence of themes within the Jewish moral tradition or something more? Since both *Ep. Arist.* 207 and Q 6:27–45 allude to the famous words on reproof in Lev 19:17, do we have here some sort of exegetical tradition? Or should we entertain the possibility that one of the contributors to Q was influenced by the *Epistle of Aristeas*?

34. James L. Kugel, "On Hidden Hatred and Open Reproach: Early Exegesis of Leviticus 19:17," HTR 80 (1987), pp. 43–62; Bilhah Nitzan, "The Laws of Reproof in 4QBerakhot (4Q286–290) in Light of Their Parallels in the Damascus Covenant and Other Texts from Qumran," in *Legal Texts and Issues: Proceedings of the Second Meeting of the International Organization for Qumran Studies, Cambridge 1995* (ed. Moshe Bernstein, Florentino García Martínez, and John Kampen; STDS 23; Leiden/New York/Cologne: Brill, 1997), pp. 149–65.

neighbor, he is obliged to reprove him? Because it is said, "You will surely rebuke" (Lev 19:17). If he rebuked him and he did not accept it, whence do we know that he must rebuke him again? The text states, "surely rebuke" all ways. One might assume [this to be obligatory] even though his face blanched, therefore the text states, "You will not bear sin because of him" (Lev 19:17). It was taught [in a baraitha]: R. Tarfon said, "I wonder whether there is any one in this generation who accepts reproof, for if one says to him, 'Remove the mote from between your eyes,' he would answer, 'Remove the beam from between your eyes.' "

In this passage the rabbinic equivalent of Q 6:41–42 is used precisely to explicate the ruling on rebuke in Lev 19:17.[35] That Lev 19:17 lies behind Q 6:41–42 is further supported by the striking fact that the only other time "brother" (ἀδελφός) appears in Q is in 17:3, where, as we shall see, the ruling on reproof in Lev 19:17 is taken up again.

(v) Q 6:37–38 tells disciples not to judge (μὴ κρίνετε) lest they be judged. It is unclear what exactly a hearer of Q is supposed to make of this in the light of 6:42 ("then you will see clearly to cast out the speck from the eye of your brother") and 17:3 ("If your brother sins, warn him"), which endorse the imperative to rebuke in Lev 19:17.[36] But there is also a striking contrast with Lev 19:15, where the LXX commands, κρινεῖς τὸν πλησίον σου, "you will judge your neighbor" (MT: תשפט עמיתך). Q 6:37–38 is qualifying Lev 19:15 or at least dissenting from a common application of it.

(vi) This tension between Q 6:37–38 and Leviticus is part of a wider pattern, for the allusions to the holiness code constitute a provocative rewriting of it:

Leviticus 19	Q 6:27–38
demand to be holy because God is holy	demand to be merciful because God is merciful
command to judge one's neighbor	command not to judge others
the golden rule (negative form) (so Pseudo-Jonathan)	the golden rule (positive form)
love your neighbor	love your enemy
instructions for repairing fraternal relations (ἀδελφόν σου in v. 17)	it is not enough to do good to "brothers" (ἀδελφοὺς ὑμῶν in v. 33)

If one reads Q 6:27–36 with Leviticus 19 in mind, a new dimension appears. We have something similar to the supertheses of Mt 5:21–48, which are of course partly based on Q 6:27–45. Jesus is modifying and adding to the Mosaic demands. He substitutes mercy for holiness, enjoins his hearers not to judge, uses a positive form of the golden rule instead of a negative

---

35. A related tradition appears in *b. B. Bat.* 15b, where Leviticus 19 is not in view.
36. See further below, pp. 65–68, on Q 17:3.

one, speaks of love of enemy rather than love of neighbor, and says it is not enough to have right fraternal relations (the subject of 19:17), for even Gentiles do that.

This sort of provocative inversion of Mosaic legislation is not without parallel. From its eschatological point of view, Isa 56:1–8, for instance, recasts Pentateuchal language (see Num 16:9; 18:2–6) in order to promote the new idea of "the inclusion of foreigners and the physically maimed in the service of the holy Temple of the future."[37] We shall, in a later chapter, see many additional examples of the reversal of hypotexts in old Jewish literature.[38]

(vii) The command to be merciful even as God is merciful, Q 6:36, reproduces a traditional Jewish sentiment, one that was associated with the holiness code of Leviticus:

> My people, sons of Israel, just as I am merciful in heaven, so will you be merciful on earth (Tg. Ps.-J. on Lev 22:28)

> Said R. Yose b. R. Bun, "It is not good to imply that God's traits [are derived from his attribute of] mercy. Those who translate [Lev 22:28 as follows:] 'My people, sons of Israel, just as I am merciful in heaven, so will you be merciful on earth: A cow or a ewe you will not kill both her and her young in one day' — that is not good, for it implies that God's traits [are derived from the attribute of] mercy" (y. Ber. 5:3)[39]

The tradition in these two texts shares four features with Q 6:36: (a) the imperative to be merciful, (b) justification through the imitation of God's mercy, (c) address to "sons" (υἱοί, בני), and (d) association with the Levitical holiness tradition.[40]

(viii) In Q 6:30, Jesus demands that his followers turn the other cheek when they are struck and that they not withhold shirt when their coat is taken. These memorable illustrations of nonretaliation are thematically related to Lev 19:18: "You will not take vengeance or bear a grudge against any of your people." But the continuity may be disrupted by Q 6:32–33, where Jesus' disciples are told that it is not enough to love those who love them or to greet (so Mt 5:47) or to do good (so Lk 6:33) to their compatriots. Lev 19:18, on the other hand, explicitly limits the application of nonretaliation to "any of your people" (LXX: τοῖς υἱοῖς τοῦ λαοῦ σου), and *Sifra* 200 ad loc. takes this to mean that "you may take vengeance and bear a grudge against others." Is Q's Jesus eliminating precisely this interpretation of the Levitical prohibition of vengeance?

---

37. Michael Fishbane, "The Hebrew Bible and Exegetical Tradition," in *Intertextuality in Ugarit and Israel* (ed. Johannes C. de Moor; OS 40; Leiden/Boston/Cologne: Brill, 1998), pp. 27–28.

38. See pp. 192–97.

39. The same tradition appears in *y. Meg.* 4:10.

40. For Q this last element appears from the context, which otherwise plays off Leviticus 19.

(ix) LXX Lev 19:14 (οὐ κακῶς ἐρεῖς, "you will not revile"; MT: לֹא־תְקַלֵּל) and Q 6:28 (τοὺς καταρωμένους ὑμᾶς, "those who curse you")[41] speak of hurtful speech, while LXX Lev 19:17 (οὐ μισήσεις τὸν ἀδελφόν σου, "you will not hate your brother"; לֹא־תִשְׂנָא אֶת־אָחִיךָ) and Q 6:27 (τοῖς μισοῦσιν ὑμᾶς, "to those who hate you") refer to hatred. The Levitical texts are prohibitions whereas the Q texts are descriptions of the disciples' opponents. So the oppressors do precisely what Leviticus 19 commands they should not do — that is, they curse and hate. Jesus' disciples go beyond the holiness code while their enemies transgress it.

(x) *T. Gad* 4–6 is a partial rewriting of LXX Leviticus 19. Rather than reprint the entire text here, I shall just note that there is a large overlap in vocabulary — including the key words "love" (ἀγαπάω), "brother" (ἀδελφός), "sin" (ἁμαρτία), "mind" (διάνοια), "(take) revenge" (ἐκδίκησις/ἐκδικάζω), "hate" (μισέω), and "neighbor" (πλησίον)[42] — as well as an overlap of main themes — avoiding vengeance, loving others, speaking to those who have offended. There are, moreover, crystal clear allusions. Thus both *T. Gad* 4:2 ("Hatred does not want to hear repeated his commands concerning love of neighbor") and 6:1 ("Each of you love his brother. Drive hatred out of your hearts") plainly recall Lev 19:17–18 ("You will not hate in your heart anyone of your kin... but you will love your neighbor as yourself").[43]

Ancient literature offers additional adaptations of Leviticus 19. Jacob Bernays long ago demonstrated that *Ps.-Phoc.* 9–41 is a creative transformation of Leviticus 19,[44] and Luke Timothy Johnson has more recently shown that the book of James repeatedly returns to the same chapter.[45]

---

41. That τοὺς καταρωμένους ὑμᾶς (which appears in Luke but not Matthew) stood in Q is established by the related sayings in Rom 12:14 (εὐλογεῖτε καὶ μὴ καταρᾶσθε); Polycarp, *Ep.* 2.2–3 (κατάραν ἀντὶ κατάρας); and *Did.* 1:3 (εὐλογεῖτε τοὺς καταρωμένους). The latter two belong to blocks that are relatives of Q's Sermon on the Plain, and they probably do not depend upon Luke.

42. ἀγαπάω (*T. Gad* 6:1, 3; Lev 19:18, 34), ἀδελφός (*T. Gad* 4:3; 6:1; Lev 19:17), ἁμαρτία (*T. Gad* 6:5; Lev 19:8, 17, 22), διάνοια (*T. Gad* 6:1; Lev 19:17), ἐκδίκησις/ἐκδικάζω (*T. Gad* 6:7; Lev 19:18), μισέω (*T. Gad* 6:5; Lev 19:17), πλησίον (*T. Gad* 4:2; Lev 19:11, 13, 15, 16, 17, 18).

43. See further Kugel, "Hidden Hatred," pp. 49–52.

44. Jacob Bernays, *Über das phokylideische Gedict: Ein Beitrag zur hellenistischen Litterature* (Berlin: Hertz, 1856), pp. 228–33. Cf. Pieter W. van der Horst, *The Sentences of Pseudo-Phocylides* (SVTP 4; Leiden: Brill, 1978), pp. 66–67; and Karl-Wilhelm Niebuhr, *Gesetz und Paränese: Katechismusartige Weisungsreihen in der frühjüdischen Literatur* (WUNT 2/28; Tübingen: Mohr Siebeck, 1987), pp. 20–26.

45. Luke Timothy Johnson, "The Use of Leviticus 19 in the Letter of James," *JBL* 101 (1982), pp. 391–401. He sees the following parallels:

Lev 19:12//Jas 5:12	Lev 19:16//Jas 4:11	Lev 19:18b//Jas 2:8
Lev 19:13//Jas 5:4	Lev 19:17b//Jas 5:20(?)	
Lev 19:15//Jas 2:1, 9	Lev 19:18a//Jas 5:9 (?)	

To these parallels should be added Jas 2:2–4, which takes up a tradition attested in *t. Sanh.* 6:2; *Sifra Lev* 200 on Lev 19:15–16; *b. Šeb.* 30a, 31a; and *Deut Rab.* 5:6, among other places; see R. B. Ward, "Partiality in the Assembly: James 2:2–4," *HTR* 62 (1969), pp. 87–97. This

Early portions of the *Didache* also consistently use Leviticus 19 as an intertext:[46]

Did. 1:2 (part of the programmatic opening): "Love your neighbor as yourself"; cf. Lev 19:18

Did. 1:2: the golden rule; see point (iii) above

Did. 2:2: "You will not steal" (οὐ κλέψεις); cf. Lev 19:11 (οὐ κλέψεις)

Did. 2:2: "You will not practice magic"; cf. Lev 19:26, 31 (prohibitions of augury, witchcraft, mediums, and wizards)

Did. 2:3: "You will not commit perjury, you will not bear false witness"; cf. Lev 19:12 ("you will not swear falsely")

Did. 2:5: "Your speech will not be vain or false" (ψευδής); cf. Lev 19:11 ("you will not deal falsely [ψεύσεσθε]; and you will not lie to one another") and 12 ("you will not swear falsely")

Did. 2:7: "You will not hate (μισήσεις) anyone but some you will reprove (ἐλέγξεις) and for some you will pray, and some you will love (ἀγαπήσεις) more than your own life"; cf. Lev 19:17, 18 (with οὐ μισήσεις, ἐλέγξεις, and ἀγαπήσεις)

Did. 3:4: "Regard not omens" (μὴ γίνου οἰωνοσκόπος); cf. Lev 19:26 (οὐκ οἰωνιεῖσθε, "you will not heed omens")

Did. 3:4: warning against idolatry (εἰδωλολατρίαν, εἰδωλολατρία); cf. Lev 19:4 (οὐκ ἐπακολουθήσετε εἰδώλοις, "you will not follow idols")

Did. 3:4: "Be not an enchanter" (ἐπαοιδός); cf. Lev 19:31 (τοῖς ἐπαοιδοῖς οὐ προσκολληθήσεσθε, "you will not attach yourselves to enchanters")

Did. 3:5: "Be not a liar" (μὴ γίνου ψεύστης); cf. Lev 19:11 (οὐ ψεύσεσθε, "you will not lie")

Did. 4:3: "You will give righteous judgment" (κρινεῖς δικαίως); cf. Lev 19:15 (ἐν δικαιοσύνῃ κρινεῖς, "in justice you will judge")

Did. 4:3: "You will favor no one's person (οὐ λήψῃ πρόσωπον) in reproving (ἐλέγξαι) transgression"; cf. Lev 19:15, 17 (the two classic texts on impartiality and reproof; both οὐ λήμψῃ πρόσωπον and ἐλέγξεις appear)

Did. 4:8: "You will not turn away the needy but will share everything with your brother"; cf. Lev 19:9–10 (instruction on leaving the gleanings for the poor and aliens)

---

tradition was firmly associated with Lev 19:15 (e.g., *t. Sanh.* 6:2 cites the verse and the passage from *Sifra* is commentary on it).

46. Cf. with what follows John S. Kloppenborg, "The Transformation of Moral Exhortation in *Didache* 1–5," in *The* Didache *in Context: Essays on Its Text, History, and Transmission* (ed. Clayton N. Jefford; NovTSupp 77; Leiden/New York/Cologne: Brill, 1995), pp. 102–4. But his list is incomplete.

These parallels are all the more interesting given that *Did.* 1:3–5 has so much material in common with Q's Sermon on the Plain.[47]

In the light of the comparative material, the proposal that Q 6:27–45 rewrites Leviticus 19 puts the Q unit firmly within a tradition.[48] This tradition, it should be noted, concentrates on the ethical imperatives of Leviticus 19. Most of the other commandments are typically not assimilated. The focus is never long off of 19:15–18, where "all of the things enjoined are very difficult to enforce simply by legal fiat — they ultimately depend on the heart of each individual and a desire to comply even when, sometimes, noncompliance is undetectable."[49]

(xi) Given the extensive parallels between the central portion of the Sermon on the Plain and Leviticus 19, one wonders whether it is coincidence that Q 6:27–45 concludes with a statement about the heart: "For from an abundance of the heart (καρδίας) the mouth speaks." Lev 19:17 also refers to the heart: "Hate not your brother *in your heart.*" Although the LXX has τῇ διανοίᾳ σου ("in your thought"), the MT has בלבבך, and καρδία is the usual translation of (ב)לב. Moreover, the Aldine edition of Lev 19:17 has τῇ καρδίᾳ σου, and both the rewriting of Lev 19:17 in 1QS 5:24–6:1 (with לבבו) and the allusions to it in *T. Gad* 6:1, 3, and 7 (with καρδιῶν ὑμῶν…καρδίας…καρδίας) mention the heart.

One may further wonder whether it is coincidence that both Q 6 and Leviticus 19 speak of the blind, of fruit, and of measures. Q 6:38 says that the measure (μέτρῳ) you give will be the measure you get,[50] whereas Leviticus 19 concludes with a section on honest weights and measures (LXX, μέτροις, vv. 35–37). Q 6:43–46 uses fruit (καρπός, thrice) as a metaphor of words and deeds, whereas Lev 19:23–25 offers instruction on what fruits (LXX, καρπός, thrice) to eat and not eat. And if Q 6:39 refers to the blind (τυφλός) leading the blind (τυφλόν), Lev 19:14 cautions against putting a stumblingblock before the blind (LXX, τυφλοῦ). We are not here dealing with meaningful thematic parallels, but maybe the common words and images are intended to help further associate the two passages.

•

---

47. See Dale C. Allison, Jr., *The Jesus Tradition in Q* (Harrisburg, Pa.: Trinity Press International, 1997), pp. 89–92.

48. Note also the use of Leviticus 19 in *ARN* A 26 ("Rabbi Akiba says: If one weds a woman that is unfit for him, he transgresses five negative commandments: You will not take vengeance [Lev 19:19], Nor bear any grudge [ibid.], You will not hate your brother in your heart [Lev 19:17], But you will love your neighbor as yourself [Lev 19:18], That your brother may live with you [Lev 25:36]") and the citation of four verses from Leviticus 19 in Cyprian, *Test.* 3.81–85 (CSEL 3/1, ed. G. Hartel, pp. 173–74). For the argument that Leviticus 19 lies beneath part of 1 Peter 1–2, see William L. Schutter, *Hermeneutic and Composition in 1 Peter* (WUNT 2/30; Tübingen: Mohr Siebeck, 1989), pp. 95–99.

49. Kugel, "Hidden Hatred," p. 45.

50. The traditional saying was often associated with Isa 27:8 (cf. the targum); see H. P. Rüger, "'Mit welchem Mass ihr messt, wird euch gemessen werden,'" *ZNW* 60 (1969), pp. 174–82. No such link is made in Q.

The creative adaptations of Leviticus 19 in the *Testament of Gad, Pseudo-Phocylides*, James, and the *Didache* point to the popularity of the chapter in antiquity.[51] So too does the fact that the New Testament cites its central verse, the famous 19:18, more than any other line from the Pentateuch.[52] Jewish sources likewise favor this commandment,[53] which Akiba, according to tradition, called the great principle in the Torah.[54] Further, according to *Sifre* 193 on Lev 19:1, "This chapter was spoken in the assembly of all Israel" because "most of the principles of the Torah depend upon its contents." *Lev Rab.* 24:5 says the same thing: "R. Hiyya taught: This section was spoken in the presence of a gathering of the whole assembly because most of the essential principles of the Torah are attached to it. R. Levi said: Because the ten commandments are included in it." That this idea goes back to the first century seems probable given Pieter van der Horst's conclusion that the author of *Pseudo-Phocylides* saw Leviticus 19 as "a kind of summary of the Torah or a counterpart of the Decalogue."[55] The link between Leviticus 19 and the Ten Commandments is understandable given the extensive overlap between them,[56] a fact that may also help explain why Lev 19:18 was commonly reckoned a summary of the second half of the Decalogue.[57] The point of all this is simply that Leviticus 19 was a central text for ancient Judaism. This much encourages us to surmise that the sort of links observed herein between it and Q 6:27–45 would not have been missed by informed listeners.

Q 7:27 // Exod 23:20; Mal 3:1. Here Jesus uses a citation formula: "This [John the Baptist] is he about whom it has been written: 'Behold, I am sending my messenger in front of you, who will prepare your way before you.'" The relation between this marked citation and the LXX may be set forth thus:

Q 7:27   ἰδοὺ   ἀποστέλλω τὸν ἄγγελόν μου πρὸ προσώπου σου
LXX Exod 23:20   ἰδοὺ ἐγὼ   ἀποστέλλω τὸν ἄγγελόν μου πρὸ προσώπου σου[58]
LXX Mal 3:1   ἰδοὺ ἐγὼ ἐξαποστέλλω τὸν ἄγγελόν μου[59]

---

51. Niebuhr, *Gesetz und Paränese*, shows the influence of Leviticus 18–20 on additional texts.

52. Mt 5:43; 19:19; Mk 12:31 par.; 12:33; Rom 12:9; 13:9; Gal 5:14; Jas 2:8. Cf. *Gos. Thom.* 25; *Did.* 1:2; *Gos. Naz.* frag. 16; *Sib. Or.* 8:481.

53. See Ecclus 13:15; *Jub.* 7:20; 20:2; 36:4, 8; CD 6:20; 1QS 5:25; *T. Reub.* 6:9; *T. Iss.* 5:2; *T. Gad* 4:2; *T. Benj.* 3:3–4.

54. *Sifre* 200 on Lev 19:18; *Gen Rab.* 24:7.

55. van der Horst, *Pseudo-Phocylides*, p. 66.

56. See Lev 19:3 (cf. the fourth and fifth commandments), 4 (cf. the second commandment), 11 (cf. the eighth commandment), 12 (cf. the third commandment), 16 (cf. the ninth commandment). These are only the more obvious connections. Others have seen allusions to all of the Ten Commandments in Leviticus 19.

57. The evidence is gathered in Dale C. Allison Jr., "Mark 12:28–31 and the Decalogue," in *The Gospels and the Scriptures of Israel* (ed. Craig A. Evans and W. R. Stegner; JSNTSS 104/Studies in Scripture in Early Judaism and Christianity 3; Sheffield: JSOT Press, 1994), pp. 270–78.

58. MT: ‫הנה אנכי שלח מלאך לפניך.‬

59. MT: ‫הנני שלח מלאכי.‬

Q 7:27   ὃς κατασκευάσει τὴν ὁδόν σου ἔμπροσθέν σου.
LXX Exod 23:20b   ἵνα φυλάξῃ σε ἐν τῇ ὁδῷ ("in order to guard you in the way")[60]
LXX Mal 3:1   καὶ ἐπιβλέψεται ὁδὸν πρὸ προσώπου μου ("and he will survey the way before me")[61]

Q's first eight words are apparently from LXX Exod 23:20, although there is also resemblance to LXX Mal 3:1. The second half of Q's marked citation, however, departs from both LXX texts. It is much closer to MT Mal 3:1b: וּפִנָּה־דֶרֶךְ לְפָנָי, "and prepare the way before me."[62] We appear to have here a conflated quotation.[63] The association of Exod 23:20 and Mal 3:1, which is also attested in Mk 1:2 and *Exod Rab.* 32:9,[64] would be natural. The two verses are very similar, and it may even be that Mal 3:1 depends upon Exod 23:20. The former almost surely depends upon Isa 40:3, which in turn also recalls Exod 23:20.

Those who perceive in Q 7:27 an allusion to Exodus 23, where the Lord's messenger goes before the people during the exodus, will, especially given the citations from Deuteronomy in Q 4:1–13, think typologically: the eschatological events associated with the Baptist and thereafter with Jesus recapitulate the foundational events of the exodus. Already in Isa 52:12 the language of "going before" is also part of an exodus typology.[65]

Those who are also, or instead, sent to Malachi 3, which contains an eschatological prophecy about judgment and fire (see vv. 2–3 and cf. Q 3:16), may remember that the messenger of Mal 3:1 was famously identified, already in the book of Malachi itself (see 4:5), with "the prophet Elijah," who will be sent "before the great and terrible day of the Lord." It will

---

60. MT: לִשְׁמָרְךָ בַּדָּרֶךְ.

61. MT: וּפִנָּה־דֶרֶךְ לְפָנָי.

62. Cf. David S. New, *Old Testament Quotations in the Synoptic Gospels, and the Two-Document Hypothesis* (SCS 37; Atlanta: Scholars Press, 1993), pp. 59–64. The older commentators mention Malachi much more often than Exodus when commenting on Mt 11:10 = Lk 7:27; see, e.g., Paschasius Radbertus, *Exp. Mt libri XII (V–VIII)* ad loc. (CCCM 56A, ed. B. Paulus, pp. 623–24); Theophylact, *Comm. Mt* ad loc. (PG 23.252A); Euthymius Zigabenus, *Exp. Mt* ad 11:10 (PG 129:350C); Albertus Magnus, *Super Mt cap. I–XIV* ad loc. (Opera Omnia 21/1, ed. B. Schmidt, p. 350); J. A. Bengel, *Gnomon of the New Testament* (Philadelphia: Perkinpine & Higgins, 1864), vol. 1, ad loc. Eusebius, *Ecl. proph.* 1.11 (PG 22.1057A), does, however, associate the synoptic text with the ἄγγελος of Exodus 23.

63. For additional examples of conflated quotations — quite common in ancient Jewish and Christian sources — see LXX Exod 15:3 (which borrows from LXX Hos 2:20); 11QTemple 23:13–4 (which combines the similar Ezek 43:20 and Lev 4:25); 66:8–11 (which mixes Exod 22:15–6 and Deut 22:28); Mt 22:24 (cf. Gen 38:8; Deut 25:5); Mk 1:2–3 (cf. Exod 23:30; Isa 40:3; Mal 3:1); Jn 12:15 (cf. Isa 35:4; 40:9; Zech 9:9); Acts 3:22–3 (cf. LXX Deut 18:15–20; Lev 23:29); 2 Cor 6:16 (which fuses Lev 26:12 with Ezek 37:27). Discussion and additional examples in Michael Klein, "Associative and Complementary Translation in the Targumim," *Eretz-Israel* 16 (1982), pp. 134*-40*; and J. Koenig, "L'herméneutique analogique du Judaïsme antique d'après les témoins textuelles d'Isaïe," *VTSupp* 33 (1982), pp. 1–103, 199–291.

64. Jacob Mann, *The Bible as Read and Preached in the Old Synagogue* (Cincinnati: Jewish Publication Society, 1940), vol. 1, p. 479, observes that the haftarah when Exod 23:20 was read included Mal 3:1.

65. See Willey, *Remember the Former Things*, pp. 132–35.

follow that John the Baptist should be identified with the eschatological Elijah. This is plainly how Matthew read our text (Mt 11:14).

(Although there was much speculation about the "angel" of Exod 23:20,[66] one is unable to see that any of it illumines Q's evaluation of the Baptist. One could, given how often Jews and Christians compared the righteous to angels,[67] suggest that the association of John with Exod 23:20 and the use of ἄγγελος — which means "angel," not "messenger," in Q 4:10 and 12:8–9 — make him angelic. Moreover, there are texts that liken prophets to angels,[68] and Origen, *Comm. Jn* ad 2:31, took the Baptist to be an angel. One cannot see, however, that such speculation really illumines the text of Q.)

Q 7:34 // Deut 21:20. Jesus says that in the eyes of others the Son of man, who has come "eating and drinking," is a "glutton and drunkard" (φάγος καὶ οἰνοπότης). The phrase recalls Deut 21:18–22, a passage containing legislation regarding "a stubborn and rebellious son who will not obey his father and mother."[69] His parents are to take him before the elders at the gate and declare, "This son of ours is stubborn and rebellious. He will not obey us. He is a glutton and a drunkard" (זולל וסבא; cf. 11QTemple 64:5). Then "all the men of the town will stone him to death. So you will purge the evil from your midst." Interestingly enough, Jer 5:21–24 takes up the language of Deut 21:18–22 and reapplies it to wayward Israel.[70]

LXX Deut 21:20 translates the MT's זולל וסבא with συμβολοκοπῶν οἰνοφλυγεῖ, "he is given to feasting and drunkenness." Q 7:34 is closer to the targums, all of which, in various ways, clarify that the MT's ambigu-

---

66. James L. Kugel, *Traditions of the Bible: A Guide to the Bible As It Was at the Start of the Common Era* (Cambridge, Mass./London: Harvard University Press, 1998), pp. 584–85, 735–36. In *b. Sanh.* 38b this angel is said to be Metatron, but in an Aramaic amulet found in Horvat Marish, he is called חטועי; see Joseph Naveh and Shaul Shaked, *Magic Spells and Formulae: Aramaic Incantations of Late Antiquity* (Jerusalem: Magnes, 1993), p. 43.

67. See esp. Charles A. Gieschen, *Angelomorphic Christology: Antecedents and Early Evidence* (AGJU 42; Leiden/Boston/Cologne: Brill, 1998).

68. Gieschen, *Angelmorphic Christology*, pp. 161–69. See esp. 2 Chr 36:15–16; Hag 1:12–13; *Liv. Proph.* Mal 2–3; *Lev Rab.* 1:1.

69. Cf. John Gill, *Gill's Commentary* (Grand Rapids: Baker, 1980), vol. 1, p. 768; S. T. Bloomfield, *Recensio Synoptica: Annotationis Sacrae* (London: C. and J. Rivington, 1826), p. 147; Adolf Schlatter, *Der Evangelist Matthäus: Seine Sprache, sein Ziel, seine Selbständigkeit* (Stuttgart: Calwer, 1948), p. 373 (also citing Prov 23:20–21); Gundry, *Old Testament*, pp. 80–81; Joachim Jeremias, *The Parables of Jesus* (2d rev. ed.; New York: Charles Scribner's Sons, 1972), p. 160; I. H. Marshall, *Commentary on Luke* (NIGTC; Grand Rapids: Eerdmans, 1978), p. 302 ("The description resembles that of the unruly son in Dt. 21:20 MT who is to be stoned; thus a proverbial expression for apostasy is being applied to Jesus"); John P. Meier, *A Marginal Jew: Rethinking the Historical Jesus* (ABRL; New York: Doubleday, 1994), vol. 2, pp. 161, 212; Crispin H. T. Fletcher-Louis, *Luke-Acts: Angels, Christology, and Soteriology* (WUNT 2/94; Tübingen: Mohr Siebeck, 1996), p. 241; Howard Clark Kee, "Jesus: A Glutton and Drunkard," in B. Chilton and Craig A. Evans, eds. *Authenticating the Words of Jesus* (NTTS 28/1; Leiden: Brill, 1999), pp. 328–30. The connection does not to my knowledge appear in patristic commentaries.

70. Fishbane, *Biblical Interpretation*, pp. 314–16.

ous זולל means "gluttony"[71] and translate סבא with a word for "drinker" followed by a word for "wine" (cf. Q's οἰνοπότης, from οἶνος + πότης):

Pseudo-Jonathan	גרגרן בבישרא ושתאי בחמרא = "glutton in meat and drinker in wine"
Onqelos	זליל בסר וסבי חמר = "glutton for meat and drinker of wine"
Neofiti	אכל בבשרה ושתי בחמר = "glutton in meat and drinker in wine"

One suspects that Q 7:34 goes back to an Aramaic original that was influenced by a targumic tradition.[72] Hearers of Q and the Greek Bible, however, might still catch the allusion, especially if they took Q 7:34 to mean that Jesus did not heed the voices of others,[73] because this is the sin in Deuteronomy.

Perceiving such an allusion might prod one to reflect on two things. The first is that, in Deuteronomy 21, the rebellious son is stoned, which is the punishment of the prophets in Q 13:34. So the accusation that Jesus is a glutton and drunkard is no light matter but rather a grave indictment that, if he continues in his ways, others will think that the law commands his execution. A second thought is that the legislation on the rebellious son (Deut 21:18–21) is followed immediately by the law that enjoins the bodies of executed criminals to be hung on a tree (Deut 21:22–23), a law that in time came to be understood as having to do with crucifixion.[74] So a hearer of Q, familiar with the story of Jesus' crucifixion (cf. Q 14:26), might associate Q's allusion to Deut 21:20 with Jesus' fate: the elders did in fact put to death one they perceived to be a rebellious son and a "glutton and drunkard."

Q 10:4 // Exod 12:11, 34–36 (?). Q 10:4 probably had Jesus forbid silver (ἀργύρ-),[75] bag (πήραν — presumably for bread),[76] sandals (ὑποδήματα), and staff (ῥάβδον).[77] This was then probably followed by the prohibition against greeting others, which is presumably motivated by the pressing need of the hour.[78] Q may also have prohibited two tunics (χιτῶνας).[79] Now all of these elements famously appear in the departure from Egypt under

---

71. Maybe under the influence of Prov 23:20 ("Do not be among winebibbers or among gluttonous eaters of meat," אל־תהי בסבאי־יין בזללי בשר); cf. *m. Sanh.* 8:2, which uses Prov 23:20 to explicate Deut 21:20. So too *Sifre* 219 on Deut 21:20.

72. So also Gundry, *Old Testament*, pp. 80–81.

73. For this interpretation, see W. D. Davies and Dale C. Allison, Jr., *A Critical and Exegetical Commentary on the Gospel according to Saint Matthew* (ICC; Edinburgh: T. & T. Clark, 1988, 1991), vol. 2, pp. 261–62.

74. Joseph A. Fitzmyer, "Crucifixion in Ancient Palestine, Qumran Literature, and the New Testament," *CBQ* 40 (1978), pp. 493–513.

75. Mt 10:9: ἄργυρον; Lk 9:3: ἀργύριον.

76. W. Michaelis, *TDNT* 6 (1968), pp. 120–21.

77. Cf. Risto Uro, *Sheep among the Wolves: A Study on the Mission Instructions of Q* (Annales Academiae Scientiarum Fennicae Dissertationes Humanarum Litterarum 47; Helsinki: Suomalainen Tiedeakatemia, 1987), pp. 76–77. All but the prohibition of the sandals are, however, in brackets in the IQP text.

78. See Uro, *Sheep among the Wolves*, pp. 77–78, and below, pp. 145–47.

79. So Mt 10:10 and Lk 9:3, but in agreement with Mk 6:9. Cf. Uro, *Sheep among the Wolves*, p. 77.

Moses, as Tertullian, *Adv. Marc.* 4.24, realized. Ambrose, moreover, found the key to Lk 10:4 in its several contrasts with Moses and the departure from Egypt,[80] and the sandals at least reminded Isho'dad of Merv of the exodus.[81] Then there is the purported exegesis of the Marcionite Megethius, as preserved in the anonymous dialogue *De recta in Deum fide* (from the early fourth century?):

> The God of Genesis commanded Moses in the going up from Egypt saying, "Make ready with loins girded, having sandals on feet, staffs in your hands, and traveller's bags upon you. Carry away the gold and silver and all the other things of the Egyptians." But our good Lord, sending his disciples out into the world, says, "Neither sandals on your feet, nor traveller's bag, nor two cloaks, nor money in your belts. See how clearly the good one opposes the teachings of that one."[82]

Exod 12:11 — a verse drawn upon in Q 12:35 — tells us that Moses commanded the Israelites to eat the Passover hurriedly, with sandals (LXX: ὑποδήματα) on their feet and staff (LXX: βακτηρίαι) in hand, and Exod 12:34–36 — which appears to be foretold in Gen 15:14 and typologically transformed in 1 Samuel 4–6[83] — recounts that they went forth with bread, with silver (LXX: ἀργυρᾶ), with gold, and with clothing.[84] Is it coincidence that Jesus' disciples are similarly to be in a hurry but even more so, so that they take even less than the fleeing Israelites did? As with Q 10:4's allusion to 2 Kgs 4:29, to be considered in a later chapter,[85] one could urge that once more Q is drawing an analogy precisely in order to surpass it.

Interestingly enough, Exod 12:11 is naturally associated with 2 Kgs 4:29, to which Q 10:4 surely alludes. Both verses contain the following:

- loins are to be girded —

  Exod 12:11: "This is how your are to eat it: your loins girded (מתניכם חגרים)."

  2 Kgs 4:29: "Gird up your loins (חגר מתניך)."

---

80. Ambrose, *Traité sur l'Évangile de S. Luc* 7.57–60 (SC 52, ed. Tissot, pp. 27–29).

81. E.g., Isho'dad of Merv, *Comm. Mt* 7 (ed. Gibson, pp. 74–75). Cf. Dionysius bar Salibi, *Comm. Ev.* ad Mt 10:10 (CSCO 77, Scriptores Syri 33, ed. J. Sedlacek and J.-B. Chabot, p. 281; with reference to the staff he mentions Moses and Passover), and Paschasius Radbertus, *Exp. Mat. libri XII (V–VIII)* ad Mt 10:10 (CCCM 56A, ed. B. Paulus, p. 585).

82. *Der Dialog des Adamantius* ΠΕΡΙ ΤΗΣ ΕΙΣ ΘΕΟΝ ΟΡΘΗΣ ΠΙΣΤΕΩΣ (GCS 4; ed. W. H. van de Sande Bakhuyzen; Leipzig: J. C. Hinrich, 1901), p. 22. Modern commentators on Mark have also occasionally noted the parallel; see, e.g., Joel Marcus, *Mark 1–8: A New Translation with Introduction and Commentary* (AB 27A; Garden City, N.Y.: Doubleday, 2000), pp. 388–89.

83. Allison, *New Moses*, pp. 32–33. Note also the *Jeremiah Apocryphon* (ed. Migana), p. 184, lines 14ff.

84. Note also Deut 8:4 and 29:5, which relate that the Israelites' clothing was indestructible: they did not need more than the one set they had on (cf. Justin, *Dial.* 131.6 [PTS 47, ed. M. Marcovich, p. 298]).

85. See below, pp. 145–47.

- staff is to be in the hand —

  Exod 12:11: "your staff in your hand (מקלכם בידכם)"

  2 Kgs 4:29: "Take my staff in your hand (משענתי בידך)."

- all is to be done hurriedly —

  Exod 12:11: "You will eat it hurriedly."

  2 Kgs 4:29: "If you meet anyone, give no greeting."

Moreover, when Tertullian, in assailing Marcionism, interpreted Luke 10, he was reminded both of Exodus 12 and 2 Kings 4:

> When the children of Israel went out of Egypt, the creator brought them forth laden with their spoils of gold and silver vessels, and with loads besides of raiment and unleavened dough; whereas Christ commanded his disciples not to carry even a staff for their journey. The former were thrust forth into a desert, but the latter were sent into cities. Consider the difference presented in the occasions and you will understand how it was one and the same power that arranged the mission of his people according to their poverty in the one case and their plenty in the other. He cut down their supplies when they could be replenished through the cities, just as he had accumulated them when exposed to the scantiness of the desert. Even shoes he forbade them to carry. For it was he under whose protection the people wore out not even a shoe (Deut 29:5), even in the wilderness for the space of so many years. "No one," he says, "will you greet by the way." What a destroyer of the prophets is Christ, seeing it is from them that he received his precept. When Elisha sent on his servant Gehazi before him to raise the Shunammite's son from death....[86]

One hesitates, however, to endorse Tertullian's exegesis without misgiving. For one thing, there does not seem to have been any exegetical habit of associating 2 Kgs 4:29 with Exod 12:11. The ancient and modern commentaries, to the extent of my research, pass over the parallels in silence. For another, the text of Q 10:4 remains quite doubtful. The IQP prints most of it in brackets, indicating uncertainty. So I must reluctantly reckon the parallel between Q 10:4 and Exod 12:11, 34–36 an open question.[87]

Q 10:21–22 // Exod 33:11–23. After Jesus thanks his father for the revelation given to babes but hidden from the wise and discerning, he declares, "Everything has been handed over to me by my Father; and nobody knows the Son except the Father, (nor) . . . the Father except the Son and any one to whom the Son wishes to reveal him." This claim to be the exclusive revealer of divine knowledge is best read, despite the scant verbal links, against the backdrop of Exod 33:11–23 and the related traditions about Moses as the

---

86. Tertullian, *Adv. Marc.* 4.24 (CCSL, ed. Florentis, p. 607).

87. Recent debates regarding Q and Cynics have often discussed the significance of Q's words about equipment but have done so without recognizing the possible exodus motif in the background.

unique mediator of divine revelation (esp. Num 12:6–8 and Deut 34:40).[88] Here are the reasons:

(i) Mt 11:25–27 and Lk 10:21–22 have as a matter of exegetical history reminded readers of Moses. According to P. Dabeck, Moses, who alone knew God face to face (Deut 34:10), is the *Vorbild* of the Matthean Son of God, who alone knows the Father and reveals his secrets in Mt 11:27.[89] Martin Hengel has written similarly:

> The statement at the end of the Torah (Deut 34.10): "And there has not arisen a prophet since in Israel like Moses, whom the Lord knew face to face, none like him for all the signs and wonders which the Lord sent him to do" is corrected by Jesus in terms of John the Baptist in Luke 16.16 and in terms of himself in Matt. 11.27 = Luke 10.22.[90]

For P. Pokorný, "In terms of content it [Matt. 11:27 par.] is a reinterpretation of the saying about the unsurpassingly close relationship between Moses and God attested in Deut. 34.10."[91] Werner Grimm has spoken of the interrelationship between Mt 11:27 (= Q 10:22) and Exod 33:12ff.; Num 12:6–8; and Deut 34:10.[92] These writers have, as far as I am aware, come to their common conclusion independently of one another. There is also no reason to think that they are under the influence of Eusebius, who associated Mt 11:27 ("All things have been handed over to me by my Father," etc.) with the experience of Moses in Exod 33, or of Bruno, Bishop of Segni (d. 1123), who cited Exod 33:13 ("Now if I have found favor in your sight, show me your ways, so that I may know you") when expounding the same Matthean verse.[93]

(ii) Exod 33:11–23 (where we read that "the Lord used to speak to Moses face to face"); Num 12:1–8 (which affirms that "my servant Moses . . . is entrusted with all my house. With him I speak mouth to mouth, clearly, and not in dark speech; and he beholds the form of the Lord"); and Deut 34:10–

---

88. For a parallel one may refer already to 1 Kings 19, which models Elijah on the Moses of Exodus 33; see Allison, *New Moses*, pp. 39–45.

89. P. Dabeck, " 'Siehe, es erscheinen Moses und Elias' (Mt 17,3)," *Bib* 23 (1947), p. 177.

90. Martin Hengel, *The Son of God* (Philadelphia: Fortress, 1976), pp. 68–69.

91. P. Pokorný, *The Genesis of Christology* (Edinburgh: T. & T. Clark, 1987), p. 55, n. 138.

92. Werner Grimm, *Jesus und das Danielbuch, Band I: Jesu Einspruch Gegen das Offenbarungssystem Daniels (Mt 11,25–27; Lk 17,20–21)* (ANTJ 6/1; Frankfurt am Main/Bern/New York: Peter Lang, 1984), pp. 68–69. He unfortunately does not develop this. Note also P. Levertoff, "Matthew," in *A New Catholic Commentary on Holy Scripture* (ed. C. Gore, H. C. Goudge, and Al Guillame; London: Macmillan, 1928), p. 156; and A. E. J. Rawlinson, *The New Testament Doctrine of the Christ* (London: Longmans, Green, 1926), p. 263. Paul Hoffmann, *Studien zur Theologie der Logienquelle* (3d ed.; NTAbh 8; Münster: Aschendorff, 1982), p. 127, cites Exod 33:33 in passing when discussing Q 10:22.

93. Eusebius, *Ecl. proph.* 1.12 (PG 22.1064C–1035B); Bruno of Segni, *Comm. Mt* ad loc. (PL 165.173A). Cf. also Cyril of Alexandria, *Comm. Lk* 66 (CSCO 70, Scriptores Syri 27, ed. J.-B. Chabot, p. 258; he contrasts the revelation of Lk 10:22 with the law through Moses); and Bonaventure, *Expositio in Evangelium Sancti Lucae* ad loc. (Opera Omnia 10, ed. A. C. Peltier, p. 500). For Tertullian, see below, p. 46.

12 ("Never since has there arisen a prophet in Israel like Moses, whom the Lord knew face to face") are thematically related.[94] Each has to do with the reciprocal knowledge between God and the lawgiver.[95] They are in addition verbally linked:

	MT	LXX
"face to face"		
Exod 33:11	פָּנִים אֶל־פָּנִים	ἐνώπιος ἐνωπίῳ
Deut 34:10	פָּנִים אֶל־פָּנִים	πρόσωπον κατὰ πρόσωπον
"mouth to mouth"		
Num 12:8	פֶּה אֶל־פֶּה	στόμα κατὰ στόμα
"know"		
Exod 33:12–13	אֵדָעֲךָ, יְדַעְתִּיךָ	οἶδα, γνωστῶς ἴδω
Num 12:6	אֶתְוַדַּע	γνωσθήσομαι
Deut 34:10	יְדָעוֹ	ἔγνω
Moses as "prophet"		
Num 12:6	נְבִיאֲכֶם	προφήτης
Deut 34:10	נָבִיא	προφήτης

It is only natural that the three verses, which together fostered much speculation regarding the delicate issue of how anyone could see God, were often associated and considered in the light of one another.[96]

This matters for the interpretation of Q 10:21–22 because "All has been handed to me by my Father; and no one knows the Son except the Father, and no one knows the Father except the Son" is a claim to exclusive and reciprocal divine knowledge. This is precisely what the well-known Exodus 33 claims for Moses when read, as it traditionally was, in the light of Numbers 12 and Deuteronomy 34: God knew (LXX: οἶδα; MT: יְדַעְתִּיךָ) Moses, Moses prayed that he might know (LXX: γνωστῶς ἴδω; MT: אֵדָעֲךָ) God, whereupon God dramatically revealed himself in a unique and unprece-

---

94. Deut 34:9–12 was probably composed with Exodus 33 in mind.

95. Cf. the paraphrase of Exod 33:13 in Philo, *Poster C.* 13: τοῦ ὁρᾶν καὶ πρὸς αὐτοῦ ὁρᾶσθαι: "to see God and to be seen by him."

96. E.g., in LXX Num 12:8, we read that Moses "saw (εἶδεν) the glory (δόξαν) of the Lord." But in the MT Moses "sees" (יביט) the form (הַתְּמֻנָה) of the Lord." The substitution of "glory" for "form" and the use of an aorist (adverting to some past occasion) imply that the translator construed Num 12:8 as a reference to Moses' vision of God's glory as told in Exodus 33–34. The same interpretation is made by Tg. Ps.-J. on Num 12:8, which mentions "the back of the Shekinah," an unmistakable allusion to Exodus 33.

The LXX ties Num 12:6–8 not only to Exodus 33 but also to the end of Deuteronomy. LXX Deut 34:5 renders the MT's עֶבֶד־יהוה ("servant of the Lord") not with ὁ παῖς τοῦ θεοῦ, as one might have expected, but with οἰκέτης κυρίου ("household slave of the Lord"), which depends upon Num 12:7 (Moses is "faithful with all my house"). Additional texts that link the relevant Pentateuchal verses include Ecclus 45:3–5; Philo, *Leg. all.* 3.100–103; Philo, *Quis rerum* 262; Ps.-Clem. *Hom.* 17.18 (GCS, ed. B. Rehm, p. 239); Tertullian, *Adv. Prax.* 14 (ed. E. Evans, pp. 105–106); *Sifre Deut* 357 on 34:10–13; Chrysostom, *Hom. Mt* 78.4 (PG 58.716); *Memar Marqah* 5:3; and (for a much later example) Moses Maimonides, *Guide for the Perplexed* 2.45.

dented fashion, with the result that reciprocal knowledge ("face to face") was gained.[97]

(iii) The declaration of reciprocal knowledge in Q 10:22 is made in a prayer (cf. Q 10:21: "I thank you Father," etc.). Similarly, in Exod 33:12–13 it is in a prayer that Moses confesses God's knowledge of him and then asks to know God ("Moses said to the Lord").

(iv) The words of Q 10:22, "nor does anyone know the Father," are related to Exod 33:20 and the tradition there encapsulated: God said to Moses, "No one shall see me and live."[98] Tertullian at least drew the connection: "With regard to the Father, the very gospel... will testify that He was never visible, according to the word of Christ: 'No one knoweth the Father, except the Son.' For even in the Old Testament He had declared, 'No one will see me and live.' "[99]

(v) On Tertullian's reading, Mt 11:27 stands very near to Jn 1:18: "No one has seen God at anytime. God the only Son, who is in the bosom of the Father, he has made him known." The meaning of this last has been expressed by Raymond Brown as follows:

> Naturally it is the failure of Moses to have seen God that the author wishes to contrast with the intimate contact between Son and Father. In Exod xxxiii 18 Moses asks to see God's glory, but the Lord says, "You cannot see my face and live...." Against this OT background that not even the greatest representatives of Israel have seen God, John holds up the example of the only Son who has not only seen the Father but is ever at His side.[100]

This interpretation of Jn 1:18, which is congruent with the express contrast with Moses in Jn 1:17, parallels Tertullian's interpretation of Mt 11:27 (see above); and Marie-Émile Boismard has recently made the convincing case that Jn 1:14–18 should be interpreted by way of its contrast with the story of Moses in Exodus 33–34.[101] The point is so important because many

---

97. According to Exodus, God revealed only God's back, so while Moses' petition was answered, it was not answered as anticipated. Hence some interpreters have urged that God really denied Moses what he sought; so Philo, *Poster C.* 13; *Spec. leg.* 1.42–43; *Fug.* 164–65; *Mut. nom.* 7–10; cf. Jn 1:18. But Ps 103:7 declares that God showed God's ways (cf. Exod 33:13) to Moses, and that is the dominant interpretation in the history of exegesis; cf. Deut 34:5–10 (v. 10 explicitly speaks of God knowing Moses: "whom the Lord knew [MT: אשר ידעו יהוה; LXX: ὃν ἔγνω κύριος αὐτόν] face to face"; this construes Moses' entreaty, "Show me your ways, so that I may know you," as having been fulfilled in a mutual act of knowing on Sinai: God knew Moses and Moses knew God); Heb 11:27; *b. Ber.* 71; Gregory of Nyssa, *Vit. Mos.* 219–20 (Opera 7/1, ed. H. Musurillo, p. 110); Theodoret of Cyrrhus, *Hist. Rel.* 2.13 (SC 234, ed. P. Canivet and A. Leroy-Molinghen, p. 222).

98. This verse and its theme generated much reflection; see Judg 13:22; *Sib. Or.* 3:17; Jn 1:18; 5:37; 6:46; 1 Tim 6:16; 1 Jn 4:12; *Asc. Isa* 3:8–9; also the references in the previous fn.

99. *Adv. Marc.* 2.27 (SC 368, ed. R. Braun, pp. 162, 164); cf. idem, *Adv. Prax.* 24 (TU 31, ed. K. Ter-Měkěrttschian and E. Ter-Minassiantz, pp. 119–20).

100. Raymond E. Brown, *The Gospel according to John (i–xii)* (AB 29; Garden City, N.Y.: Doubleday, 1966), p. 36.

101. Marie-Émile Boismard, *Moses or Jesus: An Essay in Johannine Christology* (Louvain/Minneapolis: Peeters/Fortress, 1993), pp. 93–98.

have supposed that Jn 1:14–18 is among the Johannine sayings indebted to the tradition preserved in Q 10:21–22.[102] If they are right, then Jn 1:14–18 indicates that an early interpreter of that tradition was moved to reflect upon Moses.

(vi) The πάντα in "All has been handed over to me by my Father" is comprehensive: Jesus has the whole revelation of God.[103] This is another Mosaic trait, for the Moses of the haggadah came to enjoy practical omniscience. The wedding of all written and oral Torah to Sinai entailed the unsurpassed learning of its human channel. What was not known by the man who, among other things, wrote a book that was understood to recount the creation of the world, prophesy messianic events,[104] and describe much in between, including his own death?[105] Already the *Exagōgē* of Ezekiel has Moses testify to this: "I beheld the entire circled earth, both beneath the earth and above the heaven; and a host of stars fell at my feet, and I numbered them all"; and the text goes on to announce that Moses saw all "things present, past, and future."[106] The assertion that Moses numbered the stars especially startles because in Jewish tradition it is precisely this that human beings, with their comparatively feeble mental powers, cannot do.[107] In representing Moses as a repository of encyclopedic learning, the *Exagōgē* does not stand alone: many are the texts that proclaim the lawgiver's far-reaching, supernatural knowledge.[108] All knowledge, according to tradition, had been handed over

---

102. See the survey of opinion in M. Sabbe, "Can Mt 11,25–27 and Lc 10,22 Be Called a Johannine Logion?" in *LOGIA: Les Paroles du Jésus — The Sayings of Jesus. Mémorial Joseph Coppens* (ed. Joël Delobel; BETL 59; Louvain: Peeters/Louvain University Press, 1982), pp. 363–71. Ecclesiastical commentators on Mt 11:27 or Lk 10:22 have often cited Jn 1:17–18 and vice versa; see, e.g., Albertus Magnus, *Super Mt cap. I–XIV* ad loc. (Opera Omnia 21/1, ed. B. Schmidt, p. 363); and Martin Bucer, *In sacra quatuor evangelia* (Strasbourg: Roberti Stephani, 1553), p. 108.

103. That Q 10:21 and 23–24 have to do with things that have been revealed and that v. 22b is about knowledge imply that "all has been handed over to me by my Father" (v. 22a) concerns revelation, not authority or power.

104. For Moses as a prophet, see Deut 18:15, 18; 34:10; Hos 12:13; Ecclus 46:1; Wisd 11:1; *T. Mos.* 1:5; 3:11; 11:16; 12:7; *Asc. Isa* 3:8; Josephus, *Ant.* 2.327; 4.165; *2 Bar.* 59:4–11; *m. Soṭa* 1:9; *1 Clem.* 43:6; Justin, *1 Apol.* 32.1 (PTS 38, ed. M. Marcovich, p. 78); etc.

105. See Deut 34:5–6 and the comments on this by Josephus, *Ant.* 4.326, and Rabbi Meir in *Sifre Deut* 357 on 34:5–6.

106. Preserved in Eusebius, *Praep. ev.* 9.29 (GCS 43/1, ed. K. Mras, p. 529).

107. Gen 15:5; 22:17; Deut 1:10; Ps 147:4; Isa 40:26; *1 En.* 93:14; *LAB* 21:2; *b. Sanh.* 39a; *Gk. Apoc. Ezra* 2:32; etc. The rule is, only God can count stars.

108. See, e.g., *Jub.* 1:4 (God revealed to Moses "what [was] in the beginning and what will occur [in the future]," cf. 1:26); *Ep. Arist.* 139 (Moses "understand[s] all things"); *LAB* 19:10, 14–16 (after God showed Moses how much "time has passed and how much remains," Moses "was filled with understanding"); *2 Bar.* 59:4–11 (a catalogue of things heavenly and things future known by Moses); *Sifre* 357 on Num 12:8 (God "showed him [Moses] all the world from the day it was created until the day when the dead will come to life"); *b. Meg.* 19b ("The Holy One, blessed be he, showed Moses the minutiae of the Torah, the minutiae of the scribes, and the innovations which would be introduced by the scribes"); *Midr. Ps* 24:5 (Moses "knew the upper as well as the nether worlds"); *Memar Marqah* 5:1 ("His [Moses'] span includes the knowledge of the beginning and it goes on to the day of vengeance").

to the lawgiver. So when Q 10:22 makes the same claim for Jesus, it is setting him beside Moses.

(vii) The order of the two major clauses in Mt 11:27 = Lk 10:22 has often been thought a bit peculiar: only the Father knows the Son, only the Son knows the Father. The natural tendency — shared by certain Christian scribes, as the textual traditions of Matthew and Luke attest — is to put the subject of God's unknowability first: it is the greater mystery. But in Exod 33:12–13 the statement of God's knowledge of Moses prefaces Moses' request to know God: "You have said, 'I know you [Moses] by name' " introduces "Show me your ways, so that I may know you." This explains Q's order. The clause about knowledge of the Son comes before that about knowledge of the divine Father because the Q text replicates the order of Exod 33:12–13, where God's knowledge of Moses is indicated before Moses asks to know God.[109]

(viii) Paul writes in 1 Cor 13:12: "For now we see in a mirror dimly, but then face to face. Now I know in part; then I shall understand fully even as I have been fully understood." This differs from Q 10:22 in that full knowledge still belongs to the future and knowledge is not exclusive, for all the elect will someday understand. Nonetheless, Q 10:22 and 1 Cor 13:12 are conceptually very close, which matters because the latter contains an allusion to Moses.[110] Paul opens his remarks about knowing and being known with a contrast between seeing in a mirror dimly and seeing face to face. In doing so he is, as is generally recognized, drawing upon Num 12:8, where God speaks "mouth to mouth" to Moses,[111] not in dark speech (MT: ולא בחידת; LXX: οὐ δι' αἰνιγμάτων)[112] but rather, according to the Hebrew, מראה. This last is usually read as מַרְאֶה, as in BDB, s.v. This is the vocalization behind the NRSV: "clearly." There are, however, rabbinic passages that take מראה to mean מַרְאָה, "mirror."[113] This explains 1 Cor 13:12: the passage presupposes the exegetical tradition according to which Num 12:8 means that God spoke to Moses "(as) in a mirror." Thus δι' ἐσόπτρου ἐν αἰνίγματι is the antithesis of מראה ולא בחידת: Paul borrowed the phrase about Moses and simply removed the negation. So when ruminating upon the subject of knowing and being known by God, which is also the subject of Q 10:22, Paul turned his thoughts to the lawgiver.

---

109. One may compare Jn 10:15: "The Father knows me and I know the Father." This surely is a variant of Q 10:22; see C. H. Dodd, *Historical Tradition in the Fourth Gospel* (Cambridge: Cambridge University Press, 1963), pp. 359–60.

110. See already Tertullian, *Adv. Prax.* 14 (TU 31, ed. K. Ter-Měkěrttschian and E. Ter-Minassiantz, pp. 105–6). Cf. Bede, *In epist. sept. cath.* on 3:2 (CCSL 121, ed. D. Hurst, p. 302); Gregory the Great, *Exp. vet. ac novi test.* 1.55 (PL 79.749B-750C).

111. Paul changed "mouth to mouth" to "face to face" (cf. Exod 33:11; Num 14:14; Deut 5:4; 34:10; Ecclus 45:5; *Barn.* 15:1; *Memar Marqah* 5:3; etc.) because his subject was sight, not speech, and because Jewish tradition had long associated Num 12:8 (which has "mouth to mouth") with Exod 33:11 and Deut 34:10 (which have "face to face"); see n. 96.

112. BDB, s.v., defines חידה as "riddle, enigmatic, perplexing saying or question."

113. See SB 3:452–54.

(ix) The verb used for the transmission of revelation from the Father to the Son in Q 10:22 is παραδίδωμι — "all has been handed over (παρεδόθη) to me by my Father." This verb and the related simplex, δίδωμι, like the Hebrew מסר, were, in certain contexts, technical terms for the transmission of Torah, and they were used both for the handing over of the law to Moses and for Moses' bequeathing that law to others.[114] Just as "Moses received the Torah from Sinai and handed it on to Joshua" (*m. 'Aboth* 1:1), so Jesus in Q 10:22 receives revelation directly from God and passes it on to others.[115] Jesus and Moses are both the fountains of their respective traditions.

(x) Q 10:21 ends with, "Yes, Father, for such was well pleasing before you." The Greek is εὐδοκία ἐγένετο ἔμπροσθέν σου. This is an obvious Semitism,[116] and there are good parallels in rabbinic texts (יהי רצון מלפניך)[117] and the targumim (יהי רעוה מן קדם).[118] The point for us is that thrice in Exod 33:12–13 Moses uses the expression "favor in your [God's] eyes," and it is repeated in vv. 16 ("How will it be known that I have found favor in your sight?") and 17 ("You [Moses] have found favor in my sight"):

v. 12	חן בעיני	χάριν[119] ἔχεις παρ᾽ ἐμοί
v. 13	חן בעיניך	χάριν ἐναντίον σου
v. 13	חן בעיניך	χάριν ἐναντίον σου
v. 16	חן בעיניך	χάριν παρὰ σοί
v. 17	חן בעיני	χάριν ἐνώπιόν μου

Although the LXX renders the idiom with χάριν + παρά or ἐνώπιον or ἐναντίον,[120] the dictionaries give "favor" as a meaning for both חן and εὐδοκία,[121] so εὐδοκία ἔμπροσθεν σου is a perfectly good equivalent for חן בעיניך. Moreover, an expression that occurs five times within the space of a few verses — and then again in the next chapter (34:9) — clearly calls attention to itself. One wonders, then, given the other links between Q 10:21–22 and Exodus 33, whether εὐδοκία ἐγένετο ἔμπροσθεν σου is not also among them.

---

114. Relevant texts include LXX Deut 10:4; Ecclus 45:5; *LAB* 11:2; *m. 'Aboth* 1:1; *Apost. Const.* 8.12.25 (ed. F. X. Funk, p. 504); *Apoc. Paul* 8; and PGM 12.92–94.

115. For ἀποκαλύπτω with reference to Moses, see the preface to the *Apocalypse of Moses*: "The narrative and life of Adam and Eve the first-made, revealed (ἀποκαλυφθεῖσα) by God to Moses his servant when he received the tables of the law."

116. BDF §214.6. The only other instances of εὐδοκία ἔμπροσθεν that I have been able to find are in patristic quotations of our texts, such as Clement of Alexandria, *Paed.* 1.6.32 (GCS 12, ed. O. Stählin, p. 109).

117. See SB 1, p. 607.

118. E.g., Tg. Neof. 1 on Num 22:13; 23:27; Tg. Isa 53:6.

119. χάρις can translate רצון (e.g., LXX Prov 10:32; 11:27; 12:2), and as already noted the rabbinic יהי רצון מלפניך = Q's εὐδοκία ἔμπροσθεν σου.

120. The omission of "eyes" might be explained as due to a desire to avoid anthropomorphisms when possible.

121. See, e.g., Jastrow, s.v.; and BAGD, s.v., respectively.

(xi) Mt 11:25–30 expands the tradition in Q 10:21–22. Among the items added are these:

a promise of rest: "and I will give you rest"
an invitation to take up a yoke: "take my yoke upon you"
a claim to meekness: "I am meek and lowly in heart"

It is scarcely coincidence that all three items readily associate themselves with traditions about Moses. "And I will give you rest" (κἀγὼ ἀναπαύσω ὑμᾶς) is close to Exod 33:14, where God says to Moses, "and I will give you rest" (LXX: καὶ καταπαύσω σε; MT: והנחתי לך). "Yoke" (ζυγός = עול) was associated above all with the Torah that Moses passed on.[122] And if Jesus is meek (πραΰς), Moses, on the basis of Num 12:3 (LXX with πραῢς σφόδρα; MT: ענו מאד), was Judaism's great exemplar in meekness, something not forgotten by Christians.[123] It seems clear, then, that at least Matthew espied in Q 10:21–22 parallels between Jesus and Moses and that he added to them.[124]

Some readers, incidentally, have found the antithesis between "labor and are heavy laden" and "my yoke is easy and my burden is light" (Mt 11:28–29) also to be exodus language. Pharaoh put slave masters over the Israelites. He ruthlessly forced them into hard labor, and he made their lives bitter with hard labor in brick and mortar and with all kinds of work in the fields (Exod 1:11–14; cf. 2:11). Photius, *Hom.* 14.3, referred to Mt 11:30 and then went on, "No need for your to suffer toils, to undergo sleepless vigils, distressed all day and all night, or to dig a ditch, or erect a mound of earth, or to work in clay and brick-making, which the Egyptians devised against the Jews." And in "A Soliloquy of One of the Spies Left in the Wilderness," Gerard Manley Hopkins wrote this:

Give us the tale of bricks as heretofore;
To plash with cool feet the clay juicy soil.
Who tread the grapes are splay'd with stripes of gore,
    And they who crush the oil

---

122. See Jer 5:5; Acts 15:10; Gal 5:1; and *2 Bar.* 41:3 (cf. *2 En.* 48:9). Rabbinic literature also attests to this: "yoke of the Torah" and "yoke of the commandments" are frequent. See, e.g., *m. 'Aboth* 3:5 and *m. Ber.* 2:2; additional texts in SB 1:608–10. One understands why J. C. Fenton, *Saint Matthew* (Baltimore: Penguin, 1963), p. 187, found in Mt 11:29a "the idea of Jesus as the second Moses, the teacher of the new law."

123. Cf. Ecclus 45:4; Philo, *Mos.* 1.26; *Mek.* on Exod 20:21; *b. Ned.* 38a; *Tanhuma* Bereshit l; Origen, *Hom. Exod.* 11.6 (SC 321, ed. M. Borret, p. 348); Jerome, *Ep.* 82.3 (CSEL 55, ed. I. Hilberg, p. 110); Chrysostom, *Hom. Mt* 78.4 (PG 58.716); Chromatius of Aquileia, *Tract. Mt* 3.4 (CCSL 9, ed. V. Bulhart, p. 398 — citing Num 12:3 in commenting on Mt 11:29); Theodoret of Cyrrhus, *Rel. hist.* 11.2 (SC 234, ed. P. Canivet and A. Leroy-Molinghen, p. 456); *Apophthegmata Patrum* Syncletica 11 (PG 65.425B); John the Persian 4 (PG 65.237D).

124. Cf. Jean Miler, *Les Citations d'Accomplissement dans l'Évangile de Matthieu: Quand Dieu se rend présent en toute humanité* (AnBib 140; Rome: Pontifical Biblical Institute, 1999), p. 132, n. 27.

> Are splatter'd. We desire the *yoke* we bore,
> The *easy burden* of yore.

I also have in my possession a letter in which W. D. Davies says he has always associated Mt 11:28 with the burdens of the slaves in Egypt.[125]

•

If, near the opening of Q, Jesus relives the experience of the exodus (Q 4:1–13) and revises a portion of the holiness code (Q 6:27–45), here, a bit later, in 10:22, he makes himself out to be a revealer of Mosaic stature. His prayer recapitulates the experience of Moses on Sinai, the revealer who uniquely knew and was known by God and was entrusted with the fullness of the divine paradosis. Q in its own way anticipates the rabbinic declaration, "As the first redeemer was, so shall the latter redeemer be" (*Eccles Rab.* 1:28).

Q 11:3 // Exod 16:1–36. The familiar line from the Lord's Prayer τὸν ἄρτον ἡμῶν τὸν ἐπιούσιον δὸς ἡμῖν σήμερον contains not only a great lexicographical puzzle — What is the derivation and meaning of ἐπιούσιον? — but has given rise to a host of conflicting interpretations. Those issues need not be addressed here. What is relevant for our purposes is the probable allusion to the well-known story in Exodus 16, where God is the source of manna (called "bread" in Num 21:5 and elsewhere)[126] for the day to come, a story referred to several times in the Tanak[127] and already alluded to in Q 4:1ff. In the LXX account ἡμέρα appears repeatedly (vv. 1, 4, 5, 22, 26, 27, 29, 30), and δίδωμι is used (vv. 8, 15, 29; cf. LXX Ps 77:24; Jn 6:32).[128] Further, Luke's redactional "daily" (τὸ καθ᾽ ἡμέραν) appears in LXX Exod 16:5, and the apparent allusion to τὸν ἄρτον ἡμῶν τὸν ἐπιούσιον δὸς ἡμῖν σήμερον in Jn 6:34 occurs as part of a discussion about Moses and the manna.[129]

Expositors have often perceived a link with Exodus, as Jean Carmignac has documented. His list of representative exegetes includes Tertullian,

---

125. As the Jesus of Q 10:21–22 is "the Son," one might want to add to the parallels between Jesus and Moses by observing that in Ezekiel the Tragedian's *Exagōgē*, God says to Moses, "Take courage, son" (θάρσησον, ὦ παῖ; preserved in Eusebius, *Praep. ev.* 9.29.8 [GCS 43/1, ed. K. Mras, p. 530]). But I cannot see that anywhere else in pre-Christian literature is Moses called God's "son."

I have passed over the common association of Mt 11:25–30 with Ecclesiasticus 51 because most of the parallels appear in Mt 11:28–30, which is not Q material. Moreover, there is no firm evidence of literary dependence even there. The similarities are due to the independent incorporation of motifs commonly connected with Torah and Wisdom.

126. See n. 8 on p. 26.

127. The story is told in Exodus 16 and Numbers 11 and then referred to in Deut 8:3, 16; Neh 9:20; Ps 78:24; 105:40; and Wisd 16:20. The tradition also may lie behind 1 Kgs 17:6.

128. See further P. Grelot, "La quatrième demande du 'Pater' et son arrière-plan sémitique," *NTS* 25 (1975), pp. 299–314.

129. Barnabas Lindars, "Discourse and Tradition: The Use of the Sayings of Jesus in the Discourses of the Fourth Gospel," *JSNT* 13 (1981), p. 88.

Origen, Ildefonsus of Toledo, Paschasius Radbertus, Hugh of Saint Victor, Albert the Great, Dante, Luther, Calvin, Cornelius à Lapide, Grotius, F. H. Chase, F. Spitta, Alfred Seeberg, F. Hauck, W. Foerster, R. E. Brown, Michael D. Goulder, and Jacques Dupont.[130] To this one may add that Lancelot Andrews's use of "angels' food" in his paraphrase of the Lord's Prayer alludes to Ps 78:25, where the manna of the desert is called "the bread of angels,"[131] and further that J. D. M. Derrett has observed that just as Moses commanded there to be no hoarding of the manna, so the Lord's Prayer "renounces the possibility of hoarding."[132] Still others have found a background in the wilderness traditions for the Lord's Prayer clause about temptation.[133] Whether in this they should be followed — the question may remain open — it is clear that Jesus' prayer for bread has moved many to recall the famous story of the manna in the wilderness. Here then we have a likely allusion.

How does this allusion affect interpretation? The story of the manna depicts God providing food for the faithful when they were hungry and could not find sufficient food for themselves. For itinerants who had to live off the charity of others, so that the source of their food might be uncertain from day to day (cf. Q 10:7–8), the memory of God having fed the saints of old would be great reassurance. To all this there would be a parallel in Deut 8:1–10, where the manna is an object lesson in the humility that is appropriate for those who depend upon God.

Another possibility for those who remember the miracle of the manna when praying the Lord's Prayer is that it might encourage them in an eschatological reading of the Lord's Prayer. In Judaism, manna was not just a memory but a future hope, as in *2 Bar.* 29:8, where we read that when the earth is transformed in the latter days, "the treasury of manna will come down again from on high, and they will eat of it in those years because they are they who have arrived at the consummation of time."[134] So one might, like Raymond Brown and Joachim Jeremias, who in this particular follow

---

130. Jean Carmignac, *Recherches sur le "Notre Père"* (Paris: Letouzey & Ané, 1969), pp. 200–210. Cf. Heinz Schürmann, *Das Lukasevangelium, Zweiter Teil: Erste Folge: Kommentar zu Kapitel 9,51–11,54* (HTKNT 3/2; Freiburg/Basel/Vienna: Herder, 1994), pp. 192, 194; and Keener, *Matthew*, pp. 221–22.

131. Lancelot Andrews, *The Private Devotions of Lancelot Andrews* (New York: Meridian, 1961), p. 284.

132. J. D. M. Derrett, *The Ascetic Discourse: An Explanation of the Sermon on the Mount* (Eilsbrunn: Ko'amar, 1989), p. 48.

133. E.g., C. B. Houk, "ΠΕΙΡΑΣΜΟΣ, The Lord's Prayer, and the Massah Tradition," *SJT* 19 (1966), pp. 216–25. Cf. R. F. Cyster, "The Lord's Prayer and the Exodus Tradition," *Theology* 64 (1961), pp. 377–81. The lengthy retelling of the manna tradition in Psalm 78 emphasizes both Israel's testing of God (vv. 18, 41, 56) and the forgiveness of sins (vv. 38–39). Cf. also Exod 16:4, where the giving of manna is a test ("that I may prove them, whether they will walk in my law or not").

134. Related expectations appear in *Sib. Or.* frag. 3, 49; 7:149; *LAB* 19:10; Rev 2:17; *Mek.* on Exod 16:25.

the *Gospel of the Nazaraeans* as reported by Jerome,[135] take the prayer for bread to be akin to the prayer for the coming of the kingdom.[136]

Q 11:20 // Exod 8:19. In debate with opponents, the Jesus of Q 11:20 evidently said, "But if I by the finger of God (ἐν δακτύλῳ θεοῦ) cast out demons, then the kingdom of God has come upon you."[137] The expression "the finger of God" appears thrice in the Tanak:

Exod 8:19: "And the magicians [who could not produce gnats as had Moses] said to Pharaoh, 'This is the finger of God (LXX: δάκτυλος θεοῦ; MT: אצבע אלהים).' "

Exod 31:18: "When God finished speaking with Moses on Mount Sinai, he gave him the two tablets of the covenant, tablets of stone, written with the finger of God (LXX: τῷ δακτύλῳ τοῦ θεοῦ; MT: באצבע אלהים)."

Deut 9:10: "And the Lord gave me [Moses] the two stone tablets written with the finger of God (LXX: ἐν τῷ δακτύλῳ τοῦ θεοῦ; MT: באצבע אלהים); on them were all the words that the Lord had spoken to you at the mountain out of the fire on the day of the assembly."[138]

All three texts have to do with Moses and his story. So if the hearer recalls one or more of them, the exodus typology established in Q 4:1–13 and carried forward in Q 6:27–45; 7:27; 10:4 (?), 21–22; and 11:3 will be furthered.

The closest parallel thematically to Q's saying is Exod 8:19, where one of the ten plagues worked through Moses is attributed to the finger of God. Here, as in Q, the finger of God works a miracle.[139] Q thus prods us to set the miracles of Jesus beside the miracles of Moses.[140] Eusebius naturally thought that the parallel made Jesus like Moses. After quoting Exod 8:19 he continued: "In like manner did Jesus the Christ of God say to the Pharisees, 'If I by the finger of God cast out devils.' "[141] In our own day Norman

---

135. Jerome, *Comm. Mt* on 6:11 (SC 242, ed. É. Bonnard, p. 132): in the *Gospel of the Nazaraeans* Jerome "found *mahar*, which means 'of tomorrow,' so that the sense is: 'Our bread of tomorrow — that is, of the future — give us this day.' "

136. Raymond E. Brown, "The Pater Noster as an Eschatological Prayer," in *New Testament Essays* (Garden City, N.Y.: Doubleday, 1968), pp. 275–320; Joachim Jeremias, *The Prayers of Jesus* (SBT 2/6; London: SCM, 1967), pp. 82–107.

137. So Lk 11:20 and the IQP. Cf. Meier, *A Marginal Jew*, vol. 2, pp. 410–11. Matthew has "by the Spirit of God," which Catchpole, *Quest for Q*, p. 12, n. 27, reckons original.

138. Ps 8:4 refers to the heavens being "the work of your fingers," which probably means God's "hand."

139. Cf. Philo, *Vit. Mos.* 1.112; *Migr. Abr.* 85; *Mek.* on Exod 14:30 (the exegesis here reappears in the *Passover Seder*); *b. Sanh.* 67b; *Pirqe R. El.* 48; *Penitence of Cyprian* 17 (when Jannes and Jambres "practiced magic [they] acknowledged the finger of God").

140. See further Pieter W. van der Horst, " 'The Finger of God': Miscellaneous Notes on Luke 11:20 and its *Umwelt*," in *Sayings of Jesus: Canonical and Non-Canonical: Essays in Honour of Tjitze Baarda* (ed. William L. Petersen, Johan S. Vos, and Henk J. de Jonge; NovTSup 89; Leiden/New York/Cologne: Brill, 1997), pp. 89–103. On p. 102 he concludes: "Pagan traditions about the finger of a god can hardly have played a role in the mind of Luke (or Jesus)"; rather, "it is the Jewish interpretation of God's finger in Ex. 8:15 as an invincible power in the struggle against (demonic) evil" that our text has in mind.

141. *Dem. ev.* 3.2 (PG 22.173B). Cf. Bede, *Luc. exp.* ad loc. (CCSL 70, ed. D. Hurst, p. 233); the same comments appear in Sedulius Scotus, *Kommentar zum Evangelium nach Matthäus*

Perrin, calling attention to the parallel in *Exod Rab.* 10.7,[142] paraphrased the meaning of Q 11:20 this way: "This is not the work of demons, but of God, and if God is at work in this manner, then you are even now experiencing the New Exodus: the Kingdom of God has come upon you."[143]

Since the immediate context of Q 11:20 offers a critique of exorcists other than Jesus (11:24–26)[144] and uses the word σημεῖον ("sign"),[145] it is also natural to think, as did Ainsworth,[146] that Jesus' relationship to other wonderworkers is akin to that of Moses and the magicians of Egypt, whose deeds are recorded in Exodus 7–9, where Pharaoh demands a σημεῖον of Moses.[147] If Jesus is accused of casting out demons by the prince of demons, Pharaoh's magicians, known to popular legend as Jannes and Jambres,[148]

11,2 bis *Schluß* ad 12:28 (ed. B. Löfstedt, pp. 332–33); also Bonaventure, *Exp. Luc.* ad loc. (Opera Omnia 10, ed. A. C. Peltier, p. 530); cf. Albertus Magnus, *Enarrationes in secundum partem Evangelium Lucae (X–XXIV)* ad loc. (Opera Omnia 23, ed. A. Borgnet, p. 151); Lindars, "Image of Moses," p. 131; David Flusser, "Hillel and Jesus: Two Ways of Self-Awareness," in *Hillel and Jesus: Comparisons of Two Major Religious Leaders* (ed. James H. Charlesworth and Loren L. Johns; Minneapolis: Fortress, 1997), p. 97.

142. "When the magicians saw that they could not produce the lice, they recognized immediately that the happenings [the plagues] were the work of God and not the work of demons."

143. Norman Perrin, *Rediscovering the Teaching of Jesus* (New York: Harper & Row, 1976), p. 67. He depends here upon T. W. Manson, *The Teaching of Jesus: Studies in Its Form and Content* (2d ed.; Cambridge: Cambridge University Press, 1935), pp. 82–83. Manson remarked that Jesus uses "the finger of God" in a way that presupposes its context in Exodus 8 and shows that his "acquaintance with the Hebrew Bible was not only wide...but also very intimate and detailed."

144. Allison, *Jesus Tradition in Q*, pp. 120–32.

145. So Lk 11:16 ("Others, to test him, kept demanding from him a sign from heaven") — which, because of its non-Lukan features, should probably be assigned to Q; see Joachim Jeremias, *Die Sprache des Lukasevangeliums: Redaktion und Tradition im Nicht-Markusstoff des dritten Evangeliums* (MeyerK; Göttingen: Vandenhoeck & Ruprecht, 1980), p. 199.

146. Henry Ainsworth, *Annotations on the Pentateuch* (Edinburgh: Blackie & Sons, 1843), vol. 1, p. 275: "To this speech [Exod 8:19] Christ hath reference when he refuted those that withstood his miracles, as these magicians did Moses.... Here the confession of Jannes and Jambres...condemned Pharaoh and themselves."

147. 7:9: "When Pharaoh says to you, 'Perform a wonder' (LXX: σημεῖον ἢ τέρας; Tg. Onq.: אתא ["sign"]; Tg. Neof. 1: סימן [for MT's מופת, "wonder"]), then you shall say to Aaron, 'Take your staff and throw it down before Pharaoh, and it will become a snake.' " Cf. Artapanus *apud* Eusebius, *Praep. ev.* 9.27.27 (Texts and Translations 20/Pseudepigrapha Series 10, ed. C. R. Holladay, p. 220): "The king then told Moses to perform some sign (σημεῖον) for him"; Tg. Onq. on Exod 8:5 ("Then Moses said to Pharaoh, 'Ask for a mighty deed' " [גבורא]).

The connection between Moses and "sign" is regular in the LXX; see Exod 4:8, 9, 17, 28, 30; 7:3; 8:23; 10:1, 2; 11:9, 10; Num 14:22; Deut 7:19; 11:3; 26:8; 34:11; Ps 77:43; 134:9; Bar 2:11; Wisd 10:16; Ecclus 36:5; 45:3. Cf. Ezekiel the Tragedian *apud* Eusebius, *Praep. ev.* 9.29.31 (GCS 43/1, ed. K. Mras, p. 523); Philo, *Vit. Mos.* 1.210; Josephus, *Ant.* 2.276, 280, 284; Jn 6:30–34; Acts Pilate 5:1.

148. Jannes and Jambres were not obscure figures. 2 Tim 3:8–9 refers to them without explanation, and fragments of a book about them have survived. They are also mentioned in CD 5:18–19; *T. Sol.* 25:3–4; Numenius *apud* Eusebius, *Praep. ev.* 9.8 (GCS 43/1, ed. K. Mras, p. 494); *Quaest. Barth.* Latin 2, 4.50; Acts Pilate 5:1; *b. Menah.* 85a; Tg. Ps.-J. on Exod 1:15; 7:11; Num 22:22. Cf. Pliny, *N. H.* 30.2.11; and Apuleius, *Apol.* 90, among other places.

were said to have been in league with the devil.[149] So Jesus' rebuttal to the accusation made against him is that he is not like Jannes and Jambres, who did magic by demonic means, but rather like Moses, through whom the finger of God worked.[150]

The book known as *Jannes and Jambres* has, unfortunately, survived only in fragments, but one extant portion of it is relevant for our purposes:

Pap. Chester Beatty XVI 26a^r	*Pap. Vindobonensis Gk 29456^v*
Emissaries from the king arrived who said, "Come quickly and withstand Moses the Hebrew who is doing signs (σημεῖα)	withstand Moses the Hebrew who is doing signs (σημεῖα) and wonders
so that all are amazed (θαυμάζειν)." And Jannes came to the king and withstood Moses and his brother by doing whatever they had done. But immediately his fatal illness tormented him again with a tumor. So he went into the hedra and after....	so that all are amazed (θαυμάζειν). And when he had come to the king he withstood Moses and his brother Aaron by doing whatever they had done. But immediately his fatal illness tormented him again with a serious tumor. Into the hedra he went to find a way to get rid of it. Then
he sent word to the king, saying, "This thing is God's active power (ἡ ἐνεργοῦσα δύναμις)."	he sent word to the king saying, "This is the power (δύναμις) of God; I am not able to accomplish anything [except what is?] not unto death."[151]

The final sentence includes a paraphrase of Exod 8:19, with "power" substituted for "finger."[152] So we have here, in a possibly pre-Christian book that presumably both collected lore about Jannes and Jambres and added to

---

149. Cf. *T. Sol.* 25:3–4: the demon Abezethibou claims, "I am the one whom Jannes and Jambres, those who opposed Moses in Egypt, called to their aid." According to A. Pietersma, *The Apocryphon of Jannes and Jambres the Magicians* (RGRW 119; Leiden/New York/Cologne: Brill, 1994), p. 210, "That Jannes as a μάγος would possess or would be possessed by a demon is a foregone conclusion." Already CD 5:18–19 has this: "Moses and Aaron stood by the hand of the Prince of Lights and Belial raised up יחנה and his brother in his plotting, when Israel was first saved." And in *Jub.* 48:9 we read that Mastema helped the Egyptian sorcerers in their competition with Moses. Also relevant is *Quaest. Barth.* Latin 2, 4.50 (Satan says, "Jannes and Mambres are my brothers"). For later notices, see Palladius, *H. Laus.* 18.5–8 (TS 6/2, ed. J. A. Robinson, p. 49: demons guard their tomb); and Aelfric, *De auguriis* 17.114–17 (see Pietersma, p. 34: they acted "through the devil's art"). Already Exod 8:18 says that the magicians produced gnats "by their secret arts" (MT: בלטיהם; LXX: ταῖς φαρμακείαις), and *Exod Rab.* 10:7 assumes this implies demonic aid, and Tg. Ps.-J. ad loc. sees here "spells" or "charms" (לחשיהון). *Exod Rab.* 10:7 also speaks in this connection of witchcraft: "As soon as the magicians realized that they were unable to produce gnats, they recognized that the deeds were those of a God and not witchcraft, they no longer compared themselves to Moses."

150. Interestingly enough, the citation of Exod 8:19 in *b. Sanh.* 67b follows a discussion of sorcerers who do works through demons.

151. I follow here the restoration and translation of Pietersma, *Jannes and Jambres*.

152. Cf. other interpretations of "the finger of God:"

Philo, *Vit. Mos.* 1.112–"the hand of God"
Mt 12:28 – "Spirit of God" (πνεύματι θεου)
Tg. Onq. on Exod 8:19(15) — "a plague (מחא) from before the Lord"

it,[153] the same cluster of motifs that we find in Q 11:14ff. — signs, amazement, competing miracle workers, allusion to Exod 8:19, and superiority of the hero to his competitor(s). The parallels between Q 11:14ff. and the traditions stemming from the context of Exod 8:19 may, then, be displayed this way:

Q 11:14–26	*The Moses traditions*
Jesus performs a miracle, 11:14	Moses does miracles, Exodus 7ff.
people marvel, 11:14	people marvel, *Jannes and Jambres*
he is accused of doing this by Beelzebul, 11:15	Jannes and Jambres do their magic through allegiance with the devil (see n. 149)
there are competing miracle workers who do what Jesus does, 11:19, 24–26	there are competing miracle workers who do what Moses does, Exod 7:11, etc.
Jesus is asked to perform a sign, 11:17	Moses is asked to perform a sign, Exod 7:9 (see n. 147)
Jesus works his miracles by the finger of God, 11:20	Moses works his miracles by the finger of God, Exod 8:19
Jesus' competitors fail, 11:24–26 (see n. 144)	Moses' competitors fail, *Jannes and Jambres* (already implicit in Exodus)

Sometimes in Jewish literature, when this or that hero resembles Moses, or when this or that event is likened to the exodus, the reason is a typological correlation between beginning and end: the latter things are as the first. So it is no surprise to learn that, in some circles, the idea of an eschatological prophet like Moses, an idea inspired by Deut 18:15, 18, emerged, as well as the notion that the Messiah might be like Moses.[154] Q 11:20 offers an illustration of this sort of eschatological typology, for Jesus' Mosaic likeness introduces an eschatological declaration: "If I by the finger of God cast out demons, then the kingdom of God has come upon you." Here the activities

---

Tg. Neof. 1 on Exod 8:19(15) — "the finger of might (אצבע דגבורה) from before the Lord"

Tg. Ps.-J. on Exod 8:19(15) — "a plague (מחא) sent from before the Lord"

Neofiti's "might" is akin to the "power" of *Jannes and Jambres;* and Clement of Alexandria, *Strom.* 6.16.133.1 (GCS 15, ed. O. Stählin, p. 499), comments that the finger of God is the power of God. Cf. also Josephus, *Ant.* 2.291, where Moses says, "It is from no witchcraft or deception of true judgment, but from God's providence and power that my miracles proceed."

153. Origen, *Comm. Mt* ad 27:3–10 (GCS 38, ed. E. Klostermann, p. 250) knew the book and said 2 Tim 3:8 was based upon it. Presumably the book was composed in the second century C.E. or earlier.

154. Allison, *New Moses*, pp. 73–90.

of one like Moses coincide with the coming of the eschatological kingdom.[155] Indeed, this Mosaic claim to be the instrument of the finger of God seems to be the necessary clue to interpreting the verse. Without it one wonders how on earth one exorcist's activities can mean the coming of the kingdom while the activities of other exorcists do not have such meaning.

Q 11:29–30 // Deut 1:35.[156] The expression "this generation" occurs seven times in Q:

7:31: "To what will I liken this generation (τὴν γενεὰν ταύτην)?"

11:29: "This generation (ἡ γενεὰ αὕτη) is an evil generation (γενεὰ πονηρά)."

11:30: "For as Jonah became a sign to the Ninevites, so shall the Son of man be to this generation (τῇ γενεᾷ ταύτῃ)."

11:31: "The queen of the South will be raised at the judgment with this generation (τῆς γενεᾶς ταύτης) and will condemn it."

11:32: "The people of Nineveh will be raised at the judgment with this generation (τῆς γενεᾶς ταύτης) and will condemn it."

11:50–51: "The blood of all the prophets which has been shed from the foundation of the world will be required of this generation (τῆς γενεᾶς ταύτης)"; the blood from Abel to Zechariah "will be required of this generation (τῆς γενεᾶς ταύτης [so Luke])" or "will come upon this generation (τὴν γενεὰν ταύτην [so Matthew])."

"This generation" rejects John and Jesus (7:31), it is "evil" (11:29), it will stand condemned at the last judgment (11:30–31), and it will overflow the allotted measure of divine wrath (11:50–11). There are several reasons for supposing that people steeped in Jewish tradition would take these consistently pejorative uses of "this generation" as typological, as hinting at an analogy between the latter days on the one hand and the days of Noah (cf. 17:26–27) and of Moses on the other. The Greek ἡ γενεὰ αὕτη, with its postpositive pronoun, is a Hebraism (BDF §292). It translates הדור הזה, which occurs often in the rabbis but only twice in the Bible, once with reference to the time of Noah, the other with reference to the time of Moses:

---

155. See further below, pp. 70–72. Perhaps it is worth noting that the plagues upon Egypt, which were worked through the finger of God, could become eschatological types. Thus in *Apocalypse of Abraham* 30–31 the end-time woes are ten in number, and they partly replay what happened in Moses' day — distress through want, the burning of cities, destruction of cattle through pestilence, starvation, earthquake and sword, hail and snow, animal attacks, famine and pestilence, sword and flight in terror, thunder and earthquakes.

156. In Luke the words about Jonah's being a sign to the Ninevites (11:29–30) are separated from the saying about their resurrection (11:32) by the material on Solomon and the queen of Sheba (11:31). In Matthew all the words about the Ninevites are together (12:39–41). Most have thought Luke's arrangement, which is comparable with *m. Ta'an.* 2:4, to be original; see Kloppenborg, *Q Parallels,* p. 100.

Gen 7:1: "Then the Lord said to Noah, 'Go into the ark, you and all your household, for I have seen that you alone are righteous before me in this generation (MT: בדור הזה; LXX: ἐν τῇ γενεᾷ ταύτῃ).' "

Deut 1:35: "Not one of these — not one of this evil generation [of the wilderness; MT: הדור הרע הזה; LXX omits] — will see the good land that I swore to give to your ancestors."

In rabbinic literature the generation of Noah (דור המבול) and of the wilderness (דור המדבר) came to be reckoned as especially corrupt and headed for damnation.[157] When one adds (1) that those two generations became types for the last generation,[158] (2) that the generation of the wilderness is called "that generation" in LXX Ps 94:10 (τῇ γενεᾷ ἐκείνῃ; MT: בדור), and (3) that Q elsewhere compares the latter days with the days of Noah (see on 17:26–27) as well as with the events of the exodus, it is natural to surmise that Q's "this generation" echoes stories of primordial sins.

It accords with this suggestion that other early Christian sources clearly model their γενεά expressions upon Pentateuchal texts having to do with the generation in the wilderness:

Mk 8:38: "this adulterous and sinful generation (τῇ γενεᾷ ταύτῃ τῇ μοιχαλίδι καὶ ἁμαρτωλῷ)"; cf. LXX Deut 32:5: "They have sinned (ἡμάρτοσαν) . . . a crooked and perverse generation (γενεά; MT: דור)"

Mk 9:19: "O faithless generation (γενεὰ ἄπιστος)"; cf. Deut 32:20: "a perverse generation (LXX: γενεά; MT: דור), children in whom there is no faithfulness (LXX: πίστις; MT: אמן)"

Mt 17:17 = Lk 9:41 diff. Mk 9:19: "O faithless and perverse generation (γενεὰ ἄπιστος καὶ διεστραμμένη)"; cf. Deut 32:5: "a crooked and perverse generation (LXX: γενεὰ σκολιὰ καὶ διεστραμμένη; MT: דור עקש ופתלתל)"

Acts 2:40: "Save yourselves from this crooked generation (γενεᾶς τῆς σκολιᾶς)"; cf. Deut 32:5: "a crooked generation (LXX: γενεὰ σκολιά; MT: דור עקש)"

Phil 2:15: "children of God without blemish in the midst of a crooked and perverse generation" (γενεᾶς σκολιᾶς καὶ διεστραμμένης); cf. Deut 32:5: "a crooked and perverse generation (LXX: γενεὰ σκολιὰ καὶ διεστραμμένη; MT: דור עקש ופתלתל)"

---

157. See, e.g., *m. Sanh.* 10:3; *Mek.* on Exod 15:1; *b. Nid.* 61a. Additional texts and discussion in Evald Lövestam, *Jesus and 'This Generation': A New Testament Study* (ConB 25; Stockholm: Almqvist & Wiksell, 1995), pp. 11–17.

158. See, e.g., *Jub.* 23:14 ("the evil generation"), 15 ("this evil generation"), 16 ("this generation"), 22 ("that generation"); *1 En.* 93:9 ("a perverse generation"). The expression in the Dead Sea Scrolls, "the last generation" (הדור האחרון), as in 1QpHab 2:7 and 1QpMic frags. 17–18 5, takes up Deut 32:20: "I will see what their end (אחריתם) will be; for they are a perverse generation (דור)" — a verse cited as illustrating Lk 11:29 by both Albertus Magnus, *En. sec. part. Luc. (X–XXIV)* ad loc. (Opera Omnia 23, ed. A. Borgnet, p. 177); and Bonaventure, *Exp. Luc.* ad loc. (Opera Omnia 10, ed. A. C. Peltier, p. 536).

We find the same thing already in Ps 78:8: "they should not be like their ancestors [in the wilderness], a stubborn and rebellious generation, a generation whose heart was not steadfast, whose spirit was not faithful to God:"

MT: דור סורר ומרה דור לא־הכין לבו ולא־נאמנה את־אל רוחו

LXX: γενεὰ σκολιὰ καὶ παραπικραίνουσα, γενεά, ἥτις οὐ κατηύθυνεν τὴν καρδίαν αὐτῆς καὶ οὐκ ἐπιστώθη μετὰ τοῦ θεοῦ τὸ πνεῦμα αὐτῆς

With this one may again compare Deut 32:5 and 20 (see above).[159]

Although Q 7:31 and 11:50–51 do not have any particular scripture in view, only the proverbial wickedness of the olden generations of Noah and Moses, it is different with 11:29–32. Like *Jub.* 23:14,[160] "this generation is an evil generation (ἡ γενεὰ αὕτη γενεὰ πονηρά ἐστιν)" reminds one specifically of Deut 1:35 (הדור הרע הזה, "this evil generation").[161] Also close is Num 32:13: "And the Lord's anger was kindled against Israel, and he made them wander in the wilderness for forty years, until all the evil generation (LXX: πᾶσα ἡ γενεὰ οἱ ποιοῦντες τὰ πονηρά; MT: כל־הדור העשה הרע) had disappeared." So in Q 11:29–32, Jesus' generation, which has not heeded his proclamation, resembles the generation of the wilderness, which grumbled and rebelled in the wilderness despite God's mighty salvific acts.[162]

Q 12:35–38 // Exod 12:11. Although there is only a distant Matthean parallel (Mt 24:42–51), many have assigned Lk 12:35–38 to Q, and the arguments of B. Kollmann and Claus-Peter März for this conclusion are convincing.[163] The section begins with this: "Let your loins be girded (ἔστωσαν ὑμῶν αἱ ὀσφύες περιεζωσμέναι) and your lamps lit." This, as so many commentators remark, is very close to the language of Exodus's instructions for eating the Passover: "This is how you will eat it: your loins girded (αἱ ὀσφύες ὑμῶν περιεζωσμέναι),[164] your sandals on your feet, and your staff in your hand; and you shall eat it hurriedly. It is the passover of the Lord."[165]

---

159. Note also how John 6, through the use of γογγύζω ("grumble," vv. 41, 43, 61; cf. LXX Exod 16:7, 8, 9, 12), implicitly compares Jesus' contemporaries with the wilderness generation.

160. Here the eschatological woes "will come in the evil generation."

161. The LXX omits. The targums retain the expression (Neofiti 1: דרה בישה; Onqelos and Ps.-Jonathan: דרא בישא).

162. See further Lövestam, *Generation*, pp. 18–20.

163. B. Kollmann, "Lk 12.35–38 — ein Gleichnis der Logienquelle," *ZNW* 81 (1990), pp. 254–61; and Claus-Peter März, "... *lasst eure Lampen brennen!*" *Studien zur Q-Vorlage von Lk 12,35–14,24* (ETS 20; Leipzig: St. Benno, 1991), pp. 58–71. Cf. John Dominic Crossan, *In Fragments: The Aphorisms of Jesus* (San Francisco: Harper & Row, 1983), pp. 58–59. There is a brief survey of opinion in Kloppenborg, *Q Parallels*, p. 136 (citing more who favor assigning it to Q than oppose such).

164. MT: מתניכם חגרים. Frg. Tg. P V interpret this to mean: "Your loins girded with the commandments of the Torah." Here, as in Q, we have a metaphorical application.

165. Cf. Cyril of Alexandria, *Comm. Lk* 92; Albertus Magnus, *En. sec. part. Luc. (X–XXIV)* ad loc. (Opera Omnia 23, ed. A. Borgnet, p. 243); Joseph A. Fitzmyer, *The Gospel accord-*

There are indeed other places in the LXX where ὀσφύς ("waist, loins") and περιζώννυμι/ύω ("gird") appear together. All save one of these, however, includes an object.[166] And the exception, Jer 1:17 (σὺ περίζωσαι τὴν ὀσφύν σου: "You, gird up your loins"), distinguishes itself in other respects from Q 12:35: the second person is singular, not plural; τὴν ὀσφύν is also singular; and the form of the verb is different, and it does not follow but precedes the object. Beyond all that, Exod 12:11 and Lk 12:35 are the only places in the Greek Bible where we find precisely the plural αἱ ὀσφύες with possessive ὑμῶν followed by the nominative plural feminine perfect passive participle περιεζωσμέναι.

Q's borrowing from Exod 12:11 is not decoration. On the contrary, we have here the old belief that the last redemption will be reminiscent of the first, and almost certainly even the belief that the Messiah will return on Passover night.[167] Q speaks about lamps burning (12:35) as well as of watches in the night (12:38: "in the second watch or in the third"), so the picture is of the Messiah coming at night. Now according to *Mek.* on Exod. 12:42, "In that night were they redeemed [from Egypt] and in that night will they be redeemed in the future — these are the words of R. Joshua." The same conviction appears in the old Passover poem "The Four Nights," preserved in Frg. Tg. P on Exod 15:18 and in Tg. Neof. 1, Tg. Ps.-J., and Frg. Tg. V on Exod 12:42.[168] Moreover, according to Jerome, "It is a tradition of the Jews that the Messiah will come at midnight according to the manner of the time in Egypt when the Passover was celebrated. Whence I think also the apostolic tradition has persisted that on the day of the paschal vigils it is not permitted to dismiss before midnight the people who are expecting the advent of Christ."[169]

One may observe that the Hebrew Bible itself already takes up and transforms Exod 12:11 into an eschatological exodus typology. Isa 52:11–12 reads:

> Depart, depart, go out [צאו — the verb for the "exodus" from Egypt] from there! Touch no unclean thing; go out (צאו) from the midst of it, purify yourselves, you who carry the vessels [כלי — cf. Exod 12:35, where the Israelites go forth with gold and silver כלי, vessels, of the Egyptians] of the Lord. For you shall not go out (תצאו) in haste [לא בחפזון — contrast the 'in haste' (בחפזון)

ing to Luke (X–XXIV) (AB 28A; Garden City, N.Y.: Doubleday, 1985), p. 987; François Bovon, *Das Evangelium nach Lukas 2. Teilband: Lk 9,51–14,35* (EKKNT 3/2; Zurich and Düsseldorf/Neukirchen-Vluyn: Benziger/Neukirchener, 1996), p. 325; Joel B. Green, *The Gospel of Luke* (NIGTC; Grand Rapids/Cambridge, U.K.: Eerdmans, 1997), p. 500. On the possibility that Q 10:4 already alludes to Exod 12:11, see above, pp. 41–43.

166. σάκκος ("sackcloth"): 3 Βασ 21:32; Isa 32:11; Jdt. 4:14. ζώνη ("girdle"): 4 Βασ 1:8; Job 12:18; Ezek 9:11. βυσσίνῳ ("with fine linen"): LXX Dan 10:5. χρυσίῳ Ωφαζ ("with gold Ophaz"): Theod. Dan 10:5.

167. Bovon, *Lukas 2. Teilband: Lk 9,51–14,35*, pp. 325–26, also interprets the text against a Passover background.

168. Cf. *Exod Rab.* 18:12: "On the day when I wrought salvation for you, on that very night know that I will redeem you."

169. *Comm. Mt* on 25:6 (SC 259, ed. É. Bonnard, p. 215).

of Exod 12:11; Deut 16:3], and you shall not go in flight; for the Lord will go before you, and the God of Israel will be your rear guard [cf. Exod 13:21 ("the Lord went in front of them") and 14:19 ("the angel of the Lord who was going before the Israelite army moved and went behind them")].

This likens the forthcoming redemption to the previous one[170] and at the same time adds something new: whereas in former times the Israelites went out "in haste (בחפזון)," at the new exodus they will not flee or go out "in haste."[171] So even if the interpretive moves are different, Isa 52:11–12 and Q 12:35–38 both turn Exod 12:11 into a foreshadowing of future redemption.

One may also compare Q's reapplication of Exod 12:11 with what some have found in 1 Peter 1–2, for here there seems to be a series of allusions to the exodus, including Exod 12:11:[172]

1 Pet 1:13	girded loins	Exod 12:11
1 Pet 1:13, 22	obedience	Exod 15:26; 19:8
1 Pet 1:14	former desires	Exod 16:3
1 Pet 1:18	redemption	Exod 6:6
1 Pet 1:19	blood of lamb	Exod 12:5
1 Pet 2:9	kingdom of priests	Exod 19:6
1 Pet 2:9	holy nation	Exod 19:6

If one regards these parallels as substantial,[173] then there is a second Christian text that transfers the imagery of Exod 12:11 to eschatological preparation. The point would be all the more forceful if, as some have suggested, 1 Pet 1:13 itself depends upon the Jesus tradition, for then we would have early evidence that someone construed the tradition preserved in Q 12:35–38 in terms of a new exodus typology.

Beyond the borrowing from Exod 12:11, there are two additional ways in which a new exodus typology informs Q 12:35–38. First, the disciples are to be "waiting" (προσδεχομένοις), on the alert (γρηγοροῦντας), and keeping watch (φυλακῇ). It is not coincidence that Passover was to be a night of vigil: "That was for the Lord a night of vigil (LXX: προφυλακή; MT: שמרים), to bring them out of the land of Egypt. That same night is a vigil (LXX: προφυλακή; MT: שמרים) to be kept for the Lord by all the Israelites throughout their generations" (Exod 12:42). Second, when the master (κύριος) comes home in Q, he finds the faithful servants awake and ready for a meal with

---

170. Cf. already the use of "haste" in Josh 4:10, although here the new exodus is not eschatological.

171. Cf. Fishbane, *Biblical Interpretation*, p. 364. See further Willey, *Remember the Former Things*, pp. 132–37.

172. Paul E. Deterding, "Exodus Motifs in First Peter," *Concordia Journal* 7 (1981), pp. 58–65.

173. According to Paul J. Achtemeier, *1 Peter: A Commentary on First Peter* (Hermeneia; Minneapolis: Fortress, 1996), p. 115, the exodus parallels are "surely present," even if they do not "dominate" the passage.

him (12:37). This is exactly the eschatology of Passover: the Messiah comes during the evening meal.

Q 14:26 // Exod 20:12 = Deut 5:16; Deut 33:8–9 (?). (i) The command to hate father and mother almost inevitably raises the question of how to relate it to the commandment to "honor your father and mother" (Exod 20:12; Deut 5:16). Commentaries old and new have consistently wrestled with the tension. Chrysostom asked,

> What then? Are not these things contrary to the Old Testament?...It is a sacred duty to render them [parents] all other honors; but when they demand more than is due, one ought not to obey.... [Jesus is] not commanding simply to hate them, since this were quite contrary to the law, but rather "When one desires to be loved more than I am, hate him in this respect."[174]

Ulrich Luz, in summarizing the history of the interpretation of Mt 10:37 = Lk 14:26, remarks that, in ecclesiastical tradition, there is an order of those to be loved: God, father, mother, children, and "only in cases of necessity should one transgress the command to love parents. As a matter of principle the first table of the ten commandments comes before the second, at the beginning of which stands the command to love parents. Only then, when parents hinder us from doing the will of God may the fourth commandment be rescinded."[175]

Given that our line has, over the centuries, incessantly put commentators in mind of the Decalogue, one cannot but wonder whether it was intended to do so, whether it was not provocatively formulated in deliberate contrast to the commandment to honor father and mother. This would seem to be the case, for not only does the content make one ponder the relationship to Exod 20:12 = Deut 5:16, but the sentence's very structure moves us to do this, as may be seen at a glance:

Q 14:26	εἴ τις οὐ μισεῖ τὸν πατέρα ἑαυτοῦ καὶ τὴν μητέρα
LXX Exod 20:12	τίμα τὸν πατέρα σου καὶ τὴν μητέρα[176]
LXX Deut 5:16	τίμα τὸν πατέρα σου καὶ τὴν μητέρα σου[177]

Both lines consist of a verb + τὸν πατέρα + personal pronoun ending in -ου + καὶ + τὴν μητέρα. This construction occurs in the Greek Bible in LXX Exod 20:12 = Deut 5:16, in quotations of that line (Mk 7:10; 10:19; Lk 18:20), in Lk 14:26 (Q),[178] and, to judge by a TLG search, nowhere else.

---

174. Chrysostom, *Hom. Mt* 35.3 (PG 57.406). Cf. Poole, *Commentary*, vol. 3, p. 243.

175. Ulrich Luz, *Das Evangelium nach Matthäus (Mt 8–17)* (EKK 1/2; Zurich/Neukirchen-Vluyn: Benziger/Neukirchener, 1990), p. 141.

176. MT: כבד את־אביך ואת־אמך. Cf. Tg. Onq.: יקר ית אבוך וית אימך. Pseudo-Jonathan and Neofiti 1 rewrite the imperative.

177. MT: כבד את־אביך ואת־אמך. Tg. Onq.: יקר ית אבוך וית אימך. Neofiti 1: יוקר כל אנש מנכון ית אבוי וית אמיה. Pseudo-Jonathan rewrites.

178. The easier Mt 10:37 ("The one who loves father or mother more than me is not worthy of me") is universally reckoned to be secondary vis-à-vis Lk 14:26, even if some construe it as correct interpretation. Against the IQP, Luke's ἑαυτοῦ is Q; see Jeremias, *Sprache*, 241.

According to Martin Hengel, Q 14:26 means "the annulment of the Fourth Commandment."[179] One should, with all due respect, query this reading. Evidently in Q our saying was shortly followed by Q 16:17, which declares that it is easier for heaven and earth to pass away than for any part of the law to fall away. Moreover, the notion that two moral imperatives might clash with one another without nullifying the authority of either is hardly a modern notion. It is what the commentators on our text have traditionally said,[180] and Jews knew well enough that conflicting claims were sometimes upon them, a sad circumstance that entailed not deconstruction of Torah but the subordination of one commandment to another. This was the problem the Maccabees faced when they struggled with fighting on the day of rest (1 Macc 2:39–41), and the issue appears again in *m. Yoma* 8:6, which rules that taking care of endangered life overrides sabbath observance. There is also *b. Yeb.* 5b, where it is argued that one commandment can supersede another commandment, and the illustrations include instances in which one should not obey father and mother.[181] Even more to the point is *b. Yeb.* 90b: "Come and hear: Him you will listen to (Deut 18:15), even if he tells you, 'Transgress any of all the commandments of the Torah' as in the case for instance of Elijah on Mount Carmel [in 1 Kings 18 Elijah sacrifices outside the temple], obey him in every respect in accordance with the needs of the hour."

One fails to understand why Q 14:26, just because it appears in a Christian source, should not be understood along the same lines as these texts within Judaism. The provocative demand to follow God's eschatological prophet may require leaving and disobeying parents, but this is no more an annulment of Torah than "Leave the dead to bury their own dead" is a general, antinomian prohibition of burial.[182] The Jesus of Q 14:26 does not exit the parental roof of the law but remains under it.

(ii) If Mt 10:37 = Lk 14:26 regularly sends Christians back to the Decalogue, it has also often called to mind another Pentateuchal text, Deut 33:8–9: "Give to Levi your Thummim, and your Urim to your loyal one, whom you tested at Massah, with whom you contended at the waters of Meribah; who said of his father and mother, 'I regard them not'; he

---

179. Martin Hengel, *The Charismatic Leader and His Followers* (New York: Crossroad, 1981), p. 13, n. 31

180. See Luz, as in n. 175. Cf. Cyril of Alexandria, *Comm. Lk* 58 (CSCO 70, Scriptores Syri 27, ed. J.-B. Chabot, pp. 214–21).

181. Cf. *Mek.* on Exod 31:14; *Sifra* 195 on Lev 19:1–4; *m. Šabb.* 16:1–7; 18:3; 19:1–3; *m. Pesah.* 6:1–2; *t. Šabb.* 15:10–17; *b. Šabb.* 129b, 132b; *b. Yoma* 85b. Note also that in *m. B. Meṣ.* 2:11; *t. B. Meṣ.* 2:30; and *t. Hor.* 2:5, one is supposed to show greater honor to one's master than to one's parents.

182. I do not share the widespread notion that "Leave the dead to bury their own dead" opposes the Torah, and I note that at least Matthew, who could have Jesus say he came not to abolish the Law and the Prophets (5:17–20), did not drop it. See further Markus Bockmuehl, " 'Let the Dead Bury Their Dead' (Matt. 8:22/Luke 9:60): Jesus and the Halakah," *JTS* 49 (1998), pp. 553–81; and Davies and Allison, *Matthew*, vol. 2, pp. 57–58.

ignored his brothers, and did not acknowledge his children. For they observed your word, and kept your covenant." Chrysostom, in expounding Mt 10:37, thought Deut 33:9 showed harmony between the law and Jesus' command,[183] and, in our own day, I. H. Marshall has judged that "behind the saying lies the expression of Levi's devotion to the Torah expressed in Dt. 33:9."[184] Marshall's verdict is a possibility, especially given that Deut 33:8–9 was not a neglected text: it is cited and alluded to elsewhere in old Jewish and Christian sources.[185] We do not know, however, exactly what followed in Q after the injunction to hate father and mother. Matthew and Luke disagree to some extent on what is to be hated (or, as Matthew has it, loved less), and neither series agrees exactly with Deut 33:9:

Matthew[186]	Deuteronomy	Luke
father/πατέρα	father/πατρί/אביו	father/πατέρα
mother/μητέρα	mother/μητρί/אמו	mother/μητέρα
son/υἱόν	brothers/ἀδελφούς/אחיו	wife/γυναῖκα
daughter/θυγατέρα	sons/υἱούς/בניו[187]	children/τέκνα
		brothers/ἀδελφούς
		sisters/ἀδελφάς

So whether Q 14:26 in effect plays Deut 33:8–9 against the Decalogue is an open question.

Q 16:18 // Deut 24:1–4. There are no significant verbal links between Jesus' prohibition of divorce and Deut 24:1–4, the pertinent Mosaic legislation on divorce. But the scripturally informed can hardly hear Jesus' imperative without thinking of the Mosaic legislation that concerns divorce and remarriage.[188] This is all the more so in that Q 16:18 is introduced by a statement about Torah (16:17: "It is easier for heaven and earth to pass away than for one stroke of a letter to drop from the law"). Already Mat-

---

183. Chrysostom, *Hom. Mt* 10.37 (PG 57.406–407). Cf. Albertus Magnus, *En. sec. part. Luc. (X–XXIV)* ad Lk 14:26 (Opera Omnia, ed. A. Borgnet, p. 360). Cf. also the use of Deut 33:9–10 in the fragment of Apollinaris of Laodicea's commentary on Mt 19:28–29 (TU 61, ed. J. Reuss, pp. 33–34); and in Rupert of Deutz, *Comm. Mt* ad 8:22 (PL 168.1469B).

184. I. H. Marshall, *Luke*, p. 592. Cf. John Trapp, *A Commentary or Exposition upon All the Books of the New Testament* (2d ed., ed. W. Webster; London: Richard D. Dickinson, 1865), p. 158; Henry Alford, *The Greek Testament*, vol. 1, *The Four Gospels* (Chicago: Moody, 1958), p. 111; M.-J. Lagrange, *Évangile selon Saint Luc* (EB; Paris: J. Gabalda, 1927), p. 408; Fitzmyer, *Luke (X–XXIV)*, p. 1063 ("For the Old Testament background ... see Deut 33:9").

185. Quotations: 4Q175 14–20; Philo, *Leg. all.* 2.51; *Det. pot. ins.* 67; *Ebr.* 72; *b. Yoma* 66b; *Num Rab.* 1:12; *Eccles Rab.* 4:8. Allusions: Philo, *Sacr. AC* 129; *T. Reub.* 6:8.

186. The IQP here favors the originality of Matthew.

187. The targums here follow the MT, at least with regard to the four relatives named.

188. See, e.g., Tertullian, *Adv. Marc.* 4.34 (PL 2.441–42); Jerome, *Comm. Mt* ad 5:31–32 (SC 242, ed. É. Bonnard, p. 120); Poole, *Commentary*, vol. 3, p. 24; Catchpole, *Quest for Q*, p. 237; Tuckett, *Q*, p. 408; Darrell L. Bock, *Luke*, vol. 2, 9:51–24:53 (Grand Rapids: Baker, 1996), p. 1356; Green, *Luke*, pp. 603–4.

thew introduces Jesus' prohibition of divorce by quoting Deut 24:1. This is a rare case where subject matter alone suffices to recall a specific text.

How Q's contributors and audiences related the two authoritative texts is unknown. Perhaps they understood Jesus' prohibition as does Mk 10:1–12, which distinguishes between the primeval will of God revealed in Genesis 2–3 and the will of God modified for hardness of heart (Deut 24:1–14). Certainly Jewish Christians would have been familiar with this sort of distinction. In contrast with Gen 1:29 ("I have given you every plant yielding seed which is upon the face of the earth, and every tree with seed in its fruit; you will have them for food"), Gen 9:3 grants permission for the post-Edenic world to eat meat. Similar is the law of the king in Deut 17:14–20: this accepts kingship and promulgates divine precepts for it, yet other portions of Scripture regard the institution of kingship as God's reluctant concession to Israel's frailty (cf. Judg 8:22–23; 1 Sam 8:4–22). So the Torah can be — and has been — viewed as containing divine concessions to or compromises for human sin, concessions or compromises which stand only in this world, not in the world to come.[189] In any case Q 16:18, with its assertion of the abiding force of the Law and Prophets, shows that it was possible to join Jesus' word against divorce with a belief in the law's continuing validity.

One should also not forget that the Torah itself, in Mal 2:16 ("I hate divorce, says the Lord, the God of Israel"),[190] may have raised a question mark over divorce. Although many commentators have understood this to be about spiritual unfaithfulness rather than divorce, *b. Giṭ.* 90b takes it otherwise, and LXX ℵ B A and Q Mal 2:16 seemingly oppose divorce.[191] Moreover, CD 4:19–21, as is well known, contains this: "The builders of the wall...will be caught in unchastity twice, by taking two wives in their lifetime whereas the principle of creation is 'Male and female created he them'; also, those who entered the ark went into it two by two." Some have thought that this particular text prohibits not just polygamy but also divorce. But whether or not this interpretation is warranted by the facts,[192] it remains that one's understanding of Q 16:18 cannot be arrived at without reflection upon the tension with Deut 24:1–4: what is Jesus doing to Moses?

Q 17:3–4 // Lev 19:17. Earlier we saw that Q 6:27ff. revises the demands of the holiness code. Here, in Q 17:3–4, Jesus adds to the famous rule of Lev 19:17, as many commentators have appreciated:[193]

---

189. David Daube, "Concessions to Sinfulness in Jewish Law," *JJS* 10 (1959), pp. 1–13.

190. MT: ‫שׂנא שׁלח אמר יהוה אלהי ישׂראל‬.

191. D. C. Jones, "A Note on the LXX of Malachi 2.16," *JBL* 109 (1990), pp. 683–85. Contrast the targum: "But if you hate her, divorce her, says the Lord God of Israel."

192. For doubts see Gershon Brin, "Divorce at Qumran," in *Legal Texts and Issues: Proceedings of the Second Meeting of the International Organization for Qumran Studies, Cambridge 1995* (ed. Moshe Bernstein, Florentino García Martínez, and John Kampen; STDS 23; Leiden/New York/Cologne: Brill, 1997), pp. 231–49.

193. Cf. Tertullian, *Adv. Marc.* 4.35 (CCSL 1, pp. 639–40); Basil the Great, *Reg. brev.* 47 (PG 31.1113A-B); Bede, *Luc. exp.* ad loc. (CCSL 70, ed. D. Hurst, p. 308); Hesychius

MT Lev 19:17: "You will not hate your brother (אָחִיךָ) in your heart; you will reprove (הוֹכֵחַ תּוֹכִיחַ) your neighbor (עֲמִיתֶךָ), or you will incur guilt (חֵטְא) yourself."[194]

LXX Lev 19:17: "You will not hate your brother (τὸν ἀδελφόν σου) in your heart; you will reprove (ἐλεγμῷ ἐλέγξεις) your neighbor or you will incur guilt (ἁμαρτίαν) because of him."

Mt 18:15, 21–22: " 'If your brother (ὁ ἀδελφός σου) sins (ἁμαρτήσῃ), go and reprove (ἔλεγξον), and if he listens to you, you have gained the brother (τὸν ἀδελφόν σου)'.... Then Peter came up and said to him, 'Lord, how often shall my brother (ἀδελφός) sin (ἁμαρτήσει) against me, and I forgive him? As many as seven times?' Jesus said to him, 'I do not say to you seven times, but seventy times seven.' "

Lk 17:3–4: "If your brother (ὁ ἀδελφός σου) sins (ἁμάρτῃ), rebuke (ἐπιτίμησον) him, and if he repents, you must forgive, and if he sins (ἁμαρτήσῃ) against you seven times in the day, and turns to you seven times, and says, 'I repent,' you must forgive him."

Although Matthew's ἔλεγξον is closer to LXX Lev 19:17, and although it was Matthew's wont to conform the Jesus tradition to the Bible, Mt 18:15 here probably reproduces Q, for ἐλέγχω is a Matthean *hapax legomenon*, while Luke's ἐπιτιμάω is redactional in Lk 4:39 diff. Mk 1:31; Lk 4:31 diff. Mk 1:34; and Lk 23:40 diff. Mk 15:32 and without parallel in Lk 9:55 and 19:39. For the rest, however, Luke is probably on the whole closer to Q. The IQP reconstructs this text: "If your brother sins, rebuke him, and if [[he listens to you, forgive him]]. And if seven times a day he should sin against you, seven times also forgive him."[195]

As in the Sermon on the Plain, Q 17:3–4 takes up a Mosaic imperative but goes its own way. Lev 19:17 demands that one reprove a brother, and

of Jerusalem, *In Lev* 6.19 (PG 93.1029A-1031A); Bonaventure, *Exp. Luc.* ad loc. (Opera Omnia 11, ed. A. C. Peltier, p. 51); Albertus Magnus, *En. sec. part. Luc. (X–XXIV)* ad Lk 17:4 (Opera Omnia, ed. A. Borgnet, p. 461); Cornelius à Lapide, *The Great Commentary of Cornelius à Lapide* (2d ed.; London: John Hodges, 1874–87), vol. 2, p. 297 ("Christ alludes to Leviticus xix. 17"); Trapp, *Commentary*, vol. 5, p. 212; John Lightfoot, *A Commentary on the New Testament from the Talmud and Hebraica* (Oxford: Oxford University Press, 1859), vol. 2, p. 254; Ainsworth, *Annotations*, vol. 1, p. 601 (commenting on Lev 19:17: "The same law is given by Christ, in Luke xvii.3"); Alford, *Greek Testament*, vol. 1, p. 187; Alfred Plummer, *A Critical and Exegetical Commentary on the Gospel according to S. Luke* (ICC; Edinburgh: T. & T. Clark, 1922), p. 400; Dieter Zeller, *Die weisheitlichen Mahnsprüche bei den Synoptikern* (FB 17; Würzburg: Echter, 1977), pp. 61–62, 152; Catchpole, *Quest for Q*, pp. 135–50; Tuckett, *Q*, pp. 433–34; Wolfgang Wiefel, *Das Evangelium nach Matthäus* (THKNT 1; Berlin: Evangelische Verlagsanstalt, 1988), p. 323.

194. Onqelos and Neofiti 1 stay close to the Hebrew. Ps.-Jonathan has this: "You will not speak flattering words with your mouth while hating your brother in your heart. You will reprove your neighbor; but if he is put to shame you will not incur guilt because of him."

195. But for the argument that Mt 18:16 and 17 come from Q, see Catchpole, *Quest for Q*, pp. 135–50.

with this Q 17:3–4 agrees. But Jesus' emphasis lies elsewhere, namely, on forgiveness. If the one who is rebuked heeds the rebuke, then forgiveness should be granted. Not only that, but Q adds the difficult demand to forgive seven times a day. Jesus is less interested in correction than in long-suffering: one is to forgive and forgive.

The demand for repeated forgiveness is probably an intentional reversal of an exegetical tradition surrounding the הוכח תוכיח of Lev 19:17. For *Sifra* 200 on Lev 19:17 contains this: "And how do we know that if one has rebuked him four or five times, he should still go and rebuke him again? Scripture says, 'Reproving you will reprove (הוכח תוכיח) your neighbor.' Should one suppose that this is to be done even if his countenance blanches when he is rebuked? Scripture says, 'or you will incur guilt yourself.'" *b. B. Meṣ.* 31a offers a similar exegesis: "One of the Rabbis said to Raba: [You will not hate your brother in your heart but] הוכח תוכיח (you will surely reprove) your neighbor. Perhaps הוכח means once, תוכיח twice? He replied, הוכח implies even a hundred times." If this exegetical tradition, which may lie behind Targum Pseudo-Jonathan,[196] is presupposed by Q 17:3–4, then Jesus is again turning things upside down: what he demands is not repeated rebukes but repeated acts of forgiveness.[197]

It is possible that there are additional ways in which Q 17:3–4 reflects a traditional exegesis of Lev 19:17. Particularly interesting for comparison is *T. Gad* 6:1–7:[198]

> 1. Now, my children, each of you love his brother. Drive hatred out of your hearts. Love one another in deed and word and inward thoughts. 2. For when I stood before my father I would speak peaceably about Joseph, but when I went out, the spirit of hatred darkened my mind and aroused my soul to kill him. 3. Love one another from the heart, therefore, and if anyone sins against you, speak to him in peace. Expel the venom of hatred, and do not harbor deceit in your heart. If anyone confesses and repents, forgive him. 4. If anyone denies his guilt, do not be contentious with him, otherwise he may start cursing, and you would be sinning doubly. 5. In a dispute do not let an outsider hear your secrets, since out of hatred for you he may become your enemy, and commit a great sin against you. He may talk to you frequently but treacherously, or be much concerned with you, but for an evil end, having absorbed from you the venom. 6. Even if he denies it and acts disgracefully out of a sense of guilt, be quiet and do not become upset. For he who denies will repent, and avoid offending you again; indeed he will honor you, will respect you and be at peace. 7. But even if he is devoid of shame and persists in his wickedness, forgive him from the heart and leave vengeance to God.

---

196. So Kugel, "Hidden Hatred," pp. 56–57.

197. Maybe the number seven is also part of the reversal, for Lev 19:17 is joined to 19:18, which prohibits vengeance, and vengeance and seven were famously associated (Gen 4:15, 24). See further pp. 92–93 below.

198. In addition to what follows, see p. 35.

Kugel has demonstrated that although the relationship is not at first obvious, this is indeed an extended rewriting of Lev 19:17–18.[199] Given that this is the case, there are several interesting correlations with Q 17:3–4. Both texts

- speak explicitly of the offender sinning:

  T. Gad 6:3: "if anyone sins against you"
  ἐὰν ἁμάρτῃ εἴς σε

  Q 17:3: "if your brother sins"
  ἐὰν ἁμαρτήσῃ ὁ ἀδελφός σου

- command forgiveness:

  T. Gad 6:3: "forgive him"
  ἄφες αὐτῷ

  Q 17:3: "forgive him"
  ἄφες αὐτῷ

- require forgiveness even in the face of repeated offenses:

  T. Gad 6:7: "even if he … persists in his wickedness, forgive him"
  ἐάν … ἄφες αὐτῷ

  Q 17:4: "if seven times a day he should sin against you, seven times also forgive him"
  ἐάν … ἀφήσεις αὐτῷ

It is admittedly possible that *T. Gad* 6 has been rewritten by a Christian hand familiar with Matthew 18, Luke 17, or the traditions behind them: the provenance of the *Testaments of the Twelve Patriarchs* is a complex issue. There is, however, no compelling sign here of dependence upon the Gospels, and so it may just as well be that the agreements between Q 17:3–4 and *T. Gad* 6 take us back to Jewish tradition associated with Lev 19:17.

II. Synthesis

(i) Q cites or alludes to the following texts from Exodus through Deuteronomy:

Exodus

8:19 — Q 11:20 (allusion)
12:11 — Q 12:35–38 (allusion)
12:11, 34–36 — Q 10:4 (allusion?)
16:1–36 — Q 11:3 (allusion)
20:12 — Q 14:26 (allusion)
23:20 — Q 7:27 (marked quotation)
33:11–23 — Q 10:21–22 (allusion)

---

199. Kugel, "Hidden Hatred," pp. 50–52.

Leviticus

19:2 — Q 6:36 (allusion)
19:17 — Q 6:37–38 (allusion)
      Q 17:3–4 (allusion)
19:18–Q 6:27 (allusion)

Deuteronomy

1:35 — Q 11:29–30 (allusion)
5:16 — Q 14:26 (allusion)
6:13 — Q 4:8 (quotation)
6:16 — Q 4:12 (quotation)
8:3 — Q 4:4 (quotation)
21:20 — Q 7:34 (allusion)
24:1–4 — Q 16:18 (allusion)
33:8–9 — Q 14:26 (allusion?)
34:1–4 — Q 4:5–7 (allusion)

Most of these references fall into one of three categories. In the first are those passages in which the Pentatetuchal subtexts make Q's narrative a new exodus. In the second category are those texts that liken Jesus to Moses. In the third are those places in which Jesus issues commandments that revise the Mosaic legislation. In these Jesus speaks authoritatively and with a novel twist on matters that the lawgiver received from Sinai and handed on:

New Exodus

in Q 4:1–13 Jesus recapitulates the experience of Israel in the desert, when the people were led by God and tempted by hunger and idolatry for forty years

in Q 7:27 Jesus' forerunner is identified as τὸν ἄγγελόν μου who goes "in front" in order to prepare the way, words that mix Mal 3:1 with Exod 23:20, an exodus text

in Q 11:3 Jesus' disciples ask God for daily bread, on the analogy with Israel's daily reception of bread in the wilderness (Exodus 16)

in Q 11:29–30 Jesus' generation is spoken of with language characteristic of the generation of Moses (Deut 1:35)

in Q 12:35–38 Jesus' followers are to prepare for the coming of the Son of man by girding their loins, waiting, and keeping watch in the night, all of which corresponds to Jewish tradition about observance of the Passover (cf. esp. Exod 12:11, 42)

Likeness to Moses

in Q 4:5–7 Jesus is shown, from the top of a mountain and by a supernatural character, all the kingdoms of the world, and the language is reminiscent of Moses' vision from the top of Pisgah (Deut 34:1–4; cf. Num 27:12–14; Deut 3:27; 32:48–52)

in Q 10:21–22 Jesus, like the Moses of Exod 33:11–23, uniquely knows God and is known by God, and is thus the unequaled recipient and dispenser of divine revelation

in Q 11:20 Jesus casts out demons by the finger of God, just as Moses worked his miracles by the same finger of God (Exod 8:19)

Modifications of Mosaic Commandments

in Q 6:27–45 Jesus revises an important part of the Mosaic Torah, Leviticus 19

in Q 14:26 Jesus' command to hate father and mother is an ironic reversal of the Decalogue's requirement to honor father and mother

in Q 16:17 Jesus offers a controversial ruling on divorce that inevitably invites comparison with Deut 24:1–4

in Q 17:3–4 Jesus clarifies the commandment on rebuking one's neighbor, Lev 19:17

These three intertextual patterns are complementary and, taken together, remind one of the book of Joshua, where the son of Nun is very much like Moses[200] and the Israelites miraculously cross the Jordan and experience a second exodus.[201] One is also put in mind of the *Jeremiah Apocryphon*, where Jeremiah is a new Moses who leads the remnant home from Babylon.[202] Indeed, there are quite a few books that replay the exodus and feature a Mosaic hero.[203] Here, then, Q is doing little original: it is rather plugging Jesus into a much-used outline.

Whereas Joshua and the *Jeremiah Apocryphon* turn past events into a new exodus, other texts project the pattern onto the future.[204] From the Tanak alone one may mention Deutero-Isaiah; Jer 16:14–15; Ezek 20:33–38; Hos 2:14–16; 11:10–11; and Mic 7:14–15. All of these liken the future redemption to the first redemption from Egypt.[205] So typology becomes eschatology. From a later period one may mention the targumic traditions on

---

200. See 1:5, 17; 4:14. Cf. Josh 5:15 with Exod 3:5; the intercession of Joshua for Israel in Joshua 7 with Moses' intercession for Israel in Deuteronomy 9; Joshua's raising his hands for victory in Joshua 8 with Moses' raising of his staff for victory in Exodus 17; Joshua's farewell speech in Joshua 23–24 with Moses' farewell speech in Deuteronomy 1–34; Joshua's mediation of a covenant in Joshua 24 with Moses' mediation of a covenant in Exodus 24.

201. See 4:23. Cf. the sending of spies in Joshua 2 with the sending of spies in Numbers 13; Josh 2:9 with Exod 15:15–16; the "dry ground" of Josh 3:17; 4:18, 22 with Exod 14:16, 21, 29; the "haste" of Josh 4:10 with Exod 12:11 (cf. Isa 52:12); the "heap" of Josh 4:10 with Exod 15:8; the Passover celebration under Joshua in Josh 15:10–13 with the Passover celebration under Moses in Exodus 12.

202. See Allison, *New Moses*, pp. 54–55.

203. Allison, ibid., passim.

204. On this see esp. Michael Fishbane, *Text and Texture: Close Readings of Selected Biblical Texts* (New York: Schocken, 1979), pp. 121–40.

205. For Deutero-Isaiah, see esp. Isa 40:3–5; 41:17–20; 43:1–3, 14–21; 48:20–21; 51:9–10; 52:11–12. Lit.: Bernard W. Anderson, "Exodus Typology in Second Isaiah," in *Israel's Prophetic Heritage: Essays in Honor of James Muilenburg* (ed. Bernard W. Anderson and Walter Harrelson; New York: Harper & Row, 1962), pp. 177–95; C. Stuhlmueller, *Creative Redemption in Deutero-Isaiah* (AnBib 43; Rome: Biblical Institute, 1970), pp. 60–93; Klaus Kiesow, *Exodustexte im Jesajabuch* (OBO 24; Freiburg/Göttingen: Éditions Universitaires/Vandenhoeck&Ruprecht, 1979); Marvin A. Sweeney, "The Book of Isaiah as Prophetic Torah," in *New Visions of Isaiah* (ed. Roy F. Melugin and Marvin A. Sweeney; JSOTSS 214;

Exod 12:42 and 15:18, quoted above, as well as *Tanhuma 'Ekeb* 7, where the days of the Messiah will last forty years in analogy with the period of wandering in the desert, and *Eccles Rab.* 1:8, which offers several illustrations of the principle that the last redeemer (Messiah) will be like the first (Moses).[206] Q stands in this interpretive tradition too, although in it the eschatological scenario unfolds over time, so that the eschatological typology covers not only the future but also the present as well as the past of Jesus. There is an analogy to this in the Dead Sea Scrolls, where the sect's history, its current experience, and its expectations are all eschatological, and everything falls under the exodus pattern.[207] But the closest parallels belong of course to the New Testament, especially to Matthew, Luke-Acts, and Paul, where the eschatological coming of Jesus inaugurates a new exodus.[208] Q's new exodus typology appears to have been a common theme of primitive Christian theology.

That Q's new exodus typology is indeed thoroughly eschatological, as assumed in the previous paragraph, appears from at least three texts. The first is Q 7:27, which conflates Exod 23:20 with Mal 3:1, the latter of which clearly carries eschatological sense: it is bound up with prophecies about "the day of his coming," "refiner's fire," and "judgment," and already the secondary addition in Mal 4:5 identifies the messenger of Mal 3:1 with the eschatological Elijah. The second text that links exodus and eschatology is Q 11:20. For here Jesus' ability to cast out demons by the finger of God, in imitation of the great Moses (Exod 8:19), is above all a sign that "the kingdom of God has come." Finally, there is Q 12:35–38, which enjoins hearers to ready themselves for the return of the Son of man with the words

---

Sheffield: Sheffield Academic Press, 1996), pp. 50–67; Willey, *Remember the Former Things*, pp. 34–37, 132–37.

206. Note also Bar 5:5–9; Ecclus 36:1–17.

207. It suffices to recall their textually inspired location in the wilderness (1QS 8:12–14, citing Isa 40:3; cf. 1QS 9:19–20; 1QM 1:3), the parallels between the War Scroll and arrangements in the Pentateuch (cf., e.g., 1QM 2:16–4:17 with Num 2:2 and 10:2 and 1QM 7:3–7 with Deut 23:10–15), and the eschatological interpretation of Deut 18:15, 18 in 4QTestimonia (cf. 1QS 9:11).

208. For Matthew, see Allison, *New Moses*. For Luke, see D. P. Moessner, *The Lord of the Banquet: The Literary and Theological Significance of the Lukan Travel Narrative* (Minneapolis: Fortress, 1989). For Paul, see W. D. Davies, "Paul and the New Exodus," in *The Quest for Context and Meaning: Studies in Biblical Intertextuality in Honor of James A. Sanders* (ed. Craig A. Evans and Shemaryahu Talmon; Leiden/New York/Cologne, 1997), pp. 443–63; Sylvia C. Keesmaat, *Paul and His Story: (Re)Interpreting the Exodus Tradition* (JSNTSup 181; Sheffield: Sheffield Academic Press, 1999); and Harald Sahlin, "The New Exodus of Salvation according to St. Paul," in *The Root of the Vine* (ed. A. Fridrichsen et al.; New York: Philosophical Library, 1953), pp. 81–95. There are also important parallels in John; see T. Francis Glasson, *Moses in the Fourth Gospel* (SBT 40; London: SCM, 1963); and Wayne A. Meeks, *The Prophet-King: Moses Traditions and the Johannine Christology* (NovTSup 14; Leiden: Brill, 1967). Although it is not so obvious, there is also a new exodus/new Moses typology in Mark; see Marcus, *Mark 1–8*, pp. 388–89, 483–85, and the index, s.v., "Exodus typology," "Moses," and "Sinai."

of Exod 12:11 ("your loins girded"). Here again, as so often in Judaism, exodus language is eschatological language.

That one or more of the contributors to Q reckoned Jesus to be the eschatological fulfillment of Deut 18:15 and 18, verses that foretell the coming of a prophet like Moses who must be heeded, is nowhere explicitly evidenced. But the possibility must be seriously reckoned with. (*a*) Some Jews, including the author of 4QTestimonia, took the oracle in Deuteronomy to foretell an eschatological figure.[209] (*b*) Q's hero sounds very much like a prophet, and the earliest Christians generally reckoned Jesus to be such.[210] The antiquity of this notion is well nigh guaranteed by the overwhelming probability that "prophet" was part of Jesus' own self-conception.[211] (*c*) Q knows Deuteronomy well, for it quotes from the book three times and alludes to it on at least five further occasions. (*d*) Some Christians — Matthew, for example, and whoever composed Acts 3:12–26[212] — clearly took Jesus to be the fulfillment of Deut 18:15, 18.

(ii) The materials that make up Q's new exodus typology run across the entire document, as can be seen at a glance:

Q 4:4 — Deut 8:3 (quotation)
Q 4:5–7 — Deut 34:1–4 (allusion)
Q 4:8 — Deut 6:13 (quotation)
Q 4:12 — Deut 6:16 (quotation)
Q 6:27 — Lev 19:18 (allusion)
Q 6:36 — Lev 19:2
Q 6:37–38 — Lev 19:17 (allusion)
Q 7:27 — Exod 23:20 (quotation)
Q 7:34 — Deut 21:20 (allusion)
Q 10:4 — Exod 12:11, 34–36 (allusion?)
Q 10:21–22 — Exod 33:11–23 (allusion)
Q 11:3 — Exod 16:1–36 (allusion)
Q 11:20 — Exod 8:19 (allusion)
Q 11:29–30 — Deut 1:35 (allusion)
Q 12:35–38 — Exod 12:11 (allusion)
Q 14:26 — Exod 20:12 = Deut 5:16 (allusion); Deut 33:8–9 (allusion?)
Q 16:18 — Deut 24:1–4 (allusion)
Q 17:3–4 — Lev 19:17 (allusion)

If one categorizes these eighteen texts according to the influential compositional history of Q defended by Kloppenborg,[213] seven belong to his first

209. Allison, *New Moses*, pp. 73–84.
210. Oscar Cullmann, *The Christology of the New Testament* (rev. ed.; Philadelphia: Westminster, 1965), pp. 13–50.
211. R. H. Fuller, *The Foundations of New Testament Christology* (London: Collins, 1969), pp. 125–29.
212. For Matthew, see Allison, *New Moses*, pp. 243–48. On Acts 3, see R. F. Zehnle, *Peter's Pentecost Discourse* (SBLMS 15; Nashville: Abingdon, 1971), pp. 75–89. Cf. Acts 7:37, 52.
213. In his book *Formation of Q*.

stage (6:27, 36, 37; 10:4; 11:3; 14:26), four to his third stage (4:4, 5–7, 8, 12), and the rest to passages that he assigns to the second stage of Q or fails to assign at all (7:27, 34; 10:21–22; 11:20, 29–30; 12:35–38; 16:18; 17:3). On my own very different reconstruction of Q's history, things fall out this way: three texts from stage one (10:4, 21–22; 11:3), four from stage two (12:35–38; 14:26; 16:18; 17:3), and eleven from stage three (4:4, 5–7, 8, 12; 6:27, 36, 37–38; 7:27, 34; 11:20, 29–30). Neither compositional history reveals a stage without the new exodus theme. So if one theory or the other is close to the truth, that theme was apparently present at Q's genesis as well as at its subsequent expansions.

Chapter 3

Pentateuch II

Genesis

I. Texts and Analysis

Q 3:5 // Genesis 19 (?). According to Mk 1:5, all those in the Judean countryside and all the people in Jerusalem went out to see John the Baptist. Matthew, in rewriting this verse, adds that "all the (people from the) region around the Jordan" were also there (Mt 3:5: πᾶσα ἡ περίχωρος τοῦ Ἰορδάνου). Moreover, Lk 3:3 declares that John "went into all the region around the Jordan" (εἰς πᾶσαν περίχωρον τοῦ Ἰορδάνου). This agreement between Matthew and Luke against Mark has often been taken to preserve a fragment of Q's introduction, which is otherwise lost.[1] The importance of this for our purposes is that "all the region of the Jordan" might, in view of several verses in Genesis, remind one of Sodom and Gomorrah:

LXX Gen 13:10: "Lot, lifting his eyes, saw the region around the Jordan (πᾶσαν τὴν περίχωρον τοῦ Ἰορδάνου)."

LXX Gen 13:11: "Lot chose for himself all the region around the Jordan (πᾶσαν τὴν περίχωρον τοῦ Ἰορδάνου)."

LXX Gen 19:17: "Do not look back or stop anywhere in the surrounding region (ἐν πάσῃ τῇ περιχώρῳ)."

LXX Gen 19:25 v.l.: "He overthrew those cities, and all the surrounding region (πᾶσαν τὴν περίχωρον)."

LXX Gen 19:28: "He looked on Sodom and Gomorrah and on the face of the surrounding region (τῆς περιχώρου)."

That "all the region around the Jordan" was firmly associated with the story of Lot and Sodom appears from two later texts:

Jub. 16:5: "The Lord executed the judgment of Sodom and Gomorrah and Zeboim and all of the region around the Jordan."

1 Clem. 11:1: "For his hospitality and piety Lot was saved out of Sodom when the whole surrounding region (τῆς περιχώρου πάσης) was judged by fire and brimstone."

---

1. So, e.g., the IQP. See the review of opinion in Kloppenborg, *Q Parallels*, p. 6.

One might object that in 2 Chr 4:17 the relevant phrase has nothing to do with the story in Genesis: "In the region around the Jordan (LXX: ἐν τῷ περιχώρῳ τοῦ ᾿Ιορδάνου) the king [Solomon] cast them [implements for the temple] in the clay ground between Succoth and Zeredah." But this is not a sufficient rebuttal. For one thing, *Jub.* 16:5 and *1 Clem.* 11:1 do establish that "the region around the Jordan" was a stock phrase in retelling the famous story. For another, 2 Chr 4:17 does not use πᾶς ("all"): it remains the case that the only two places in the LXX featuring πᾶς + περίχωρος + τοῦ ᾿Ιορδανοῦ (Gen 13:10–11) are associated with Lot and Sodom and that Genesis 19 uses an abbreviated form of the expression a full three times. Moreover, aside from Gen 13:10, 11; Mt 3:5; Lk 3:3; and patristic texts dependent upon the latter two, there may indeed be no further examples in Greek literature of πᾶς + περίχωρος + τοῦ ᾿Ιορδανοῦ.[2]

So the question becomes whether there are corroborative markers in the text, additional words or themes that might remind hearers of Sodom and Gomorrah. John S. Kloppenborg has urged that there are.[3] He observes that the Baptist's speech speaks of flight (Q 3:7), which is a prominent motif in Genesis 19 (vv. 17, 19, 20, 22); that the theme of fiery destruction unites Q 3 and Genesis 19 (Q 3:9, 16, 17; Gen 19:24, 28); and that if Q 3:8 refers to children of Abraham, Lot is Abraham's kin. To all this one may add that John refers to God's "wrath" (ὀργή, 3:7) and that Deut 29:20–23 cites the destruction of Sodom and Gomorrah as an illustration of God's "wrath" (LXX: ὀργή, vv. 20, 23, 24; ὀργίζω, v. 27). Kloppenborg further observes that Q elsewhere refers to the destruction of Sodom (Q 10:12; 17:28–30), and we shall see below that the allusion to Lot's wife in Lk 9:62 probably belonged in Q and that the express mention of her in Lk 17:32 may have.[4] So Q's general interest in Genesis 19 is established.

But is this enough to procure confidence that Q 3 would have turned the thoughts of scripturally literate Jewish-Christians to Genesis and Sodom and Gomorrah? Two considerations, beyond the customary failure of the commentators on Matthew and Luke to think of Genesis 19, make one hesitate. The first is that beyond the coincidence of wording in "the region around the Jordan," there are no other arresting markers. "Flight," "fire,"

---

2. Neither Philo nor Josephus ever uses περίχωρος + ᾿Ιορδάνης, and a TLG search through the third century C.E. has failed to supply any additional examples of the expression, except thirteen instances in Origen, who is in every case referring to the activity of the Baptist. John's Gospel uses πέραν τοῦ ᾿Ιορδάνου for the location of the Baptist's activities: 1:28; 3:26; 10:40.

3. John S. Kloppenborg, "City and Wasteland: Narrative World and the Beginning of the Sayings Gospel," *Semeia* 52 (1990), pp. 145–60. Cf. Bovon, *Lukas*, vol. 1, p. 170 ("Denkt Lukas an Lot und Abraham, wenn er Johannes und Jesus trennt?"); and R. Uro, "John the Baptist and the Jesus Movement," in *The Gospel behind the Gospels: Current Studies in Q* (ed. Ronald A. Piper; NovTSup 75; Leiden/New York/Cologne, 1995), pp. 61–64. For criticism, see Frans Neirynck, "The Minor Agreements," in *The Gospel behind the Gospels: Current Studies in Q* (ed. Ronald A. Piper; NovTSup 75; Leiden/New York/Cologne: Brill, 1995), pp. 67–71; and C. H. Talbert, "Beginning to Study 'How Gospels Begin,'" *Semeia* 52 (1991), p. 190.

4. See below, pp. 78–81, 95–98.

and "wrath" show up in dozens of eschatological prophecies with no eye
on Sodom and Gomorrah, and the mention of Abraham in Q 3:8 takes
one back not to Genesis but, as we shall see, to Isa 51:1–2.[5] One should
also keep in mind that the Jordan and its vicinity, while associated with the
legend about Sodom and Gomorrah, were also associated with other famous
biblical episodes, such as the crossing into the Promised Land (Joshua 1–
3) and certain miracles of Elijah and Elisha (e.g., 2 Kings 2). The other
difficulty concerns the content of Q: doubt hangs over the proposition that
the agreement between Mt 3:5 and Lk 3:3 (πᾶς + περίχωρος + ᾿Ιορδάνου)
is a remnant from Q. We just might have here instead a piece of independent
editing.[6] So the verdict on Kloppenborg's case is *non liquet*.

Q 6:23 // Gen 15:1. The beatitudes that open the Sermon on the Plain
contain this closing promise: "Your reward will be great in heaven." This is
close to Gen 15:1, where God says to Abram, "Do not be afraid, Abram, I
am your shield; your reward will be very great."

MT Gen 15:1	שכרך הרבה מאד
Tg. Onq.	אגרך סגי לחדא[7]
LXX Gen 15:1	ὁ μισθός σου πολὺς ἔσται σφόδρα
Mt 5:12	ὁ μισθὸς ὑμῶν πολὺς ἐν τοῖς οὐρανοῖς
Lk 6:23 (= IQP Q)	ὁ μισθὸς ὑμῶν πολὺς ἐν τῷ οὐρανῷ

The parallel, while it may seem fleeting, should probably be classified not
as a coincidence but instead as an allusion. (*a*) There is verbal as well as
formal agreement: both lines consist of ὁ μισθός + second person pronoun
in the genitive case + πολύς + further specification. Moreover, while the
pertinent clauses in Q 6:23 and MT Gen 15:1 are independent, both lack
verbs: one must in each case supply a form of "to be" (as do the LXX and
English versions). (*b*) There is likewise conceptual concordance: both lines
are about receiving future reward from God. (*c*) Gen 15:1 and Mt 5:12
par. share an unusual combination of words. These two places are the only
ones in the Greek Bible which qualify μισθός with πολύς, an otherwise rare
combination.[8] (*d*) Readers of Mt 5:12 and Lk 6:23 have as a matter of
record been reminded of Gen 15:1. Grotius commented simply on Mt 5:12:
"*Ex Genesi* xv, I."[9] Others have thought the same thing,[10] and Gen 15:1

---

5. See below, pp. 101–4.

6. Or, according to Gundry, *Matthew*, p. 46 (who accepts the existence of Q), a sign of
Luke's use of Matthew.

7. Tg. Ps.-J. and Neof. 1 rewrite; see below.

8. The language of Ps.-Ignatius, *Mar.* 4.3 ("the expected reward is great," προσδοκώμενος
μισθὸς πολύς), presumably depends upon the New Testament.

9. Hugo Grotius, *Operum theologicarum* (Amsterdam: Joannis Blaev, 1679), vol. 2, pt. 1,
p. 32.

10. E.g., Adolf Schlatter, *Das Evangelium des Lukas aus seinen Quellen erklärt* (2d ed.;
Stuttgart: Calwer, 1960), p. 247; and Gundry, *Old Testament*, p. 72. Cf. Hugh of Saint Cher,
Comm. Mt ad 5:12 (Opera Omnia 6, p. 17); Nicholas of Gorran, *In quatuor evangelia com-*

has been in the margins of Mt 5:12 in the various Nestle-Aland editions of the Greek New Testament.

Interestingly enough, both Tg. Neof. 1 and Tg. Ps.-J. on Gen 15:1 insert a conversation between Abram and God in which Abram worries that he has received his reward already in this world. God responds with reassurance: Abram's reward for his good works is prepared before God "in the world to come":

> Tg. Ps.-J.: "The reward of your good works is kept and prepared before me for the world to come, very great (reward)."

> Neof. 1: "The reward of your good works is prepared for you before me in the world to come."

In these places then the "great reward" of Gen 15:1 has become eschatological (cf. the future tense of the LXX, ἔσται, "will be"). One suspects that a common exegetical tradition underlies these targumic readings and Q 6:23, where the reward is also eschatological.[11] If so, in Q there is a revised application. The promise is now for the followers of Jesus: it is they who gain Abraham's eschatological reward in heaven (cf. Q 3:8).

It is no objection to all this that Q 6:23 goes on to say, "For so they persecuted the prophets." For widespread haggadic legends (including the targumic traditions on Genesis 15)[12] make Abraham a prophet who saw far into the future, and there are legends about how the Chaldeans — on account of the patriarch's monotheism and opposition to idols — persecuted him.[13]

Discerning an allusion to Gen 15:1 in Q 6:23 creates a thematic link with Q 13:28–29, where the saints enjoy the eschatological feast in the company of Abraham. If Q 6:23 holds forth the abstract promise of being rewarded as Abraham will be, Q 13:28–29 offers a concrete picture of the redeemed sharing the same future as the patriarchs.

There is also a potentially meaningful link with Q 3:9, where John the Baptist rebukes those who think that they will be, because of their ancestry, the beneficiaries of Abraham's merit: "And do not presume[14] to say in

---

mentarius (Antwerp: Ioannem Keerbergium, 1617), p. 35; Albertus Magnus, *Super Mt cap. I–XIV* ad loc. (Opera Omnia 21/1; ed. B. Schmidt, p. 117); Bonaventure, *Exp. Luc.* ad loc. (Opera Omnia 10, ed. A. C. Peltier, p. 370); Johann Jakob Wettstein, *Novum Testamentum Graecum* (Amsterdam: Ex officina Dommeriana, 1751–52), vol. 1, p. 291.

11. Cf. Gundry, *Old Testament*, p. 72. It should be observed, however, that the rewriting of Gen 15:1 in 1QapGen 29:31 shows no sign of this interpretation (cf. *Jub.* 14:1).

12. In Gen 15:13–16, Abram learns that his descendants will go down into Egypt and then come out with great possessions and that he himself will live to a good old age. Tg. Onq. 1 on Gen 15:1 says the word of the Lord spoke with Abram "in a prophecy." Tg. Neof. 1 on Gen 15:4 says that "a word of prophecy" came upon Abram. Tg. Ps.-J. on Gen 15:12 has Abram foresee the rise of Babylon and Greece, among other things.

13. Abraham as prophet: Philo, *Rer. div. her.* 258, 266; *4 Ezra* 3:13–14; *Apoc. Abr.* 9:1–6; 27–29; *Mek.* on Exod 20:18; Tg. Neof. on Gen 15:1, 12; *Gen Rab.* 44:21. Persecution of Abra(ha)m: Jdt 5:8; *Jub.* 12:7; Josephus, *Ant.* 1.157; *T. Levi* 6:9; *LAB* 6:15–18; *ARN* A 33; Tg. Ps.-J. on Gen 11:28; 15:7; Tg. Neof. on Gen 11:31; 15:7; *Gen Rab.* 34:9; etc.

14. So Matthew (δόξητε). Luke has "begin," ἄρξησθε.

yourselves, 'We have Abraham for our father,' for I tell you that God is able from these stones to raise up children to Abraham."[15] Here people are being apprised that while they may think themselves the rightful heirs of the patriarch, their fate may tell a very different story. The warning is reinforced by Q 6:23, when it is understood as an allusion to Gen 15:1, for here the reward of Abraham is clearly bestowed on the basis of something other than physical descent from the patriarch.

Q 9:61–62 // Gen 19:17, 26. Mt 8:18–22 and Lk 9:57–60 recount two call stories with challenging punch lines. Luke alone has a third such story in which Jesus engages a would-be disciple: "Another said: 'I will follow you, Lord; but let me first say farewell to those at my home.' Jesus said to him, 'No one who puts his hand to the plough and looks back is fit for the kingdom of God' " (Lk 9:61–62). Despite its being attested only in Luke, the unit is, with good reason, often assigned to the Sayings Source.[16] As Kloppenborg has written, "Of all the Lukan *Sondergut*, this has the strongest probability of deriving from Q since it is found in a Q context, the saying coheres with the preceding sayings formally, and it evinces the same theology of discipleship typical of other Q sayings."[17] To this it may be added that the unit contains features that, according to Joachim Jeremias, should be classified as non-Lukan[18] and further that an explanation as to why Matthew might have omitted Q 9:61–62 is not far to seek: Q 9:61–62 is so close to Q 9:59–60 that Matthew's well-known penchant for abbreviating and removing redundancy readily accounts for his inclusion of only one of the two passages.[19]

We shall see in a subsequent chapter that the concluding pronouncement of Q 9:61–62 — "No one who puts his hand to the plow and looks back (βλέπων εἰς τὰ ὀπίσω) is fit for the reign of God" — is quite similar to 1 Kgs 19:19–21, where Elijah calls Elisha.[20] Now one of the key words of 1 Kgs 19:19–21 is "after" (ὀπίσω = אַחֲרֵי):

> 20   "he ran after (LXX: ὀπίσω; MT: אַחֲרֵי) Elijah"
> 20   "I shall follow after (LXX: ὀπίσω; MT: אַחֲרֶיךָ) you"
> 21   "he went after (LXX: ὀπίσω; MT: אַחֲרֵי) Elijah"

---

15. See on this further the discussion below, pp. 101–4.

16. For a place in Q see Karl Löning, "Die Füchse, die Vögel und der Menschensohn (Mt 8,19f par Lk 9,57f)," in *Vom Urchristentum zu Jesus: Für Joachim Gnilka* (ed. Hubert Frankemölle and Karl Kertelge; Freiburg: Herder, 1989), pp. 83–84; and Schürmann, *Lukasevangelium, Zweiter Teil*, pp. 44–47. For a Lukan origin, see Harry T. Fleddermann, "The Demands of Discipleship: Matt 8,19–22 par. Luke 9:57–62," in *The Four Gospels 1992: Festschrift Frans Neirynck* (ed. F. Van Segbroeck et al.; BETL 100; Louvain: Louvain University Press/Peeters, 1992), vol. 1, pp. 541–61. Sato, *Q und Prophetie*, p. 55, assigns the unit to Q^{Lk}.

17. Kloppenborg, *Q Parallels*, p. 64.

18. Jeremias, *Sprache*, pp. 182–83.

19. See further Kloppenborg, *Q Parallels*, p. 64.

20. See below, pp. 142–45.

One might think this suffices to explain the striking phrase in Q 9:62, βλέπων εἰς τὰ ὀπίσω, literally, "looking at the things behind." But in 1 Kgs 19:19–21 ὀπίσω is not associated with sight. Moreover, there is a very famous story in Genesis about one who looked at the things behind — the story about Lot's wife.

According to Gen 19:26, ותבט אשתו מאחריו ותהי נציב מלח. The NRSV has this: "Lot's wife, behind him, looked back, and she became a pillar of salt." The Hebrew is difficult because it is not clear what "from behind him" (מאחריו) should mean. The NRSV takes the word as independent and then translates תבט with "looked back," even though it does not have a preposition. All would be clear if we could instead read מאחריה ("from behind her"). This would give us "his wife looked behind her" and link up with 19:17, where God says, "Do not look behind you" (אל־תביט אחריך). Interestingly enough, this is the reading presupposed by the fragment targums and Neofiti.[21] More importantly for us, it is what lies behind the LXX, which in v. 17 has μὴ περιβλέψῃς εἰς τὰ ὀπίσω ("Do not look at the things behind") and in v. 26 ἐπέβλεψεν...εἰς τὰ ὀπίσω ("she looked at the things behind"). The importance of this for Q 9:62 can be seen at once:

Q 9:62	βλέπων	εἰς τὰ ὀπίσω
LXX Gen 19:17	μὴ περιβλέψῃς	εἰς τὰ ὀπίσω
LXX Gen 19:26	ἐπέβλεψεν...	εἰς τὰ ὀπίσω

The correlation is not a fluke. Rather Q 9:62 should be construed as an allusion to the fatal mistake of Lot's wife, for the following reasons:

(i) εἰς τὰ ὀπίσω appears in connection with (περι-/ἐπι-)βλέπω five times in the LXX. Two of these belong to the story of Lot's wife, where the words are a key part of the narrative. In the other three places, the phrase is incidental to the plot and not repeated, the stories they belong to are not nearly so renowned, and ὀπίσω is directly followed by a personal pronoun.[22]

(ii) The brief Gen 19:26 captured the imagination of ancient hearers and received much attention (just as it does in later ecclesiastical commentaries, where comments on this verse often dwarf comments on the other verses of Genesis 19). People wanted to know what was so wrong about what Lot's wife did as well as why she did it and why her punishment was to become a pillar of salt. Legends grew up around these topics.[23] Josephus even claimed

---

21. Neofiti: אסתכלת לבתרה למחמי. Fragment targums: או)י(סהכלה מן בתרה למ)י(חמי.

22. See Josh 8:20 ("and when the inhabitants of Gai looked round behind them," περιβλέψαντες οἱ κάτοικοι Γαὶ εἰς τὰ ὀπίσω αὐτῶν); 1 Βασ 24:9 ("and Saul looked behind him," ἐπέβλεψε Σαοὺλ εἰς τὰ ὀπίσω αὐτοῦ); 2 Βασ 2:20 ("Abenner looked behind him," ἐπέβλεψεν Ἀβεννὴρ εἰς τὰ ὀπίσω αὐτοῦ).

23. See Harry Sysling, *Tehiyyat Ha-Metim: The Resurrection of the Dead in the Palestinian Targums of the Pentateuch and Parallel Traditions in Classical Rabbinic Literature* (TSAJ 57; Tübingen: Mohr Siebeck, 1996), pp. 91–103.

to have seen the pillar of salt.[24] Just maybe there was a spot somewhere southwest of the Dead Sea where people were shown the pillar that was once Lot's wife.

(iii) The targums imply that Lot's wife looked behind her, in disobedience to the divine command (Gen 19:17), because she was sentimentally attached to her family and past.[25] Philo tells us that she was "enamored of Sodom"[26] and desired to "gaze round at the old familiar objects."[27] In analogous fashion, the sin of the disciple unfit for the kingdom of God in Q 9:61–62 is attachment to his old life (cf. the jarring Q 9:60: "Leave the dead to bury their own dead").

(iv) The very next section of Q, the missionary discourse, refers to the story of Sodom (Q 10:12), and Q returns to that tale again in 17:28–29 (+ 31–32).

(v) Whether or not one assigns all or part or none of Lk 17:31–32 to Q, the verses as they stand say this: "In that day anyone on the housetop who has belongings in the house must not come down to take them away; and likewise anyone in the field must not turn back (εἰς τὰ ὀπίσω). Remember Lot's wife." Here indisputably someone has associated the phrase, εἰς τὰ ὀπίσω, with the story of the pillar of salt.

(vi) Many readers have indeed caught an allusion here, beginning with Tertullian, who commented that when Christ "forbids the man 'to look back' who would first 'bid his family farewell,' he only follows out the rule of the Creator. For he had not wanted those he rescued from Sodom to look back."[28] Bede had the same thought when remarking upon Lk 9:62: "If anyone having begun . . . delights with Lot's wife to look back to the things he has left, he is deprived of the gift of the future kingdom."[29] Origen, Cyprian, Athanasius, Albertus Magnus, Bonanventure, Luther, Grotius, Maldonatus, and others have made similar remarks.[30]

---

24. *Ant.* 1.203. Cf. *1 Clem.* 11:2; Irenaeus, *Adv. haer.* 4.31.1 (SC 100, ed. A. Rousseau, p. 788).

25. Tg. Ps.-J. on Gen 19:26 (she "looked behind . . . to know what would be the end of her father's house. She was one of the daughters of the Sodomites"); Tg. Neof. 1 on Gen 19:26 ("because Lot's wife was from the daughters of Sodomites she looked back to see what would be the end of her father's house").

26. *Leg. all.* 3.213. Cf. also *Fug.* 121–22; *Som.* 1.246–48.

27. *Ebr.* 164. Cf. *Leg. all.* 3.213; *Quaest. Gen* 4.52; *1 Clem.* 11:1–2; Clement of Alexandria, *Prot.* 10(103) (SC 2, ed. C. Mondésert, pp. 171–72); Augustine, *Civ. Dei* 10.8; 16.30 (CSEL 40, ed. E. Hoffmann, 1, p. 458, 2, pp. 180–81).

28. *Adv. Marc.* 4.23 (CCSL, ed. Florentis, p. 607).

29. Bede, *Luc. exp.* ad loc. (CCSL 70, ed. D. Hurst, p. 214).

30. Origen, *Hom. Gen* 5.1 (SC 7, ed. L. Doutreleau, p. 166, citing Lk 9:62 and 17:32 when discussing Lot's wife); idem, *Hom. Jer* 13.3 (SC 238, ed. P. Natuin, p. 60); Cyprian, *Ep.* 11.7(7.7) (CSEL 3/2, ed. G. Hartel, pp. 500–501); Athanasius, *Vit. Ant.* 20.1 (SC 400, ed. G. J. M. Bartelink, p. 188); Albertus Magnus, *En. prim. part. Luc. (I–IX)* ad loc. (Opera Omnia 22, ed. A. Borgnet, p. 700); Bonaventure, *Exp. Luc.* ad loc. (Opera Omnia 10, ed. A. C. Peltier, p. 487); Martin Luther, *Martin Luthers Evangelien-Auslegung, Dritter Teil. Markus-und Lukasevangelium (Mark. 1–13; Luk. 3–21)* (ed. E. Mülhaupt; Göttingen: Vandenhoeck &

Because Gen 19:12–26 and the other text alluded to here, namely, 1 Kgs 19:19–21, both repeat the word, ὀπίσω = אחר, one strongly suspects that the allusion to Genesis 19 in Q 9:61–62 entered the tradition when someone reflecting upon 1 Kgs 19:19–21 was led to Genesis 19 through word association. The rabbis later on spoke of גזירה שוה, a hermeneutical principle that encouraged them to associate two passages with common words or expressions. Is not some such procedure implicit in the intertextual background of Q 9:61–62? One may compare Q 7:27, which conflates Exod 23:20 and Mal 3:1 because they contain similar wording.[31]

Q 10:12 // Gen 19:1–29. Jesus warns that it will be more tolerable for Sodom on the day of judgment than for those who reject the emissaries of the kingdom of God.[32] This prophetic denunciation not only refers to the story we know from Genesis 19 (a chapter just alluded to if Lk 9:62 belonged to Q) but also reflects exegetical and haggadic traditions about Sodom and its proverbial wickedness:

(i) Sodom's inhospitality was, in accord with Genesis 19,[33] infamous, as appears from the following:

> Ezek 16:49–50: "This was the guilt of your sister Sodom: she and her daughters had pride, excess of food, and prosperous ease, but did not aid the poor and needy. They were haughty, and did abominable things before me; therefore I removed them when I saw it."

Ruprecht, 1961), p. 137; Grotius, *Operum theologicarum*, vol. 2, pt. 1, p. 395; Juan Maldonatus, *Commentarii in Quatuor Evangelistas* (London/Paris: Moguntiae, 1853–54), vol. 2, p. 181. Note also Clement of Alexandria, *Strom.* 7.16 (SC 428, ed. A. Le Boulluec, p. 284); Wettstein, *Novum Testamentum Graecum*, vol. 1, p. 718; Schlatter, *Lukas*, p. 273; and Michael D. Goulder, *Luke — A New Paradigm*, vol. 2, pt. 2 (Cont.), *Commentary: Luke 9:51–24:53* (JSNTSS 20; Sheffield: JSOT Press, 1989), p. 464. According to William Dodd, *A Commentary on the Books of the Old and New Testament* (London: R. Davies, 1770), vol. 3, ad Lk 9:62, Jesus was either citing a popular proverb or alluding to Lot's wife. Christian commentators on Gen 19:26 have also recalled Lk 9:62; so, e.g., Rabanus Maurus, *Comm. Gen* 2.23 (PL 107.558B); Martin Luther, *Luther's Commentary on Genesis* (Grand Rapids: Zondervan, 1958), vol. 1, p. 355; Augustin Calmet, *Commentarium literale in omnes ac singulos tum Veteris cum Novi Testamenti libros* (n.p.: Augustae Vindelicorum & Graecii, 1735), vol. 1, p. 161; Ainsworth, *Annotations*, vol. 1, pp. 104–5; and *A Commentary upon the Holy Bible from Henry & Scott; with Numerous Observations and Notes from Other Writers* (London: The Religious Tract Society, n.d.), p. 60.

31. See further above, pp. 38–40.

32. Luke (following Q according to the IQP) names only Sodom, Matthew both Sodom and Gomorrah. For "Sodom and Gomorrah" (in that order) see Gen 10:19; 13:10; 14:10–11; 18:20; 19:24, 28; Deut 29:23; 32:32; Isa 13:19; Jer 49:18; 50:40; Amos 4:11; Zeph 2:9; *Jub.* 16:5; Mk 6:11; 2 Pet 2:6; Jude 7; *4 Ezra* 2:8; *Asc. Isa.* 3:10; *Gk. Apoc. Ezra* 2:19; etc. But the *Testaments of the Twelve Patriarchs* (exception in *T. Levi* 14:6), Josephus, and the rabbis prefer the singular "Sodom." Cf. Lam 4:6; Ezek 16:44–58.

33. On the theme of inhospitality in Genesis 19, which shares motifs central to Joshua 2 and Judges 19–21, see esp. Weston W. Fields, *Sodom and Gomorrah: History and Motif in Biblical Narrative* (JSOTSS 231; Sheffield: Sheffield Academic Press, 1997), esp. pp. 127–33. Note also Chrysostom, *Hom. Gen* 43.7(32) (PG 54.405). Does Judges 19 already rewrite Genesis or a closely related tradition? See Robert Alter, *The World of Biblical Literature* (New York: HarperCollins, 1992), pp. 111–12.

Wisd 19:13–14: The Sodomites "had refused to receive strangers when they
came to them, but made slaves of guests who were their benefactors."

Josephus, *Ant.* 1.194: The Sodomites "hated foreigners (μισόξενοι) and declined all converse with others."

Sifre on Deut 11:13–17 (43): "The Sodomites rebelled against God. . . . [They]
said, 'Lo, we have food near at hand, lo, we have silver and gold near to
hand. Let us go and wipe out the law of the wayfarer from our land."

b. Sanh. 109a: The Sodomites said: "Why should we suffer wayfarers, who
come to us only to deplete our wealth? Come, let us abolish the practice
of travelling in our land."

b. Sanh. 109b: The Sodomites "had beds upon which travellers slept. If [the
guest] was too long, they shortened him [by cutting off the feet]. If too
short, they stretched him out. . . . They made this agreement among themselves, that whoever invites one [a stranger] to a feast shall be stripped
of his garment."

Pirqe R. El. 25: "They announced in Sodom that anyone who gave bread to
the poor, the sojourner, or the destitute would be burned. Now Pelotit
was Lot's daughter, and she was married to one of the leaders of Sodom.
She saw a poor man afflicted in the public square and she was sorely
grieved for him. What did she do? Every day, when she went to draw
water, she would take some food from her house and put it in her pitcher,
and so would feed the poor man. The people of Sodom wondered, How
is this poor man managing to live? When they found out, they took
[Pelotit] to be burned."

Unlike Abraham, who was (because of Gen 18:1–15) renowned for his hospitality, the Sodomites were notorious for the opposite. This illuminates Q
10:12 because the sin it records is precisely the sin of inhospitality.[34] The
itinerants shake off their feet the dust of the town that has not "received"
them (μὴ δέχωνται ὑμᾶς, Q 10:10–11), the town that will fare worse on
judgment day than Sodom.

   (ii) In Jewish tradition Sodom and Gomorrah typically serve as symbols
of wickedness and of complete destruction,[35] which is why they also become
symbols of eschatological annihilation, as in Q 10:12. Typical are *Jub.* 16:6

---

34. Cf. the comments of Eusebius and Bede preserved in Aquinas, *Catena Aurea* on Lk 10:9;
also Rupert of Deutz, *Comm. Mt* ad 10:15 (PL 168.1491C-92D); and Judith H. Newman, "Lot
in Sodom: The Post-Mortem of a City and the Afterlife of a Biblical Text," in *The Function of
Scripture in Early Jewish and Christian Tradition* (JSNTSS 154; Sheffield: Sheffield Academic
Press, 1998), pp. 34–44.

35. Cf. J. A. Loader, *A Tale of Two Cities: Sodom and Gomorrah in the Old Testament,
Early Jewish and Early Christian Traditions* (Contributions to Biblical Exegesis and Theology
1; Kampen: J. H. Kok, 1990), p. 71. Note 4Q180 frags. 2–4 col. 2; Rom 9:29, quoting Isa
1:9; also Deut 29:23; Isa 13:19–22; Jer 50:40; Zeph 2:9 ("a waste forever"); 2 Pet 2:6–
7 ("extinction"); 4 Ezra 2:8–9. 4Q252 3:2–6 puts Sodom and Gomorrah under the ban of
Deuteronomy 13, which demands that a city be a "perpetual ruin." See George J. Brooke, "The
Deuteronomic Character of 4Q 252," in *Pursuing the Text: Studies in Honour of Ben Zion*

("the Lord will execute judgment like the judgment of Sodom on places where they act according to the pollution of Sodom"); 16:9 ("just like the judgment of Sodom so that he [God] will not leave seed of man for him on the earth in the day of judgment"); and *Gk. Apoc. Ezra* 7:12 ("Those who do not believe this book will be burned like Sodom and Gomorrah").[36] The legend about Sodom was already popular with the canonical Jewish prophets, who used it as an everlasting warning about divine judgment.[37]

(iii) Q 10:12 is not alone in polemically likening certain Jews to Sodomites.[38] Particularly interesting for comparison is Ezek 16:43–52. This memorably promises that God will restore the fortunes of Sodom and employs the proverbial wickedness of the city to assert that Jerusalem is even worse than her "younger sister," Sodom.

(iv) In asserting that the final judgment will be more tolerable for Sodom than for the cities that reject Jesus' messengers, Q 10:12 may be related not only to Ezek 16:43–52 but also to a debate recorded in *m. Sanh.* 10:3:

> The people of Sodom have no share in the world to come, for it is written, "Now the people of Sodom were wicked and sinners against the Lord exceedingly" (Gen 13:13) — wicked in this world, and sinners in the world to come. But they will stand in the judgment. R. Nehemiah says: Neither of them [neither the Sodomites nor the generation of the flood] will stand in the judgment, for it is written: "Thus the wicked will not stand in the judgment nor sinners in the congregation of the righteous" (Ps 1:5). "Thus the wicked will not stand in the judgment" — this is the generation of the flood. "Nor sinners in the congregation of the righteous" — these are the people of Sodom. They said to him: They will not stand in the congregation of the righteous, but they will stand in the congregation of the ungodly.

Does Q 10:12 agree with the authorities who say that the citizens of Sodom will be resurrected for judgment? Against R. Nehemiah and others who thought that only the righteous would be resurrected,[39] Q expects a resurrection of just and unjust,[40] for Matthew's version of Q 12:5, which refers to the one "who can destroy both soul and body in hell" (Mt 10:28), more likely preserves Q than does Luke's Hellenized version ("who, after he has

---

Wacholder on the Occasion of His Seventieth Birthday (ed. John C. Reeves and John Kampen; JSNTSS 184; Sheffield: Sheffield Academic Press, 1994), p. 123.

36. Note also *Jub.* 22:22; 36:10; 2 Pet 2:6; Jude 7; and *Gk. Apoc. Ezra* 2:18–19; and see Jacques Schlosser, "Les jours de Noé et Lot: A propos de Luc, XVII, 26–30," *RB* 80 (1973), pp. 13–36.

37. See Isa 1:9; 3:9; 13:19; Jer 23:14; 49:18; 50:40; Lam 4:6; Amos 4:11; Zeph 2:9. Cf. 3 Macc 2:5 ("You consumed with fire and sulfur the people of Sodom who acted arrogantly, who were notorious for their vices; and you made them an example to those who should come afterward").

38. Cf. Isa 1:10; 3:9; Amos 4:11; *Asc. Isa.* 3:10 (referring to the verses in Isaiah).

39. See, e.g., *Psalms of Solomon* 3; *1 Enoch* 83–90; Josephus, *Bell.* 2.163; *2 Bar.* 30:1–5.

40. Cf. *Sib. Or.* 4:179–90; *T. Benj.* 10:8; Jn 5:28–29; Acts 24:15; *4 Ezra* 7:32.

killed, has power to cast into hell").[41] In Mt 10:28 the destruction of a body in hell seemingly assumes that an individual has been raised from the dead, condemned at the judgment, and then cast bodily into the place of punishment. In other words, Q apparently taught the resurrection of the righteous and unrighteous, and this may be presupposed in Q 10:12, the word about Sodom.

Q 11:49–51 // Gen 4:8–16.[42] "The blood of all the prophets that has been shed from the foundation of the world" will be "required of this generation," from "the blood of Abel" to "the blood of Zechariah [son of Barachia],[43] who perished between the altar and the house." This text presupposes that readers (*a*) know the story of Cain and Abel in Genesis 4 and (*b*) can identify Zechariah — he is according to the vast majority of commentators the Zechariah killed in 2 Chr 24:20–22[44] — and can recall his story, which is not for us a particularly prominent one. It may also (*c*) reflect a scriptural corpus that, like the MT, concludes with Chronicles (cf. *b. B. Bat.* 14b) so that Cain and Zechariah are the first and the last in a series.[45] At any rate "the presupposition of this Q saying seems to be that the era of 'biblical' history is one on which to look back, as a closed era of the past."[46]

---

41. Cf. Joachim Gnilka, *Das Matthäusevangelium* (HTKNT I/1, 2; Freiburg: Herder, 1986), vol. 1, pp. 384–85.

42. In addition to what follows, see below, pp. 149–52, on the extensive dependence of Q 11:49–51 upon 2 Chr 24:17–25.

43. Was this added by Matthew as clarification? Or was it omitted by Luke as problematic?

44. See R. Beckwith, *The Old Testament Canon of the New Testament* (Grand Rapids: Eerdmans, 1985), pp. 211–22. This is confirmed by the dependence of Q 11:49–51 + 13:34–35 upon 2 Chr 24:17–25; see below, pp. 85–86. With regard to Matthew's "son of Barachia" (υἱοῦ Βαραχίου), Zech 1:1 refers to the book's author as Zechariah, son of ברכיה/Βαραχίου. There is, however, no biblical evidence of his death as a martyr, and, as Jerome observed, the temple was in ruins in his time. The one biblical martyr named Zechariah is the son of Jehoiada, the priest whose story appears near the end of Chronicles. Still other candidates have been forwarded — most often either the father of the Baptist (Lk 1:5–23) or the son of Baris (or Bariscaeus or Baruch), who was martyred in the temple during the Jewish war (Josephus, *Bell.* 4.334–44). There is also, among the many biblical Zechariahs, the son of Jeberechiah (LXX: Βαραχία) of Isa 8:2, who is called a "faithful witness." Given, however, that tradition, which could merge two distinct persons (cf. Phineas and Elijah), conflated the prophet Zechariah with the son of Jehoiada (e.g., ms. E2 of the *Lives of the Prophets;* Tg. on Lam 2:20) and given that the death of the latter became the popular subject of legends (see n. 55), we may assume that Matthew's "son of Berechiah," whether from Q or redactional, already attests to the conflation. Moreover, Q's specification of exactly where Zechariah was killed corresponds to the fact that rabbinic sources on the Zechariah of 2 Chronicles 24 contain quite a bit of discussion of this subject; see Anna Maria Schwemmer, *Studien zu den frühjüdischen Prophetenlegenden* Vitae Prophetarum (TSAJ 50; Tübingen: Mohr Siebeck, 1996), vol. 2, pp. 297–301. The identity of Q's Zechariah, rightly understood by Matthew, seems reasonably clear.

45. One must be very cautious, however, about the shape of the Hebrew canon in the first century. See Lee M. McDonald, *The Formation of the Christian Biblical Canon* (rev. ed.; Peabody, Mass.: Hendrickson, 1995), esp. pp. 46–49.

46. So Tuckett, "Scripture in Q," p. 7. Codex Marchalianus (Cod. Vaticanus Gk. 2125) of *Lives of the Prophets* concludes with the narrative about Zechariah, so too the Latin and Arabic versions. See Schwemmer, *Studien*, vol. 2, pp. 27–33. Schwemmer concludes that this is how the document originally ended.

Abel and Zechariah may not just belong together because they come at the beginning and the end of the sacred literature. Q's threefold use of "blood"[47] reminds the informed hearer that the Bible refers to the blood of both of these characters, and precisely in the context of the need for them to be avenged.[48] In Gen 4:10 God says to Cain, "Your brother's blood is crying from the ground!" In 2 Chr 24:22 Zechariah cries out as he dies, "May the Lord see and avenge!" and 24:25 refers to "the blood of the son of the priest Jehoiada." Once more then there are additional reverberations for those who bring to the text a knowledge of tradition. Indeed, one with such knowledge might see several parallels between Abel and Zechariah:

- one is a temple priest; the other is killed because of jealousy over a sacrifice he has offered;

- both of their narratives speak of their "bloods" (plural);[49]

- Abel's blood cries from the ground for vengeance, and as Zechariah dies, he says, "May the Lord see and avenge," and the king who had him murdered is himself killed "because of the blood of the son of the priest Jehoiada";[50]

- both are killed with a stone (see below).

There has been much discussion about what in Q immediately followed 11:49–51, whether or not Matthew's order (Mt 23:34–39 = Q 11:49–51+ 13:34–35) is original. I have argued elsewhere that it is.[51] This conclusion is reinforced by the fact that Q 13:34, which in Matthew immediately follows the lines about Abel and Zechariah, describes Jerusalem as killing prophets and stoning (λιθοβολοῦσα) those sent to the city. According to Jewish tradition, both Cain and Zechariah were stoned. 2 Chr 24:21 says, "They stoned (ἐλιθοβόλησαν) him [Zechariah] to death." Gen 4:8 says only that "Cain rose up against his brother Abel and killed him." But since the Bible "does say that the murder occurred 'when they were in the field' (Gen 4:8), some

---

47. Although the use of ἐκχύννομαι with "blood" (Q 11:50) is from neither LXX Genesis 4 nor 2 Chronicles 24, it does have a parallel in the summary of Zechariah's martyrdom in *Liv. Proph. Zech* 23:1.

48. Cf. Grotius, *Operum theologicarum*, vol. 2, pt. 1, p. 218. Note also *1 En.* 22:7: "This is the spirit which had left Abel, whom Cain, his brother, had killed; it continues to sue him until all of Cain's seed is exterminated from the face of the earth, and his seed has disintegrated from among the seed of the people."

49. MT Gen 4:10: דמי. The LXX has the singular αἵματος. MT 2 Chr 24:25: דמי. In this case the LXX has the plural αἵμασιν.

50. Sheldon Blank, "The Death of Zechariah in Rabbinic Literature," *HUCA* 13 (1938), pp. 336–38: "Even as the blood of Abel cried unto God from the ground so the blood of Zechariah cried to Him for vengeance from the pavement of the Temple where he had been stoned. The association of the death of this Zechariah with that of Abel in the Gospels is thoroughly logical."

51. Allison, *Jesus Tradition in Q*, pp. 201–3: Matthew followed Q in putting the unit at the end of the woes, and Luke moved the piece so that it would follow Jesus' remark that a prophet should not perish away from Jerusalem (Lk 13:33).

interpreters saw in this detail a hint concerning the weapon: it must have been something likely to be found in a field, namely, a stone."[52] *Jub.* 4:31 says that Cain "killed Abel with a stone," and *Pirq. R. El.* 21 says that Cain "took a stone and drove it into his [Abel's] forehead and killed him."[53] So when Q 11:49–51, with its two murders by stoning, introduces the declaration that Jerusalem has stoned those sent to it, a nice thematic link is forged.[54]

Q 11:51 may presuppose not only extrabiblical tradition about the weapon with which Abel was murdered but also additional legends about him, as well as later legends about Zechariah. These points are worth noting:

(*i*) The passing mention of Zechariah assumes that his story was not obscure. This is confirmed by Jewish sources, which have much to say about this incident.[55] Maybe Lam 2:20 ("Should priest and prophet be killed in the sanctuary of the Lord?") already alludes to it.

(*ii*) The mention of Zechariah's blood may be intended to recall not just 2 Chr 24:25 but vivid legends about that blood, if such were already in circulation in the first century. The plural "bloods" in 2 Chr 24:25 (MT: יְמֵי; LXX: αἵμασιν) activated the haggadic imagination.[56] *Midr. Num* 30:15 says it was splashed on the wall of the temple.[57] *b. Giṭ.* 57b says that it bubbled up for years afterwards.[58]

(*iii*) In *m. Sanh.* 4:5, one interpretation of Abel's "bloods" is that it includes the life of his potential descendants, and Tg. Neof. 1 on Gen 4:10 has this: "the voice of the blood (אדמהון) of the righteous multitudes that

---

52. James L. Kugel, *Traditions of the Bible: A Guide to the Bible As It Was at the Start of the Common Era* (Cambridge, Mass./London: Harvard University Press, 1998), p. 152. Cf. the singular אבן = "stone" in MT 2 Chr 24:21.

53. The stoning of Abel is also recorded in Tg. Ps.-J. on Gen 4:8; *Gen Rab.* 22:8 (here several opinions are given; that a rock was used is the opinion of "the rabbis"); *Tanhuma*, Bereshit 9; Didymus of Alexandria, *Comm. Gen* 126 (SC 233, ed. P. Nautin, p. 296); *Cave of Treasures* 5:29 (CSCO 486, ed. Su-Min Ri, p. 47); *Conflict of Adam and Eve*, p. 72 (ed. Dillmann); *History of the Forefathers* 23–25 (SVTP 14, ed. M. Stone, p. 192); *Abel* 3:4–6 (SVTP 14, ed. M. Stone, pp. 148–49). But for other conjectures about the weapon, see Johannes Bartholdy Glenthøj, *Cain and Abel in Syriac and Greek Writers (4th–6th Centuries)* (CSCO 567 Subsidia 95; Louvain: Peeters, 1997), pp. 149–50, 229–30.

54. This has also been seen by Kee, "Jesus: A Glutton and Drunkard," p. 330.

55. See Blank, "Death of Zechariah," pp. 327–46; SB 1, pp. 940–42. Along with Jeremiah (see *Par. Jer* 9:25–32; etc.), Zechariah may be in mind in Heb 11:37. I have not had access to J.-D. Dubois, "Études sur l'Apocalypse de Zacharie et sur les traditions concernant la mort de Zacharie" (Ph.D. dissertation, Oxford University, 1978). It does not seem that the north wall of the Dura Europos synagogue depicts Zechariah's martyrdom; see Schwemmer, *Studien*, vol. 1, pp. 257–59.

56. Note the mention of Zechariah's blood in the brief summary of his martyrdom in *Liv. Proph. Zech* 23:1.

57. Is it only coincidence that the plural in Gen 4:10 ("your brother's bloods [דְמֵי] are crying out to me from the ground") also raised exegetical possibilities, among them this: "his blood had been spattered over tree and stone" (*m. Sanh.* 4:5)? Interestingly enough, *Gen Rab.* 4:10 associates Abel's "bloods" with Zechariah's "bloods."

58. Cf. *b. Sanh.* 96b; *Eccles Rab.* 3:16; 10:4; *Lam Rab.* proem 23; *Pesiq. Rab. Kah.* 15:7.

were to arise from Abel your brother is crying against you before me from the earth." Both of these rabbinic texts enlarge the scope of Abel's murder, which is analogous to its role in the Synoptics. Is this a coincidence?

(*iv*) Q 11:51 follows the saying about the sending of prophets, and in Josephus, *Ant.* 9.169, and subsequent tradition, Zechariah was a prophet.[59] Already 2 Chr 24:20 says that "the Spirit of God took possession of Zechariah," and it goes on to record a prophetic condemnation: "Thus says God.... Because you have forsaken the Lord, he has also forsaken you." Moreover, *b. Sanh.* 96b says that Zechariah "foretold the destruction of Jerusalem."

Q 12:42–46 // Genesis 39. LXX Gen 39:4–5 says that "Joseph found favor in his lord's sight and was pleasing to him, and he appointed him over his house, and all that he had he gave into Joseph's hand. And it happened that after he appointed him over his house, and over all that was his, the Lord blessed the house of the Egyptian."[60] The similarity of this to Q's rhetorical question "Who then is the faithful and wise servant whom the lord appointed over his house to give (them) food on time?" has been observed by many others.[61] One can see why at a glance:

---

59. *Liv. Proph. Zech* 23:1; *b. Giṭ.* 57b; *b. Sanh.* 96b; Tg. on Lam 2:20; *Midr. Num* 30:15; *Eccles Rab.* 3:16; 10:4; *Lam Rab.* proem 23; *Pesiq. Rab. Kah.* 15:7. Abel is also a prophet in Tg. Neof. 1 on Gen 4:8, where he foretells the last judgment.

60. MT: "And Joseph found favor in his [lord's] sight and he served him, and he appointed him over his house, and all that was his he gave into his hand. And it happened from the time that he appointed him over his house and over all that was his, that the Lord blessed the house of the Egyptian." The targums do not introduce major changes.

61. Ecclesiastical commentaries on Mt 24:45 or Lk 12:44 that cite Gen 39:4–5 or refer to Joseph, or commentaries on Gen 39:4–5 that cite Mt 24:45 or Lk 12:44, include Albertus Magnus, *Super Mt cap. XV–XXVIII* ad loc. (Opera Omnia 21/1, ed. B. Schmidt, p. 581); idem, *En. sec. part. Luc. (X–XXIV)* ad loc. (Opera Omnia 23, ed. A. Borgnet, p. 260); Grotius, *Operum theologicarum*, vol. 2, pt. 1, p. 235; Matthew Henry, *Commentary on the Whole Bible*, vol. 1, *Genesis to Deuteronomy* (New York/London/ Edinburgh: Fleming H. Revell, n.d.), p. 221; Calmet, *Commentarium*, vol. 7, p. 299; Wettstein, *Novum Testamentum Graecum*, vol. 1, p. 506; Ainsworth, *Annotations*, vol. 1, p. 196; Paul Gaechter, *Das Matthäus Evangelium: Ein Kommentar* (Innsbruck/Vienna/Munich: Trolia, 1963), p. 796; and Gnilka, *Matthäusevangelium*, vol. 2, p. 343 ("Prototyp des treuen Verwalters ist der ägyptische Josef, dessen Einsetzung in LXX Gn 39,4 mit ähnlich Worten beschrieben wird"). Ulrich Luz, *Das Evangelium nach Matthäus (Mt 18–25)* (EKKNT 1/3; Zurich/Neukirchen-Vluyn: Benziger/Neukirchener, 1997), p. 462, citing Gen 39:4; 41:37–46; and Ps 105:21, thinks that Mt 24:45 reminds one of "die biblische Josefsgeschichte." He cites as support J. Brenz, *In scriptum ... Matthaei de rebus gestis ... Jesu Christi commentarius* (Tübingen: Ulrici Morhardi, 1566), p. 726, to which I have not had access. Gen 39:4–5 is cited in the margins of Mt 24:45 (but not the Lukan parallel) in the Nestle-Aland versions of the Greek New Testament. According to C. F. Evans, *Saint Luke* (TPINTC; London/Philadelphia: SCM/Trinity Press International, 1990), p. 336, "Behind this language [in Lk 12:42] may lie the figure of Joseph, the Jewish model of the wise one (*phronimos*: prudent), who was set by Pharaoh over his household (*therapeia*, v. 42; cf. Gen. 45[16]; 41[33,39f.]; Ps. 105[21]), and who dispenses supplies (Gen 47[12–14], *sitometrein*, only there in the LXX)." Cf. B. T. D. Smith, *The Parables of the Synoptic Gospels: A Critical Study* (Cambridge: Cambridge University Press, 1937), p. 157: the one who "faithfully discharges his duties in the absence of his lord, will be rewarded by being given a position such as was Joseph's in Egypt (Gen. xxxix.4)."

Q 12:42   κατέστησεν   ... ἐπὶ τῆς οἰκετείας αὐτοῦ[62]
LXX Gen 39:4   κατέστησεν αὐτὸν ἐπὶ τοῦ οἴκου   αὐτοῦ[63]
LXX Gen 39:5   τὸ κατασταθῆναι αὐτὸν ἐπὶ τοῦ οἴκου   αὐτοῦ[64]

These are the only places in the Greek Bible where καθίστημι is followed by ἐπί + οἰκ-.[65] In addition, the following texts show us how naturally the language of Gen 39:4–5 (and related verses from the story of Joseph)[66] suggested itself to Jews writing about Joseph; indeed, the words of those verses became a sort of refrain in retellings of his story:

LXX Ps 104:21: The king "appointed him lord over his house (κατέστησεν αὐτὸν κύριον τοῦ οἴκου αὐτοῦ)."

Jub. 39:3: Potiphar "appointed (*ašēmo*) Joseph over all of his house (*diba kʷellu betu*)."

Jub. 40:7: Pharaoh made Joseph "ruler over all of his house (*diba kʷellu betu*)."

Philo, *Jos.* 37: Joseph "received authority over (ἐπί) his fellow-servants and the charge of the whole household (τῆς οἰκίας)."

Philo, *Jos.* 38: "appointed (καθίστατο) him steward of his household (τῆς οἰκίας)"

Philo, *Jos.* 117: "take charge of my house (οἰκίας) and the superintendence of all Egypt"

T. Jos. 2:1: "This chief officer of Pharaoh entrusted to me his household (τὸν οἶκον αὐτοῦ)."

T. Jos. 11:6: "He entrusted me with his household (τὸν οἶκον αὐτοῦ)."

Josephus, *Ant.* 2.39: Potiphar "committed the charge of his household (τὸν οἶκον) into his hands."

Jos. Asen. 4:7: "Pharaoh appointed (κατέστησεν) him ruler of all our land."

---

62. So Mt 24:45, which the IQP here prefers. Lk 12:42 has κατ αστήσει...ἐπὶ τῆς θερ απείας αὐτοῦ. θεραπεία (Mt: 0; Mk: 0; Lk: 2) is redactional in Lk 9:11 diff. Mk 6:34. Matthew's οἰκετεία is a NT *hapax legomenon*.

63. MT: יפקדהו על־ביתו.

64. MT: הפקיד אתו בביתו.

65. The nearest parallel is Ps 104:21. But there are also further parallels from the story of Joseph; see next note.

66. From the LXX:

> Gen 41:33: "Set him over (κατάστησον αὐτὸν ἐπί) the land of Egypt"
> Gen 41:40: "You shall be over my house (ἐπὶ τῷ οἴκῳ μου)."
> Gen 41:41: "I have set you over (καθίστημί σε ἐπί) all the land of Egypt."
> Gen 41:43: "He set him over (κατέστησεν αὐτὸν ἐφ') all the land of Egypt."
> Gen 45:8: "He has made me...lord of all his house (τοῦ οἴκου αὐτοῦ)."

Gen 41:33 is cited as a parallel to Lk 12:43–44 by Edward William Grinfield, *Scholia Hellenistica in Novum Testamentum* (London: Gulielmus Pickering, 1848), vol. 1, p. 151.

Jos. Asen. 20:9: Pharaoh "appointed (κατέστησεν) me chief over (ἐπί) the whole land of Egypt."

Acts 7:9–10: Pharaoh "appointed (κατέστησεν) him ruler over Egypt and over all his household (ἐφ᾽ ὅλον τὸν οἶκον αὐτοῦ)."[67]

There is also an Aramaic magic text that quotes Gen 39:4 and turns it into an incantation:

> In the name of Barqiel and in the name of Qedusiel, and in the name of Hasin Yah, may you give N son of N beauty and grace and mercy in the eyes of all those who see him, and his hand has found as a nest the riches of the people, and "Joseph found grace in his eyes, and he served him. And he made him overseer over his house, and all that he had he put into his hand."

This is immediately followed by part of the quotation from Gen 39:4 being repeated backwards: "And he served in his eyes grace Joseph and he found."[68] Clearly Joseph was well remembered as the servant who had been appointed over the entire house of first Potiphar and then Pharaoh.[69]

What about the rest of Q 12:42? For our purposes there are four key words: "the lord" (ὁ κύριος), "wise" (φρόνιμος),[70] "servant" (δοῦλος),[71] and "ration of grain" (τὸ σιτομέτριον).[72] Each of these terms has its counterpart in the traditions about Joseph. He is appointed by Potiphar, his "lord" (κύριος, LXX Gen 39:3–4, etc). He is particularly "wise" (φρόνιμος, LXX Gen 41:33, 39; in LXX Ps 104:21 we read that Joseph taught wisdom [σοφίσαι] to the elders of Egypt).[73] He is his lord's "servant" (παῖς,

---

67. This belongs to a very short summary of Joseph's career, which shows how central the event indicated was thought to be.

One may also observe that Daniel 2 is modeled in part upon the story of Joseph in Pharaoh's court (see John J. Collins, *Daniel: A Commentary on the Book of Daniel* [Hermeneia; Minneapolis: Fortress, 1993], pp. 39–40) and that there we read: "The king promoted Daniel . . . made him ruler over the whole province of Babylon and chief prefect over all the wise men of Babylon" (v. 48).

68. Naveh and Shaked, *Magic Spells and Formulae*, p. 236.

69. On the great popularity of the Joseph cycle, see Shalom Goldman, *The Wiles of Women/The Wiles of Men: Joseph and Potiphar's Wife in Ancient Near Eastern, Jewish, and Islamic Folklore* (Albany: SUNY Press, 1995).

70. φρόνιμος appears only here in Q (assuming its presence in Mt 7:24 is redactional).

71. δοῦλος appears in Mt 24:45 and 46 and in Lk 12:43, οἰκονόμος (Mt: 0; Mk: 0; Lk: 4) in Lk 12:42 (where it is redactional).

72. On the originality of σιτομέτριον (Lk 12:42) over τροφήν (Mt 24:45), see below, pp. 238–39.

73. Joseph's wisdom was proverbial: Artapanus, frag. 2 = Eusebius, *Praep. ev.* 9.23.1 (φρονήσει) (GCS 43,1, ed. K. Mras, p. 516); *Jub.* 40:5; Philo, *Jos.* 117 (φρονίμος); Josephus, *Ant.* 2.9 (φρονήσει); Acts 7:10; Tg. Onq. on Gen 37:3 ("he was a wise son"). See further Louis H. Feldman, *Josephus's Interpretation of the Bible* (Berkeley: University of California Press, 1998), pp. 346–51, who documents that Josephus "uses [of Joseph] no fewer than six different synonyms — σοφία, σύνεσις, δεξιότης, φρόνησις, φρόνημα, and λογισμός. It is the quality of φρόνησις, with its connotations of intelligence, sagacity, practical wisdom, and understanding, that Josephus ascribes to Joseph over and over again" (p. 347).

LXX Gen 39:17, 19; 41:12).[74] And it is Joseph who supplies the rations of grain for Egypt (Gen 41:53–57).

Regarding this last point, although the substantive τὸ σιτομέτριον ("ration of grain") is never used in the LXX, σῖτος ("grain") is one of the key words in the story of Joseph,[75] and the related verb, σιτομετρέω ("deal out rations of grain"), does appear in the LXX — on two occasions only, and in both Joseph is the subject (Gen 47:12, 14).[76] Artapanus, moreover, tells us that it was Joseph who discovered food rationing (μέτρα, frag. 2 *apud* Eusebius, *Praep. ev.* 9.23.3), and Q's δοῦναι/διδόναι + τὸ σιτομέτριον recalls expressions that appear in several accounts of Joseph's deeds:

LXX Gen 42:19: "your gift of grain (σιτοδοσίας)"

LXX Gen 42:33: "the gift of grain (σιτοδοσίας)"

Jos. Asen. 4:8: "He is giving grain (σιτοδοτεῖ) to the whole land."

Jos. Asen. 25:6: "He is king of the whole land of Egypt and savior and grain giver (σιτοδότης)."

Jos. Asen. 26:3: "I too will go to my grain giving (σιτοδοσίαν) and will give grain (δώσω σῖτον)."

Jos. Asen. 26:4: "Joseph went away to his grain giving (σιτοδοσίαν)."

Josephus, *Ant.* 2.124: Joseph "ordered his steward to give them their measures of grain (σῖτον…δοῦναι μεμετρημένον)."

Josephus, *Ant.* 2.189: "Joseph still gave them grain (σῖτον…διδόντος)."

The vocabulary is not all that Q 12:42–46 shares with the traditions about Joseph. The situation of the servant in Q 12:42–46 is similar to that of Joseph, for not only, as Grotius observed, does the history of Joseph in Genesis 39 show us a servant becoming an overseer,[77] but according to Gen 39:16, the lord's wife kept Joseph's garment "until his lord came (LXX: ἕως ἦλθεν ὁ κύριος)[78] home." Clearly Joseph faced temptation while his master was gone.[79] Moreover, *T. Jos.* 3:5–6 has the patriarch say this, "If my master was absent (ἀπεδήμει), I drank no wine; for three-day periods

---

74. Although the LXX uses παῖς of Joseph, the *Testament of Joseph* uses δοῦλος of him repeatedly: 1:5; 11:2, 3; 13:6, 7, 8; 15:2, 3. Cf. Philo, *Jos.* 37, 47, 51, 66.

75. LXX Gen 41:35, 49; 42:2, 3, 25, 26; 43:2; 44:2; 47:12, 13, 14. Cf. Aristobulus, frag. 2 *apud* Eusebius, *Praep. ev.* 9.23.4 (GCS 43,1, ed. K. Mras, p. 517); Philo, *Jos.* 180, 190, 197, 207, 212, 258; *Jos. Asen.* 1:3; 4:7; 25:5; 26:3, 4; Josephus, *Ant.* 2.77, 88, 90, 94, 95, etc.; *Sib. Or.* 11:27.

76. Grotius, *Operum theologicarum*, vol. 2, pt. 1, p. 408, sees the connection. Cf. Lagrange, *Saint Luc*, p. 369; and Bovon, *Lukas*, vol. 2, p. 334.

77. Grotius, *Operum theologicarum*, vol. 2, pt. 1, p. 235.

78. MT: עד־בוא אדניו. Cf. the formulation in Josephus, *Ant.* 2.55: ἐλθόντι δὲ τἀνδρί.

79. Tradition, expanding upon Gen 39:11, made this plain. Cf. Josephus, *Ant.* 2.45: on the day that Potiphar's wife tried to seduce Joseph, everyone else had gone to a public festival. *b. Soṭ.* 36b reports the same.

I would take no food but give it to the poor and the ill. I would awaken early and pray to the Lord, weeping over the Egyptian woman of Memphis because she annoyed me exceedingly and relentlessly." This presupposes that Joseph sometimes carried out his supervisory duties while his lord was away. This is precisely the situation in Q 12:42–46, where we find the phrase ἐλθὼν ὁ κύριος, which corresponds to the ἦλθεν ὁ κύριος of LXX Gen 39:16.[80]

If any doubt were left regarding the dependence of Q 12:42–46 upon the Joseph traditions, it is closed by Q 12:44. Here we read of the lord's returning and finding his servant doing well. Jesus declares, "I tell you that he will appoint him over all his possessions." This is a variation of the original declaration, "Who then is the faithful and wise servant whom the lord put over his household to give (them) food on time?" We find exactly the same sort of variation in Genesis 39. After we twice read that the master appointed Joseph over all of his house (39:4–5a), the text continues: "The blessing of the Lord was upon all that he had, in house or field." The LXX rendering of "all that he had" (MT: כל־אשר יש־לו) lines up neatly with our Q text:

> Q 12:44   ἐπὶ πᾶσιν τοῖς ὑπάρχουσιν αὐτοῦ
> LXX Gen 39:5b   ἐν πᾶσιν τοῖς ὑπάρχουσιν αὐτῷ

The phrase πᾶσιν τοῖς ὑπάρχουσιν occurs only one other place in the LXX. That one place is Jdt 8:10, where, unlike Gen 39:5b and Q 12:44, it is not prefaced by a preposition, not succeeded by a masculine pronoun, and not preceded by two occurrences of καθίστημι. And in any case the story of Judith 8 is and was, it goes without saying, not so readily called to mind as words from the celebrated and unforgettable account of Joseph fleeing his lord's wife.

The informed hearer of Q, who as a follower of Jesus is waiting for the returning master, should find in Joseph, as did the author of the *Testament of Joseph*, a role model[81] — especially as tradition emphasized the eschatological consequences of Joseph's faithful service. Joseph was a prominent illustration of the faithful servant who is eventually rewarded — as in Acts 7, where "Stephen recounts Joseph's story in order to introduce the theme of vindication by God."[82] Other parallels include *Jub.* 39:6 ("He did not surrender himself but he remembered . . . that there is a judgment of death

---

80. MT: עד־בוא אדניו.

81. Cf. Gnilka, *Matthäusevangelium*, vol. 2, p. 343. Cf. also 1 Macc 2:51–53; 4 Macc 2:2–4; Wisd 10:13–14; *T. Benj.* 3:1. Discussion in H. W. Hollander, *Joseph as an Ethical Model in the Testaments of the Twelve Patriarchs* (SVTP 6; Leiden: Brill, 1981).

82. H. Alan Brehm, "Vindicating the Rejected One: Stephen's Speech as a Critique of the Jewish Leaders," in *Early Christian Interpretation of the Scriptures of Israel: Investigations and Proposals* (ed. Craig A. Evans and James A. Sanders; JSNTSS 148; Sheffield: Sheffield Academic Press, 1997), p. 279.

which is decreed in heaven before the Lord Most High. And the sin is written concerning him in the eternal books always before the Lord"); Tg. Ps.-J.
on Gen 39:10 ("lest he be declared guilty with her on the day of the great
judgment in the world to come"); and *b. Yoma* 35b (Joseph "would not
listen to her — not to lie with her in this world nor to be with her in the
world to come").[83]

An informed hearer of Q 12:42–46 might also think that the servant
who says, "My lord is delayed," and then begins to beat others and eat and
drink (Q 12:45) is the antithesis of the good and trustworthy Joseph, for if
the faithless servant of Q 12:42–46 eats and drinks and gets drunk,[84] the
traditions about Joseph go beyond Genesis in telling us that he fasted and
refused to drink wine.[85] Philo has him tell his master's wife that he will not
be a drunkard (μεθύω, *Jos*. 45).[86]

Q 17:3–4 // Gen 4:15, 24 (?). In Mt 18:21–22, Peter asks Jesus,
"If my brother sins against me, how often should I forgive? As many
as seven times?" Jesus responds, "I say to you, not seven times, but
seventy-seven times." The Greek ἑβδομηκοντάκις ἑπτά, translated here as
"seventy-seven times,"[87] occurs also in LXX Gen 4:24: "If Cain is avenged
sevenfold [cf. Gen 4:15], truly Lamech ἑβδομηκοντάκις ἑπτάς " (for the
MT's שבעים ושבעה). Clearly Matthew is alluding to one of the classic texts
about vengeance. As T. W. Manson remarked, Gen 4:24 refers to a blood
feud "carried on without mercy and without limit. The reply of Jesus in v. 22
says: Just as in those old days there was no limit to hatred and vengeance,
so among Christians there is to be no limit to mercy and forgiveness."[88]
Naturally the commentators on Mt 18:21–22 have, through the centuries,
seen the point and cited Gen 4:24 as well as 15 ("Whoever kills Cain will
suffer a sevenfold vengeance").[89]

---

83. One might also draw a parallel with *Gen Rab.* 93:10, which applies another verse from
the story of Joseph, Gen 45:3, to the eschatological coming of God: "Joseph was the youngest
of the tribal ancestors, yet his brothers could not withstand his rebuke....How much more
then when the Holy One, blessed be he, comes and rebukes each man according to his deserts?"
84. Mt 24:49: ἐσθίῃ δὲ καὶ πίνῃ μετὰ τῶν μεθυόντων, "eats and drinks with the drunken"
    Lk 12:45: ἐσθίειν τε καὶ πίνειν καὶ μεθύσκεσθαι, "eat and drink and get drunk"
85. *T. Jos.* 3:4–5; 10:1.
86. Is it also relevant that the drunken servant beats other servants (Q 12:45) while tradition
tells us that Joseph was beaten (*T. Jos.* 2:3; 13:9; 14:1, 2 — all with τύπτω, the verb used in Q
12:45)?
87. This is probably the meaning, rather than "seventy times seven"; see Gundry, *Old
Testament*, p. 140.
88. T. W. Manson, *The Sayings of Jesus* (London: SCM, 1949), p. 212.
89. See, e.g., Tertullian, *Orat.* 7.3 (CCSL 1, p. 262); Origen, *Comm. Mt* ad loc. (GCS 40,
ed. E. Klostermann, p. 282); Hilary of Poitiers, *Comm. Mt* ad loc. (SC 258, ed. J. Doignon,
p. 84); Chromatius of Aquileia, *Tract LIX in Mt* ad Mt 18:22 (CCSL 9A, ed. R. Étaix and
J. Lemarié, p. 494); Paschasius Radbertus, *Exp. Mt libri XII (V–VIII)* ad Mt 18:22 (CCCM
56A, ed. B. Paulus, p. 899); Maldonatus, *Comentarii*, vol. 1, p. 250; Lapide, *Commentary*,
vol. 2, p. 310; Bengel, *Gnomon*, ad loc.; Alford, *Greek Testament*, vol. 1, p. 189; Schlatter,
Matthäus, p. 559; Gundry, *Old Testament*, p. 140; Gnilka, *Matthäusevangelium*, vol. 2, p. 145;

The Lukan parallel, which is more often than not thought to be closer than Matthew to Q,[90] is rather different: "And if the same person sins against you seven times a day, and turns back to you seven times and says, 'I repent,' you must forgive" (17:4). But this line also has directed some commentators to Gen 4:15 and 24.[91] One understands why. Lk 17:3–4 is about a "brother" (ἀδελφός — a key word in LXX Genesis 4; see vv. 2, 8 [*bis*], 9 [*bis*], 10, 11, 21) who "sins" (ἁμαρτάνω; cf. LXX Gen 4:7: "Have you not... sinned [ἥμαρτες]?");[92] and the sevenfold vengeance in Gen 4:15 and 24 has its antithesis in Q's sevenfold forgiveness, while the theme of forgiveness appears in LXX Gen 4:13 ("My crime is too great for me to be forgiven," ἀφεθῆναι) and in the targumic modifications of Gen 4:7 and 13. That Q 17:3–4 led at least one of its early auditors to Genesis 4 is plain from Matthew's redactional work.

There is, nonetheless, no room for confidence in the matter. For the number seven is linked with vengeance, forgiveness, and related themes in texts that do not clearly allude to Genesis 4. Lev 16:14, 19 (sevenfold sprinkling of blood for the sins of the people); 26:18 ("I will continue to punish you sevenfold for your sins"; cf. vv. 21, 24); 2 Βασ 12:6 (sevenfold restoration of stolen property); 4Q5111 frag. 35 (purification seven times); and *LAB* 6:6 (a span of seven days for repentance) are examples.

Q 17:26–27 // Genesis 6–9. As it was in "the days of Noah," so will it also be in the days of the Son of man, for "they were eating, drinking, marrying, being given in marriage, until the day Noah entered the ark and the flood came and took them all." These words, which take up the old biblical formula, "Just as it was... so" (כ... כאשר),[93] do not just refer to the story of Noah: they also borrow from the vocabulary of the LXX version:

Genesis 6–9	*Q 17:26–27*
εἰσῆλθεν + Νῶε + εἰς τὴν κιβωτόν, 7:7, 13	εἰσῆλθεν Νῶε εἰς τὴν κιβωτόν
ὁ κατακλυσμός, 7:6, 7, 10, etc.	ὁ κατακλυσμός

This correlation of the primeval history with the story of the end grows out of Jewish tradition, in which the flood is a prototype of the last judgment or the end of the world.[94]

Wiefel, *Matthäus*, p. 329; Luz, *Matthäus*, vol. 3, p. 62. Cf. Philoxenus, *Comm. Lk* frag. 56 (CSCO 392, Scriptores Syri 171, ed. J. W. Watt, p. 84).

90. See p. 66 herein.

91. Note, e.g., Ambrose, *Comm. Lk* 8.24 (SC 52, ed. G. Tissot, p. 110); and Crossan, *In Fragments*, p. 275.

92. This element of the story is emphasized in the targums on Gen 4:7 and Tg. Ps.-J. on 4:24.

93. See, e.g., Josh 3:7; 4:14, 23; Isa 11:16. One may also note that ὥσπερ...οὕτως occurs over twenty times in LXX Proverbs: 10:26; 11:22; 12:4; 17:3; 19:12; etc.

94. Isa 24:18; *Jub.* 20:5–6; *1 Enoch* 1–16; 67:10; 93:4 (the flood is "the first consummation"); Ecclus 16:7; 2 Macc 2:4; *LAB* 3:1–3, 9–10; 49:3; Josephus, *Ant.* 1.72–6; 2 Pet 2:5; 3:6–7; *2 En.* J 70:10; *Apoc. Adam* 3:3; *3 En.* 45:3; *Mek.* on Exod 18:1; *b. Sanh.* 108a.

Even though it goes its own way in focusing neither upon the sins of Noah's generation nor upon his righteousness but instead upon the unexpected nature of the past and the coming cataclysm, our saying presupposes the flood's use as an eschatological type and the traditional disparaging of Noah's generation.[95] Indeed, informed hearers might understand the activities of eating, drinking, and marrying to be other than morally neutral, for "eating and drinking" could carry pejorative connotations (as in Q itself: see 7:34), and "marrying and being given in marriage," when used of Noah's generation, could have brought to mind the many legends surrounding the giants of Gen 6:1–4 and their intercourse with human women. Theophylact wrote: "When the Antichrist comes, people will be giving themselves over to pleasure, reclining at weddings and feasts in a most arrogant manner, just as the giants did in the time of Noah."[96]

It is possible that Q 17:26–27 helps us with the section that follows it, for the nearby Q 17:34–35 contains the enigmatic assertion about one being taken (παραλαμβάνεται) and another left (ἀφίεται). This probably envisages, not the wicked being removed and condemned, but rather the righteous being taken to meet Jesus in the air. This is the dominant interpretation of the Matthean and Lukan texts in Christian history,[97] and the image of angels taking the saints to meet the returning Jesus has parallels elsewhere in early Christianity.[98] Moreover, ἀφίμι means "abandon" or "forsake" in Q 9:60 and 13:35. If this is the correct interpretation, then those left behind (ἀφίεται) are like the people who were left behind to perish in the flood.

There may be yet a further link with the Genesis narrative. Ancients well knew that, despite the wickedness of the era preceding the flood, there was one individual who "walked with God,"[99] namely, Enoch (Gen 5:21–24). Moreover, the cryptic expression of Gen 5:24, "God took him" (לקח

---

95. Noah's contemporaries — the rabbinic "generation of the flood" (דור המבול), who were excluded from the world to come (*m. Sanh.* 10:1) — were remembered as great sinners who did not foresee God's wrath (SB 1, pp. 961–64). See further p. 58.

96. *Comm. Mt* ad loc. (PG 123.420). Cf. Chrysostom, *Hom. Mt* 77.2 (PG 58.704); *Glossa Ordinaria* on Mt 24:38 (PG 114.162) and on Lk 17:27 (PG 114.321–22); Poole, *Commentary*, vol. 3, p. 117 ("a time of great security and debauchery"); Trapp, *Commentary*, 5:251 ("Their wits they had buried in their guts, their brains in their bellies"). Contrast John Calvin, "The Epistle of James," in *A Harmony of the Gospels Matthew, Mark and Luke, Volume III, and the Epistles of James and Jude* (ed. David W. Torrance and T. F. Torrance; Grand Rapids: Eerdmans, 1972), p. 101: "In this passage he is not directly condemning the intemperance of those times."

97. See, e.g., Theophylact, *Comm. Mt* ad loc. (PG 123.420); Bengel, *Gnomon*, ad loc.; John Wesley, *Explanatory Notes upon the New Testament* (New York: T. Mason and G. Lane, 1839), p. 81; Gnilka, *Matthäusevangelium*, vol. 2, p. 338. Contrast Dieter Zeller, *Kommentar zur Logienquelle* (SKKNT 21; Stuttgart: Katholisches Bibelwerk, 1984), p. 91, who thinks that the image is rather of the wicked being swept away in judgment (cf. Mt 24:39).

98. Cf. 1 Thess 4:17. Ecclesiastical commentators have sometimes associated this last verse with our text; see, e.g., Isho'dad of Merv, *Comm. 1 Thess* ad loc. (Hoarae Semiticae 11, ed. M. D. Gibson, p. 128).

99. The LXX has εὐηρέστησεν Ἐνὼχ τῷ θεῷ — Enoch was pleasing to God.

אֹתוֹ אֱלֹהִים; LXX: μετέθηκεν αὐτὸν ὁ θεός), was understood to mean that Enoch was transported to heaven.[100] So a hearer of Q 17:34–35, having just finished thinking about the generation of Noah, might draw yet another correlation between the beginning and the end: just as in Genesis God snatched from the midst of a wicked generation a righteous individual so that he escaped judgment, so shall it be in the end, when some will be lifted out of the eschatological flood, others left.

Q 17:28–29 (+ 31–32), 33 // Genesis 19. Following 17:27, Luke continues with a parallel passage about Lot. It should probably be assigned to Q:[101] the language is not especially Lukan,[102] Q is fond of coordinated sayings,[103] Noah and Lot and their generations were traditionally paired,[104] Q elsewhere refers to Sodom (10:12), and Matthew, who so often abbreviates, may similarly have omitted the second half of the double saying in Q 15:3–10 (the lost sheep and the lost coin). The cause of Matthew's omission can only be guessed. Perhaps he desired brevity in an already lengthy discourse (Matthew 24–25). Or perhaps he perceived tension with 11:23–4, where those in Sodom fare better than others. Or perhaps, if Matthew was copying a written Q, he was a victim of *homoioteleuton*: the end of Luke 17:29 is identical with the end of Luke 17:27. Or maybe the evangelist deemed only the flood story — of universal scope — truly parallel to the *parousia*. The disaster at Sodom was local.

Q 17:28–29, like Q 17:26–27, succinctly summarizes a story from Genesis with the vocabulary of the LXX:

Gen 19:24–26	Q 17:28–29
ἔβρεξειν…θεῖον καὶ πῦρ	ἔβρεξεν πῦρ καὶ θεῖον
ἐκ τοῦ οὐρανοῦ…	ἀπ' οὐρανοῦ…
πᾶσαν…πάντας…πάντα	πάντας

The transplanted language adds to the feeling of familiarity. One should note, however, the reversal of θεῖον καὶ πῦρ. Maybe Q's order, which is

---

100. See, e.g., *1 En.* 14:8; 70:1–3; *Jub.* 4:23; 10:17; Ecclus 49:14; Philo, *Mut. Nom.* 38; *LAB* 1:15–16; Heb 11:5; *Asc. Isa* eth. 9:9; Tg. Ps.-J. on Gen 5:24; etc. Contrast Tg. Onq. on Gen 5:24; *Gen Rab.* 25:1.

101. Review of opinion in Kloppenborg, *Q Parallels*, pp. 192–94. On the omission of this passage from the IQP text, see Kirk, *Composition*, p. 256, n. 398.

102. Jeremias, *Sprache*, p. 269.

103. E.g., Q 6:44 (figs and grapes); 7:33–34 (John the Baptist and the Son of man); 11:31–32 (Solomon and the queen of the South and Jonah and the Ninevites); 12:24–28 (ravens and lilies); 13:18–21 (mustard seed and leaven); 15:4–9 (lost sheep and lost coin); 17:34–5 (two on the couch, two at the mill).

104. *Jub.* 20:5; Wisd 10:3–8; 3 Macc 2:4–5; *T. Naph.* 3:4–5; Josephus, *Bell.* 5.566; 2 Pet 2:4–8; Jude 6–7; Irenaeus, *Adv. haer.* 4.36.3 (SC 100, ed. A. Rousseau, p. 888); Tertullian, *Apol.* 40 (CSEL 10, ed. H. Hoppe, p. 97); Eunomius, *Exp. fidei* 3 (OECT, ed. R. P. Vaggione, p. 154); *m. Sanh.* 10:3; etc. See further Dieter Lührmann, "Noah und Lot (Lk 17 26–29) — ein Nachtrag," *ZNW* 63 (1972), pp. 130–32; and Schlosser, "Les jours de Noé et Lot."

attested in other sources,[105] indicates nothing more than that πῦρ καὶ θεῖον sounded more natural because it had been heard more often than θεῖον καὶ πῦρ, just as "fire and brimstone" and "Sodom and Gomorrah" sound, because of the Authorized Version and its influence, more natural to speakers of English than "brimstone and fire" and "Gomorrah and Sodom." One may also wonder, however, whether "fire" is in first place because of Q's special interest in πῦρ. The Sayings Source after all begins with reiterated warnings of eschatological fire (3:9, 16, 17); indeed, the bringing together of Noah and Lot, who witnessed destruction by water and fire respectively, might prod a hearer to recall John's prophecy of a baptism of fire.

Q 17:28–29 features an interesting contrast between the activities remarked upon as typical of Noah's generation in Q 17:27 and those typical of the Sodomites in Q 17:28:

activities of Noah's generation	*activities of the people of Sodom*
ate and drank	ate and drank
married and given in marriage	bought and sold
	planted and built

Do these differences reflect exegetical tradition? Noah's generation was, as already noted, notorious for its unlawful marriages: the sons of God took for themselves wives from among human daughters (Gen 6:1–2). This may partly account for the text of Q 17:27 ("They were eating and drinking, marrying and being given in marriage"). In like manner, the statement that the people of Sodom "bought and sold" could allude to the tradition, based upon Ezek 16:49–50,[106] that the Sodomites were wealthy and stingy.[107]

What then about the remark that the Sodomites "planted and built" (ἐφύτευον, ᾠκοδόμουν)? The former verb at least reflects biblical tradition about Sodom, for Gen 19:25 says that the fire and brimstone destroyed "everything that grew in the ground," and Gen 13:10 says that Lot saw "that the plain of the Jordan was well watered everywhere like the garden of the Lord...this was before the Lord destroyed Sodom and Gomorrah." So Sodom was remembered as having been a "fruitful place,"[108] "rich in corn and well wooded and teeming with fruits" (Philo, *Abr.* 227), a place that, after the fire and sulphur fell from heaven, had "plants (φυτά) bearing

---

105. See Ps 11:6 and Ezek 38:22, both MT and LXX; also LXX Isa 30:33 a[1] and 3 Macc 2:5. Cf. Rev 14:10; 20:10; 21:8.

106. "This was the guilt of your sister Sodom: she and her daughters had pride, excess of food, and prosperous ease, but did not aid the poor and needy. They were haughty, and did abominable things before me; therefore I removed them when I saw it."

107. See, e.g., Josephus, *Ant.* 1.194–95; *m. 'Aboth* 5:10; Tg. Onq. on Gen 13:13; *Pirqe R. El.* 25. Cf. Eusebius in Aquinas, *Catena Aurea* ad loc.

108. *Apost. Const.* 8.12.22 (ed. F. X. Funk, p. 503).

fruit that does not ripen" (Wisd 10:7). According to Josephus, *Ant.* 1.195, Sodom yielded "neither plant (φυτόν) nor fruit whatsoever." Already Deut 29:22–23 underlines this memory: "The next generation ... will see the devastation of that land and the afflictions with which the Lord has afflicted it — all its soil burned out by sulfur and salt, nothing planted, nothing sprouting, unable to support any vegetation, like the destruction of Sodom and Gomorrah" (cf. Philo, *Abr.* 140).

Lk 17:31–32, which appears only in Luke, adds this: "On that day, anyone on the housetop who has belongings in the house must not come down to take them away; and likewise anyone in the field must not turn back (καὶ ὁ ἐν ἀγρῷ ὁμοίως μὴ ἐπιστρεψάτω εἰς τὰ ὀπίσω). Remember Lot's wife." This is sometimes assigned to Q.[109] Like Lk 9:62, it lifts the language of Gen 19:17: "Do not look back or stop anywhere in the plain."[110] But then it makes the allusion explicit by instructing readers to "remember Lot's wife."[111] No elaboration is offered. The text clearly assumes that hearers know about Lot and his wife and, having just been reminded about the fate of Sodom, will recall the tale that she was turned into a pillar of salt (Gen 19:23–26).

Gen 19:26 explains that Lot's wife became a pillar of salt because she "looked back." Later interpreters, as we have seen, often took this to mean that she sinned by remaining attached to her past.[112] In line with this, Q 17:33 warns that one must be willing to lose one's life. But there is also another lesson here associated with the Sodom traditions. Q 17:24 stresses that one needs to be prepared because the end will come unexpectedly, like lightning, and Irenaeus, *Adv. haer.* 4.36.3, interpreted Lk 17:26ff. in the light of this: the judgment of Sodom is a lesson to be ever vigilant, for the Son of man may return when not expected. In line with this, Lam 4:6, which seemingly conflates Genesis 19 with the story about Korah's sudden destruction (Num 16:21), speaks of Sodom being "overthrown in a moment." Further, Deut 32:32–35 mentions Sodom and Gomorrah and then speaks of doom coming swiftly. Already in Gen 19:22 the angel tells Lot to "hurry."

---

109. Survey of opinion in Kloppenborg, *Q Parallels*, p. 195. Some think 17:31 comes from Mk 13:15–16. Kloppenborg, *Formation of Q*, pp. 154–58, argues this, and also that 17:32 is Lukan redaction.

110. MT: אל־תביט אחריך ואל־תעמד בכל־הככר. LXX: μὴ περιβλέψῃς εἰς τὰ ὀπίσω μηδὲ στῇς ἐν πάσῃ τῇ περιχώρῳ.

111. Lot's wife is not named in the Bible, and she becomes "Idit" only in late tradition (*Pirqe R. El.* 25; *Tan. B. Wayyera* 8). Luke's designation of her as γυναικὸς Λώτ is the usual one: Philo, *Fug.* 121 (γυναῖκα Λώτ); Josephus, *Ant.* 1.203 (Λώτου γυνή); Tg. Neof. 1 on Gen 19:26 (אתתה דלוט); etc.

112. Philo, *Ebr.* 164; *Leg. all.* 3.213; *Quaest. Gen* 4.52; *1 Clem.* 11:1–2; Clement of Alexandria, *Prot.* 10(103) (SC 2, ed. C. Mondésert, pp. 171–72); Athanasius, *Vit. Ant.* 20.1 (SC 400, ed. G. J. M. Bartelink, p. 188); Augustine, *Civ. Dei* 10.8; 16.30 (CSEL 40, ed. E. Hoffmann, 1, p. 458, 2, pp. 180–81); Tg. Ps.-J. on Gen 19:26; Tg. Neof. 1 on Gen 19:26.

In Q the words about Lot may have been followed by Q 17:33:

Mt 10:39: "The one who finds his life will lose it, and the one who loses his life for my sake will find it," ὁ εὑρὼν τὴν ψυχὴν αὐτοῦ ἀπολέσει αὐτήν, καὶ ὁ ἀπολέσας τὴν ψυχὴν αὐτοῦ ἕνεκεν ἐμοῦ εὑρήσει αὐτήν

Lk 17:33: "Whoever seeks to gain his life will lose it, but whoever loses his life will preserve it," ὃς ἐὰν ζητήσῃ τὴν ψυχὴν αὐτοῦ περιποιήσασθαι ἀπολέσει αὐτήν, ὃς δ' ἂν ἀπολέσῃ ζῳογονήσει αὐτήν[113]

Perhaps this line is an extension of Q's intertextuality, for we find the following in the story of Lot and Sodom:

Gen 19:17: "Flee for your life" (MT: המלט על־נפשך; LXX: "Save your life," σῴζε τὴν σεαυτοῦ ψυχήν)

MT Gen 19:19: "You have shown me great kindness in saving my life" (להחיות את־נפשי); LXX: "You have magnified your righteousness, in what you do to me, so that my soul might live" (ζῆν τὴν ψυχήν μου)

Gen 19:20: "and my life will be saved" (MT: ותחי נפשי; LXX: ζήσεται ἡ ψυχή μου; LXX A adds "for your sake," ἕνεκέν σου; cf. Mt 10:39's ἕνεκεν ἐμοῦ)

Does the saying about finding and losing one's life (ψυχή) trail the mention of Lot's wife because Genesis 19 is precisely the story of one person finding life and another losing it?[114]

II. Synthesis

(i) Q makes use of the following passages from Genesis:

Gen 4:8–16 — Q 11:49–51 (explicit reference)
Gen 4:15, 24 — Q 17:3–4 (allusion?)
Genesis 6–9 — Q 17:26–27 (explicit reference)
Gen 15:1 — Q 6:23 (allusion)
Gen 19:1–29 — Q 3:5 (allusion?)
                         Q 10:12 (explicit reference)
                         Q 17:28–29 (+ 31–32), 33 (explicit reference)

---

113. The IQP reckons Matthew here closer to Q, for it prints: "The [[one who finds]] his life will lose it, and the [[one who]] loses his life [[for my sake]] will [[find]] it," ὁ [[εὑρὼν]] τὴν ψυχὴν αὐτοῦ [[ ]] ἀπολέσει αὐτήν, καὶ ὁ [[ ]] ἀπολέσ[[ας]] τὴν ψυχὴν αὐτοῦ [[ἕνεκεν ἐμοῦ εὑρ]]ήσει αὐτήν.

114. Cf. Lars Hartman, "Reading Luke 17,20–37," in *The Four Gospels 1992: Festschrift Frans Neirynck* (ed. F. Van Segbroeck et al.; BETL 100; Louvain: Louvain University Press/Peeters), vol. 2, pp. 1668–69; and M. Morgen, "Lc 17,20–37 et Lc 21,8–11.20.20–24: Arrièe-fond scripturaire," in *The Scriptures in the Gospels* (ed. C. M. Tuckett; BETL 131; Louvain: Louvain University Press/Peeters, 1997), p. 316. John Dominic Crossan, *In Fragments: The Aphorisms of Jesus* (San Francisco: Harper & Row, 1983), p. 275, notes the possibility of connecting our saying with Gen 19:17 but then goes on to argue that we do not know where the saying stood in Q: both Matthew and Luke moved it from its Q context.

Gen 19:17, 26 — Q 9:62 (allusion)
Genesis 39 — Q 12:42–46 (allusion)

Two of these references have to do with the story of Cain and Abel (Q 11:49–51; 17:3–4), one with the story of Noah and the flood (Q 17:26–27), one with the story of Abraham (Q 6:23), three or four with the story of Sodom and Gomorrah (Q 3:5; 9:61–62; 10:12; 17:28–29 [+ 31–32], 33), and one with the story of Joseph (Q 12:42–46). Even though several of these nine texts have to do with Sodom or Lot's wife, Q's handful of references span almost the entirety of Genesis. There is, however, one striking omission. Q nowhere has occasion to refer to the creation story or the legend of Adam and Eve (Genesis 1–3). So the Sayings Source, as opposed to Paul and the Gospel of Mark, has no Adam typology.

(ii) Q's references to Genesis are consistently in the service of eschatology. In Q 6:23, the pledge of descendants for Abraham from Gen 15:1 is turned into a promise of heavenly reward for the righteous. In Q 9:61–62, looking at the things behind, which is what Lot's wife foolishly did, disqualifies one for the kingdom of God. In Q 10:12, Sodom stands as a warning of coming judgment. In Q 11:49–51, the blood of Abel and all the martyrs will be avenged upon "this generation," which is the last generation. In Q 12:42–46, Joseph is the model for faithful servants waiting for their returning Lord. In Q 17:26–27, the tale of the flood is a foreshadowing of eschatological peril. So too is it with Q 17:28–29 (+ 31–32), 33: the fate of Sodom is a warning for those facing the possibility of eschatological judgment. So Q finds in Genesis a collection of patterns or types for the final days: the future consists largely of revised memories.

All this is in line with both Jewish and early Christian tradition, in which, as is well known, the *Urzeit* and the *Endzeit* are correlates: eschatology regularly recapitulates protology.[115] For instance, in Isa 54:9–10 and elsewhere, Deutero-Isaiah makes the days of Noah and the flood paradigmatic for the hopeful exiles.[116] *4 Ezra* 7:30 prophesies that "the world will be turned back to primeval silence for seven days, as it was at the first beginnings. . . . " 2 Pet 2:4–10, very much like Q, recalls the fallen giants of Genesis 6, the tale of Noah's flood, and the overthrow of Sodom and Gomorrah in order to encourage the godly and admonish the unrighteous. Rev 22:1–5 depicts the future as a return to Eden: just as God, in the beginning, created a paradise with a tree of life in it (Gen 2:9; 3:22, 24), so too will a second paradise be created with another tree of life (Rev 22:2); and just as God, in the be-

---

115. See Nils Alstrup Dahl, *Jesus in the Memory of the Early Church* (Minneapolis: Augsburg, 1976), pp. 120–40. For the evidence that "a *Urzeit /Endzeit* typology of the Eden stories was already developed in the sectarian writings of Qumran," see F. García Martínez, "Man and Woman: Halakhah Based upon Eden in the Dead Sea Scrolls," in *Paradise Interpreted: Representations of Biblical Paradise in Judaism and Christianity* (ed. Gerard P. Luttikhuizen; Leiden/Boston/Cologne: Brill, 1999), pp. 98–99.

116. David M. Gunn, "Deutero-Isaiah and the Flood," *JBL* 94 (1975), pp. 493–508.

ginning, set a river in Eden (Gen 2:10), so too will a river be set in the New Jerusalem of a new earth (Rev. 22:1). According to *Barn.* 6:13, God "make[s] the last things as the first." In all of these places, as in so many others, the primordial past is projected onto the future, whether for comfort or for warning. Thus Q's references to Genesis belong to a well-established tradition.

(iii) Q does not just generally reflect the common imaginative correlation of beginning and end: its particular readings are, in every case, paralleled elsewhere. Q 6:23's eschatological application of the word to Abraham in Gen 15:1 has a parallel in Tg. Neof. 1 and Tg. Ps.-J. on Gen 15:1. The use of Lot's wife in Q 9:62 (and 17:31–32 + 33) to illustrate the dire consequences of attachment to the past appears, as we have seen, several times in Philo as well as elsewhere. When Q 10:12 and 17:28–29 turn Sodom into an archetype of inhospitality and a parable of eschatological judgment, they are keeping company with Isa 1:9; Ezek 16:49–50; Wisd 19:13–14; *Jub.* 16:6; and a host of other texts. Q 11:49–51 probably presupposes several exegetical legends about Abel and Zechariah, including that the former was stoned (*Jub.* 4:31; etc.). The use of Joseph as a model of ethical behavior, whose service of his earthly lords fittingly symbolizes service of the heavenly Lord, was commonplace, so that in this respect at least Q 12:42–46 offers little new. And when Q 17:26–27 turns Noah's flood into a dire eschatological admonition, it is reproducing a Jewish topos.

(iv) The results of this chapter do not help us with the source criticism of Q. On Kloppenborg's analysis of Q's history, the allusions in Q 6:23 (Abraham) and 9:61–62 (Lot's wife) come from the first stage of Q while the allusions in Q 10:12 (Sodom); 11:49–51 (Abel); 12:42–46 (Joseph); 17:26–27 (Noah and the flood); and 17:28–29 (Sodom) come from Q's second stage. On my own hypothesis, Q 6:23 (Abraham) and 11:49–51 (Abel) come from Q^3, Q 9:61–62 (Lot's wife) and 10:12 (Sodom) from Q^1, and Q 12:42–46 (Joseph) and 17:26–27 (Noah and the flood), 28–29 (+ 31–32), 33 (Sodom and Lot's wife) from Q^2. So on neither reconstruction are the references to Genesis associated exclusively with any one stage of the tradition. The same can even be said for the three or four uses of the story of Sodom. This may imply either that something is wrong with the two theories or, as this writer thinks, that there was more theological and social continuity between the various phases of Q than some have imagined.[117]

---

117. On this topic see further F. Gerald Downing, "Word-Processing in the Ancient World: The Social Production and Performance of Q," *JSNT* 64 (1996), pp. 29–48.

Chapter 4

Prophets I

Isaiah

I. Texts and Analysis

Q 3:8 // Isa 51:1–2. John the Baptist, after demanding fruit worthy of repentance, warns his hearers that they should not presume to say to themselves, "We have Abraham as our father," because "God is able from these stones (λίθων) to raise up children to Abraham." Many exegetes have thought that this line alludes to Isaiah 51:1–2: "Look to the rock[1] from which you were hewn, and to the quarry from which you were dug. Look to Abraham your father and to Sarah who bore you; for he was but one when I called him, but I blessed him and made him many." Already Chrysostom brings the two texts together: the Baptist "reminds them of this prophecy [Isa 51:1–2], showing that if at the beginning he [God] made him [Abraham] a father, as marvelously as if he had made him so out of stones, it was possible for this now also to come to pass."[2] Dionysius bar Salibi says something similar,[3] and many other exegetes have made the connection. In our own time, for example, Joachim Jeremias, observing that Q's ἐγείρειν ἔκ τινος is a Semitism meaning "to cause to be born,"[4] wrote that the "strange image" of lifeless stones with "the power to bring forth men" is "based on Isa 51:1–2, where Abraham is compared with a rock, and his descendants with stones hewn out of the rock."[5]

---

1. MT: צור. LXX: τὴν στερεὰν πέτραν ("the solid rock"). Targum: טינרא.
2. *Hom. Mt* 11.3 (PG 57.195). Does Theophylact, *Comm. Mt* ad loc. (PG 123.176A-B) allude to Isa 51:1–2 when, in his commentary on Mt 3:9, he speaks of Sarah's womb being a "stone" (λίθος ἦν καὶ ἡ μήτρα τῆς Σάρρας διὰ τὴν στείρωσιν)?
3. Dionysius bar Salibi, *Commentarii in Evangelia* ad loc. (CSCO 77, Scriptores Syri 33, ed. J. Sedlacek and J.-B. Chabot, p. 151): "Just as Adam was created from dust and the wife of Lot became a pillar, so also says the prophet: Look to the rock from whence you were hewn, that is, to Abraham, and to the quarry from which you were dug, that is, to Sarah."
4. See, e.g., Deut 18:15, 18; 2 Sam 7:12; Acts 13:23.
5. *TDNT* 4 (1967), p. 271. Cf. Albertus Magnus, *Super Mt cap. I–XIV* ad loc. (Opera Omnia 21/1, ed. B. Schmidt, p. 73); Bonaventure, *Exp. Luc.* ad loc. (Opera Omnia 10, ed. A. C. Peltier, p. 288); Grotius, *Operum theologicarum*, vol. 2, pt. 1, p. 23; Lapide, *Commentary*, vol. 1, p. 115; Cornelius Jansen, *Tetrateuchus sive Commentarius in sancta Jesu Christi Euangelia* (Brussels: Francisci t'Serstevens, 1776), p. 23; Plummer, *Luke*, p. 90; Lagrange, *Saint Luc*, p. 107; R. Kratz, *EDNT* 2 (1991), p. 352; R. Alan Culpepper, "Luke," in *The New Inter-*

This interpretive verdict seems warranted by the facts. The notion of stones being turned into people is sufficiently startling as to call for some special explanation, and for this Isa 51:1–2 is to hand. It is true that the "strange image" of rocks giving birth to Israel appears also in Deut 32:18. There, however, God is the originating rock. It is only in Isa 51:1–2 and in texts dependent upon those two verses, such as *LAB* 23:4,[6] that Abraham is given this metaphorical role.[7]

That Q 3:8 alludes to Isa 51:1–2, which itself seemingly draws upon a traditional saying,[8] is supported by the recognition that John's words are an attack on the familiar notion of זכות, or "merit." The Q text entails that "one cannot... expect inherited *zekhut;* it has to be earned individually in the present time by each person in his or her own life; only then can s/he truly continue the spirit of Abraham."[9] While commentators have often enough seen this point, they have seemingly been unaware that the rabbinic idea of זכות was regularly associated not only with the fathers, Abraham, Isaac, and Jacob,[10] but also with rocks and mountains. *Mek.* on Exod 17:12 asks, "What did he [Moses] do? He turned to the deeds of the forefathers. For it is said: 'And they took a stone (אבן) and put it under him,' which refers to the deeds of the fathers." Tg. on Cant 2:8 contains the phrase "for the sake of the merits of their fathers, who are like the mountains (טורייא)."[11] Frg. Tg. P on Gen 49:26 reads: "The blessings of your father will be added

---

preter's Bible (Nashville: Abingdon, 1995), vol. 9, p. 84; Green, *Luke,* p. 176. William Dodd, *Commentary,* vol. 3, ad Mt 3:9, attributes this view to "many." Contrast Bovon, *Lukas,* vol. 1, p. 172, who rejects an allusion to Isa 51:1–2, at least on the level of Lukan redaction.

6. *LAB* 23:4: "Thus says the Lord: 'There was one rock from which I hewed out your father. The hewing-out of that rock bore two men whose names are Abraham and Nahor, and out of the hollowed-out place were born two women whose names are Sarah and Melcha, and they lived together across the river. And Abraham took Sarah, and Nahor took Melcha.' " Although this text is difficult, it is clearly a new version of Isa 51:1–2. See Howard Jacobson, *A Commentary on Pseudo-Philo's Liber Antiquitatum Biblicarum, with Latin Text and English Translation* (AGJU 31; Leiden/New York/Cologne: Brill, 1996), vol. 2, p. 713. On the pertinent rabbinic texts see below.

7. The reference to Abraham is also part of the reason for looking first to Jewish sources rather than to those Greco-Roman tales (such as those about the Gorgons) that recount the metamorphosis of human beings into stone.

8. See Ezek 33:24, and Moshe Greenberg, *Ezekiel 21–37* (AB 22A; New York: Doubleday, 1997), pp. 688–90. Here too a prophet rebukes people for putting their confidence in identification with Abraham.

9. Joan E. Taylor, *The Immerser: John the Baptist within Second Temple Judaism* (Grand Rapids/Cambridge, U.K.: Eerdmans, 1997), p. 130. See further R. Menahem, "A Jewish Commentary on the New Testament: A Sample Verse," *Immanuel* 21 (1987), pp. 43–54. There are of course Hebrew Bible parallels to this sort of warning; see, e.g., Jer 9:24–25 and the exposition of Richard C. Steiner, "Incomplete Circumcision in Egypt and Edom: Jeremiah (9:24–25) in the Light of Josephus and Jonckheere," *JBL* 118 (1999), pp. 497–505.

10. See A. Marmorstein, *The Doctrine of Merits in Old Rabbinical Literature* (New York: Ktav, 1968).

11. Jastrow, s.v., gives the meaning of the Aramaic טור as "mount, mountain," but it is closely related to the Hebrew צור, which means "rock" or "cliff" (so BDB, s.v., for biblical Hebrew, and Jastrow, s.v., for rabbinic Hebrew). For the equation of "rock" (צור) with "stone" (אבן; cf. Q's λίθων), see *Est Rab.* 7:10 (citing Isa 51:1).

to the blessings that Abraham and Isaac blessed you, they being likened unto mountains" (טווריא). And Tg. Neof. 1 on Num 23:9 interprets, "For from the top of the crags (צרים) I see him, from the hills I behold him," with reference to the merits of the patriarchs and matriarchs: "For I see this people being led and coming for the merits of the just fathers who are comparable to the mountains (טווריה), Abraham, Isaac, and Jacob, and for the merits of the just mothers who are comparable to the hills, Sarah, Rebekah, and Leah."[12] The point for us is that the link between rocks, mountains, and merit was made because Abraham, whose merit was so great, is a rock (צור) in Isa 51:1–2.[13] When God "saw Abraham who was going to arise, he said, 'Behold, I have found a rock (פטרא)[14] upon which to build and establish the world.' Therefore he named Abraham a rock" (צור, Isa 51:1; *Yalqut Shimon* on Num 23:9).[15]

The antithetical relationship between the rabbinic texts that associate Abraham with rocks or mountains and merit on the one hand and Q 3:8 on the other may be set forth in this way:

The rejected conviction (Isa 51:1–2)	*John the Baptist's declaration (Q 3:8)*
In the past God raised up	In the future God can raise up
from the rock that is Abraham	from "these stones" on the ground[16]
children to Abraham	children to Abraham
Israel benefits from its ancestor's merit	Israel does not benefit from its ancestor's merit

Although Isa 51:1–2 holds out the hope that Israel will be restored because of the promises to Abraham, John declares that descent from the patriarch does not necessarily mean inclusion in Israel.

One wonders whether the exegetical background of Q 3:8 may be further clarified by Tg. Neof. 1 on Deut 33:15. This speaks of a land "producing good fruits by the merits of our fathers — who are like the rocks (טווריא), Abraham, Isaac, and Jacob, and by the merits of the mothers, who are

---

12. Cf. Frg. Tg. P V and Ps.-J. on Num 23:9; also *Sifre* 353 on Deut 33:13–17 ("the patriarchs and matriarchs are called mountains and hills"); *Mek.* on Exod 17:9–10 ("the top" [Exod 17:10] refers to "the deeds of the fathers" and "the hill" [ibid.] refers to "the deeds of the mothers"); b. Roš. Haš. 11a ("leaping upon the mountains" [Mic 6:2] means "for the merit of the patriarchs" and "skipping upon the hills" [ibid.] means "for the merit of the matriarchs"); etc.

13. N. A. van Uchelen, "The Targumic Versions of Deuteronomy 33:15: Some Remarks on the Origin of a Traditional Exegesis," *JJS* 31 (1980), p. 199.

14. Cf. the use of *petra* (*bis*) in *LAB* 23:4, where Isa 51:1–2 is rewritten.

15. Cf. *Midr.* on Ps 53:4, where "the rock (צור) is removed out of his place" (Job 14:18) is taken to refer to Abraham's leaving the region of Sodom (Gen 20:1).

16. The suggestion that "these stones" adverts to the twelve stones planted in the Jordan in Josh 4:1–9 — Calmet, *Commentarium*, assigns this view to Anselm, Remig, and Pineda (the latter two unknown to me); cf. Paschasius Radbertus, *Exp. Mt* 2.3 (PG 120.159A-B); Rupert of Deutz, *Comm. Mt* ad loc. (PL 168.1361A); Geoffrey Babion (?), *En. Mt* ad Mt 3:8 (PG 162.1264A); Erasmus Schmid, *Opus sacrum posthumum* (Nuremberg: Michaelis Endteri, 1658), p. 55 — does not persuade, in part because we cannot be certain that Q mentioned the Jordan.

like the hills, Sarah, Rebekah, Rachel, and Leah."[17] This, just like Q 3:8, concerns the merit of the fathers, refers to bearing fruit, names Abraham, and (in dependence upon Isa 51:1–2) associates him with rocks. That this is not coincidence is strongly suggested by 1QIsa[a] 51:2, which, against the MT, has God say of Abraham, "I made him fruitful" (אפרהו): this shows that the link between Abraham as a rock and fruitfulness is ancient. So perhaps Q is rejecting the conventional thought that good fruit would be produced by the merits of Abraham, the rock from which Israel was hewn (Isa 51:1–2). In other words, Q 3:8 may not just provocatively use Isa 51:1–2 as a foil but may also set itself against a traditional exegesis of that passage and its equation of Abraham with a rock (צור). In this case Q 3:8 would turn that tradition on its head: far from the merit of Abraham guaranteeing good fruit, the divine ax is about to hack at the root of the trees (Q 3:9).

Q 6:20–23 // Isa 61:1–2. In their Matthean form, the four beatitudes found in Q 6:20–23 draw upon Isaiah 61.[18] "Blessed are the poor (πτωχοί) in spirit, for theirs is the kingdom of heaven" (5:3) is related to Isa 61:1: "The Spirit of the Lord is upon me, because the Lord has anointed me, to preach good news (εὐαγγελίσασθαι/לבשר) to the poor (πτωχοῖς/ענוים)" (in the synoptic tradition the object of εὐαγγελίζομαι is "the kingdom," βασιλεία; cf. Isa 52:7).[19] "Blessed are those who mourn (πενθοῦντες), for they will be comforted (παρακληθήσονται)" (5:4) alludes to Isa 61:2 ("to comfort all who mourn," παρακαλέσαι πάντας τοὺς πενθοῦντας/לנחם כל־אבלים). "Blessed are you when people revile you and persecute you and utter all kinds of evil against you falsely on my account; rejoice and be glad (ἀγαλλιᾶσθε)..." (5:11–12) has thematic parallels in Isa 61:3 and 10 (the latter of which uses, in the LXX, ἀγαλλιάσθω). Moreover, if Matthew's Jesus blesses the poor, those who mourn, and those who are hated, excluded, re-

---

17. Cf. Tg. Ps.-J. on Deut 33:14–15: "And from the abundance of fine fruits and produce that his land ripens by the gift of the sun, and from the abundance of the first fruits of the trees that his land produces at the beginning of each and every month, and from the abundance of the mountain tops, the birthright that the blessing of the fathers, who resemble the rocks (טוורייא), caused him to inherit, and from the abundance of the heights whose produce never ceases that the blessing of the matriarchs from eternity, who resemble the hills."

18. This is the consensus of the modern commentaries; see, e.g., Hühn, *Alttestamentlichen Citate*, p. 6; Theodor Zahn, *Das Evangelium des Matthäus* (Wuppertal: R. Brockhaus, 1984), p. 183; R. Guelich, "The Matthean Beatitudes: 'Entrance Requirements' or Eschatological Beatitudes?," *JBL* 95 (1976), pp. 415–34; and Hans Dieter Betz, *The Sermon on the Mount: A Commentary on the Sermon on the Mount, Including the Sermon on the Plain (Matthew 5:3–7:27 and Luke 6:20–49)* (Hermeneia; Minneapolis: Fortress, 1995), pp. 121, 123–24. Patristic and medieval commentators observe the links less frequently, but they are nonetheless obvious to Tertullian, *C. Marc.* 4.14 (PL 2.390B-C); cf. Eusebius, *Dem. ev.* 3.1 (88b-c); 9.10 (442a-d) (GCS 23, ed. I. A. Heikel, pp. 94, 426–27); idem, *Comm. Isa* 2.51 (GCS Eusebius 9, ed. J. Ziegler, pp. 379–80); idem, *Ecl. proph.* 4.32 (PG 22.1253D-56A); Jerome, *Comm. Mt* 1.425–32 (CCSL 77, p. 24); idem, *Comm. Isa* 17.53ff. (CCSL 73A, ed. M. Adriaen and F. Glorie, p. 707); Paschasius Radbertus, *Exp. Mt libri XII (I-IV)* ad Mt 5:3 (CCCM 56, ed. B. Paulus, p. 285); Bruno Astensius, *Comm. Lk* 1.15 (PL 165.370C).

19. 11QMelch 2:15–16 and 23–24 bring together words from Isa 52:7 and Isa 61:1–3.

proached, and spoken evil of, in Isaiah the poor and those who mourn are oppressed, despised, forsaken, and hated (Isa 60:14).

The strongest of the Isaian points of contact is with Mt 5:4, "Blessed are those who mourn for they will be comforted" (cf. Isa 61:2). But the corresponding beatitude in Luke is: "Blessed are you that weep now, for you will laugh" (6:21: μακάριοι οἱ κλαίοντες νῦν ὅτι γελάσετε). If Luke were reckoned original, then one might doubt that Q 6:20–23 alluded clearly or at all to Isaiah: one could ascribe the intertextuality to Matthean redaction.[20] Yet this, despite the opinion of some to the contrary, would probably be the wrong judgment. (*a*) The strongest contacts between Mt 5:3–12 and Isaiah 61 are in precisely those beatitudes that stood in Q. Matthew's other five beatitudes show no assimilation to Isaiah. (*b*) Apart from the beatitudes and Mt 11:5 (also from Q), Matthew nowhere else uses Isaiah 61. (*c*) Q 7:22 ("and good news is preached to the poor") is immediately followed by a beatitude, so Q indisputably drew upon the prophetic text about good news for the poor and further associated that text with the makarism form. (*d*) On the basis of word statistics one may suspect Luke's οἱ κλαίοντες νῦν of being redactional,[21] whereas neither Matthew's παρακαλέω nor πενθέω is clearly characteristic of the First Evangelist.[22] (*e*) Luke's first woe has παράκλησιν (6:24), his third woe πενθήσετε (6:25), which has been taken to suggest that the woes presuppose the Matthean form of Q 6:21, where both words occur.[23] This is a particularly strong argument if we assign Lk 6:24–26 to Lukan redaction or to Q^Lk and so keep them out of Q, for this would eliminate the possibility that Matthew revised Q 6:21 on the basis of the woes.

The allusive way in which Q 6:20–23 draws upon Isa 61:1–2 has a near parallel in 1QH 23(18):12–15: "You have opened a spr[ing] to rebuke the creature of clay for his way, the guilt of the one born of woman according

---

20. Doubt regarding the background of the pre-Matthean beatitudes in Isaiah 61 is expressed by Hubert Frankemölle, "Jesus als deuterojesajanischer Freudenbote? Zur Rezeption von Jes 52,7 und 61,1 im Neuen Testament, durch Jesus und in den Targumim," in *Jüdische Wurzeln christlicher Theologie* (BBB 116; Bodenheim: Philo, 1998), pp. 143–44. In "Die Makarismen (Mt 5,1–2; Lk 6,20–23): Motive und Umfang der redaktionellen Komposition," *BZ* 15 (1971), pp. 52–75, Frankemölle argues that the possible allusions to Isaiah come from Matthew, not Q. See also now the review of the discussion in Frans Neirynck, "Q 6,20b-21; 7,22 and Isaiah 61," in Tuckett, ed., *Scriptures in the Gospels*, pp. 27–64.

21. κλαίω: Mt: 2; Mk: 3; Lk: 10; νῦν: Mt: 4; Mk: 3; Lk: 14. γελάω, however, appears only twice in Luke, in 6:21 (a beatitude) and 6:25 (a woe).

22. παρακαλέω: with the sense of "comfort" this verb occurs again only in Mt 2:18, where it is from LXX A Jer 38:15. πενθέω: Mt: 2 (redactional in 9:15 diff. Mk 2:19); Mk: 0; Lk: 1.

23. "Although the language of παρακαλεῖν and παράκλησις is predominately Lucan in the NT (9–9–7 + 23; 0–0–2 + 4), it represents the reversal of ills in the context of the poverty/prosperity divide, cf. Luke 16:25, and never [other than Lk 6:24] the original prosperity of the rich as such. An explanation has to be found for the naturalness of the παρακαλεῖν usage in Matt 5:4 and the contrivedness of the παράκλησις usage in Luke 6:24. If the one [Lk 6:24] is an infelicitous echo of the other [Matthew's form] this explanation is found." So Catchpole, *Quest for Q*, p. 85, n. 85. See further Tuckett, *Q*, pp. 223–26.

to his deeds, to open the sp[rin]g of your truth to the creature whom you
have supported with your power, to [be,] according to your truth, a herald
(מבשר) [...] of your goodness, to proclaim to the poor (לבשר ענוים) the
abundance of your compassion... from the spring [... the bro]ken of spirit,
and the mourning (אבלים) to everlasting joy."[24] "To proclaim to the poor"
is taken straight from Isa 61:1 (לבשר ענוים), "mourning" is the key word
of Isa 61:2–3, appearing there three times (אבלים...אבלי...אבל), and the
theme of joy in 1QH 23(18):15 ("to everlasting joy") has its counterpart in
Isaiah's comment that "the oil of gladness" and "the mantle of praise" will
replace "mourning" and "a faint spirit."

This sort of allusive use of the beginning of Isaiah 61 appears also in
another Qumran text. Column 2 of 11QMelchizedek contains, as is well
known, a series of expressions from Isa 61:1–3:

11QMelch 2:4: the interpretation concerns "the captives (השבויים)"; cf. Isa
61:1 ("to proclaim liberty to the captives [לשבוים]")

11QMelch 2:6: "proclaim liberty to them (וקרא להמה דרור)"; cf. Isa 61:1
("to proclaim [לקרא] to the captives liberty [דרור]")

11QMelch 2:9: "year of favor (שנת הרצון)"; cf. Isa 61:2 ("the year [שנת] of
the Lord's favor [רצון]")

11QMelch 2:13: "will exact the ven[geance] [נקם)(ת] of E[l's] judgments"; cf.
Isa 61:2 ("the day of vengeance [נקם]")

11QMelch 2:17: "[all the mourners of Zion] ([אבילי ציון])"; cf. Isa 61:2–3
("to comfort all who mourn, to provide for those who mourn in Zion
[לאבלי ציון]")

11QMelch 2:18: "the herald (המבשר) i[s the one an]nointed (מ[שיח]) of the
spir[it] ([הרו[ח)"; cf. Isa 61:1 ("The spirit [רוח] of the Lord is upon me
because the Lord has anointed [משח] me; he has sent me to bring good
news [לבשר]")

11QMelch 2:20: "to comfo[rt the] m[ourners of Zion] ([לנח]ם א[בילי ציון])";
cf. Isa 61:2–3 ("to comfort all who mourn [לנחם כל־אבלים], to provide
for those who mourn in Zion [לאבלי ציון]")

Evidently those who wrote the Dead Sea Scrolls found it altogether natural
to create compositions with multiple allusions to the opening of Isaiah 61.[25]
Do Q's beatitudes then stand in some sort of exegetical tradition?

---

24. Apparently first observed by David Flusser, "Blessed Are the Poor in Spirit...," *IEJ* 10
(1960), pp. 1–13.

25. Johannes Zimmermann, *Messianische Texte aus Qumran: Königliche, priesterliche und
prophetische Messiasvorstellungen in den Schriftfunden von Qumran* (WUNT 104; Tübingen:
Mohr Siebeck, 1998), pp. 377–78, also sees allusions to Isa 61:1–3 in 4Q521. But aside from
the clear borrowing in frag. 2 12 ("to preach good news to the poor") and the mention of an
"anointed one" (משיחו) in line 1 (cf. Isa 61:1: "the Lord has anointed [משח] me"), his proposed
allusions are doubtful.

Those who discern an allusion to Isaiah 61 in Q 6:20–23 may think two things that those who miss the intertext may not think, things that contribute to the eschatology, Christology, and literary unity of Q. First, they may see the beatitudes as laying claim to the fulfillment of an eschatological prophecy: what Isaiah foresaw is now happening in Jesus' ministry (cf. Lk 4:16–21).[26] Indeed, they may hear in Jesus' words an implicit claim to be the anointed herald of Isaiah 61 (cf. again Lk 4:16–21): he is the expected prophet who comforts those who mourn and brings good news to the poor.

Second, they may associate Q 6:20–23 with Q 7:22, a text to which we shall revert in due course: here Jesus, in answering John's question about the coming one (Q 7:19; cf. 3:16), plainly alludes to Isaiah 61. That is, Q 6:20–23 may be read as anticipating Q 7:18–23, and Q 7:18–23 may be read as confirming the intertextual reading of Q 6:20–23. Understood thus, Q 6:20–23 belongs to a sequence in which Jesus' identity becomes increasingly clear:

Q 3:16–17: John prophesies one who is to come (Q 3:16).

Q 6:20–23: Jesus implicitly associates himself with Isaiah 61 and so insinuates that he is Isaiah's eschatological figure.

Q 7:18–23: Jesus, in answer to John's question whether he is the coming one, associates himself with Isaiah 61 and other texts and so implicitly equates the figure of John's expectation with the anointed prophet of Isa 61:1–2.

Q 13:34–35: Jesus explicitly identifies himself as "the one who comes" with reference to his eschatological return; so Jesus' earthly ministry is only the beginning of fulfillment (cf. Q 7:18–23); the Baptist's prophecy will be brought to completion when Jesus comes as the Son of man.[27]

Q 6:29–30 // Isa 50:6, 8. William Manson observed that Mt 5:39–40 shares several Greek words with LXX Isa 50:6, 8:[28]

Mt 5:39–40: "Do not resist (ἀντιστῆναι) an evildoer. But if anyone strikes (ῥαπίζει) you on the right cheek (σιαγόνα), turn (στρέψον) the other also; and if anyone wants to sue (κριθῆναι) you and take your coat, give your cloak as well.... To the one asking give (δός), and do not turn away from (ἀποστραφῇς) anyone who wants to borrow from you."

LXX Isa 50:6, 9: "I gave (δέδωκα) my back to scourges, my cheeks (σιαγό-νας) to slaps (ῥαπίσματα), and I did not turn away (ἀπέστρεψα) my face

---

26. For the eschatological interpretation of Isaiah 61, see James A. Sanders, "From Isaiah 61 to Luke 4," in *Christianity, Judaism and Other Greco-Roman Cults: Studies for Morton Smith at Sixty, Part One: New Testament* (ed. Jacob Neusner; SJLA 12; Leiden: Brill, 1975), pp. 75–106.

27. Q's interest in Isaiah 61 would be even more evident if one could assign Lk 4:18–19 to Q; but notwithstanding Tuckett, *Q*, pp. 226–37, the case for this is too uncertain to build upon.

28. William Manson, *Jesus the Messiah: The Synoptic Tradition of the Revelation of God in Christ: With Special Reference to Form-Criticism* (London: Hodder & Stoughton Ltd., 1943), pp. 30–32.

from the shame of spitting. . . . Who is the one who pleads (κρινόμενος)
for me? Let that one stand up against me (ἀντιστήτω). . . . You will wax
old as a garment (ἱμάτιον)."[29]

Manson claimed that the similarities had not "been noticed or discussed by
any critic or commentator." But earlier exegetes, such as Albertus Magnus,
John Trapp, and Matthew Poole, certainly did cite the parallel.[30] Further,
Gundry has since followed Manson, and Werner Grimm appears to have
espied the parallel independently.[31] The Nestle-Aland editions of the Greek
New Testament now cite the verse in the margin.

As Manson noted, ῥαπίζει, στρέψον, and κριθῆναι are absent from the
Lukan parallel, Lk 6:29–30, so he went on to argue either that Luke muted
the intertextual links or that Matthew multiplied them. One suspects, however, that both are true at the same time. On the one hand, Matthew's
ῥαπίζει and στρέψον, with parallels in Isaiah, are usually reckoned to repro-
duce Q,[32] in which case Luke dropped them. On the other hand, Matthew
in all likelihood was responsible for adding ἀντιστῆναι and κριθῆναι,[33]
words that increase the parallelism with Isaiah.[34] The upshot, then, is that
Q contained ῥαπίζω, σιαγών, στρέφω, δίδωμι, and ἱμάτιον, which together
could readily function as an allusion to Isa 50:6, 8, especially because the
text was popular with early Christians[35] and because the theme of Q 6:29–
30 is the same as Isa 50:6, 8: both are about insults being endured, not
returned. Furthermore, one of our two earliest commentators on Q, namely
Matthew, evidently perceived such an allusion and enhanced it.

How might an allusion to Isa 50:6, 8 augment the meaning of Q 6:29–
30? If one were familiar with traditions identifying Jesus as the suffering
servant of Deutero-Isaiah, then one could think that the disciple who turns

29. Isa 50:6 itself depends upon Lam 3:30 (see Willey, *Remember the Former Things*,
pp. 215–19), a text sometimes cited in discussions of Mt 5:39–40 and its Lukan parallel;
see, e.g., Johann Ludwig Wolzogen, *Commentarius in Evangelium Matthaei* (Opera Omnia;
Amsterdam: n.p., 1656), p. 227; and Wettstein, *Novum Testamentum Graecum*, vol. 1, p. 309.

30. Albertus Magnus, *Super Mt cap. I–XIV* ad loc. (Opera Omnia 21/1, ed. B. Schmidt,
p. 155); Poole, *Commentary*, vol. 3, p. 25; Trapp, *Commentary*, vol. 5, p. 77.

31. Gundry, *Old Testament*, pp. 72–73; Werner Grimm, *Weil Ich Dich Liebe: Die
Verkündigung Jesu und Deuterojesaja* (ANTJ; Bern/Frankfurt am Main: Herbert Lang/Peter
Lang, 1976), pp. 183–86. Note also Marshall, *Luke*, p. 260; and Catchpole, *Quest for Q*,
pp. 110–11.

32. According to the initial publication of the IQP, Q 6:29 had ῥαπίζ…σε εἰς τὴν σιαγόνα
[[ ]] στρέφον.

33. The former belongs to the introductory generalization (μὴ ἀντιστῆναι τῷ πονηρῷ) that
allows Matthew to assimilate the material to the traditional form in 5:21–26: old teaching/new
teaching/illustrations. See Ulrich Luz, *Matthew 1–7: A Commentary* (Minneapolis: Augsburg,
1989), pp. 323–24.

34. Isa 50:8 seems to envisage a court, as does Mt 5:40 ("and if anyone wants to sue you").
But as there is no Lukan parallel, one does not know whether this additional parallel belonged
to Q or was added by the First Evangelist.

35. See, e.g., Mt 26:67; *Barn.* 5:14; 6:1; *Gos. Pet.* 3(9); Justin, *1 Apol.* 38 (PTS 38, ed.
M. Marcovich, p. 86); *Sib. Or.* 8:290; Apollinarius of Laodicea, *Comm. Mt* frag. 138 (TU61,
ed. J. Reuss, p. 49). Cf. *Ps. Sol.* 10:2.

the other cheek when slapped is like Jesus. This idea of Jesus as an implicit model of faithful discipleship would be all the more obvious to those familiar with the passion traditions in which Jesus is struck, has his clothes taken from him, and does not resist (Mk 14:65; 15:29–32). Matthew, one may surmise, puts two and two together: the evangelist alludes to Isa 50:6 not only in the Sermon on the Mount but also in his passion narrative.[36] Thus he fuses the image of the suffering servant in Isa 50:6 with both master and disciple.[37]

Q 7:18–23 // Isa 26:18–19; 29:18–19; 35:5–6; 42:18; 61:1–2. This pericope has important links with several other Q texts. John's question whether Jesus is "the coming one" takes us back to 3:16–17, where the Baptist foresees "the one coming after me,"[38] and it anticipates 13:34, where Jesus' return is accompanied by the response, "Blessed is he who comes in the name of the Lord." Q 7:18–23 further harks back to 6:20–23, where Jesus' words allude to Isaiah 61. As the commentators recognize, in Q 7:18–23 Jesus answers John's question by referring to the activities of his own ministry, and in doing so he transforms several texts from Isaiah, most prominently Isa 35:5–6 and 61:1–2:[39]

---

36. Mt 26:67; cf. 27:30. Cf. Justin Martyr, *1 Apol.* 38 (PTS 38, ed. M. Marcovich, p. 86); Irenaeus, *Adv. haer.* 4.33.12 (Fontes Christiani 8/4, ed. N. Brox, p. 270); Jerome, *Comm. Mt* 4.1641–46 (CCSL 77, p. 269); Apollinarius of Laodicea, *Comm. Mt* frag. 138 (TU 61, ed. Joseph Reuss, p. 49); Ps.-Epiphanius, *Testim.* 48.3 (Texts and Translations 4, Early Christian Literature Series 1, ed. Robert V. Hotchkiss, p. 48); Isidore of Seville, *Fide cath. ex vet.* 13 (PLSuppl. 4.1832); Sedulius Scotus, *Kommentar zum Evangelium nach Matthäus, 11,2 bis Schluß* (ed. Bengt Löfstedt; Freiburg: Herder, 1991), p. 590; Gundry, *Old Testament*, p. 61; and most modern commentators.

37. Dale C. Allison Jr., "Anticipating the Passion: The Literary Reach of Matthew 26:47–27:56," *CBQ* 56 (1994), pp. 701–14. Although others would demur, it is not methodologically suspect to ask whether those who produced and heard Q knew more than the traditions preserved in Q, traditions we ourselves know only from other early Christian writings. For one thing, Q 7:18–23 and 10:13–15, with their references to deeds of Jesus otherwise not narrated in Q, assume familiarity with more stories than the Sayings Source relates. For another, we know that Matthew and Luke represent groups who knew and used Q alongside many other sayings and stories. There is also the good possibility that Q was never intended to be read verbatim but instead functioned as an aid for oral proclamation, so its message was never confined to what the Sayings Source explicitly says. For this possibility with regard to the *Shepherd of Hermas*, see Carolyn Osiek, "The Oral World of Early Christianity in Rome," in *Judaism and Christianity in First-Century Rome* (ed. Karl P. Donfried and Peter Richardson; Grand Rapids/Cambridge, U.K.: Eerdmans, 1998), pp. 151–72. Additional relevant observations in Susan Niditch, *Oral World and Written Word: Ancient Israelite Literature* (Louisville: Westminster/John Knox, 1996). See also n. 55 on p. 17.

38. Because there is no evidence that "the coming one" was a recognized title, the article in Q 7:19 ("*the* coming one") is probably anaphoric: it refers back to 3:16.

39. Cf. Isidore of Seville, *Fide cath. ex vet.* 10 (PLSuppl. 4.1831); Paschasius Radbertus, *Exp. Mt* 2.3 (PG 120.457D); Geoffrey Babion (?), *En. Mt* ad Mt 11:5 (PG 162.1349C); Bonaventure, *Exp. Luc.* ad loc. (Opera Omnia 10, ed. A. C. Peltier, pp. 400–401); Lucas Osiander, *Sacrorum Bibliorum* (Tübingen: Georgium, 1592), vol. 3, p. 48; Calvin, *Harmony*, vol. 2, p. 3 (Jesus "refers to one place in Isaiah 35, and to another in Isaiah 61"); Maldonatus, *Commentarii*, vol. 1, p. 158; Lapide, *Commentary*, vol. 2, pp. 51–52; Jansen, *Tetrateuchus*, p. 104; Poole, *Commentary*, vol. 3, p. 48; Zachary Pearce, *A Commentary on the Four Evangelists and the Acts of the Apostles* (London: E. Cox, 1777), vol. 1, p. 72; Dittmar, *Vetus*

the blind see

Q 7:22	τυφλοὶ ἀναβλέπουσιν
Isa 29:18	ὀφθαλμοὶ τυφλῶν βλέψονται, עיני עורים תראינה
Isa 35:5	ἀνοιχθήσονται ὀφθαλμοὶ τυφλῶν, תפקחנה עיני עורים
(Isa 42:7	ἀνοῖξαι ὀφθαλμοὺς τυφλῶν, (לפקח עינים עורות
Isa 42:18	οἱ τυφλοί ἀναβλέψατε ἰδεῖν, העורים הביטו לראות
Isa 61:1	τυφλοῖς ἀνάβλεψιν, ולאסורים פקח־קוח

the lame walk

Q 7:22	χωλοὶ περιπατοῦσιν
Isa 35:6[40]	ἁλεῖται ὡς ἔλαφος ὁ χωλός, ידלג כאיל פסח

the deaf hear

Q 7:22	κωφοὶ ἀκούουσιν
Isa 29:18	ἀκούσονται ... κωφοί, החרשים ... ושמעו
Isa 35:5	ὦτα κωφῶν ἀκούσονται, ואזני חרשים תפתחנה
Isa 42:18	οἱ κωφοί, ἀκούσατε, החרשים שמעו

the dead are raised

Q 7:22	νεκροὶ ἐγείρονται
Isa 26:19[41]	ἀναστήσονται οἱ νεκροί καὶ ἐγερθήσονται οἱ ἐν τοῖς μνημείοις, יחיו מתיך נבלתי יקומון

the poor have good news preached to them

Q 7:22	πτωχοὶ εὐαγγελίζονται
Isa 29:19	ἀγαλλιάσονται πτωχοί, ויספו ענוים
Isa 61:1	εὐαγγελίσασθαι πτωχοῖς, לבשר ענוים[42]

Testamentum, p. 12; Rudolf Pesch, *Jesu Ureigene Taten? Ein Beitrag zur Wunderfrage* (QD 52; Freiburg/Basel/Vienna: Herder, 1970), pp. 41–43 ("scheint Is 61,1 den Rahmen, Is 35,5–6 die Reihenfolge der Aufzählung zu bestimmen"); Cesare Marcheselli Casale, " 'Andate e annunciate a Giovanni ciò che udite e vedet' (Mt. 11,4; Lc. 7,22)," in *Testimonium Christi: Scritti in onore di Jacques Dupont* (Brescia: Paideia, 1985), pp. 264–69. Justin, *1 Apol.* 48.2 (PTS 38, ed. M. Marcovich, p. 99), already cites 35:6 as fulfilled in Jesus. Cf. Eusebius, *Ecl. proph.* 4.16 (PG 22.1220D–1221A); Ps.-Epiphanius, *Testim.* 4.3; 12.2; 33.2; 87.1 (Texts and Translations 4, Early Christian Literature Series 1, ed. Robert V. Hotchkiss, pp. 16, 32, 40, 66).

40. According to William L. Holladay, "Was Trito-Isaiah Deutero-Isaiah After All?," in *Writing and Reading the Scroll of Isaiah: Studies of an Interpretive Tradition* (VTSup 70,1; ed. Craig C. Broyles and Craig A. Evans; Leiden/New York/Cologne: Brill, 1997), vol. 1, pp. 214–15, 35:5–6 itself may rewrite Jer 31:8–9. For an eschatological reading of the verse, see *b. Sanh.* 91b, where it is linked with the resurrection of the dead.

41. This may itself grow out of a rewriting of Hos 13:14; see John Day, "The Dependence of Isaiah 26:13–27:11 on Hosea 13:4–14:10 and Its Relevance to Some Theories of the Redaction of the 'Isaiah Apocalypse,' " in Broyles and Evans, eds., *Writing and Reading the Scroll of Isaiah*, vol. 1, pp. 357–68. However one understands the original intent of Isa 26:29, it soon came to be understood as a prophecy of the resurrection on the last day, as in the targum: "You are he who brings alive the dead, you raise the bones of their bodies. All who were thrown in the dust will live and sing before you.... And the wicked to whom you have given might, and they transgressed against your Memra, you will hand over to Gehenna." See also below, p. 120.

42. Some would add that Q's "lepers are cleansed" has a parallel in Isa 35:8 ("A highway will be there, and it will be called the Holy Way; the unclean will not travel on it"), but surely this is a stretch. Others have been reminded of 2 Kgs 5:1–27 (the cure of Naaman's leprosy), especially as Elisha also raised the dead (2 Kgs 4:18–37; cf. Q 7:22).

Jesus' answer to John presupposes that hearers have knowledge of two things. One is that Jesus healed the blind, made the lame walk, and so on. But Q itself, which recounts from the store of early Christian miracle stories only the healing of the centurion's son (7:1–10) and an unmemorable exorcism (11:14), hardly justifies Jesus' extravagant response.[43] At this point, then, Q implies that it is part of a larger Jesus tradition.

The other thing Q 7:18–23 presupposes is the ability of hearers to recognize that Jesus' list of accomplishments alludes to verses from Isaiah, for it is only such recognition that allows the implicit argument to work:

Question	Is Jesus the coming one?
Answer	The blind see, the lame walk, etc.
Recognition	These deeds were prophesied by Isaiah.
Conclusion	Jesus is the fulfillment of scriptural/eschatological prophecy.

Without the scriptural intertexts, one cannot conclude that Jesus has brought "to pass those things that were prophesied long before" (Cyril of Alexandria).[44]

4Q521 2 + 4 ii 12 (4QMessianic Apocalypse) contains a fascinating parallel:

> [For the heav]ens and the earth will listen to his Messiah, [and all] that is in them will not turn away from the holy precepts. Be encouraged, you who are seeking the Lord in his service! Will you not, perhaps, encounter the Lord in it, all those who hope in their hearts? For the Lord will observe the devout, and call the just by name, and upon the poor he will place his spirit, and the faithful he will renew with his strength. For he will honor the devout upon the throne of eternal royalty, releasing prisoners, giving sight to the blind, lifting up those who are bowed down. Ever shall I cling to those who hope. In his mercy he will jud[ge,] and from no one will the fruit [of] good [deeds] be delayed, and the Lord will perform marvelous acts such as have not existed, just as he sa[id], for he will heal the badly wounded and will make the dead live, he will proclaim good news to the meek, give lavishly [to the needy], lead the exiled and enrich the hungry. [. . .] and all [. . .].

This list of eschatological expectations is based upon Psalm 146 with secondary influence from Isaiah, including Isa 61:1–2:[45]

"heaven and earth . . . and all that is in them (השׁ[מים והארץ...[וכל א[שר בם])"; cf. Ps 146:6 (the God of Jacob "made heaven and earth, the sea, and all that is in them [שמים וארץ...ואת־כל־אשר־בם]")

---

43. Lk 7:21 ("Jesus had just then cured many people of diseases, plagues, and evil spirits, and had given sight to many who were blind") is presumably redactional; see Bovon, *Lukas*, vol. 1, p. 370.

44. Cyril of Alexandria, *Comm. Lk* 37 (CSCO 70, Scriptores Syri 27, ed. J.-B. Chabot, p. 80).

45. The association is natural: Ps 146:7–8 says that "the Lord sets the prisoners (אסורים) free," and Isa 61:1–2 proclaims "liberty to the captives, release to the prisoners (אסורים)."

"the Lord . . . will call the righteous (צדיקם) by name"; cf. Ps 146:8 ("the Lord loves the righteous [צדיקם]")

"upon the throne of an eternal kingdom" (מלכות עד); cf. Ps 146:10 ("the Lord will reign forever [ימלך . . . לעולם]")

"releasing prisoners" (מתיר אסורים); cf. Ps 146:7 ("sets the prisoners free [מתיר אסורים]"); Isa 42:7 ("to bring out the prisoner [אסיר] from the dungeon"); and 61:1–2 ("to announce to the captives liberty and to the prisoners [לאסורים] freeing from the dark")

giving sight to the blind (פוקח עורים); cf. Ps 146:8 ("the Lord opens the eyes of the blind [פקח עורים]"); Isa 29:18 ("the eyes of the blind [עורים] will see"); 42:7 ("to open the eyes of the blind [לפקח עינים עורות]"); 42:18 ("you that are blind [העורים] look up and see"); 61:1–2 (see above)

"lifting up those who are bowed down (זוקף כ[פופים])"; cf. Ps 146:8 ("the Lord lifts up those who are bowed down [זקף כפופים]"); Isa 35:5–6 ("then the lame will leap like a deer")

"give life to the dead" (מתים יחיה); cf. Isa 26:19 ("your dead will live [יחיו מתיך]; their corpses will rise")

"preach good news to the poor" (ענוים יבשר); cf. Isa 61:1 ("bring good news to the oppressed [לבשר ענוים]")

"enrich the hungry" (רעב[ין]ם); cf. Ps 146:7 (God "gives food to the hungry [רעבים]")

The list in 4Q521 is far from identical with the recitation of Jesus' deeds in Q, and the parallels should not be exaggerated. Yet it does appear that phrases from Isa 61:1–2 were sometimes brought into connection with other scriptural sentences from Isaiah and elsewhere in order to paint a picture of the eschatological future. That is, like 11QMelchizedek,[46] 4Q521 shows us not only that Q's eschatological interpretation of Isa 61:1–2 was nothing new but, beyond that, that even the form of Q 7:22 — a short catalog of scriptural phrases construed as prophecies — must be judged conventional.[47] Perhaps indeed Tuckett is correct in suggesting that Q's beatitudes, like 4Q521, also conflate Isa 61 with Psalm 146, for in addition to its parallels with Isaiah 61 (see above), Q 6:20–23 shares with Psalm 146 the

---

46. See above, pp. 105–6, on Q 6:20–23.

47. Karl-Wilhelm Niebuhr, "4Q 521,2 II — Ein eschatologischer Psalm," in *Mogilany 1995: Papers on the Dead Sea Scrolls Offered in Memory of Aleksy Klawek* (ed. Z. J. Kapera; Qumranica Mogilanensia 15; Kraków: Enigma, 1998), pp. 151–68. Some have found the same phenomenon already in Ezra 9:8–9; see Harm W. M. van Grol, "Exegesis of the Exile — Exegesis of Scripture?" in de Moor, *Intertextuality in Ugarit and Israel*, pp. 49–61. Cf. J. G. McConville, "Ezra-Nehemiah and the Fulfillment of Prophecy," *VT* 36 (1986), pp. 205–24. From a later time, note the (noneschatological) use of three phrases from Psalm 146 in *b. Yoma* 35b; *ARN* A 16; and *Gen Rab.* 87:9.

beatitude form (v. 5; MT: אשרי; LXX: μακάριος), and both speak of God giving food to the hungry (v. 7; MT: לרעבים; LXX: πεινῶσιν).[48]

Three notes may be added. First, commentators have long remarked upon the absence from the list in Q 7:22–23 of the notion of vengeance, which is prominent in Isa 60:1 (cf. 11QMelch 2:13). Does this signal a contrast with the message of the Baptist? Perhaps. Once an intertext is established, differences may be as meaningful as similarities.[49] We must be cautious, however, for 4Q521, with its focus on God's salvific acts, makes the very same omission, and given the vengeance we find elsewhere in the scrolls, few presumably would want to make much of this.

Second, Mt 11:2 tells us that John's question was sent through disciples because John was in prison. Lk 7:18–20 agrees that John made the inquiry not directly but indirectly, through his disciples. What exactly stood in Q cannot be recovered. But even if Matthew's "in prison" (ἐν τῷ δεσμωτηρίῳ) is redactional (which is hardly obvious),[50] the fact that John communicates only through intermediaries and that Christian tradition put John in prison during Jesus' ministry (Mk 1:14) might have encouraged hearers of Q to assume what is explicit in Matthew: John was in prison when he sent to Jesus. If so, it is striking that release of captives is featured in Isa 61:1 ("liberty to the captives and release to the prisoners")[51] — and that our text passes over this in silence. An astute audience, one with a knowledge of both Isa 61:1–2 and John's fate, might take the omission to be prescient: Jesus did not set John free from prison.

Third, Q's allusions to Isa 61:1–2 are followed immediately by a passage whose climax is the identification of John the Baptist with Elijah (Q 7:24–27). One wonders whether this juxtaposition might not have a polemical edge. Not only has John J. Collins argued that the anointed figure of 4Q521, who fulfills the expectations of Isaiah 61, is Elijah or an Elijah-like figure,[52] but Tg. Ps.-J. on Num 25:12 has this: "In an oath I [God] say to him [Phinehas = Elijah] in my name: Behold, I have decreed to him my covenant of peace (שלם), and I will make him a messenger of the covenant (מלאך קיים), and he will live eternally[53] to announce the redemption (למבשרא גאולתא) at the end of days." This clearly borrows from Mal 3:1

---

48. Tuckett, "Scripture in Q," pp. 23–25.

49. See pp. 29–37, on Q 6:27–45 and Leviticus 19.

50. δεσμωτήριον is a Matthean *hapax legomenon*.

51. Cf. 4Q521 and 11QMelch 2:4, 6. The LXX renders the MT's ולאסורים פקח־קוח with καὶ τυφλοῖς ἀνάβλεψιν. The Hebrew belongs to synonymous parallelism: לקרא לשבים דרור ולאסורים פקח־קוח, "to announce to the captives liberty and to the prisoners freeing from the dark" (cf. Isa 42:7 and the targum on Isa 61:1). LXX readers, on the other hand, can see two different forecasts — liberty to the captives and sight for the blind. See the discussion of James A. Sanders, "From Isaiah 61 to Luke 4," pp. 81–85. The LXX nonetheless retains the image of prisoners being freed.

52. John J. Collins, "The Works of the Messiah," *DSD* 1 (1993), pp. 1–15.

53. Recall the story of Elijah's ascension: 2 Kings 2.

("I am sending my messenger [identified in 4:5–6 with Elijah]... the messenger of the covenant [וּמַלְאַךְ הַבְּרִית]"). But it appears equally to allude to Deutero-Isaiah's eschatological messenger who brings good news (Isa 52:7: "the messenger who announces peace [שָׁלוֹם], who brings good news [מְבַשֵּׂר טוֹב], who announces salvation"; 61:1: "the Lord has sent me to bring good news [לְבַשֵּׂר]"). If then in some circles Elijah was identified with Deutero-Isaiah's herald of salvation, Q 7:19–27, which on the contrary differentiates the two by identifying Jesus's ministry with prophecies from Isaiah and John the Baptist with Malachi's messenger, might be a statement of exegetical dissent: the eschatological Elijah and the anointed prophet of Isaiah 61 are two separate figures, not one.

Q 10:15 // Isa 14:13, 15. "And you, Capernaum, will you be exalted to heaven? You shall be brought to Hades" appears to be built upon Isa 14:13, 15 ("You said in your heart, 'I will ascend to heaven.... But you are brought down to Sheol' "):[54]

MT Isaiah

אַתָּה אָמַרְתָּ בִלְבָבְךָ

הַשָּׁמַיִם אֶעֱלֶה...

אַךְ אֶל־שְׁאוֹל תּוּרָד

Q	LXX Isaiah
καὶ σύ, Καφαρναούμ,	σὺ δὲ εἶπας ἐν τῇ διανοίᾳ σου
μὴ ἕως οὐρανοῦ ὑψωθήσῃ;	εἰς τὸν οὐρανὸν ἀναβήσομαι ...
ἕως [[τοῦ]] ᾅδου καταβήσῃ	νῦν δὲ εἰς ᾅδου καταβήσῃ

Targum Isaiah

וְאַתְּ אֲמַרְתְּ בְּלִיבָּךְ

לְרוֹמָא אִיסַק...

בְּרַם לִשְׁאוֹל תִּיתְחַת

So far from scaling the heights, Jesus' own city is poised for eschatological judgment. We may have here little more than a borrowing of a familiar figure of speech, although recognition of the scriptural intertext would enhance the solemnity.[55] But there might also be more.

(i) George Nickelsburg has documented an exegetical tradition that applies the language of Isa 14:12–17 (sometimes in conjunction with allusions

---

54. Cf. Albertus Magnus, *Super Mt cap. I–XIV* ad Mt 11:23 (Opera Omnia, ed. B. Schmidt, p. 357); Nicholas of Gorran, *In quatuor evangelia commentarius*, p. 35; Grotius, *Operum theologicarum*, vol. 2, pt. 1, p. 121; Schlatter, *Matthäus*, p. 379; Gundry, *Old Testament*, p. 81; R. T. France, *Jesus and the Old Testament: His Application of Old Testament Passages to Himself and His Mission* (London: Tyndale, 1971), pp. 74, 241; David Hill, *The Gospel of Matthew* (NCB; London: Oliphants, 1977), p. 203; Daniel J. Harrington, *The Gospel of Matthew* (Sacra Pagina 1; Collegeville, Minn.: Michael Glazier, 1991), pp. 164–65; Donald A. Hagner, *Matthew 1–13* (WBC 22A; Dallas: Word, 1993), p. 314; Catchpole, *Quest for Q*, p. 231; Schürmann, *Lukasevangelium*, vol. 2, p. 80; Tuckett, *Q*, p. 423; Pierre Grelot, *Jésus de Nazareth, Christ et Seigneur* (LD 167; Paris: Cerf, 1997), p. 293; Luz, *Matthäus*, vol. 2, p. 193; Keener, *Matthew*, p. 344.

55. Cf. the use of the same passage in *Ps. Sol.* 1:5.

to Isaiah 52–53) to the opponents of the righteous: Dan 8:9–10; 11:36 (Antiochus Epiphanes); 2 Maccabees 9 (Antiochus Epiphanes); Wisd 4:18–19 (oppressors of the righteous); and *1 Enoch* 46 (the kings and mighty of the earth).[56] To these examples one may add *Ps. Sol.* 1:5 (the Gentile enemies of Jerusalem);[57] *Sib. Or.* 5:72 (Egypt);[58] *Apoc. Elijah* 4:11 (Antichrist);[59] and our verse, Q 10:15 (those who reject the missionaries of Jesus).[60]

(ii) Perhaps already by the first century, as for Milton and so many others later on, Isa 14:12ff. could be read as depicting the fall of Satan.[61] A reader knowing this exegetical tradition might have found even more rhetorical force in Q 10:15: Capernaum's fate is the fate of Lucifer. One may compare the later use of Isa 14:13–15 in *Gk. Apoc. Ezra* 4:29–33, where it is said of the Antichrist, whose "eye is like the Daystar" (Isa 14:12), "He has been exalted to heaven: to hell shall he descend."[62]

(iii) Luke's version of Q 10:15 is closely followed by Lk 10:18, which contains a second allusion to Isaiah 14.[63] When Luke speaks of Satan's falling from heaven (ἐκ τοῦ οὐρανοῦ πεσόντα), the commentators are reminded of Isa 14:12 (LXX: ἐξέπεσεν ἐκ τοῦ οὐρανοῦ; MT: נפלה משמים), which later readers, as noted, often referred to the devil. Did Luke recognize the intertext behind Q 10:15 and bring it into close association with a second tradition (Lk 10:18) tied to the same intertext?

(iv) Later on Isa 14:13–15 came to be associated with the similar Ezek 28:2 (e.g., Hippolytus and the Talmud).[64] One could speculate that since the latter is addressed to the king of Tyre, Q 10:13–14, with its mention of Tyre, naturally led to Q 10:15, with its allusion to Isa 14:13–15. In line with this, Q's choice of ὑψωθήσῃ as opposed to the LXX's ἀναβήσομαι could be explained as influence from LXX Ezek 28:2, 5.[65]

Q 10:23–24 // Isa 6:9–10. Jesus blesses those who see and hear what

---

56. George W. E. Nickelsburg Jr., *Resurrection, Immortality, and Eternal Life in Intertestamental Judaism* (HTS 26; Cambridge, Mass.: Harvard University Press, 1972).

57. ὑψώθησαν ἕως τῶν ἄστρων, εἶπαν οὐ μὴ πέσωσιν.

58. ἐξ ἄστρων πέπτωκας, ἐς οὐρανὸν οὐκ ἀναβήσῃ.

59. "You have fallen from heaven like the morning stars" (ⲁⲕ2ⲉ ⲉⲃⲟⲗ 2ⲛ ⲧⲡⲉ ⲛⲑⲉ ⲙⲙⲥⲓⲟⲩ ⲛ2ⲧⲟⲟⲩⲉ; cf. Job 38:7). Cf. *Gk. Apoc. Ezra* 4:32, quoted below.

60. Perhaps already the oracle against Edom in Obad 3–4 depends upon Isa 14:13–15.

61. See *LAE* 15:3; *2 Enoch* 28–30; cf. *Gk. Apoc. Ezra* 4:32; Origen, *De prin.* 1.5.5 (GCS 22, ed. P. Koetschau, p. 77); Augustine, *Civ. Dei* 11.15 (CSEL 40/1, ed. E. Hoffmann, p. 534: Isaiah "denotes the Devil in the figurative person of the Babylonian emperor"); Milton, *Paradise Lost*, bk. 1. For relevant rabbinic texts, see A. Puig Tàrrech, "Lc 10,18: La visió de la Caiguda de Satanàs," *Revista Catalana de Teologia* 3 (1978), pp. 227–30.

62. ἕως τοῦ οὐρανοῦ ὑψώθη, ἕως τοῦ ἅδου καταβήσει.

63. Tàrrech, "Lc 10,18," pp. 231–36. On p. 218 he observes that Origen and Jerome already catch the allusion.

64. Hippolytus, *Antichr.* 53 (GCS 1, 2, ed. H. Achelis, p. 35); *b. Ḥul.* 89a. For the argument that the association belongs already to the intertestamental period, see Joseph Jensen, "Helel Ben Shahar (Isaiah 14:12–15) in Bible and Tradition," in Broyles and Evans, eds., *Writing and Reading the Scroll of Isaiah*, pp. 339–56.

65. Tuckett, "Scripture in Q," pp. 17–18, suggests instead influence from LXX Isa 52:13.

many prophets and kings desired to see and did not see and to hear and did not hear. For Heinz Schürmann, these words gain force if read in the light of Isa 6:9–10: "Go to this people and say, 'Keep listening, but do not comprehend; keep looking, but do not understand. Make the mind of this people dull, and stop their ears, and shut their eyes, so that they may not look with their eyes, and listen with their ears, and comprehend with their minds.' "[66] There are some verbal links that involve more than just isolated words:

Q

οἱ ὀφθαλμοί οἱ βλέποντες
βλέποντες ἃ βλέπετε
καὶ οὐκ εἶδαν
ἀκοῦσαι ἃ ἀκούετε καὶ οὐκ ἤκουσαν

LXX Isaiah

ἀκούσετε καὶ οὐ μὴ συνῆτε
βλέποντες βλέψετε
καὶ οὐ μὴ ἴδητε
ἴδωσιν τοῖς ὀφθαλμοῖς

Also in favor of an allusion here is the popularity of Isa 6:9–10: this was a well-known text in the early Church.[67] So maybe Q 10:23–24 is contrasting those privileged to see and understand the ministry of Jesus with those denounced long ago by Isaiah as unable to see and understand.

This possibility is bolstered by Matthew's redactional activity in chapter 13. Following the parable of the sower (Mt 13:3–9 = Mk 4:3–9), he makes three alterations to his source, Mk 10:10–12. He first inserts a saying from Mk 4:25 ("For to those who have, more will be given…," Mt 13:12). Then he expands the cryptic quotation of Isa 6:9–10 in Mk 4:12 ("They may indeed see, but not perceive, and may indeed hear, but not understand, so that they may not turn again and be forgiven") by following it with a formal quotation: "With them indeed is fulfilled the prophecy of Isaiah that says: 'You will indeed listen, but never understand…' " (Mt 13:12–15). Lastly, he subjoins Q 10:23–24 to the quotation of Isa 6:9–10: "But blessed are your eyes…" (Mt 13:16–17). It seems that at least Matthew thought that Q 10:23–24 and Isa 6:9–10 belong together.[68]

Q 12:33–34 // Isa 51:8 (?). Q probably had something close to Matthew 6:19–21: "Do not store up for yourselves treasures on the earth, where moth (σής) and βρῶσις consume and where thieves break in and steal;

---

66. *Lukasevangelium*, vol. 2, p. 120. Hodgson, "On the Gattung of Q," p. 81, also cites the parallel (as well as Isa 29:14).

67. Craig A. Evans, *To See and Not Perceive: Isaiah 6.9–10 in Early Jewish and Christian Interpretation* (JSNTSup 64; Sheffield: JSOT Press, 1989). Cf. Mt 13:14–15; Mk 4:12; Lk 8:10; Jn 12:40; Acts 28:26–27; Justin, *Dial.* 12.2; 33.5 (PTS 47, ed. M. Marcovich, pp. 89–90, 124).

68. Matthew's juxtaposition may explain why Eusebius, *Comm. Isa* 42 (GCS Eusebius 9, ed. J. Ziegler, p. 44), quotes Mt 13:16 = Q 10:23 in his exposition of Isa 6:9–10.

but store up for yourselves treasures in heaven, where neither moth (σής)
nor βρῶσις consumes."[69] The word left untranslated, βρῶσις, is difficult.
It usually means "eating" (Rom 14:17) or "food" (Jn 6:27). "Decay" is
also an attested meaning (LSJ, s.v.). So many, encouraged by the parallel
in Jas 5:2–3, where "moth" and "rust" (ἰός) appear together, translate the
βρῶσις of Mt 6:19–20 with "rust." But in LXX Mal 3:11, the word means
"locust" or "grasshopper,"[70] and in Ep. Jer 10 v.l., βρῶσις is found with
ἰός, and hendiadys is doubtful.[71] Hence it seems no less likely that Q 12:33,
like its parallel in *Gos. Thom.* 76,[72] refers to two different sorts of insects
devouring costly textiles (cf. Q 12:27–28) — "where moth and devouring
insect consume." In this case, one must ask if there is an allusion to Isa
51:8, where there is likewise a contrast between something that endures
and something that perishes:

> MT Isa 51:8: "For the moth will eat them up like a garment, and the worm
> will eat them like wool (כי כבגד יאכלם עש וכצמר יאכלם סס);[73] but my
> deliverance will be forever, and my salvation to all generations."

> Tg. Isa 51:8: "They are like a garment which the moth eats, and like wool
> which the wood-worm [or: rot] attacks (ארי כלבושא דאכיל ליה עשא
> וכעמרא דאחיד ביה רקבא); but my virtue will be forever, and my salvation
> to all generations."

> LXX Isa 51:8: "For (they are) just as a garment that will be eaten up by time,
> and just as wool will be eaten up by a moth (ὡς γὰρ ἱμάτιον βρωθήσεται
> ὑπὸ χρόνου καὶ ὡς ἔρια βρωθήσεται ὑπὸ σητός); but my righteousness
> will be forever, and my salvation for all generations."

Three things are of interest. The first is that the word pair in the MT matches
the word pair in Q 12:33–34 if Q's βρῶσις is an insect. The second is
the curious fact that the ambiguity of the Greek βρῶσις is matched by the
ambiguity of the targum's רקבא, which according to Jastrow, s.v., can mean
either "wood-worm" or "rot, rust." The third is that although the devouring
pair in the LXX is "time" and "moth," the vocabulary nonetheless recalls Q:

LXX	βρωθήσεται (bis)	σητός
Q	βρῶσις	σής

69. So IQP; see W. Pesch, "Zur Exegese von Mt 6:19–21 and Lk 12,33–34," *Bib* 41 (1960),
pp. 356–61.

70. MT Mal 3:11: "I will rebuke the locust (אכל — 'devourer') for you, so that it will not
destroy the produce of your soil." The targum translates אכל with מחבלא, "destroyer."

71. So BAGD, s.v., βρῶσις. The text reads: "gods of silver and gold and wood that cannot
save themselves from rust (ἰοῦ) and devouring insect (βρωμάτων)."

72. "You also seek for the treasure that fails not, which endures, there where no moth
(ⲭⲟⲟⲗⲉⲥ) comes near to devour and no worm (ϥⲛⲧ) destroys." Cf. also *LAB* 40:6: "Let
the moth (*tinea*) consume the white garment that my mother spun.... Let the worm (*vermis*)
devour the coverlet that my skill wove of purple and crimson."

73. According to the dictionaries, עש means "moth," סס, "moth" or "worm."

So we may leave open the possibility that the scripturally literate might hear in Q 12:33–34 not just biblical language[74] but a borrowing from Isaiah in particular.[75]

Q 17:26–27 // Isa 54:9–10. LXX Isa 54:9–10 has this: "From (the time of) the water of Noah (ἀπὸ τοῦ ὕδατος τοῦ ἐπὶ Νῶε) this is my purpose: As I swore to him at that time, I will no longer be angry with the earth on account of you, nor will the mountains depart when you are threatened, nor will your hills be moved. Thus my mercy for you will not fail, nor will the covenant of your peace ever be removed." The majority of Hebrew manuscripts open with כִּי־מֵי נֹחַ ("for the waters of Noah"), which is presumably what lies behind the LXX. But some Hebrew witnesses, including importantly 1QIsaᵃ,[76] have כִּימֵי נֹחַ ("as the days of Noah"), and this is the reading presupposed by Symmachus, Theodotian, the Peshitta, the targum, and the Vulgate (and translated by the NRSV). In other words, these witnesses, just like 1 Pet 3:20 (ἐν ἡμέραις Νῶε), attest to the phrase "the days of Noah."[77]

That Isa 54:9 v.l. lies behind Q 17:26[78] seems altogether likely given that in both places "the days of Noah" are compared with the eschatological present. At the same time, there is a potentially salient contrast with Isaiah 54, where recall of the days of Noah makes a point about God's compassion: just as God, once upon a time, swore never again to flood the earth, so now God swears not to be angry with or rebuke Israel. If Q 17:26–27, which does not offer reassurance but predicts judgment, sends one back to Isaiah 54, and if one knows the prophet well, one will sense a change in Jesus' tone vis-à-vis Isaiah, who was in general known as a prophet of comfort (Ecclus 48:24). For Jesus the days of Noah serve as a warning, not solace.

II. Synthesis

(i) Q interacts with up to twelve texts from Isaiah:

Isa 6:9–10 — Q 10:23–24 (allusion?)
Isa 14:13, 15 — Q 10:15 (allusion)

---

74. Cf. LXX Job 13:28 ("One wastes away like a rotten thing, like a garment that is moth-eaten [σητόβρωτον]"); Isa 50:9; Hos 5:12; Ecclus 19:3; 29:10–11 ("Lose your silver for the sake of a brother or a friend, and do not let it rust [ἰωθήτω] under a stone and be lost. Lay up your treasure [θησαυρόν] according to the commandments of the Most High, and it will profit you more than gold"). Apart from Job 13:28, Isa 51:8 is the only place in the LXX where σής appears beside the root βρω-.

75. Cf. Grimm, *Weil Ich Dich Liebe*, pp. 159–60.

76. See Millar Burrows, *The Dead Sea Scrolls of St. Mark's Monastery,* vol. 1 (New Haven: ASOR, 1950), plate xlv.

77. "The days of Noah" also appears in Gen 9:29, but there the meaning is not "the time of Noah" but "the length of Noah's life."

78. John N. Oswalt, *The Book of Isaiah: Chapters 40–66* (Grand Rapids/Cambridge, U.K.: Eerdmans, 1998), p. 413, n. 14, speaks of an "allusion."

Isa 26:19 — Q 7:22 (allusion)
Isa 29:18-19 — Q 7:22 (allusion)
Isa 35:5-6 — Q 7:22 (allusion)
Isa 42:18 (cf. 42:7) — Q 7:22 (allusion)
Isa 50:6, 8 — Q 6:29-30 (allusion)
Isa 51:1-2 — Q 3:8 (allusion)
Isa 51:8 — Q 12:33-34 (allusion?)
Isa 54:9-10 — Q 17:26-27 (allusion)
Isa 61:1-2 — Q 6:20-23 (allusions); 7:22 (allusion)

All these references are allusions: there is not one explicit quotation, never any introductory phrase like "Isaiah said" or "It is written." There is indeed no mention of Isaiah anywhere in Q.[79] Nor do the Q verses cited in any way hint that they are borrowing from or alluding to the Jewish Bible: all the references remain implicit. So unless one knows Isaiah well, Q's dependence upon that prophet will be missed. In Isaiah's own idiom, one will see but not perceive.

One assumes, however, that many did know Isaiah well enough to catch the allusions. John Sawyer has written:

> In most extant Jewish lectionaries, which date from the early Middle Ages down to the present day, a very large proportion of the haftaroth (often about half) come from Isaiah. They include the "Consolation" readings from chapters 40–61, which were prescribed to be read on the seven sabbaths following the Fast of the Ninth of Ab. This series was almost certainly compiled in ancient times and reflects a situation that obtained many centuries earlier than our earliest evidence. We can therefore be reasonably sure that, like most Jews then and now, Jesus and his followers would be specially familiar with the Book of Isaiah.[80]

Sawyer's inference is supported by the Christian evidence he summarizes:

> The first thing that strikes one is the sheer number and variety of texts from the whole book of Isaiah that appear to be familiar to early Christian writers. Around one hundred verses from forty-five of the sixty-six chapters of Isaiah are either quoted directly or clearly alluded to, mainly in the Gospels (forty-six), Paul (thirty) and Revelation (thirty). They range from single phrases or verses, such as 7:14 in Matthew 1:23, to longer passages such as 42:1–4 in Matthew 12 or 40:3–5 in Luke 3, and cover all manner of topics from healing miracles (53:4 in Matth. 8:17) and preaching good news to the poor (61:1 in Luke 4), to hypocrisy (29:13 in Matth. 15:8–9) and hell-fire (66:24 in Mark 9:48).[81]

---

79. Contrast the naming of Isaiah in Mt 3:3; 4:14; 8:17; 12:17; 13:14, 35 v.l.; 15:7; Mk 1:2; 7:6; Lk 3:4; 4:17; Jn 1:23; 12:38, 39, 41; Acts 8:28, 30; 28:25; Rom 9:27, 29; 10:16, 20; 15:12.

80. John Sawyer, *The Fifth Gospel: Isaiah in the History of Christianity* (Cambridge: Cambridge University Press, 1996), p. 25.

81. Ibid., p. 30.

The impression left by Sawyer's general remarks is reinforced by observing that, with reference to Q in particular, most of the Isaian passages alluded to appear to have been particularly popular with Jews and/or Christians:

Isa 6:9–10 (cf. Q 10:23–24?) is quoted in Mt 13:14–15; Mk 4:12; Jn 12:40; Acts 28:26–27; Justin, *Dial.* 12.2; 33.5 (PTS 47, ed. M. Marcovich, pp. 89–90, 124); and *Mek.* on Exod 19:1–2; and Philo, *Leg. all.* 2.69, allude to it.

Isa 14:13, 15 (Q 10:15) seems to lie behind Dan 8:9–10; 11:36; 2 Maccabees 9; Wisd 4:18–19; *1 Enoch* 46; *Ps. Sol.* 1:5; *LAE* 15:3; *2 Enoch* 28–30; and *Apoc. Ezra* 4:29–33; it is cited in *Mek.* on Exod 15:1, 7–8, 11.

Isa 26:18–19 (cf. Q 7:22) is expounded in a fragment from the *Apocryphon of Ezekiel* preserved in Epiphanius, *Haer.* 4(64).70.5;[82] already Dan 12:2 is probably a transformation of Isa 26:18–19,[83] which is also taken up into 4Q521 2 + 4 ii 12; the verses may lie behind the promise of eschatological dew in *2 Bar.* 29:7 and *b. Ḥag.* 12b; and v. 19 is quoted in *Acts Pilate* 21:2.

Isa 35:5–6 (cf. Q 7:22) is alluded to in Mk 7:37; Acts 3:8; and the Slavonic addition to Josephus, *Bell.* 1.364–70 (LCL 210, ed. H. St. J. Thackery, Josephus 3, p. 637); the verses are cited in Justin, *1 Apol.* 48.2 (PTS 38, ed. M. Marcovich, p. 99); *Dial.* 69.5 (PTS 47, ed. M. Marcovich, p. 190); and *Mek.* on Exod 15:1.

Isa 50:6 and 8 (cf. Q 6:29–30) are drawn upon in Mt 26:67; 27:30 (allusions); Mk 14:65; 15:19 (allusions); Jn 19:1 (allusion); *Gos. Pet.* 3(9) (allusion); *Barn.* 5:14; 6:1; 7:8 (quotations); *1 Apol.* 38 (quotation); *Sib. Or.* 8:290 (allusion); and from the Jewish side, *Ps. Sol.* 10:2 alludes to Isa 50:6.

Isa 51:1–2 (cf. Q 3:8) is rewritten in *LAB* 23:4 and was evidently responsible for the tradition, widely attested in rabbinic literature, that the patriarchs are rocks.

Isa 61:1–2 (cf. Q 6:20–23 and 7:22) is not only frequently referred to in early Christian literature (e.g., Lk 4:18–19; Acts 4:27; 10:38; *Barn.* 14:9) but was important for those who produced the Dead Sea Scrolls (1QH 23(18):12–15; 11QMelch 2:4, 6, 9, 13, 17, 18, 20; 4Q521 2 + 4 ii 12); it is also quoted in *Mek.* on Exod 20:21.

When the contributors to Q recalled lines from Isaiah, they were evidently recalling particularly well-known texts.

(ii) Looking not at what Q cites but at what it fails to cite, we are not surprised that there is only one reference to the oracles against foreign nations (Isaiah 14–21) — 14:13, 15 in Q 10:15 — and none to the narrative

---

82. G. Dindorf, *Epiphanii Episcopi Constantiae Opera* (Leipzig: Weigel, 1859–1862), vol. 4 1862, p. 683.

83. Nickelsburg, *Resurrection, Immortality, and Eternal Life*, pp. 17–18.

section regarding Sennacherib and Hezekiah (Isaiah 36–39), for these appear to have been the least popular sections of Isaiah in antiquity. But two omissions may be less expected, even when the relative brevity of Q is taken into account. First, Q nowhere equates Jesus with the suffering servant of Deutero-Isaiah, an equation that is found in Matthew, Mark, Luke, and so many other early Christian writers.[84] It is true that one can, as suggested above, and on the assumption that Jesus is the suffering servant, augment the meaning of Q 6:29–30, which takes up the language of Isa 50:6, 8. This can be done, however, only by reading into the text, not out of it.

Second, throughout early Christian literature Isaiah is perhaps most typically cited in support of the Gentile mission.[85] Q, however, offers no illustrations of this phenomenon. This may be because the Sayings Source faithfully represents Jesus' own failure to address this issue, and/or because it reflects a stage of the new faith or a group within it that was still predominately Jewish and not yet fully engaged with the issue of missionizing non-Jews.[86]

(iii) Q's allusions to Isaiah function in several different ways. At least two texts express the conviction that prophecies of Isaiah — who, in the words of Jesus ben Sirach, "revealed what was to occur to the end of time, and the hidden things before they happened" (Ecclus 48:25) — have been fulfilled in Jesus. The beatitudes in Q 6:20–23 tacitly present Jesus' ministry as the realization of the prophecy about an anointed one who brings good news to the poor and comforts those who mourn. And Jesus' answer to John the Baptist in Q 7:22 recalls a number of prophetic phrases (Isa 26:18, 19; 35:5–6; 42:18; 61:1–2) and transfers them to the ministry of Jesus. In these two places, then, Isaiah's tomorrow is Q's today.

Matters are different in Q 3:8, where John speaks of Abraham and stones, and in Q 17:26–27, where Jesus speaks of the days of Noah. In these places Isaiah functions not as prophecy but as foil. In the former case John rebuts the idea that merit accrues to Abraham's descendants because Scripture says that they can look to him as the rock from whence they were hewn (Isa 51:1–2). In the latter case Jesus takes an expression that in Isaiah belongs to a section proffering reassurance and uses it instead to predict judgment.

A third use of Isaiah appears in Q 6:29–30 (turn the other cheek when struck; cf. Isa 50:6, 8) and in 10:15 (Capernaum will not be exalted to heaven but brought down to Hades; cf. Isa 14:13, 15). In these cases Q draws analogies; that is, scriptural individuals become models or types, in

---

84. See Joachim Jeremias, *TDNT* 5 (1967), pp. 700–717.

85. Mt 4:12–16, quoting Isa 9:1–2; Mt 12:18–21, quoting Isa 42:1–4; Mt 21:13 = Mk 11:17 = Lk 19:46, quoting Isa 56:7; Lk 1:79, alluding to Isa 9:1; Lk 2:30, 32, alluding to Isa 42:6; Acts 13:47, quoting Isa 49:6; Acts 26:18, alluding to Isa 42:7; Rom 10:20–21, quoting Isa 65:1–2; Eph 2:17, alluding to Isa 57:19; etc.

86. For the reasonable position that "Q is aware of a Gentile mission, but not actively engaged in it," see Tuckett, *Q*, pp. 393–404.

the one case positive, in the other case negative. Whether or not the hearer of Q thinks of Jesus as the suffering servant, Q 6:29–30 models the behavior of the disciples on that figure, and Q 10:15 makes Capernaum like the king of Babylon (or like the devil, if the equation of that king with Satan was known to Q's hearers).

(iv) References to Isaiah are scattered throughout Q and cannot be reckoned characteristic of any one stage. If one separates them according to either my own theory of Q's compositional history or that of Kloppenborg, this is the result:

	Kloppenborg	Allison
Q 3:8 — Isa 51:1–2 (allusion)	stage 2	stage 3
Q 6:20–23 — Isa 61:1–2 (allusions)	stage 1	stage 3
Q 6:29–30 — Isa 50:6, 8 (allusion)	stage 1	stage 3
Q 7:22 — Isa 26:18–19; 29:18–19; 35:5–6; 42:18; 61:1 (allusions)	stage 2	stage 3
Q 10:15 — Isa 14:13, 15 (allusion)	stage 2	stage 1
Q 10:23–24 — Isa 6:9–10 (allusion?)	stage 2	stage 1
Q 12:33–34 — Isa 51:8 (allusion?)	stage 1	stage 2
Q 17:26–27 — Isa 54:9–10 (allusion)	stage 2	stage 2

There are not enough references to make anything of the fact that, on my analysis, stage 1 uses texts from the early chapters of Isaiah, stage 2 texts from later chapters. It may bear remarking, however, that the christological sequence in 3:16–17; 6:20–23; 7:18–23; and 13:34–35 (see p. 107) is made up of texts that are, on my theory but not on Kloppenborg's, all from the same late stage.[87]

---

87. See Allison, *Jesus Tradition in Q*, pp. 6–7, 33–37.

Chapter 5

Prophets II

Jeremiah, Ezekiel, Minor Prophets, Daniel

I. Texts and Analysis

Q 3:17 // Mal 4:1 (?). According to Marius Reiser, the Baptist's similitude in Q 3:17 ("whose winnowing fork is in his hand, and he will clear his threshing floor, etc.") was "probably influenced by Mal. 4:1," which reads: "See, the day is coming, burning like an oven, when all the arrogant and all evildoers will be stubble; the day that comes will burn them up, says the Lord of hosts, so that it will leave them neither root nor branch."[1] Both texts have to do with judgment, with eschatological fire, and with stubble (Malachi LXX: καλάμη; MT: קַשׁ) or chaff (Q: ἄχυρον); and Q 3:17 speaks of the root (ῥίζαν) of trees being cut, while Mal 4:1 says there will be no root (LXX: ῥίζα). So there is a concatenation of similar themes and images. Beyond that, "Malachi's words are the only ones in the OT comparing the judgment of Israel to winnowing and burning the chaff,"[2] and another verse in Q plainly alludes to the end of Malachi (Q 7:27). Indeed, Mal 4:1 belongs to a section of Scripture that Q 7:27 associates specifically with John the Baptist: he is the messenger of Malachi 3–4.[3] It is, then, not hard to imagine that hearers of Q 3:17 could have been led, as was Reiser, to recall the final verses of the Book of the Twelve.

But much uncertainty remains, for other prophecies of eschatological judgment are also reminiscent of Q 3:17 and its context. Apart from the many places where the wicked are compared with chaff[4] — this is a common

---

1. Marius Reiser, *Jesus and Judgment: The Eschatological Proclamation in Its Jewish Context* (Minneapolis: Fortress, 1997), p. 180. Jeffrey A. Trumbower, "The Role of Malachi in the Career of John the Baptist," in *The Gospels and the Scriptures of Israel* (ed. Craig A. Evans and W. Richard Stegner; JSNTSS 104; Sheffield: Sheffield Academic Press, 1994), pp. 28–41, also directly links the two texts. Cf. Cyril of Alexandria, *XII Proph. in Mal* 2 (ed. P. E. Pusey, p. 619); and Poole, *Commentary*, vol. 3, p. 15.

2. So Markus Öhler, "The Expectation of Elijah and the Presence of the Kingdom of God," *JBL* 118 (1999), pp. 472–73. He adds in a footnote: "Obad 18, the only other example of this metaphor, has Edom in view."

3. See above, pp. 38–40.

4. E.g., Job 21:18; Ps 1:4; 35:5; 83:13–14 (with fire); Isa 17:13; 29:5 (with fire, cf. v. 6); Hos 13:3 (with smoke); Obad 18 (with fire); Tg. Isa 41:15–16; Tg. Jer 23:28 (with fire, cf. v. 29).

motif—the Baptist's sayings about judgment overlap, for instance, with Isa 30:27–28, which says that the Lord "comes" (LXX: ἔρχεται; cf. Q 3:7), that he is full of wrath (LXX: ὀργῆς, ὀργή; cf. Q 3:7), that his anger will devour like fire (LXX: πῦρ; cf. Q 3:9, 16, 17), and that his breath or spirit (LXX: πνεῦμα) will be like water (cf. Q 3:16: "will baptize you with holy spirit [πνεύματι] and fire"). Similarly, *1 En.* 102:1–6 refers to fire (πυρός, cf. Q 3:9, 16, 17), eschatological flight (cf. Q 3:7), and "works" (cf. the "fruit(s)" of Q 3:8), while Wisd 5:20–23 speaks of divine wrath (ὀργήν, cf. Q 3:7), judgment by water (cf. Q 3:16), a wind (πνεῦμα) of judgment (cf. Q 3:16), and winnowing (cf. Q 3:17).[5] Several texts, then, contain prophecies of judgment that unite items also united in Q 3. So John's words about judgment may not allude to any one text in particular but rather illustrate a natural concatenation of traditional eschatological motifs.[6]

Q 7:27 // Exod 23:20; Mal 3:1. Q 7:27 apparently conflates Exod 23:20 and Mal 3:1. See the discussion on pp. 38–40.

(Q 10:13–14. Although probably no specific text is called to mind by the references to the heathen Tyre and Sidon, "who would have repented long ago in sackcloth and ashes,"[7] in Isaiah 23; Amos 1:9–10; and Joel 3:4–8, the former is denounced in prophetic oracles, and in Ezekiel 28 both are rebuked and the certainty of divine judgment upon them is proclaimed.[8] Elsewhere the prophets speak of the two cities (in their Q order) as surpassing embodiments of wickedness headed for destruction.[9] Those who bring this scriptural knowledge to Q 10:13–14 will feel the full force of the rhetoric.[10] To be more wicked than Tyre and Sidon is to be wicked indeed. To fare worse at the last judgment than Tyre and Sidon is to fare ill indeed.)

Q 11:29–30 // Jonah.[11] Jesus declares that no sign will be given to an "evil generation" except "the sign of Jonah. For as Jonah became a sign to the Ninevites, so shall the Son of Man be to this generation." The meaning of this line is notorious, for the interpretation in terms of Jesus' resurrection appears only in Mt 10:40 and is almost universally supposed to be

---

5. Cf. also Ezek 38:17–23; *Ps. Sol.* 15:4–5; 1 Cor 2:12–14.

6. See further James D. G. Dunn, "John the Baptist's Use of Scripture," in Evans and Stegner, eds., *Gospels and the Scriptures*, pp. 42–54.

7. For the stereotyped "sackcloth and ashes" (only here in the New Testament), see Neh 9:1; Ezra 4:1, 3; Isa 58:5; Jer 6:26; Dan 9:3; Jon 3:6; 1 Macc 3:47; Josephus, *Ant.* 11.221; 20.123; *Jos. Asen.* 13:2; *Barn.* 3:2; 7:5; *Ps.-Clem. Hom.* 7.5.1 (GCS 42, ed. B. Rehm, p. 188); *T. Jos.* 15:2.

8. Although it does not name Tyre, Revelation repeatedly uses oracles against it in denouncing Babylon = Rome; see Fekkes, *Prophetic Traditions*, pp. 86–91.

9. Jer 25:22; 47:4; Joel 3:4; Zech 9:1–4. Cf. 2 Esdr 1:11; *Sib. Or.* 4:90 and 5:455 (both with Tyre alone). It is probably coincidence that the mention of "sackcloth" and "ashes" in Ezek 27:30–31 is immediately followed by a reference to Tyre (27:32).

10. Cf. Maldonatus, *Commentarii*, vol. 1, p. 165.

11. In Luke the words about Jonah being a sign to the Ninevites (11:29–30) are separated from the saying about their resurrection (11:32) by the material on Solomon and the queen of Sheba (11:31). In Matthew all the words about the Ninevites appear together (12:39–41). Most have thought Luke's arrangement to be original; see Kloppenborg, *Q Parallels*, p. 100.

secondary; and when one turns instead to Q, it fails to inform us exactly how the Son of man is a sign like Jonah. One can nonetheless say this much: however one interprets the saying, it will only be on the basis of what one knows about Jonah — his deliverance from the whale, his preaching to Nineveh (cf. Q 12:41), or some other part of his legend. That is, whatever one's solution to our "dark saying,"[12] one will only come to it because of intertextual knowledge brought to Q, which in this case means knowledge of the book of Jonah and/or the exegetical traditions that grew up around it.

Q 11:32 // Jonah 3. Like Q 11:29–30, this succinct summary of Jonah 3 — "The people of Nineveh...repented at the proclamation of Jonah" — assumes that hearers can fill in the blanks. They should know, for example, about the great wickedness of the Ninevites,[13] which has as its eschatological correlate the sin of "this generation." They should also know that the episode with Jonah took place in the distant past and that the Ninevites, like the citizens of Sodom (10:12) and the queen of Sheba (11:31), are no more[14] — which is why they will become actors again only after the resurrection. And they should know who Jonah was and what he proclaimed, for to say that "a greater than Jonah is here" is meaningless unless Jonah is a known entity.

The very language of 11:32 takes memories back to the book of Jonah — specifically to chapter 3 — and so helps us to hear Jesus' words in the light of that book. "The people of Nineveh" (ἄνδρες Νινευῖται) is lifted from Jon 3:5 (LXX: οἱ ἄνδρες Νινευή; MT and targum: אנשי נינוה). Q's "repented" (μετενόησαν) is appropriate because the verb μετανοέω appears three times in LXX Jonah, in 3:9, 10; and 4:2[15] — more than in any other LXX book except Jeremiah. "At the proclamation (κήρυγμα) of Jonah" also echoes LXX Jonah, which uses the verb κηρύσσω fully five times (1:2; 3:2, 4, 5, 7), once in the striking phrase κήρυξον...τὸ κήρυγμα ("proclaim...the proclamation," 3:2; MT: את־הקריאה...קרא).[16]

If Q reflects a knowledge of the text of canonical Jonah, it is also congruent with extracanonical tradition, for while the book of Jonah fails explicitly to contrast Nineveh's repentance with the disobedience of God's own people, that contrast, which is at the heart of Jesus' saying, does appear in rabbinic texts. *Mek.* on Exod 12:1, for instance, tells us that Jonah thought this: "I will go outside of the land, where the Shekinah does not reveal itself. For since the Gentiles are more inclined to repent, I might be causing Israel to

---

12. Chrysostom, *Hom. Mt* 43.2 (PG 57.458).
13. For the wickedness of the Ninevites, see Jon 1:2 and 3:8; it is implicit in Nahum and Zeph 2:13. On their evil reputation in Greco-Roman sources, see Thomas M. Bolin, *Freedom beyond Forgiveness: The Book of Jonah Re-Examined* (JSOTSS 236; Copenhagen International Seminar 3; Sheffield: Sheffield Academic Press, 1997), pp. 135–40.
14. On Nineveh as dead and gone, see Plato, *Laws* 685c; Arrian, *Indica* 42.3; Lucian, *Inspectors* 23. Cf. Zeph 2:13–14.
15. Each time for the niphal of נחם.
16. The short summary of Jonah's story in Josephus, *Ant.* 9.208–11, uses κηρύσσω twice.

be condemned." Similarly, in *y. Sanh.* 11:30b, Jonah flees because he does not want Israel to suffer by comparison when the Gentiles repent.[17]

Was Q's use of the Ninevites to shame Israel a traditional rhetorical move? The rabbinic sources are, it goes without saying, later than Q. But, as A. Feuillet once observed, there are a number of striking similarities and dissimilarities between Jonah and Jeremiah 36, where King Jehoiakim, upon hearing the prophetic warning to turn from evil, responds not with sackcloth and ashes but with burning Jeremiah's scroll.[18] And when ancient Jews heard either Jonah or Jeremiah, the correlations that Feuillet unfolded might likewise have occurred to some of them, so that they contrasted the response of Nineveh and its king to a prophet with the response of Jerusalem and its king to a prophet. So the striking contrast in Q 11:32 between Jew and Gentile, while not found in Jonah itself, may already have suggested itself to some who knew Jonah, not as an isolated book, but as part of the prophetic corpus that includes Jeremiah. That is, a canonical reading of Jonah could have helped generate the readings that we find in Q 11:32 as well as in *Mek.* on Exod 12:1 and *y. Sanh.* 11:30b.

Q 13:35 // Jer 12:7. Jesus introduces his quotation of Ps 118:26 with this: "Behold, your house is forsaken" (Q 13:35). This is reminiscent of Jer 12:7, where God says, "I have abandoned my house, I have forsaken my heritage."

Lk 13:35	ἰδοὺ ἀφίεται ὑμῖν ὁ οἶκος ὑμῶν
Mt 23:38	ἰδοὺ ἀφίεται ὑμῖν ὁ οἶκος ὑμῶν ἔρημος[19]
LXX Jer 12:7	ἐγκαταλέλοιπα τὸν οἶκόν μου, ἀφῆκα τὴν κληρονομίαν μου
MT Jer 12:7	עזבתי את־ביתי נטשתי את־נחלתי
Tg. Jer 12:7	שבקית ית בית מקדשי רטשית ית אחסנתי

The commentators on Lk 13:35 and especially Mt 23:38 are regularly put in mind of Jer 12:7, a verse that Christians from an early period associated with Jesus being rejected by Jerusalem.[20] Jerome commented on Mt 23:38–39: *"Hoc ipsum et ex persona Hieremiae iam ante dixerat: Reliqui domum meam dimisi hereditatem meam."*[21] The theme in the Synoptics and Jeremiah

---

17. See further SB 1, pp. 643–44.

18. A. Feuillet, "Les sources du livre de Jonas," *RB* 54 (1947), pp. 169–76 (he argues for the literary dependence of Jonah upon Jeremiah). Cf. Magonet, *Form and Meaning*, pp. 76–77, 93, 102–3.

19. Matthew apparently added ἔρημος, although it is omitted in B L ff² sy^s sa bo^pt. For its originality, see Michael Knowles, *Jeremiah in Matthew's Gospel: The Rejected-Prophet Motif in Matthean Redaction* (JSNTSS 68; Sheffield: JSOT Press, 1993), pp. 185–86.

20. See, e.g., Apollinaris of Laodicea, *Comm. Mt* frag. 108 (TU 61, ed. J. Reuss, p. 36), and Cyril of Alexandria, *Comm. Mt* frag. 305 (TU 61, ed. J. Reuss, p. 262). One should note that the nearby Jer 12:11 is famously alluded to in Mt 21:13 = Mk 11:17 = Lk 19:46, in the story of Jesus in the temple.

21. Jerome, *Comm. Mt* 4.350–52 (CCSL 77, p. 222). Cf. idem, *Comm. Jer* 3.7 (CCSL 74, ed. M. Adriaen and F. Glorie, p. 123).

is the same — the divine abandonment of the temple — and the LXX shares with Q both ἀφίημι and οἶκος + a personal pronoun.

One might object that the parallel is fleeting and observe, in addition, that LXX Isa 32:14 also combines οἶκος and ἀφίημι.[22] But the latter concerns "houses" (plural) and is not about the temple, so it is a much more distant parallel. Moreover, Mt 23:38 = Lk 13:35 is an instance where the commentators who perceive the proposed allusion constitute so great a cloud of witnesses that one hesitates not to join their company. As a matter of exegetical history, our line has again and again reminded readers of Jer 12:7.[23]

There is a further point to be made. Q 13:34, which in Q immediately followed 11:51,[24] speaks of the stoning of those who have been sent to Jerusalem (λιθοβολοῦσα τοὺς ἀπεσταλμένους πρὸς αὐτήν). The generalization includes Zechariah, who has just been mentioned in Q 11:51.[25] But as one can see already from Origen's lengthy discussion, the plural (τοὺς ἀπεσταλμένους) prods one to think of others also. The first prophet that usually comes to mind is Jeremiah (cf. Heb 11:37),[26] for he met severe opposition in Jerusalem, and tradition held that he was stoned.[27] It is no objection to this that some sources locate Jeremiah's martyrdom in Egypt,[28] for *4 Bar.* 8:6 and 9:22 have him stoned in Jerusalem, and Q 13:34 could well assume the latter tradition. In other words, if in Q 13:35 Jesus borrows a phrase from Jeremiah, in Q 13:34 he may well allude to Jeremiah's fate.

Finding an allusion in Q 13:35 to Jer 12:7 raises two possibilities. The first is that an echo of the honored martyr Jeremiah would reinforce the

---

22. "The houses are deserted (οἶκοι ἐγκαταλελειμμένοι); the wealth of the city they will abandon (ἀφήσουσιν), the pleasant houses (οἴκους)."

23. There is a long list of commentators on Matthew and Q in Knowles, *Jeremiah*, p. 186, n. 1: E. Huhn, W. Dittmar, W. C. Allen, A. H. M'Neile, T. Zahn, M.-J. Lagrange, H. Montefiore, B. T. D. Smith, T. H. Robinson, L. Goppelt, K. Staab, R. V. G. Tasker, A. W. Argyle, J. Schmid, J. Schniewind, W. Trilling, W. Rothfuchs, W. F. Albright and C. S. Mann, J. C. Fenton, E. Schweizer, H. B. Green, R. A. Edwards, A. Polag, J. Maier, J. P. Meier, F. W. Beare, P. Bonnard, R. H. Gundry. To these names one can add Eusebius, *Ecl. Proph.* 3.34 (PG 22 1160D-1161A); Jerome, *Comm. Mt* 4.350–52 (CCSL 77, p. 222 — see above); Albertus Magnus, *En. sec. part. Luc. (X–XXIV)* ad loc. (Opera Omnia 23, ed. A. Borgnet, pp. 323–34); Sedulius Scotus, *Kommentar zum Evangelium nach Matthäus, 11,2 bis Schluß*, p. 523; Grotius, *Operum theologicarum*, vol. 2, pt. 1, p. 220; Lapide, *Commentary*, vol. 3, p. 54; Gill, *Commentary*, vol. 3, p. 59; France, *Jesus and the Old Testament*, p. 71; and Goulder, *Luke*, vol. 2, p. 580, among others.

24. See pp. 85–86 herein.

25. See pp. 149–52 herein, where the tradition of Abel being stoned is also discussed.

26. Origen, *Comm. Mt* ad loc. (PG 13.1636B; he recalls Jeremiah first but then says he was not killed in Jerusalem); J. Jeremias, Ἰερεμίας, *TDNT* 3 (1965), pp. 219–20; M. J. J. Menken, "The References to Jeremiah in the Gospel according to Matthew (Mt. 2.17; 16.14; 27.9)," *ETL* 60 (1984), p. 19 (observing that Heb 11:37 may likewise allude to Jeremiah); Knowles, *Jeremiah*, pp. 183–84. Isaiah was remembered as a martyr in Jerusalem, but he was not stoned.

27. *4 Baruch* 9; *Liv. Proph. Jer* 2:1; *Apoc. Paul* 49. See further Schwemmer, *Studien*, vol. 1, pp. 167–70.

28. See *Liv. Proph. Jer* 2:1 and the other references in Schwemmer, *Studien*, vol. 1, pp. 165–67.

declaration of Q 11:49–51 + Q 13:34–35, according to which Jerusalem has in the past so often rejected prophets, and it would further imply that Jesus is like Jeremiah, who met such opposition in the holy city.

The second possibility, which concerns not interpretation but hermeneutical method, follows from the observation that בֵּית/οἶκος occurs not only in Jer 12:7 but likewise in Ps 118:26, which is quoted in Q 13:35 ("Blessed is the one who comes in the name of the Lord. We bless you from the house of the Lord"), as well as in 2 Chr 24:17–25, upon which Q 11:49–51 + 13:34–35 has been modeled (vv. 18, 21, 27: "the house of the Lord"). Further, if Q's "your house is forsaken" (ἀφίεται, 13:35) recalls Jer 12:7 ("I have abandoned [עֲזַבְתִּי/ἐγκαταλέλοιπα] my house, I have forsaken [נָטַשְׁתִּי/ἀφῆκα] my heritage"), it is also the case that "to forsake" recurs in 2 Chr 24:17–25:

v. 18: "They abandoned (וַיַּעַזְבוּ/ἐγκατέλιπον) the house of the Lord."

v. 20: "Because you have forsaken (עֲזַבְתֶּם/ἐγκατελίπετε) the Lord, he has also forsaken (וַיַּעֲזֹב/ἐγκαταλείψει) you."

v. 24: "They had forsaken (עָזְבוּ/ἐγκατέλιπον) the Lord."

v. 25: "When they had withdrawn, leaving (עָזְבוּ/ἐγκαταλιπεῖν) him [the king] severely wounded.... "

Maybe Q illustrates the principle that the rabbis later called גְזֵרָה שָׁוָה. Texts may be brought together on the basis of shared key words, in this case "house" (בֵּית/οἶκος) and "forsake" (עָזַב/ἐγκαταλιπεῖν).

Q 13:35	Ps 118:26	Jer 12:7	2 Chr 24:17–25
ἀφιήμι		ἀφιήμι	
		ἐγκαταλείπω	ἐγκαταλείπω
		עזב	עזב
οἶκος	οἶκος	οἶκος	οἶκος
	בית	בית	בית

Q 12:6 // Amos 3:5 (?). In Lk 12:6 Jesus says, "Are not five sparrows sold for two pennies? And not one of them is forgotten before God." The parallel in Matthew reads, "Are not two sparrows sold for a penny? And not one of them will fall to the ground without your Father's will" (10:29). The precise reconstruction of the opening question is of no concern here, only the subsequent assertion:

Lk 12:6 καὶ ἓν ἐξ αὐτῶν οὐκ ἔστιν ἐπιλελησμένον ἐνώπιον τοῦ θεοῦ

Mt 10:29 καὶ ἓν ἐξ αὐτῶν οὐ πεσεῖται ἐπὶ τὴν γῆν ἄνευ τοῦ πατρὸς ὑμῶν

Clearly Q began with καὶ ἓν ἐξ αὐτῶν and then went on to make a statement (with οὐ or οὐκ) about God. Both Matthew's "on the earth" (ἐπὶ τὴν γῆν) and "your father" (τοῦ πατρὸς ὑμῶν) are presumably redactional.[29] Luke's "is forgotten" (ἔστιν ἐπιλελησμένον) and "before" (ἐνώπιον) are also arguably editorial.[30] So if Q had, "And one of them will not fall without God" (καὶ ἓν ἐξ αὐτῶν οὐ πεσεῖται ἄνευ τοῦ θεοῦ), both Mt 10:29 and Lk 12:6 would be readily accounted for.

The reconstructed sentence might well recall Amos 3:5a —

LXX: "Will a bird fall on the earth without a fowler?"
εἰ πεσεῖται ὄρνεον ἐπὶ τὴν γῆν ἄνευ ἰξευτοῦ;

MT: "Does a bird fall into a snare on the earth when there is no trap for it?"
התפל צפור על־פח הארץ ומוקש אין לה

Targum: "Does a bird fall into a trap on the ground if there is not a fowler?"
התפול ציפרא בקולא על ארעא וצייד לית לה

Whatever stood in Q sent at least Matthew to Amos, for that is the best explanation for his addition of "on the earth" (ἐπὶ τὴν γῆν). Moreover, there was a patristic tradition that associated Mt 10:29 and Lk 12:6 with trapping, which recalls not only the trap of MT Amos 3:5a (cf. the targum) but LXX Amos 3:5b ("Does a snare [παγίς] spring up from the earth without having taken anything?"):

Ps.-Clem. Hom. 12.31.3 (GCS 42, ed. B. Rehm, p. 190): "For without the will of God, not even a sparrow can fall into a trap (ἐν παγίδι). Thus even the hairs of the righteous are numbered by God."

Origen, C. Cels. 8.70 (GCS 2, ed. P. Koetschau, p. 287): "For of two sparrows sold, as the Scripture says, for a penny, not one falls into a trap (εἰς παγίδα) without our father in heaven."

Chrysostom, Hom. Mt 34.2 (PG 57.400–401): "Are not two sparrows sold for a penny? And one of them will not fall into a trap (εἰς παγίδα) without your Father. But the very hairs of your head are all numbered."

So we know that some early Christians, like some later commentators,[31] found in Mt 10:29 = Lk 12:6 an allusion to Amos 3:5. But how might intertextuality work here? If one were familiar with the reading that refers to a "fowler" — so the LXX, the targum, and the Peshitta[32] — then one

---

29. γῆ: Mt: 43; Mk: 19; Lk: 25. πατὴρ + ἡμῶν, ὑμῶν, σου, αὐτῶν: Mt: 20; Mk: 1; Lk: 3.

30. See Jeremias, *Sprache*, pp. 212–13. Cf. Acts 10:31. Matthew's ἄνευ is a Matthean *hapax legomenon*.

31. E.g., Trapp, *Commentary*, vol. 4, ad Amos 3:5; Gundry, *Matthew*, p. 198; Alexander Sand, *Das Evangelium nach Matthäus* (RNT; Regensburg: Friedrich Pustet, 1986), p. 228; George Wesley Buchanan, *The Gospel of Matthew* (Edwin Mellen Biblical Commentary; Lewiston/Queenston/Lampeter: Mellen Biblical Press, 1996), vol. 1, p. 461.

Philip Doddridge, *The Family Expositor; or, a Paraphrase and Version of the New Testament* (Amherst, Mass.: J. S. & C. Adams & L. Boltwood, 1836), p. 142, n. a, records the opinion, with which he disagrees, that there is a reference here to the two birds of Lev 14:4–7, but I do not recall otherwise running across this opinion.

32. Do the versions go back to a Hebrew text with יקוש or מיקש ("hunter") instead of מוקש ("snare")?

would perceive an unexpected reworking of a scriptural line. Instead of hearing about a bird not falling without a fowler, one would hear about a bird not falling without God. The point would not be exegetical; rather would Jesus' assertion be rendered more forceful and memorable because it takes up the familiar only to transform it.[33]

Q 12:8–9 // Dan 7:13–14. The shape of this saying in Q has been the object of a very long debate now exhaustively documented and evaluated by the International Q Project.[34] The upshot is that Lk 12:8–9, with its mention of the Son of man, has a better chance than Mt 10:32–33, which does not mention the Son of man, of being near to Q.[35] That is, Q 12:8–9 had something close to this: "Everyone who confesses me before others, also the Son of man will confess before the angels of God, and whoever denies me before others, will be denied before the angels of God."

If this result be accepted, then we must entertain the likelihood that Q 12:8–9, like other ancient Jewish and Christian texts,[36] alludes to Dan 7:13–14 and its context.[37] Like Daniel 7, the Q saying (i) concerns the last judgment, (ii) has as its central figure the Son of man, ὁ υἱὸς τοῦ ἀνθρώπου (Daniel speaks of "one like a son of man"),[38] (iii) depicts this figure as being "before" the divine court,[39] (iv) sets the stage with angels,[40] and (v) speaks

---

33. Does Ps 91:3 (God "will deliver you from the snare of the fowler"), which *Num Rab.* 12:3 brings into connection with Amos 3:5, have anything to do with the possible transformation of Amos 3:5 in Q 12:6?

34. *Q 12:8–12: Confessing or Denying, Speaking against the Holy Spirit, Hearings before Synagogues* (ed. Christoph Heil; Documenta Q; Louvain: Peeters, 1997), pp. 1–425.

35. See further Henk Jan de Jonge, "The Sayings on Confessing and Denying Jesus in Q 12:8–9 and Mark 8:38," in *Sayings of Jesus: Canonical and Non-Canonical: Essays in Honour of Tjitze Baarda* (ed. William L. Petersen, Johan S. Vos, and Henk J. de Jonge; NovTSup 89; Leiden/New York/Cologne: Brill, 1997), pp. 106–21; and Rudolf Pesch, "Über die Autorität Jesu: Eine Rückfrage anhand des Bekenner- und Verleugnerspruchs Lk 12,8f par.," in *Die Kirche des Anfangs* (ed. Rudolf Schnackenburg, Josef Ernst, and Joachim Wanke; Freiburg: Herder, 1978), pp. 25–55.

36. E.g., *1 En.* 46:1–2; Mk 13:26; 14:62; Mt 19:28; 25:31; 28:18; Rev 1:13–16; *4 Ezra* 13:3; Justin, *Dial.* 14.8; 32.1–3; 76.1–2; 79.2; 120.1 (PTS 47, ed. M. Marcovich, pp. 94, 121, 201, 207); *b. Ḥag.* 14a; *b. Sanh.* 38b, 98a; Tg. on 1 Chr 3:24.

37. Cf. Mogens Müller, *Der Ausdruck 'Menschensohn' in den Evangelien* (Acta Theologica Danica 17; Leiden: Brill, 1984), pp. 130–32; Chrys C. Caragounis, *The Son of Man: Vision and Interpretation* (WUNT 2/38; Tübingen: Mohr Siebeck, 1986), p. 203 (the link with Daniel 7 is "obvious"); Adela Yarbro Collins, "The 'Son of Man' Tradition and the Book of Revelation," in *The Messiah: Developments in Earliest Judaism and Christianity* (ed. J. H. Charlesworth; Minneapolis: Fortress, 1992), pp. 560–61. Geza Vermes, *Jesus the Jew* (London: Fontana, 1972), p. 185, speaks of "the implicit reference to Dan 7:13" in our saying (although he thinks this a secondary intrusion).

38. LXX and Theod.: ὡς υἱὸς ἀνθρώπου; MT: כבר אנש.

39. ἔμπροσθεν τοῦ πατρός (so Matthew 2x); ἔμπροσθεν τῶν ἀγγελῶν τοῦ θεοῦ (Lk 12:8); ἐνώπιον τῶν ἀγγελῶν τοῦ θεοῦ (Lk 12:9); קדמוהי(MT Dan 7:13); ἐνώπιον αὐτοῦ (Theod. Dan 7:13).

40. According to Dan 7:10, "a thousand thousands served him, and ten thousand times ten thousand stood attending him." The commentators have always taken these to consist of or to include the heavenly angelic court.

to a situation of persecution.[41] There is also the supporting fact that the Markan parallel (8:38), with its combination of ὁ υἱὸς τοῦ ἀνθρώπου, ἔλθῃ, and δόξῃ, certainly recalls Dan 7:13–14 (LXX: υἱὸς ἀνθρώπου, ἤρχετο, δόξα; Theod.: υἱὸς ἀνθρώπου, ἐρχόμενος).

With this result in mind, one has to ask if Johannes Weiss's generalization about the Son of man in the synoptic tradition is not at least true for Q. Weiss wrote that in many cases where

> the term "Son of man" occurs, it seems to me to imply a kind of abbreviated hint of prophecy. So, for example, in the majority of parousia sayings, one might well supply something like the following: then "the prophecy that the 'Son of man' comes on the clouds of heaven will be fulfilled."[42]

Weiss's inference works for at least Q 12:8–9, 40 and 22:30. Maybe 17:24, 26, and 30 should also be included. That is, three or more times Q's language recalls to the mind's eye Daniel's vision in the night.[43]

Q 12:40 // Dan 7:13–14. Given that Q 12:8–9, as just argued, alludes to Dan 7:13–14 and its vision of one like a son of man coming on the clouds of heaven, it is natural to think that, when Q 12:40 speaks of "the Son of man coming (ὁ υἱὸς τοῦ ἀνθρώπου ἔρχεται)," this too is an allusion to Dan 7:13–14 (LXX: υἱὸς ἀνθρώπου ἤρχετο; Theod.: υἱὸς ἀνθρώπου ἐρχόμενος). If so, the Jesus of Q 12:40 is prophesying the same thing that the Tanak prophesies.

Q 12:42–46 // Hab 2:3 (?). Q 12:45 refers to a servant who says in his heart, "My lord is delayed." Concern over the delay of eschatological salvation already appears in Hab 2:3, which became a much discussed text: "For there is still a vision for the appointed time; it speaks of the end, and does not lie. If it seems to tarry, wait for it; it will surely come, it will not delay."[44] There are some intriguing correlations between this

---

41. For Daniel see 7:21 and 25. The contexts for both Mt 10:32–33 and Lk 12:8–9 concern persecution; so too the parallels in Mk 8:38 and Rev 3:5. Even in isolation, the combination of "confess" (ὁμολόγεω) and "deny" (ἀρνέομαι) could make one think of a court.

42. Johannes Weiss, *Jesus' Proclamation of the Kingdom of God* (ed. Richard H. Hiers and D. Larrimore Holland; Philadelphia: Fortress, 1971), p. 118. See further Tuckett, *Q*, pp. 266–76.

43. Lk 12:32 ("Do not be afraid, little flock, for it is your Father's good pleasure to give you the kingdom") is sometimes thought to advert to Daniel 7 (cf. Joachim Jeremias, *New Testament Theology: The Proclamation of Jesus* [New York: Charles Scribner's Sons, 1971], p. 154), and some have assigned it to Q; but as this is a distinctly minority opinion, I have omitted including it here. See Kloppenborg, *Q Parallels*, p. 132.

44. MT: כִּי־בֹא יָבֹא לֹא יְאַחֵר. The targum is plainly eschatological: "For the prophecy is ready for a time and the end is fixed, nor will it fail; if there is delay in the matter wait for it, for it will come in its time and will not be deferred (ארי בזמניה ייתי ולא יתעכב)." The LXX has ὑπόμεινον αὐτόν, which may mean "wait for him [the Messiah]." Hab 2:3 is cited in Heb 10:37, probably alluded to in 2 Pet 3:9, and interpreted in 1QpHab 7:6–8:1. For discussion of these and other texts related to Hab 2:3, see esp. A. Strobel, *Untersuchungen zum eschatologischen Verzögerungsproblem auf Grund der spätjüdisch-urchristlichen Geschichte von Habakuk 2,2f.* (NovTSup 2; Leiden: Brill, 1961).

text, which is applied to the delay of the *parousia* in Heb 10:37, and Q 12:42–46:[45]

> Both use the same words to talk about the same theme, namely, delay in the fulfillment of prophecy (LXX: ἐρχόμενος ἥξει...χρονίση; Q: ἐλθών...χρονίζει ...ἥξει).

Q 12:42–46 is about two servants, one who is "faithful" (πιστός), one who is "faithless" (ἀπίστων); Habakkuk speaks of two different sorts of people, those who "live by faith" (LXX, ἐκ πίστεως) and those whose "spirit is not right in them" (the targum refers here to "the wicked," רשיעא, v. 4; cf. v. 5: רשע).

MT Hab 2:5 says that wine is treacherous,[46] whereas in Q 12:45 the faithless servant eats and drinks and gets drunk.[47]

One must, despite the minimal support from the commentators,[48] wonder whether Q's story of the "faithful" servant who does what is right while his lord delays his coming might not have echoed for an ancient audience Hab 2:3 and its exegetical tradition. If it did, it would have comforted them with the belief that eschatological delay was itself a part of prophecy and so nothing to be surprised or too anxious about.

Q 12:51–53 // Mic 7:6. Despite the differences between Mt 10:34–36 and Lk 12:51–53, it is clear that Q 12:51–53 opened with a denial that Jesus brought peace on the earth,[49] followed with an affirmation that he instead brought a sword (Matthew) or division (Luke), and concluded with a paraphrase of Mic 7:6, one independent of the LXX.[50] Already Tertullian, in polemicizing against Marcion, observed that the battle among relatives foretold in Lk 12:51–53 "was sung by the prophet's trumpet in these very words.... Micah must have predicted it to Marcion's Christ."[51]

---

45. Cf. Catchpole, *Quest for Q*, p. 216, n. 54. He notes that the occurrences of ἥκω in Q are eschatological.

46. So too the targum but not the LXX.

47.   Mt 24:49 ἐσθίῃ   δὲ καὶ πίνῃ   μετὰ τῶν μεθυόντων
       Lk 12:45 ἐσθίειν τε καὶ πίνειν καὶ   μεθύσκεσθαι

48. But note Schlatter, *Matthäus*, p. 718.

49. "Peace on the earth" recalls LXX Lev 26:2; Jer 36:7; 1 Macc 14:11.

50. For the reconstruction of Q and its dependence upon Mic 7:6, see my article, "Q 12:51–53 and Mk 9:11–13 and the Messianic Woes," in *Authenticating the Words of Jesus* (ed. B. Chilton and C. A. Evans; NTTS 28/1; Leiden: Brill, 1999), pp. 289–310.

51. *C. Marc.* 4.29 (PG 2.435B). Cf. Jerome, *Comm. Mic* ad loc. (CCSL 76, ed. M. Adriaen and F. Glorie, p. 513); Cyril of Alexandria, *XII Proph. in Mal* 2 ad Mic 7:6 (ed. P. E. Pusey, p. 718); Rupert of Deutz, *XII Proph. in Mic* 3 ad Mic 7:6 (PG 168.517B); Euthymius Zigabenus, *Exp. Luc.* ad loc. (PG 129:343A-B); Albertus Magnus, *En. XII Proph. Min.* ad Mic 7:6 (Opera Omnia 19, ed. A. Borgnet, pp. 368–69); Sedulius Scotus, *Kommentar zum Evangelium nach Matthäus, 11,2 bis Schluß*, pp. 300, 302; Luther, *Evangelien-Auslegung, Dritter Teil*, p. 365; and nearly all modern commentaries.

MT Mic 7:6

כי־בן מנבל אב
בת קמה באמה
כלה בחמתה
איבי איש אנשי ביתו

Tg. Mic 7:6

ארי בעדנא ההוא ברא מנביל אבא
ברתא נציא עם אמה
כלתא מקלא לחמותה
סנאוהי דגברא אנשי ביתיה

LXX Mic 7:6 διότι υἱὸς ἀτιμάζει πατέρα
θυγάτηρ ἐπαναστήσεται ἐπὶ τὴν μητέρα αὐτῆς
νύμφη ἐπὶ τὴν πενθερὰν αὐτῆς
ἐχθροὶ ἀνδρὸς πάντες οἱ ἄνδρες οἱ ἐν τῷ οἴκῳ αὐτοῦ

Mt 10:35–36 ἦλθον γὰρ διχάσαι
ἄνθρωπον κατὰ τοῦ πατρὸς αὐτοῦ
καὶ θυγατέρα κατὰ τῆς μητρὸς αὐτῆς
καὶ νύμφην κατὰ τῆς πενθερᾶς αὐτῆς
καὶ ἐχθροὶ τοῦ ἀνθρόπου οἱ οἰκιακοὶ αὐτοῦ

Lk 12:52–53 ἔσονται γὰρ ἀπὸ τοῦ νῦν πέντε ἐν ἑνὶ οἴκῳ διαμεμερισμένοι
τρεῖς ἐπὶ δυσὶν καὶ δύο ἐπὶ τρισίν
διαμερισθήσονται πατὴρ ἐπὶ υἱῷ καὶ υἱὸς ἐπὶ πατρί
μήτηρ ἐπὶ τὴν θυγατέρα καὶ θυγάτηρ ἐπὶ τὴν μητέρα
πενθερὰ ἐπὶ τὴν νύμφην αὐτῆς καὶ νύμφη ἐπὶ τὴν πενθερὰν

Q's use of Mic 7:6 is much more than the ornamental use of sacred language, for Q elsewhere contains a *Naherwartung;* so if one recognizes that Mic 7:6 is being alluded to and knows that the verse was traditionally used to depict the travails of the latter days,[52] then one naturally gives Q 12:51–53 an eschatological sense. The text associates Jesus with eschatological discord rather than with eschatological peace. The disavowal about peace does not deny the eventual reality of eschatological שלם but is rather a way of saying that the new age has not yet come and that it is not coming without tribulation. Jesus, that is, comes not in the time of eschatological peace but, as the use of Mic 7:6 indicates, in the apocalyptic time of trouble. The present is the period prophesied by Dan 12:1 and many apocalypses, the period (to use the later technical term) of the "messianic woe" (חבלו של משיח), when the bitter prophecy of Mic 7:6 will come to pass.

This reading is bolstered by the fact that at least two other Q texts have been commonly understood to teach that the present is the time of the great tribulation. According to Norman Perrin, the cryptic saying about the kingdom and violence in Q 16:16 "evokes the myth of the eschatological war between God and the powers of evil and interprets the fate of John the

---

52. Mk 13:12; *4 Ezra* 5:9 arm; *m. Soṭah* 9:16; *b. Sanh.* 97; targum on Mic 7:6 (on this see D. L. Büchner, "Micah 7:6 in the Ancient Old Testament Versions," *Journal of Northwest Semitic Languages* 19 [1993], pp. 159–68); *Pesiq. R.* 15:14/15; *Pesiq. Rab Kah.* 5:9; *Song of Songs Rab.* 2:13:4. Cf. also *Jub.* 23:19; *Sib. Or.* 8:84. On the possibility that Mal 4:6 already offers an inner-biblical, eschatological interpretation of Mic 7:6, see my article, "Q 12:51–53."

Baptist, and the potential fate of Jesus and his disciples, as a manifestation of that conflict."[53] And in the view of Jeremias and many others, the final line of the Lord's Prayer (Q 11:4) envisages, not the trials or temptations of everyday life, but the final time of trouble that precedes the renewal (cf. Rev 3:10).[54]

One final comment. In Q 12:51-53 Jesus seems, at least on the surface, to distance himself from a scripturally grounded expectation, and one might even understand him to be setting Scripture (Mic 7:6) against Scripture (the prophetic promises of peace). Such a provocative reading of the Bible runs throughout Q. Here the purpose of the surprising juxtaposition, which creates an ironic tension left unresolved, functions perhaps a bit like the seemingly contradictory assertions in Abelard's *Sic et non*: the assumption is that the competing assertions can be harmonized, but hearers must achieve this for themselves. One might, for example, ask how it can be that the eschatological Elijah has returned in John the Baptist (so Q 7:27) if Jesus declares that family members are turned against one another, for Mal 4:6 says that the eschatological Elijah will turn the hearts of parents to their children and the hearts of children to their parents (cf. Ecclus 48:10; 4Q521 frag. 2 ii.2). Calvin, for example, recognizes the tension between our text and the circumstance that "the prophets always promise that under the reign of Christ there will be peace and tranquil times" as well as the problem created by John the Baptist being the fulfillment of Mal 4:6 (Q 7:27), which promises the reconciliation of parents and children.[55]

Q 13:19 // Daniel 4; Ezekiel 17; 31. The parable of the mustard seed has long been associated with three scriptural passages — Daniel 4 (the world tree with branches touching the heavens); Ezekiel 17 (God planting a cedar on Mount Zion); and Ezekiel 31 (Pharaoh being likened to a cedar in Lebanon).[56] The closest verbal parallels are with Daniel 4:

---

53. Norman Perrin, *Jesus and the Language of the Kingdom* (Philadelphia: Fortress, 1976), p. 46. Cf. Richard H. Hiers, *The Kingdom of God in the Synoptic Tradition* (Gainesville: University of Florida Press, 1970), pp. 36–42; and G. R. Beasley-Murray, *Jesus and the Kingdom of God* (Grand Rapids: Eerdmans, 1986), pp. 95–96.

54. Jeremias, *Theology*, pp. 201–2. Cf. Brown, "Pater Noster," pp. 314–19.

55. Calvin, *Harmony*, vol. 1, p. 310.

56. See Stephen L. Wailes, *Medieval Allegories of Jesus' Parables* (Berkeley: University of California Press, 1987), p. 113 (naming Bonaventure, Albert the Great, Aquinas, and Nicholas of Lyra: "all refer to Nebuchadnezzar's vision of the great tree in the Book of Daniel"); and R. C. Trench, *Notes on the Parables of Our Lord* (8th ed.; New York: D. Appleton & Co., 1856), p. 92. Cf. Euthymius Zigabenus, *Commentarius in Quatuor Evangelia. Exposito in Matthean* ad Mt 13:31 (PG 129.420B); Lagrange, *Saint Luc*, p. 386; C. H. Dodd, *The Parables of the Kingdom* (rev. ed.; New York: Charles Scribner's Sons, 1961), p. 153; Perrin, *Rediscovering the Teaching of Jesus*, p. 157; Hans Weder, *Die Gleichnisse Jesu als Metaphern: Traditions- und redaktionsgeschichtliche Analysen und Interpretationen* (FRLANT 120; Göttingen: Vandenhoeck & Ruprecht, 1984), p. 129; Tuckett, *Q*, p. 423. Peter Wolff, *Die frühe nachösterliche Verkündigung des Reiches Gottes* (FRLANT 171; Göttingen: Vandenhoeck & Ruprecht, 1999), p. 76, speaks of a "literary dependence" upon Theod Dan 4:21.

Q 13:18–19

βασιλεὶα
    δένδρον
        τὰ πετεινὰ τοῦ οὐρανοῦ
            κατεσκήνωσεν
                ἐν τοῖς κλάδοις αὐτοῦ

Daniel 4 LXX

βασιλείας (4)
βασιλείας (27)
    δένδρον (10)
    δένδρον (20)
    δένδρον (22)
    δένδρον (23)
    δένδρου (26)
        τὰ πετεινὰ τοῦ οὐρανου (12)
        τὰ πετεινὰ τοῦ οὐρανου (21)
                        κλάδοι (12)
                        κλάδοι (17a)

Daniel Theodotion

βασιλείας (17)
βασιλείας (18)
βασιλείας (25)
βασιλεία (26)
    δένδρον (10)
    δένδρον (11)
    δένδρον (14)
    δένδρον (20)
    δένδρον (23)
        τὰ ὄρνεα τοῦ οὐρανου (12)
        τὰ ὄρνεα τοῦ οὐρανου (21)
            κατεσκήνουν (12)
            κατεσκήνουν (21)
                ἐν τοῖς κλάδοις αὐτου (12)
                    κλάδους (14)
                    κλάδων (14)
                ἐν τοῖς κλάδοις αὐτου (21)

The tree in Daniel represents Nebuchadnezzar and his kingdom, and it gets cut down, just like the tree in Ezekiel 31.[57]

Thematically closer to Q's parable is Ezekiel 17 — alluded to plainly in the Markan parallel[58] — where God plants a cedar on a high and lofty

---

57. Some think Daniel here draws upon Ezekiel; so, e.g., D. S. Russell, *The Method and Message of Jewish Apocalyptic 200 BC–AD 100* (Philadelphia: Westminster, 1976), p. 189.
58. Mk 4:32 and LXX Ezek 17:23 both have ὑπὸ τὴν σκιὰν αὐτοῦ.

mountain (Zion).[59] It becomes a "noble cedar, and under it will dwell all kinds of beasts, and in the shade of its branches every sort of bird will nest. And all the trees of the field shall know that I the Lord bring low the high tree and make high the low tree" (17:23–24). The making of the low into the high is analogous to the small becoming large in Q 13:18–19. Further, the parable in the last part of Ezekiel 17, which implicitly depicts the kingdom of Israel replacing the pagan empires, invites an eschatological interpretation: commentators regularly read the chapter as expressing hope in the renewal of the Davidic dynasty (so, for example, the targum).[60] So the simile of the mustard seed, by recalling phrases from Ezekiel and Daniel, may do more for the biblically informed than just sound a scriptural ring. It may also add rhetorical force to Jesus' words by implying that they have the support of Scripture: his parabolic assurance is a new version of a prophetic promise.

John Dominic Crossan has argued that allusion to Ezekiel 17 and 31 and/or Daniel 4 is unlikely because "if one makes the mistake of actually looking up these references, one immediately senses a problem: the allusion is not very explicit and not very appropriate."[61] Two things may be said in response. On the one hand, the tree in Ezekiel 17 and 31 is a cedar,[62] so one may ask whether the use of language scripturally associated with a cedar in a parable about a mustard seed is not intentional, that is, whether the distance Crossan perceives between parable and subtext might not be deliberate. Perhaps, for example, an implied contrast with the cedar reinforces the inferences one makes from the proverbial smallness of the mustard seed. That is, allusion to the passages from Ezekiel and Daniel may be a way of surprising hearers, who do not expect a parable about a mustard seed to end with words traditionally associated with cedars.[63] Possibly in line with this, Ezekiel 31 and Daniel 4 are about ungodly pagan powers, and maybe it is not coincidence that the parable of the mustard seed is paired with the parable of the leaven, a thing so often associated with evil.[64] Perhaps

---

59. Cf. Jerome, *Comm. Ezek* 5.1240–41 (CCSL 75, ed. M. Adriaen and F. Glorie, p. 224).

60. "22. Thus says the Lord God, 'I myself will bring near a child from the kingdom of the house of David which is likened to the lofty cedar, and I will establish him from among his children's children; I will anoint and establish him by my Memra on a high and exalted mountain. 23. On the holy mountain of Israel will I establish him, and he shall gather together armies and build fortresses and become a mighty king; and all the righteous shall rely upon him, and all the humble shall dwell in the shade of his kingdom. 24. And all the kings of the nations shall know that I the Lord have humbled the kingdom which was mighty and have made mighty the kingdom which was weak. I have humbled the kingdom of the nations which was mighty as a green tree, and have made mighty the kingdom of the house of Israel, which had been as weak as a dried-up tree.' "

61. John Dominic Crossan, *In Parables: The Challenge of the Historical Jesus* (New York: Harper & Row, 1973), p. 47.

62. Daniel 4 does not identify the sort of tree it depicts.

63. Such is the reading of Robert W. Funk, *Jesus as Precursor* (SBLSS 2; Philadelphia/Missoula, Mont.: Fortress/Scholars Press, 1975), p. 23.

64. E.g., Exod 12:15–20; 34:25; Lev 2:11; Mt 16:6; Lk 12:1; 1 Cor 5:6; Ignatius, *Magn.* 10.2; Justin, *Dial.* 14.2; *Ps.-Clem. Hom.* 8.17; SB 1, pp. 728–29.

the former parable is trying to do what the latter parable is trying to do, namely, explicate the kingdom of God with ironic reference to something unexpected and indeed, in its usual symbolic uses, evil.

On the other hand, it is equally possible that there is no irony here but rather an exegetical tradition. Ezekiel 31 and Daniel 4 have both clearly influenced *Acts of Thomas* 146, where imagery from those two places is part of a parable describing the altogether positive work of Thomas.[65] That is, the imagery of Ezekiel 31 and Daniel 4 is carried over without the negative connotations in the original passages.[66] The same may be said of 1QS 14(6):14–18 and 16(8):4–13, which borrow from Ezekiel 31 and perhaps 17 as well as Daniel 4 in picturesquely describing the community and its pious hymnist.[67] In these places there does not seem to be any irony. Further, throughout the scrolls

> the position of the sect is described with the image of a young, tender plant, which is hardly noticed in the present, but which in the future will grow into a large tree which will cover the earth (cf. Isa 60:21; Ezekiel 31). In sectarian parlance the plant refers to the group of the elect and the just, now few and hidden but destined to rule the world in the future.[68]

Maybe it is the same in Q.

Q 17:24, 26, 30 // Dan 7:13–14 (?). Mention of "the day of the Son of man" in an eschatological context might be a pointer to Dan 7:13–14 given that Q alludes on at least three other occasions to Dan 7:13–14 (see the discussions in this chapter of Q 12:8–9, 40 and 22:28–30).

Q 22:28–30 // Dan 7:9–14. It is extremely difficult to determine the wording of Q's final saying. Mt 19:27–28 has this: "27. Then Peter said in reply, 'Look, we have left everything and followed you. What then will we have?' 28. Jesus said to them, 'Truly I tell you, at the renewal of all things, when the Son of man is seated on the throne of his glory, you who have followed me will also sit on twelve thrones, judging the twelve tribes of Israel.' " Lk 22:28–30 is rather different: "28. You are those who have stood by me in my trials; 29. and I confer on you, just as my Father has conferred on me, a kingdom, 30. so that you may eat and drink at my table

65. Richard Bauckham, "The Parable of the Vine: Rediscovering a Lost Parable of Jesus," *NTS* 33 (1987), pp. 84–101.

66. Is this due to the positive image in Ezekiel 17?

67. "The branch of an eternal planting" in 1QS 6:15 "seems to be taken from Ps 104:12, possibly combined with Dan. 4:8–9. The whole context in lines 15–17 is moreover largely inspired by Ezek. 31:2–12." So Svend Holm-Nielsen, *Hodayot: Psalms from Qumran* (Acta Theologica Danica 2; Aarhus, Denmark: Universitetsforlaget, 1960), p. 126. The עצי מים ("trees by the water") of 1QH 16(8):6 comes from Ezek 31:14.

68. Devorah Dimant, "Qumran Sectarian Literature," in *Jewish Writings of the Second Temple Period: Apocrypha, Pseudepigrapha, Qumran Sectarian Writings, Philo, Josephus* (ed. Michael E. Stone; CRINT 2; Assen/Philadelphia: Van Gorcum/Fortress, 1984), p. 539, citing also CD 1:7; 1QH 8:4–26; and 4QPs 1–10 II 2–11. Cf. *1 En.* 10:16; 84:6; 93:5, 10; *Jub.* 1:16; 36:6.

in my kingdom, and you will sit on thrones judging the twelve tribes of Israel." The IQP has reconstructed this original: ὑμεῖς ...οἱ ἀκολουθήσαντές μοι...καθήσεσθε ἐπὶ θρόνους κρίνοντες τὰς δώδεκα φυλὰς τοῦ Ἰσραήλ, "You...who have followed me...will sit on thrones judging the twelve tribes of Israel."[69] This reconstruction seemingly implies that Lk 22:29 is wholly Lukan, which may or may not be the case. Otherwise, however, the fragmentary reconstruction commends itself. We can only partly recover this Q saying.[70]

Given our ignorance of what exactly stood in Q, it is hazardous to be confident about any proposed intertext. Nonetheless, commentators on Matthew have often seen in Mt 19:28 an allusion to Daniel 7, for the verse has to do with the Son of man (cf. Dan 7:13), thrones (plural, cf. Dan 7:9, LXX: θρόνοι), and the saints as eschatological judges or rulers (cf. Dan 7:22).[71] Commentators on Lk 22:28–30 have likewise thought that the Lukan parallel, even though it does not name the Son of man, draws upon Daniel 7. According to Howard Clark Kee, for instance, "The analogy with the bestowal of the kingdom upon the Son of Man and the 'saints of the Most High' in Daniel 7 is unmistakable."[72]

My own judgment is that both Mt 19:28 and Lk 22:28–30 do indeed send one's thoughts to Daniel 7, and this in turn implies that Q 22:28–30 probably did the same thing. The reason is this. If, on the one hand, Matthew's "the Son of man" and Lk 22:29, where Jesus confers the kingdom to his followers, are redactional (as so many now think), the best explanation would be that Q 22:28–30 sent both evangelists to Daniel 7, for both Matthew's "the Son of man" and Lk 22:29 recall that text. If, on the other hand, one or both of those features already belonged to Q, then the probability that it intended to allude to Daniel 7 would be all the greater. In either case, an allusion to Dan 7:13–14 seems likely.

---

69. Christoph Heil, ed., *Q 22:28, 30: You Will Judge the Twelve Tribes of Israel* (Documenta Q; Louvain: Peeters, 1998). Luz, however, suggests that Matthew and Luke do not here depend upon Q but oral tradition: *Matthäus*, 3:121.

70. The variant in Rev 3:21 does not take us any further.

71. Cf. Albertus Magnus, *Super Mt cap. XV–XXVIII* ad loc. (Opera Omnia 21/2; ed. B. Schmidt, p. 496); Poole, *Commentary*, vol. 2, p. 832 (citing Mt 19:28 in illustration of Dan 7:18); Trapp, *Commentary*, vol. 5, p. 221; William Dodd, *Commentary*, vol. 3, ad Mt 19:28); Barnabas Lindars, *Jesus Son of Man* (Grand Rapids: Eerdmans, 1983), p. 126 ("It is very likely that he was conscious of the allusion to the thrones placed for the Ancient of Days and his entourage in Dan. 7.9"); Gundry, *Matthew*, p. 393; Müller, *Der Ausdruck 'Menschensohn' in den Evangelien*, pp. 116–17; Hagner, *Matthew*, vol. 2, p. 565; Luz, *Matthäus*, vol. 3, p. 121. Casey, *Son of Man*, pp. 187–89, leaves the question open.

72. Kee, "Jesus: A Glutton and Drunkard," p. 326 (he is commenting on Lk 22:29, which he evidently assigns to Q). Cf. Doeve, *Jewish Hermeneutics*, p. 142 (the text is "based directly upon Dan. vii 22"); Marshall, *Luke*, p. 818 (the disciples sitting upon thrones is "a reminiscence of Dn. 7:9"). Note also Beasley-Murray, *Kingdom*, pp. 275–76 (affirming the influence of Daniel 7 on Mt 19:28 = Lk 22:28, 30b); and Craig A. Evans, "The Twelve Thrones of Israel: Scripture and Politics in Luke 22:24–30," in *Jesus in Context: Temple, Purity, and Restoration* (Bruce Chilton and Craig A. Evans; AGAJU 39; Leiden/New York/Cologne: Brill, 1997), pp. 455–79.

That this is the right conclusion is supported by the portion of Q 22:28–30 where Matthew and Luke are closest:

Mt 19:28	*Lk 22:30*
καθήσεσθε καὶ ὑμεῖς	καὶ καθήσεσθε
ἐπὶ δώδεκα θρόνους	ἐπὶ θρόνων
κρίνοντες	
τὰς δώδεκα φυλὰς τοῦ Ἰσραήλ	τὰς δώδεκα φυλὰς
	κρίνοντες
	τοῦ Ἰσραήλ

We do not know whether Matthew added the first δώδεκα ("twelve") in order to increase the parallelism or whether Luke dropped it because of the problem created by Judas's apostasy. In either case Q referred to "thrones" (θρόνους or θρόνων). This matters because, according to Reiser, only in Dan 7:9 "or in reference to that passage, does the early Jewish tradition speak of a group of judges at the last judgment."[73] Moreover, the ancients seem to have paid some attention to Daniel's plural, "thrones." *b. Sanh.* 38b attributes to R. Akiba the view that Daniel has in view two thrones, one for God, one for David (the Messiah). But other opinions are also given — thrones for God and for the heavenly court; or one throne for justice, another for mercy; or one for justice, another for charity; or one is a throne, one a footstool (cf. *b. Ḥag.* 14a). And *Tan.* B Leviticus 7 contains this comment on Dan 7:9:

> Our rabbis say, What does "thrones" (in the plural) mean? In the time to come the Holy One, blessed be he, will take his seat, and the angels will set up thrones for the great ones of Israel, and they will be seated and will judge with the Holy One, blessed be he, the nations of the world, as it says: "The Lord enters into judgment with the elders and princes of his people."

Some interpretation like this appears to lie behind Q 22:28–30.

The allusion to Dan 7:9–14 in what most have taken to be Q's conclusion prompts three comments. First, it is appropriate that a book with so much intertextuality as Q should end with an allusion. Second, Q 22:28–30 adverts to a passage referred to earlier, in Q 12:8–9 and 40 and perhaps also in 17:24, 26, and 30. Dan 7:9–14 is in fact Q's most frequent intertext, so ending the Sayings Source with yet one more allusion to it recalls earlier portions of Q and adds to the document's literary and theological unity. Third, the reference to Daniel 7 serves to make the future that Jesus promises a fulfillment of Hebrew Bible prophecy: when Jesus' followers sit on thrones, they will bring to realization the hopes of Daniel. So Jesus' prophetic word is the Tanak's prophetic word. The result is that Q's two authorities are mu-

---

73. Reiser, *Jesus and Judgment*, p. 262. Does Dan 7:9 itself reflect Ps 122:4–5 ("there the thrones for judgment were set up, the thrones of the house of David")?

tually supporting: Jesus adds his authority to Scripture, and Scripture adds its authority to Jesus.

II. Synthesis

(i) Q's use of Jeremiah, Ezekiel, Daniel, and the Book of the Twelve may be seen at a glance:

Jer 12:7 — Q 13:35 (allusion)
Ezekiel 17; 31 — Q 13:19 (allusion)
Dan 4:10–33 — Q 13:19 (allusion)
Dan 7:9–14 — Q 22:28–30 (allusion)
Dan 7:13–14 — Q 12:8–9 (allusion)
                Q 12:40 (allusion)
                Q 17:24, 26, 30 (allusions?)
Amos 3:5 — Q 12:6 (allusion?)
Jonah — Q 11:29–30 (reference)
Jonah 3 — Q 11:32 (reference)
Mic 7:6 — Q 12:51–53 (unmarked quotation)
Hab 2:3 — Q 12:45 (allusion?)
Mal 3:1 — Q 7:27 (marked conflated quotation)
Mal 4:1 — Q 3:17 (allusion?)

Even after one leaves aside the several allusions that are uncertain, Q shows a knowledge of Jeremiah (an allusion), Ezekiel (an allusion), Daniel (several allusions), Jonah (explicit references), Micah (a loose quotation), and Malachi (a mixed quotation).

(ii) Two of the prophetic hypotexts that Q refers to are no longer predictions. Q 7:27 finds in Mal 3:1 a prophecy that has already been fulfilled in the Baptist, who prepared the way of the Lord, and Q 12:51–53 sees in Mic 7:6 a prophecy that is being realized among those who heed Jesus: father is against son, etc. So in the Sayings Source eschatology belongs to experience; it has entered history with the crisis brought by Jesus (cf. perhaps Q 11:20).

Q does not, however, feature a "realized eschatology." The allusions to Daniel's vision of one like a son of man (Q 12:8–9, 40; 22:28–40) entail that the biblical prophecies have only begun to be fulfilled. Daniel's oracle remains an expectation. Eschatology in Q is accordingly in the process of realization, and much remains unaccomplished. This includes the return of the Son of man, the resurrection of the dead, and the final judgment — and so all prophecies of those events. Q contains nothing like Mk 9:1–8 and Mt 28:16–20, which seem to present a proleptic coming of the Son of man, nor anything like the belief, recorded in 2 Tim 2:17, that "the resurrection has already taken place" (cf. Mt 27:51–53; Jn 5:25).

(iii) In addition to finding eschatological forecasts in the prophets, Q also employs prophetic texts as illustrations. Q 11:29–30, 32 draws a parallel between Jesus and Jonah and a contrast between the Jews who have heard the former and the Ninevites who heard the latter. Q 13:35 borrows from Jer 12:7 ("Your house is forsaken") and thus makes Jesus sound like the reluctant prophet of judgment, Jeremiah. And the parable of the mustard seed in Q 13:19 uses imagery from Daniel 4 and Ezekiel 17 and 31 in order to depict the unexpected manifestation of the kingdom of God.

(iv) Q, like so many other early Christian writings, offers a christological reading of Scripture: Jesus' person, work, and circumstances are the hermeneutical key to the Tanak. Thus Mal 3:1 is about Jesus' forerunner (Q 7:27) while Mic 7:6 depicts the circumstances of his disciples (Q 12:51–53). Jonah is a type for Jesus (Q 11:29–30, 32), and Jeremiah likewise foreshadows him (Q 13:35). Moreover, Dan 7:13–14 will pass from promise to fulfillment when Jesus confesses those who have confessed him and denies those who have denied him (Q 12:8–9). Whether or not one should go so far as to say that Jesus is the Tanak's telos, there is in any case a reciprocal hermeneutic: Q guides one's reading of the Tanak, and the Tanak informs one's reading of Q, which means one's understanding of Jesus.

Chapter 6

Historical Books

Samuel, Kings, Chronicles

I. Texts and Analysis

Q 9:59–62 // 1 Kgs 19:19–21. Immediately after Jesus responds to a would-be follower with the saying about the Son of man having no place to lay his head, a second individual seeks to join the cause. He says, "Lord, let me first go and bury my father (τὸν πατέρα μου)." Jesus responds with harsh words, "Follow me (ἀκολούθει μοι), and leave the dead to bury their own dead." Many commentators have been reminded of 1 Kgs 19:19–21, where Elijah calls Elisha. The latter asks whether, before following the former (LXX: ἀκολουθήσω ὀπίσω σου), he might not first go and kiss his father (LXX: τὸν πατέρα μου).[1] According to Harry T. Fleddermann, "Q undoubtedly refers to this passage but radicalizes the request by substituting the duty of burying a dead parent for leave taking."[2]

Supportive of this interpretation is Mark's Gospel. It contains three call stories that are assimilated to 1 Kgs 19:19–21: the call of Peter and Andrew (1:16–18), the call of James and John (1:19–20), and the call of Levi the toll collector (2:14).[3] All three Markan narratives have the same structure:

---

1. The MT has "my father and my mother."
2. Harry T. Fleddermann, "The Demands of Discipleship: Matt 8,19–22 par. Luke 9:57–62," in Van Segbroeck, ed., *Four Gospels*, vol. 1, p. 554. Cf. Albertus Magnus, *Super Mt cap. I–XIV* ad 8:21 (Opera Omnia 21/1; ed. B. Schmidt, p. 292); Bonaventure, *Exp. Luc.* ad loc. (Opera Omnia 10, ed. A. C. Peltier, p. 486); J. A. Findlay, "Luke," in *The Abingdon Bible Commentary* (ed. Frederick Carl Eiselen, Edwin Lewis, and David G. Downey; New York/Cincinnati/Chicago: Abingdon, 1929), p. 1042; Crossan, *In Fragments*, p. 243; Luke Timothy Johnson, *The Gospel of Luke* (Sacra Pagina 3; Collegeville, Minn.: Michael Glazier, 1991), p. 162; Löning, "Die Füchse, die Vögel und der Menschensohn," pp. 93–94; Richard A. Horsley, "Q and Jesus: Assumptions, Approaches, and Analyses," *Semeia* 55 (1992), pp. 188, 206; Bovon, *Lukas*, vol. 2, pp. 36–37; and Markus Öhler, *Elia im Neuen Testament: Untersuchungen zur Bedeutung des alttestamentlichen Propheten im frühen Christentum* (BZNW 88; Berlin/New York: de Gruyter, 1997), pp. 154–63. Trapp, *Commentary*, vol. 1, p. 582, remarks that if Elisha gave a feast after he was called by Elijah (1 Kgs 19:21), so too does Matthew/Levi in Mt 9:9–10 = Mk 2:14–15. Cf. Thomas Scott, *The Holy Bible* (Boston: Crocker & Brewster, 1844), vol. 2, ad loc.
3. Cf. Anselm Schulz, *Nachfolgen und Nachahmen: Studien über das Verhältnis der neutestamentlichen Jüngerschaft zur urchristlichen Vorbildethik* (SANT 6; Munich: Kösel, 1962), pp. 97–110; and Sato, *Q und Prophetie*, pp. 375–77.

1. Jesus is passing by.

2. He sees a person whose name is given.

3. This person is at his place of work.

4. Jesus issues a call to discipleship.

5. The person obediently responds and follows Jesus.

This common outline, as often observed, has been borrowed from 1 Kgs 19:19–21:

1. Elijah is passing by.

2. He finds Elisha.

3. Elisha is at work with a plow.

4. Elijah puts his mantle on Elisha, which is a sign of the call to prophetic office.

5. Elisha says, "I will follow after you,"[4] and asks to kiss his parents; he slaughters oxen.

6. Elisha follows Elijah.

As Chrysostom already saw, Jesus is, in Mk 1:16–20 and 2:14, as so often in the synoptic tradition, like Elijah.[5] But the parallelism underlines a contrast. Mark has no element corresponding to number 5 in the second outline (1 Kgs 19:20–21). Now in the MT and targum this part of the narrative is ambiguous. It is unclear whether Elisha is being rebuked or being given permission to see his parents before following Elijah. But in the LXX and Josephus, *Ant.* 8.354, Elijah grants Elisha permission to return home. Presumably this was a popular way of understanding the story, and with it in mind Jesus' call becomes all the more urgent and demanding. He does not permit what Elijah permitted, so one greater than Elijah is here.[6] Precisely the same point is made in Q 9:59–60 when read with 1 Kgs 19:19–21 as an intertext: discipleship to Jesus — who must like Elijah be a prophet — takes priority over duty to parents.[7]

Another reason for finding 1 Kgs 19:19–21 in the background of Q 9:59–60 appears from its Lukan context. In Lk 9:61–62 yet a third would-be disciple appears on the scene and asks to follow Jesus (ἀκολουθήσω σοι). He asks if he might first say farewell to those at home. Jesus responds, "No one who puts a hand to the plow (ἄροτρον) and looks back is fit for the kingdom of God." Here the commentators regularly discern an allusion

---

4. LXX: ἀκολουθήσω ὀπίσω σου. Cf. Mk 1:17: δεῦτε ὀπίσω μου; 2:14: ἀκολούθει μοι.

5. Chrysostom, *Hom. Mt* 14.2 (PG 57.219).

6. So Rudolf Pesch, *Das Markusevangelium 1. Teil: Einleitung und Kommentar zu Kap. 1,1–8,26* (2d ed., HTKNT 2; Freiburg/Basel/Vienna: Herder, 1977), pp. 109–12. Cf. Strauss, *Jesus*, pp. 311–12; and Sato, *Q und Prophetie*, pp. 376–77.

7. Cf. Kloppenborg, *Formation of Q*, p. 191.

to 1 Kgs 19:19–21, which has in the LXX ἀκολουθήσω ὀπίσω σου ("I will follow after you," MT: אלכה אחריך) and ἠροτρία ("ploughing," MT: חרש).[8] If the passage belonged to Q, it would clearly have cast its light forward to Q 9:59–60 and so show us that whoever put together Q 9:57–62 was thinking of Elijah's call of Elisha.

Unfortunately, Lk 9:61–62 appears only in Luke, and its place in Q is disputed. Yet even if one dismisses the argument on p. 78 herein and credits Lk 9:61–62 to Lukan creativity, the relationship between 1 Kgs 19:19–21 and Q 6:59–60 is still reinforced, for in this case the best explanation for why Luke subjoined or composed 9:61–62, a story plainly alluding to 1 Kgs 19:19–21, would be that Q 9:59–60 moved him to think of that portion of Scripture. In other words, we would here have an ancient reader perceiving the intertextuality so many later readers have perceived. In line with this, Luke's three little stories of discipleship are immediately preceded by 9:51–56, where the disciples' question, "Lord, so you want us to command fire to come down from heaven and consume them?," again regularly moves readers to think of Elijah.[9]

One last point regarding Q 9:59–62. If Jesus is here like Elijah, Q 7:27 has already identified John the Baptist with the messenger of Mal 3:1, and Mal 4:5 (and so subsequent tradition) equates that messenger with Elijah. One could, if so inclined, see Q 7:27 and 9:59–60 (+ 61–62) as contradictory and then assign them to different stages of Q's development. In one stage Jesus would have been like Elijah (Q 9:59–60 [+ 61–62]); in another stage that honor would have gone to John (Q 7:27). Although that is perhaps the correct inference, and one that harmonizes with my own account of Q's formation, according to which Q 7:27 and 9:59–62 belong to different stages, there is also another possibility. One could just as reasonably argue that implicit here in Q[10] is what we find so plainly in Matthew and in Luke, namely, the assimilation of John and Jesus one to another.[11] Maybe in fact

---

8. Cf. Albertus Magnus, *En. prim. part. Luc. (I-IX)* ad loc. (Opera Omnia 22, ed. A. Borgnet, p. 700); Theodore Beza, *Annotationes maiores in Novum Testamentum* (n.p.: Henri Estienne, 1594), p. 282; Grotius, *Operum theologicarum*, vol. 2, pt, 1, p. 395; Wolzogen, *Commentarius in Evangelium Lucae*, p. 607; Trapp, *Commentary*, vol. 5, p. 321 ("Christ here happily alludeth to that which Elisha did"); Bengel, *Gnomon*, vol. 2, p. 88 ("he seems to have in mind the example of Elisha"); Wesley, *Explanatory Notes*, p. 166 ("As Elisha did after Elijah had called him from the plough, 1 Kings xix, 19; to which our Lord's answer seems to allude"); John Peter Lange, *Commentary on the Holy Scriptures: Kings* (Grand Rapids: Zondervan, n.d.), vol. 6, p. 223; Melancthon W. Jacobs, *Notes on the Gospels, Critical and Explanatory* (New York: Robert Carter & Bros., 1872), p. 87; F. W. Farrar, *The First Book of Kings* (New York: A. C. Armstrong and Son, 1893), p. 448; Crossan, *In Fragments*, p. 243; Kloppenborg, *Formation of Q*, p. 191; Sato, *Q und Prophetie*, pp. 376–77; Wolfgang Wiefel, *Das Evangelium nach Lukas* (THKNT 3; Berlin: Evangelische Verlagsanstalt, 1988), p. 194.

9. See 2 Kgs 1:10, 12; cf. 1 Kgs 18:36–38. Cf. Lk 9:54 A C D W Θ Ψ *f*[1.13] Maj it sy[p.h] bo[pt] Marcion: "as also Elijah did."

10. Note also Q 7:32–34, where John and Jesus, despite differences, are clearly similar.

11. On Matthew, see John P. Meier, "John the Baptist in Matthew's Gospel," *JBL* 99 (1980), pp. 383–405. On Luke, see Charles H. Talbert, *Literary Patterns, Theological Themes, and the*

there was no stage in the tradition where one prophet but not the other was made out to be like Elijah. Perhaps from the outset the tradents of the Jesus tradition had no trouble thinking simultaneously of Jesus as a prophet like Elijah and of the Baptist as the eschatological Elijah of Malachi.

Q 10:4 // 2 Kgs 4:29. In Mt 10:9–10, Jesus tells his disciples not to take gold or silver or copper in their belts, nor a wallet nor two shirts nor sandals nor a staff. In Lk 10:4, purse, bag, and sandals are prohibited, and disciples are commanded to salute no one on the road. The relation of these two verses to Mk 6:8–9 (prohibition of bread, wallet, copper, two shirts, permission of staff and sandals) and Lk 9:3 (prohibition of staff, wallet, bread, silver, two shirts) is notorious and perhaps not wholly susceptible to a neat literary resolution. But three propositions seem more probable than not. First, the agreements between Matthew 10 and Luke 10 show us that Q had a version of the missionary discourse.[12] Second, that Mt 10:10 and Lk 9:3 + 10:4 agree against Mk 6:8 in prohibiting a staff and sandals is best explained if Matthew and Luke here follow Q.[13] Third, the strange imperative to greet no one on the road, although found only in Luke, surely comes from Q,[14] for we can explain why Matthew omitted it — the command seemingly contradicted Mt 5:47 ("And if you greet only your brothers...?") — whereas the best explanation for its presence in Luke is that he took it from a source. Since Mark's instructions for missionaries contain nothing of the kind, presumption places it in Q's version of the missionary discourse.

If all this is correct, then Q 10:4 ordered missionaries not to take several things, including a staff (ῥάβδον), and then ended with "Do not greet anyone" (καὶ μηδένα ἀσπάσησθε).[15] The mention of a staff followed by a prohibition of greeting has consistently reminded commentators of 2 Kgs 4:29: "He [Elijah] said to Gehazi, 'Gird up your loins, and take my staff in your hand, and go. If you meet anyone, give no greeting, and if anyone greets you, do not answer.'" According to Michael Goulder, the "sense" of Lk 10:4 is "from 4 Kgdms... the preaching of the kingdom is too urgent

---

Genre of Luke-Acts (SBLMS 20; Missoula, Mont.: Scholars Press, 1974), pp. 44–48. The motif is not so obvious in Mark, but it is still there. Mark uses both κηρύσσω and παραδίδωμι of John (1:4, 7, 14) and of Jesus (1:14; 9:31; 10:33; 14:10; etc.): both preach and then are delivered up. Both are reckoned by people to be prophets (6:15; 8:28; 11:32). Mark also says that Jesus was "bound" (δέω, 15:1) and "arrested" (κρατέω, 12:12; 14:1, 44, 46, 49, 51) and laid in a tomb (ἔθηκεν αὐτὸν ἐν μνημείῳ, 15:46), just like John (6:17, 29). And in 9:11–13 John is Jesus' forerunner in suffering and rejection. Note also 6:14, 16, where Herod suggests Jesus is John risen from the dead.

12. See Uro, *Sheep among the Wolves*, pp. 25–72.

13. See above, p. 41.

14. See esp. Iris Bosold, *Pazifismus und prophetische Provokation: Das Grußverbot Lk 10,4b und sein historischer Kontext* (SBS 90; Stuttgart: Katholisches Bibelwerk, 1978), pp. 43–51. Cf. Uro, *Sheep among the Wolves*, pp. 77–78. The IQP prints both the prohibition of staff and greeting, although it puts them in brackets.

15. The κατὰ τὴν ὁδόν in καὶ μηδένα κατὰ τὴν ὁδὸν ἀσπάσησθε is probably Lukan redaction; see Jeremias, *Sprache*, p. 184.

to allow for conventions."[16] John Gray, in his commentary on Kings, has similarly written that 2 Kgs 4:29 is "cited by Jesus in his dispatch of the seventy disciples."[17]

It is not just moderns who have made the connection. In his commentary on Luke, Isho'dad of Merv wrote on 10:4: "It is like what Elisha said to Gehazi, 'If you meet anyone, salute not, and if anyone salute you, answer not'; just as there he does not hinder him from salutation and blessing, but that he may not be delayed and kept by human things, and talk by the way; etc."[18] And Cyril of Alexandria observed that Jesus did not allow his disciples

> to receive any distraction in their work, such as interruption by greetings on their way. Hence he adds, "Greet no one on the way." This was long ago said by Elisha, as though he said, " 'Proceed straight away to your work without exchanging blessings with others.' For it is a loss to waste the time which is fitter for preaching in unnecessary things.' "[19]

The verbal links between Q 10:4 and 4 Βασ 4:29 are minimal. The two verses use different words for "staff" (LXX: βακτηρία;[20] Q: ῥάβδος) and "greet" (LXX: εὐλογέω;[21] Q: ἀσπάζομαι). Nonetheless, Lk 10:4b (= Q 10:4b) has, as observed, moved the biblically literate to think of Kings. The peculiarity of Elisha's injunction, which makes it stick in the memory, as well as the similar series of imperatives explain why:

2 Kgs 4:29	*Q 10:3–9*
"Take my staff in your hand."	"Do not carry . . . a staff."
"Go" (LXX: δεῦρο; MT: לך; Ps.-J.: איזיל).	"Go" (ὑπάγετε).[22]
"If you meet anyone, give no greeting."	"Do not greet anyone."
Elisha sends Gehazi to heal.	"Heal the sick."

16. Goulder, *Luke*, p. 467. Most modern commentaries on Luke at least mention the parallel.

17. John Gray, *I and II Kings* (2d rev. ed.; Philadelphia: Westminster, 1970), p. 498. Cf. Osiander, *Sacrorum Bibliorum*, vol. 3, p. 206; Beza, *Annotationes*, p. 283; Calmet, *Commentarium literale*, vol. 7, p. 560; Poole, *Commentary*, vol. 3, p. 226; Pearce, *Commentary*, vol. 1, p. 364; Theodor Zahn, *Das Evangelium des Lukas ausgelegt* (4th ed.; Leipzig/Erlangen: A. Deichert, 1930), p. 411, n. 66; Paul Hoffmann, *Logienquelle*, p. 267.

18. Isho'dad of Merv, *Comm. Lk* ad loc. (ed. M. D. Gibson, vol. 3, pp. 37–38).

19. *Apud* Aquinas, *Catena aurea* ad loc. = Cyril, *Comm. Lk* ad loc. (PG 72.666C-67A). Cf. Ambrose, *Traité Luc* 7.62 (SC 52, ed. Gabriel Tissot, p. 30); Euthymius Zigabenus, *Exp. Luc.* ad loc. (PG 129.958B); Dionysius bar Salibi, *Comm. Ev.* ad Lk 10:4 (CSCO 95, Scriptores Syri 47, ed. J. Sedlacek and J.-B. Chabot, p. 329); Bar-Hebraeus, *Commentary on the Gospels*, p. 114; Nicholas of Gorran, *In quatuor evangelia commentarius*, p. 636; Bonaventure, *Exp. Luc.* ad loc. (Opera Omnia 10, ed. A. C. Peltier, p. 12); Nicholas of Lyra, *Biblia cum glosa ordinaria et expositione Nicolai de Lyra* (Basel: J. Petri & J. Froben, 1498), ad loc.

20. MT: משענה. Tg. Ps.-J.: חטר. The LXX translates משענה with ῥάβδος in Exod 21:19; Judg 6:21; 4 Βασ 18:21; Isa 36:6; Zech 8:4.

21. MT: ברך. Tg. Ps.-J. here uses שאל + בשלם.

22. So Lk 10:3. Cf. Mt 10:5–6.

One may also observe that the unit that introduces Q's missionary discourse, namely, Q 9:59–62, directs attention, as we have seen, to another episode involving Elisha (see above).[23]

Q 10:4's allusion to 2 Kgs 4:29 is hermeneutically very helpful, for in Kings the injunction not to exchange greetings is clearly motivated: time is of the essence. Commentators on Luke have regularly taken this as the clue to making sense of Lk 10:4, which otherwise remains enigmatic. As Calvin wrote, the prohibition of greeting "indicates extreme haste. . . . Thus, when Elijah sent his servant to the Shunamite woman. . . . "[24] Here is a case where the interpretation of a text is fixed by its subtext, without which we would be left in the dark.[25]

Q 10:5 // 1 Sam 25:6 (?). According to Lk 10:5, when the itinerants of Jesus enter a house, they are to say, "Peace to this house" (εἰρήνη τῷ οἴκῳ τούτῳ). This expression is a rarity, its only parallels being, to my knowledge, in 1 Sam 25:6 and *Lam Rab.* proem 25. Commentators are once in a while reminded of the former.[26] Here David sends men to Nabal and tells them to salute him with the words, "Peace be to you, and peace be to your house, and peace be to all that you have." In Samuel, the king sends messengers, and they are looking for food. In Q, Jesus sends missionaries, and they too are hoping to receive food (Q 10:7–8). The analogy would be all the greater if the hearers of Q, like so many other early followers of Jesus, believed him to be the Davidic Messiah and so one like David.[27] Such an audience might in fact take the analogy to confirm Jesus' Davidic status.

But in this matter we cannot pass beyond the interrogatory, for not only is there no assurance that Luke is here the better witness to Q,[28] but the earliest Christian sources do not pay much attention to the story of David, Nabal,

---

23. Those of us (a distinct minority) who assign Mt 10:5–6 (with its prohibition of mission to Gentiles and Samaritans) to Q may wonder whether Elisha's association with Samaria (2 Kgs 2:25; 5:3; 6:19; etc.) would not have extended the intertextuality in Q 10.

24. Calvin, *Harmony* ad loc. Cf. John Pearson, *Critici sacri* (Amsterdam: Balthasaris Christophi Wustii, 1698), vol. 6, ad Lk 10:4; William Dodd, *Commentary*, vol. 3, ad Lk 9:62; and many others.

25. Calvin's interpretation need not exclude that of Bosold, *Pazifismus*, pp. 81–93; and Uro, *Sheep among the Wolves*, pp. 135–37, who think of the prohibition as a prophetic sign of provocation. That the staff is not taken is also probably explained by the need for hurriedness. See further pp. 41–43, where the possibility of a new exodus motif (cf. Exod 12:11 + 35–36) is considered.

26. So, e.g., Hodgson, "On the Gattung of Q," p. 80. The parallel is cited by Hühn, *Alttestamentlichen Citate*, p. 57, and is in the margin beside Lk 10:5 in the recent Nestle-Aland editions. Cf. Poole, *Commentary*, vol. 1, p. 573; and Scott, *Holy Bible*, vol. 2, p. 90. But Tertullian, *Adv. Marc.* 4.24 (PL 2.419A), found a parallel in 2 Kgs 4:26 (interpreted to mean, "Peace to you, peace to your husband, peace to your child") — presumably because he had just noted another parallel between Luke 10 and 2 Kings 4 (see above).

27. For this possibility for Q, see Edward P. Meadors, "The 'Messianic' Implications of the Q Material," *JBL* 118 (1999), pp. 253–77.

28. Mt 10:12–13 is different: "As you enter the house, greet it. And if the house is worthy, let your peace come upon it."

and Abigail.[29] Beyond that, the verbal link obtains only when comparison is made with the MT (בֵּיתְךָ שָׁלוֹם).[30] The LXX has, "May you and your house prosper, and may all that is yours prosper" (σὺ ὑγιαίνων καὶ ὁ οἶκός σου καὶ πάντα τὰ σὰ ὑγιαίνοντα). Is this an example of an allusion that was clearer in an earlier, Semitic stage of the tradition? Or is the affinity between Q 10:5 and 1 Sam 25:6 just the fruit of coincidence?

Q 11:31 // 2 Chronicles 9. The queen of the South will be raised at the judgment and condemn "this generation," for she "came from the ends of the earth[31] to listen to the wisdom of Solomon, and behold, something greater than Solomon is here." These words refer to the well-known story narrated in 1 Kgs 10:1–13 and 2 Chr 9:1–12. Five observations may be made. First, the Sayings Source alludes to the biblical story in the briefest possible manner. The tale is not told here because the listeners, it is assumed, already know it. Second, Q 11:31 does not explicitly identify the queen of the South as a Gentile, but this is surely assumed. We have just read about the pagan Ninevites who repented, so here Q is, as in Q 10:12–14, implicitly accusing certain Jews of being bested by Gentiles. Third, ἡ σοφία Σολομῶνος ("the wisdom of Solomon") was a conventional expression associated in particular with our story (and only later with the book of the Apocrypha known as the "Wisdom of Solomon," Σοφία Σαλωμώνος):[32]

LXX 3 Βασ 10:4	φρόνησιν Σαλωμὼν	(MT: חכמת שלמה)
LXX 3 Βασ 10:6	τῆς φρονήσεώς σου	(MT: חכמתך)
LXX 3 Βασ 10:8	τὴν φρόνησίν σου	(MT: חכמתך)
LXX 3 Βασ 10:24	τῆς φρονήσεως αὐτοῦ	(MT: חכמתו)
LXX 2 Chr 9:3	τὴν σοφίαν Σαλωμὼν	(MT: חכמת שלמה)
LXX 2 Chr 9:5	τῆς σοφίας σου	(MT: חכמתך)
LXX 2 Chr 9:6	τῆς σοφίας σου	(MT: חכמתך)
LXX 2 Chr 9:7	σοφίαν σου	(MT: חכמתך)
LXX 2 Chr 9:23	τῆς σοφίας αὐτοῦ	(MT: חכמתו)
Josephus, *Ant.* 8.168[33]	τὴν σοφίαν τοῦ Σολόμωνος	

Q agrees with LXX Chronicles against LXX Kings.

Fourth, the words "to listen to the wisdom of Solomon" echo the story of the queen of Sheba. She says in 1 Kgs 10:8 = 2 Chr 9:7, "Happy are these your servants who . . . hear your wisdom," and 1 Kgs 10:24 = 2 Chr 9:23

---

29. Sometimes 1 Sam 25:41 is cited as a parallel to Lk 7:44, and 1 Sam 25:25 as a parallel to Acts 24:5, but the resemblances are slight.

30. Cf. Tg. Ps.-J. 1 Sam 25:6: בֵּיתָךְ שְׁלָם.

31. "From the ends of the earth" (ἐκ τῶν περάτων τῆς γῆς) is a biblicism that occurs in LXX Dan 4:18; Theod. Dan 4:8, 19; Tob S 13:11; Wisd 6:1; and over ten times in LXX Psalms (e.g., 60:3: ἀπὸ τῶν περάτων τῆς γῆς, for MT's מקצה הארץ).

32. The book may not have been composed much before Q saw the light of day; a date in the first half of the first century c.e. is often suggested.

33. This is a retelling of 1 Kings 10 and 2 Chronicles 9.

apprises us that "the whole earth" (so Kings) or "all the kings of the earth" (so Chronicles) "sought the presence of Solomon to hear his wisdom:"

Q 11:31	ἀκοῦσαι	τὴν σοφίαν	Σολομῶνος
LXX 3 Βασ 10:8 οἱ	ἀκούοντες…	τὴν φρόνησίν	σου (MT: השמעים את־חכמתך)
LXX 3 Βασ 10:24 τοῦ	ἀκοῦσαι	τῆς φρονήσεως	αὐτου (MT: לשמע את־חכמתו)
LXX 2 Chr 9:7	ἀκούουσιν	σοφίαν	σου (MT: שמעים את־חכמתך)
LXX 2 Chr 9:23	ἀκοῦσαι	τῆς σοφίας	αὐτοῦ (MT: לשמע את־חכמתו)
T. Sol. 19:3 P	ἀκούσασα	τὴν σοφίαν	μου

Q's Greek is, it may be again noted, closer to Chronicles than Kings.

Finally, Kings and Chronicles speak of "the queen of Sheba" (LXX: βασίλισσα Σαβά; MT: מלכת־שבא),[34] Q of "the queen of the South" (βασίλισσα νότου). Apart from writings dependent upon the canonical Gospels, the expression seemingly appears elsewhere only in T. Sol. 19:3 and 21:1 (both times βασίλισσα νότου). Josephus, Ant. 8.165, says she was queen of Egypt and Ethiopia. Q's expression probably presumes that she was from Arabia.[35]

Q 11:49–51 + 13:34–35 // 2 Chr 24:17–25.[36] Although the Zechariah named in Mt 23:35 = Lk 11:51 has, throughout exegetical history, most often and rightly been identified with the figure whose martyrdom is related in 2 Chronicles 24,[37] the fact that Q 11:49–51 + 13:34–35 draws heavily upon 2 Chr 24:17–25 has seemingly been overlooked—although the commentators on 2 Chronicles sometimes take notice.[38] Consider the display of the parallels as shown on the following page. Q 11:49–51 + 13:34–35 is an updating of 2 Chr 24:17–22, 25: it moves the historic language of Chronicles to the eschatological time of the Jesus.

How does the recognition of the intertext affect the interpretation of Q 11:49–51 + 13:34–35? The latter implicitly constructs an analogy: As it was in the days of Zechariah, so now is it in the days of Jesus. If in the

---

34. So too the targum on Kings, but the targum on Chronicles has מלכת זמרגד, "queen of Zemargad" (cf. Tg. 1 Chr 1:9). זמרגד is a Greek loanword from σμάραγδος = "emerald," for which LSJ, s.v., gives as the second meaning, "the name of the Emerald mines in Egypt."

35. Although the Bible does not locate Sheba, modern archaeology identifies it with modern Yemen in southwest Arabia.

For the later Jewish legends about the queen of Sheba, see Lou H. Silberman, "The Queen of Sheba in Jewish Tradition," in *Solomon and Sheba* (ed. James B. Pritchard; London: Phaidon, 1974), pp. 65–84. I cannot see that they shed any light on Q. Q certainly shows no knowledge of her identification with Lilith, queen of the demons.

36. In addition to what follows, see the discussion of 11:49–51 on pp. 85–86. There it is argued that Q's order is in this rare case preserved by Matthew; that is, Mt 23:34–39 = Lk 11:49–51 + 13:34–35 corresponds to Q's sequence.

37. See above, pp. 84–87, and below, pp. 151–52.

38. E.g., F. C. Cook, *The Holy Bible*, vol. 3, *II Kings-Esther* (New York: Charles Scribner's Sons, 1886), pp. 337–38; and J. Glentworth Butler, *The Bible-Work. The Old Testament*, vol. 7, *1 Kings XII–XXII, 2 Kings, 2 Chronicles X–XXXVI, Ezra, Nehemiah, Esther, Isaiah, Four Chapters, Jeremiah, Eighteen Chapters* (New York: Butler Bible-Work, 1894), pp. 311–12.

Q 11:49–51 + 13:34–35	*2 Chr 24:17–25*
"I will send them prophets" (Lk: ἀποστελῶ εἰς αὐτοὺς προφήτας, Mt: ἐγὼ ἀποστέλλω πρὸς ὑμᾶς προφήτας), 11:49	"He sent prophets among them" (LXX: ἀπέστειλεν πρὸς αὐτοὺς προφήτας; MT: וישלח בהם נבאים), v. 19
"Some they will kill," 11:49	the stoning of Zechariah, vv. 20–22
"the blood of Zechariah (αἵματος Ζαχαρίου)," 11:51	"the blood (LXX: αἵμασιν; MT: דמי) of the son of the priest Jehoiada," that is, of Zechariah, v. 25
"who perished between the altar and the house" (οἴκου), 11:51[39]	"stoned him to death in the court of the house (LXX: οἴκου; MT: בית) of the Lord," v. 21
"required of this generation," 11:50, 51	"May the Lord see and avenge!" v. 22; cf. Tg. 2 Chr 24:25: "that the blood of the sons of Jehoiada the priest might be avenged"
"stoning (λιθοβολοῦσα) those sent to you," 13:34	"stoned (LXX: ἐλιθοβόλησαν; MT: וירגמהו אבן) him to death," v. 21
judgment upon Jerusalem, 13:34–35	Judah and Jerusalem delivered into the hands of the Syrians, vv. 23–24
"your house is forsaken (ἀφίεται ὑμῖν ὁ οἶκος)," 13:35[40]	"They forsook the house (MT: יעזבו את־בית) of the Lord," v. 18 (LXX has only "they forsook [ἐγκατέλιπον] the Lord"); "Because you have forsaken the Lord, he has forsaken (LXX: ἐγκαταλείψει; MT: יעזב) you," v. 20 (cf. v. 24); *Midr. Num* 30:15 says that the murder of Zechariah caused the Shekinah to depart from the temple.

---

39. This is Luke's version, which the IQP favors. Mt 23:35 has "between the sanctuary and the altar" (τοῦ ναοῦ καὶ τοῦ θυσιαστηρίου; cf. Ezek 8:16; Joel 2:17). Interestingly enough, the targum on 2 Chr 24:18 adds מקדשא, "sanctuary." Cf. the targum on Lam 2:20, where the question, "Should priest and prophet be killed in the house of the sanctuary of the Lord?" is answered with this: "As they slew Zechariah, the son of Iddo, the high priest and faithful prophet in the house of the sanctuary (בבית מקדשא)...." Already *Liv. Proph. Zech* 23:1 has Zechariah killed near "the altar" (θυσιαστηρίου).

40. On this phrase, see further pp. 126–28.

past Jerusalem forsook the Lord so that the Lord forsook the city, so again has this happened: the rejection of Jesus means the rejection of Jerusalem. The house is abandoned, the divine presence withdrawn ("You will not see me again . . . "). In this way tragedy wears a familiar face — from one point of view it has all happened before — and Q's verdict, however dreadful, is made both more authoritative and more palatable through contemporary circumstances being akin to 2 Chronicles 24: there is scriptural precedent.

It may also be significant that 2 Chronicles 24 is not unremittingly negative. The chapter, after narrating the martyrdom of Zechariah, the conquest of Jerusalem, and the murder of King Joash, ends by speaking of "the rebuilding of the house of God" (v. 27). This positive conclusion is of interest because while the majority of commentators have thought the conclusion of Q 11:49–51 + 13:34–35 ("You will not see me again until you say, 'Blessed is the one who comes in the name of the Lord' ") to anticipate only condemnation, others have agreed with John Wesley, who found in our text the hope that someday the Jerusalemites will receive Jesus "with joyful and thankful hearts."[41] Perhaps Wesley's interpretation is more credible when one sees that Q 13:35 belongs to a complex that rewrites 2 Chronicles 24, where there is restoration in the end.

The realization that Q 11:49–51 + 13:34–35 depends upon 2 Chronicles 24 helps with two old exegetical problems. The first concerns the debate over the identity of Zechariah. Perhaps most exegetes have, ever since Jerome, identified him with the martyr in 2 Chronicles,[42] who has sometimes been further identified with the canonical prophet whose book is known as "Zechariah."[43] But many have instead thought of the father of John the Baptist, whose name is Zechariah in Lk 1:5–23 and who is martyred in *Prot. Jas* 23.1–23.4.[44] Zwingli and others have nominated the son of Baris (or Bariscaeus or Baruch), who was martyred in the temple during the Jewish war according to Josephus, *Bell.* 4.334–44 (cf. Mt 23:35: "Zechariah the son of Barachiah").[45] And a few have confessed ignorance: for all we know

41. Wesley, *Explanatory Notes*, p. 78. For a survey of the interpretive options and a defense of the view that Q 13:34–35 envisages the repentance of Israel, see Allison, *Jesus Tradition in Q*, 192–204.

42. Jerome, *Comm. Mt* 4.286ff. (CCSL 77, pp. 219f.); Paschasius Radbertus, *Exp. Mt libri XII (IX–XII)* ad loc. (CCSL 66B, ed. p. 1138); Bonaventure, *Exp. Luc.* ad loc. (Opera Omnia 10, ed. A. C. Peltier, p. 548); Calvin, *Harmony*, vol. 3, p. 66; Maldonatus, *Commentarii*, vol. 1, pp. 321–22; Poole, *Commentary*, vol. 3, p. 111; Trapp, *Commentary*, vol. 5, p. 244; Wesley, *Explanatory Notes*, p. 77; Luz, *Matthäus*, vol. 2, pp. 373–74.

43. E.g., Jerome but not Calvin.

44. Cf. Origen, *Comm. Mt* frag. 457; Gregory of Nyssa, *Diem nat. Domini* (PG 46.1132B); Epiphanius, *Haer.* 26.12.2 (PL 41.350D), quoting the lost *The Birth of Mary;* Peter of Alexandria, *Ep. can.* 13 (PG 18.504B); Theophylact, *Comm. Mt* ad loc. (PG 123.406B-C). *Prot. Jas* 23.1–23.4 recalls the language of Mt 23:34ff. par. and so seems to be narrating the event told in Q.

45. Ulrich Zwingli, *Annotationes in Evangelium Matthaei* (Opera 6/1; ed. M. Schuler and J. Schulthess; Zurich: F. Schulthess, 1836), p. 376; Julius Wellhausen, *Das Evangelium Matthaei* (Berlin: Reimer, 1904), pp. 119–21; and Steck, *Israel*, pp. 33–40. Matthew refers to Ζεχαρίου

the text refers to a Zechariah of whom we have no knowledge.[46] When, however, one sees all the parallels between Q 11:49–51 + 13:34–35 and 2 Chronicles 24, the issue resolves itself. If Q names a certain Zechariah, and if its intertext also names a certain Zechariah, they must be one and the same.

The biblical background to Q 11:49–51 + 13:34–35 may resolve a second exegetical crux. Whereas Mt 23:34 begins with, "Therefore, behold, I send to you prophets," Lk 11:49 commences with this: "Therefore also the Wisdom of God said (διὰ τοῦτο καὶ ἡ σοφία τοῦ θεοῦ εἶπεν), 'I will send them prophets.' " Most source critics have reckoned Luke's introduction to be original, and this judgment seems sound; that is, Q probably referred to "the Wisdom of God."[47] But there has been no accord as to what this "Wisdom of God" might be. Some have suggested that it is the name of a lost Jewish apocryphon.[48] Others have understood Luke's Greek to mean "God in God's wisdom said," while still others have suggested that divine Wisdom is the speaker or that Jesus is here giving himself a novel self-designation.[49] But once one recognizes the extensive dependence of Q 11:49ff. upon 2 Chr 24:17ff., another possibility suggests itself. The identification of Sophia with Torah was prevalent,[50] and the identification of Torah with the entire Bible, not just the Pentateuch, was also known.[51] So given that Q 11:49ff. is a transformation of Scripture, of 2 Chr 24:17ff., and that Q 11:49 (Lk: ἀποστελῶ εἰς αὐτοὺς προφήτας, Mt: ἐγὼ ἀποστέλλω πρὸς ὑμᾶς προφήτας) is particularly close to 2 Chr 24:19 (LXX: ἀπέστειλεν πρὸς αὐτοὺς προφήτας), it occurs that maybe "the Wisdom of God" is a way of referring to the Bible. Certainly εἶπεν was common in formulas introducing biblical quotations.[52]

Q 12:27 // Solomonic traditions. "Even Solomon in all his glory (τῇ δόξῃ) was not arrayed" like the wild lilies. The memorable assertion gains its impact from hearers knowing that Solomon's reign was, as reported in 1 Kings, 2 Chronicles, and Ecclesiastes 2, the most splendid in Israel's history (cf. 1 Kgs 10:23; 1 Esdr 1:5; patristic commentaries regularly make Solomon's reign the most glorious not just in Israel but in human history).[53]

υἱοῦ Βαραχίου, Josephus to Ζεχαρίαν υἱὸν Βάρεις (so P A V R Lat) or Βαρούχου (M¹ C) or Βαρισκαίου (L M²).

46. E.g., J. M. Ross, "Which Zachariah?" *IBS* 9 (1987), pp. 70–73.

47. So the IQP; Sato, *Q und Prophetie*, pp. 151–54; and Schürmann, *Lukasevangelium*, vol. 2, pp. 326–27. Contrast Jeremias, *Sprache*, pp. 208–9.

48. So, e.g., Rudolf Bultmann, *The History of the Synoptic Tradition* (rev. ed.; New York: Harper & Row, 1976), p. 119.

49. For these options and proponents of them, see Marshall, *Luke*, pp. 502–3. The third is the view of most of the older ecclesiastical commentaries.

50. The evidence is reviewed in Eckhard J. Schnabel, *Law and Wisdom from Ben Sira to Paul: A Tradition Historical Enquiry into the Relation of Law, Wisdom, and Ethics* (WUNT 2/16; Tübingen: Mohr Siebeck, 1985).

51. W. Gutbrod, *TDNT* 4 (1967), pp. 1054–55.

52. Joseph A. Fitzmyer, *Essays on the Semitic Background of the New Testament* (Missoula, Mont.: Scholars Press, 1974), pp. 10–12.

53. See, e.g., Chrysostom, *Hom. Mt* 22.1 (PG 57.300).

As Josephus, *Ant.* 8.211, put it, Solomon "surpassed all other kings in good fortune, wealth, and wisdom."

Several key words or motifs in Q 12:27 are particularly appropriate in a passage naming Solomon. (i) "Glory" (δόξα) was typically associated with Solomon's reign, as appears from these places:

> 3 Βασ 3:13: "I have given you [Solomon] what you did not ask for, wealth and glory (δόξαν)."

> 1 Chr 29:25: "And the Lord magnified Solomon above all Israel, and he gave to him kingly glory (LXX: δόξαν), such as was not upon any king before him."

> 2 Chronicles: This book refers more than once to the "glory (LXX: δόξα) of the Lord" abiding in the temple during Solomon's reign (5:13, 14; 7:1, 2, 3; cf. 2:6).

> 2 Chr 1:12: "I [God] will give to you [Solomon] wisdom and understanding and riches and property and glory (LXX: δόξαν)."

> Josephus, *Ant.* 8.190: Solomon was "the most glorious (ἐνδοξότατος) of all kings."

> *T. Sol.* 5:5: "Do not ask me so many things, Solomon.... This glory (δόξαν) of yours is temporary."

> Justin, *Dial.* 36; 85.1: Justin argues that Solomon is not "the king of glory (δόξης)" of Psalm 24.[54]

(ii) The Greek word κρίνον, usually translated "lily," appears twenty-two times in the LXX, over half of them in connection with Solomon. 3 Βασ 7:19, 22, 24, 26; and 2 Chr 4:5 detail the lily decorations for Solomon's temple, and the author of Canticles (traditionally Solomon) is "a lily of the valleys" (2:1) who "pastures his flock among the lilies" (2:16; 6:3) and gathers lilies (6:2), and his lips are like lilies (5:13). Further, he speaks of the lily when talking about the beauty of his beloved (4:5; 7:2). As Cornelius à Lapide wrote in commenting upon Mt 6:28–29, that "Solomon delighted in them [lilies] is plain from his Song of Songs, where he often says of the bridegroom, 'He feedeth among the lilies.' And again, 'I am the flower of the field, and the lily of the valleys' (Vulg.)."[55] So when Q's Jesus compares Solomon and the lilies, he is taking up a traditional juxtaposition. Perhaps indeed there is irony generated by the circumstance that if Solomon equates himself with the lily (Cant 2:1), Jesus in effect says he is not a lily.

---

54. PTS 47, ed. Miroslav Marcovich, pp. 131, 216.
55. Lapide, *Commentary*, vol. 1, p. 288. Cf. Albertus Magnus, *Super Mt cap. I–XIV* ad Mt 6:28 (Opera Omni 21/1, ed. B. Schmid, p. 237); M. F. Olsthoorn, *The Jewish Background and the Synoptic Setting of Mt 6,25–33 and Lk 12,22–31* (Studium Biblicum Franciscanium Analecta 10; Jerusalem: Franciscan, 1975), p. 46; and Martin Ebner, *Jesus — ein Weisheitslehrer? Synoptische Weishheitslogien im Traditionsprozess* (HBS 15; Freiburg: Herder, 1998), p. 265.

(iii) Q's "toil" (κοπιῶσιν) may also have something to do with the traditions about Solomon. For the question "What do people gain from all the toil at which they toil under the sun?" (1:3) stands at the head of Ecclesiastes, a book thought in antiquity to have been authored by Solomon, and over and over again it speaks of labor or toil.[56] When it does so, the LXX uses μοχθεῖν and μόχθος (for עמל). But κοπιάω appears in LXX B Eccles 2:18 ("I hated the whole of my labor with which I toiled [κοπιῶ] under the sun"), and Aquila has κοπιάω and κόπος in Eccles 1:3 and 8, while Symmachus uses the latter in Eccles 2:24 and 4:6. κοπιάω and κόπος moreover appear in additional texts that the ancients thought were written by Solomon — LXX Ps 126:1 (attributed to Solomon in the superscription); Prov 4:12; Wisd 3:11; 9:10; 10:10, 17; *T. Sol.* 2:8; 10:10. So maybe Olsthoorn is right to suggest that "they neither toil nor spin" echoes Solomon's "self-criticism: his toil was of no avail: it was vanity and chasing of wind. Then we have . . . a critical saying which lines up very well with the previous saying about the powerlessness of anxiety."[57]

(iv) Q 12:22–31 is about anxiety over food, drink, and clothing, while Q 12:27 mentions the clothing of Solomon in particular. It may be relevant then to note that several texts refer to the spectacular food, drink, and clothing of Solomon's court: 1 Kgs 4:20, 22; 10:5; 2 Chr 9:4.[58] In addition, both Kings and Chronicles inform us that Solomon was given all this by God precisely because he sought other things, namely, wisdom and knowledge (1 Kgs 3:11–13; 2 Chr 1:11–12; cf. Wisd 7:10–11). This is analogous to Q 12:22–31, in which those who seek the kingdom have their physical needs met by God.

What we appear to have in Q 12:27 is what we have found elsewhere: when Q explicitly refers to a biblical person or story it sometimes reinforces the reference by incorporating words, phrases, and themes found in the biblical accounts of that person or story (cf. 11:31–32, 51).

II. Synthesis

(i) The results of this chapter may be seen at a glance:

     1 Sam 25:6 — Q 10:5 (allusion?)
     1 Kgs 19:19–21 — Q 9:59–62 (allusion)
     2 Kgs 4:29 — Q 10:4 (allusion)
     2 Chronicles 9 — Q 11:31 (explicit reference)
     2 Chr 24:17–25 — Q 11:49–51 + 13:34–35 (explicit reference)
     Solomonic traditions — Q 12:27 (explicit reference)

---

56. 1:3, 8; 2:10, 11, 18, 19, 20, 21, 22, 24; 3:13; 4:4, 6, 8, 9; 5:15, 16, 18, 19; 6:7; 8:15, 17; 9:9; 10:15.

57. Olsthoorn, *Jewish Background*, p. 48.

58. Cf. Albertus Magnus, *Super Mt cap. I–XIV* ad Mt 6:29 (Opera Omni 21/1, ed. B. Schmid, p. 237), citing 1 Kgs 10:4–5.

Q shows a knowledge of both Kings and Chronicles and maybe Samuel. There are no references to Joshua or Judges. This neglect is perhaps not surprising. A work that enjoins turning the other cheek and loving one's enemy (Q 6:27, 29) might be expected not to borrow from texts that are as brutal and bloody as Joshua and Judges.

(ii) When Q refers to the Former Prophets and Chronicles, it does not just allude to famous people and events but in every case incorporates textual details from the Tanak. Q 9:59–62 mirrors not only the circumstances of Elijah's calling of Elisha but uses the vocabulary of 1 Kgs 19:19–21 (ἀκολουθέω, ἄροτρον, ὀπίσω). Q 10:4 borrows an imperative from 2 Kgs 4:29 ("Do not greet anyone") and reflects its context, for in Q 10 the imperative to "Go" is followed by words about staff, greeting, and healing, while in 2 Kgs 4:29 Elijah says, "Take my staff in your hand and go. If you meet anyone, give no greeting… and lay my staff on the face of the child [to heal him]." If Jesus' command in Q 10:5, "Peace be to this house," comes from 1 Sam 25:6, then it is noteworthy that in both places the context has to do with a leader sending out his followers for food. Q 11:31 does not just refer to the story of Solomon and the queen of Sheba but incorporates a phrase from 2 Chr 9:7, 23 ("to listen to his wisdom"). Q 11:49–51 + 13:34–35, in referring to the martyrdom of Zechariah as told in 2 Chronicles 24, borrows most of its themes from 2 Chr 24:17–25 — the sending and murder of prophets, Zechariah's blood, perishing in the temple, vengeance, stoning, judgment upon Jerusalem, being forsaken. And Q 12:27 does not just name Solomon but uses words that biblical texts associate with him specifically — "glory," "lily," "toil." In sum, Q incorporates not vague knowledge about such figures as Elijah, Elisha, Solomon, and Zechariah but precise knowledge about particular texts.

(iii) Jesus, in issuing his call to discipleship, is like Elijah (Q 9:59–61; cf. 1 Kgs 19:19–21). Jesus' words also recall the speech of Elisha (Q 10:4; cf. 2 Kgs 4:29) and perhaps that of David (Q 10:5; cf. 1 Sam 25:6). So Q's Jesus is familiar: he beckons reminiscence. The emphasis, however, is not on continuity with the past. Q rather recalls the old in order to show that with Jesus something new has come. Thus he, unlike Elijah (LXX 1 Kgs 19:19–21; Josephus, *Ant.* 8.354), does not grant a would-be follower permission to return to parents (Q 9:59–61). And unlike Elisha (2 Kgs 4:29), Jesus' followers are not to take a staff (Q 10:5). Similarly, Q 11:31 recalls the story of the queen of Sheba in order to declare that "something greater than Solomon is here." So yet again the contrast trumps the continuity. The same is true for the transformation of 2 Chr 24:17–25 in Q 11:49–51 + 13:34–35. If the Chronicler recounts the terrible consequences of the murder of Zechariah, Q proclaims a guilt that somehow spans the mistreatment of God's envoys throughout history: "The blood of all the prophets that has been shed from the foundation of the world will be required of this generation." For Chronicles, history can continue. For Q, the end is at hand, and the future is the coming of the Son of man.

(iv) Finally, aside from a couple of references to Solomon, there is very little interest in the history of David or in texts having to do with Davidic kingship. Does this mean anything interesting? Although inferences from silence are hazardous, one might at least wonder whether the issue of Davidic messiahship was not of great importance for Q's contributors.[59]

---

59. But for other considerations that cast doubt on this inference, see Meadors, " 'Messianic' Implications of the Q Material."

Chapter 7

Psalms

I. Texts and Analysis

Q 4:10–11 // Ps 91:12. (i) Thrice in the temptation story Jesus quotes Deuteronomy,[1] but there is a fourth quotation, one not from Deuteronomy. In this instance it is the devil through whom the Scripture speaks — a fact that has always fascinated ecclesiastical commentators. When Satan takes Jesus to Jerusalem and sets him on the wing[2] of the temple, he challenges him with the words of Ps 91:11–12: "If you are the Son of God, throw yourself down, for it is written, 'He will command his angels concerning you, and on their hands they will bear you up, lest you ever dash your foot against a stone' ":

Mt 4:6	τοῖς ἀγγέλοις αὐτοῦ ἐντελεῖται περὶ σοῦ
Lk 4:10	τοῖς ἀγγέλοις αὐτοῦ ἐντελεῖται περὶ σοῦ τοῦ διαφυλάξαι σε
LXX Ps 90:11	τοῖς ἀγγέλοις αὐτοῦ ἐντελεῖται περὶ σοῦ τοῦ διαφυλάξαι σε
MT Ps 91:11	מלאכיו יצוח־לך...
Tg. Ps 91:11	מלאכוי יפקד עלך...

Mt 4:6	καὶ ἐπὶ χειρῶν ἀροῦσίν σε, μήποτε προσκόψῃς πρὸς λίθον τὸν πόδα σου
Lk 4:11	καὶ ὅτι ἐπὶ χειρῶν ἀροῦσίν σε, μήποτε προσκόψῃς πρὸς λίθον τὸν πόδα σου
LXX 90:12	ἐπὶ χειρῶν ἀροῦσίν σε, μήποτε προσκόψῃς πρὸς λίθον τὸν πόδα σου
MT Ps 91:12	על־כפים ישאונך פן־תגף באבן רגלך[3]
Tg. Ps 91:12	על תוקפיהון יטלונך דילמא תיתקל ביצרא בישא דמתיל לאבני ריגלך

One wonders whether the tempter's words add to the new exodus typology reviewed in chapter 3.[4] The devil seeks to reassure Jesus that the angels will "bear [him] up" (ἀροῦσιν) if he were to throw himself down from the "wing" (πτερύγιον) of the temple. An informed hearer might recall that, after leaving Egypt, Israel was "borne up" in the desert on "wings:"

> Exod 19:4: "You have seen what I did to the Egyptians, and how I bore you on eagles wings (LXX: πτερύγων) and brought you to myself."

> Deut 1:31: God "carried" Israel in the wilderness.

---

1. See above, pp. 25–27.
2. What exactly is meant by the "wing" of the temple remains uncertain.
3. 11Q11 6:10–11, although fragmentary, appears to agree with the MT.
4. See above, pp. 25–29.

Deut 32:11–12: God sustained Jacob "in a desert land, in a howling wilderness waste; he shielded him, cared for him, guarded him as the apple of his eye. As an eagle stirs up its nest, and hovers over its young; as it spreads its wings (LXX: πτέρυγας), takes them up, and bears them aloft on its pinions, the Lord alone guided him."

Isa 63:9: God "lifted them up and carried them all the days of old."

So Q's desire to replay the exodus might help explain the otherwise obscure use of "wing (πτερύγιον) of the temple." Maybe the devil recognizes that the Son of God is undergoing a new exodus and accordingly tempts Jesus to make God do something that God did long ago for Israel in the wilderness (cf. the temptation to produce bread, Q 4:3).

The proposal is, however, uncertain, for Q's verb, αἴρω, is not used in the Septuagintal verses of the passages just cited, and "wing" might direct one rather to Ps 91:4 ("under his wings [LXX: πτέρυγας] you will find refuge").[5] Moreover, *Midr. Rab.* on 91:11–12 seems to take "bear you up" not in a metaphorical sense (as in the passages about the exodus just cited) but literally: the angels raised Jacob in the air. Q offers the same literal reading.

Whether or not the quotation of Ps 91:12 belongs to Q's new exodus theme, there is another way in which the verse might be particularly appropriate. Some readers have taken Psalm 91 to be a royal psalm.[6] Moreover, Lk 10:19 and perhaps *T. Levi* 18:12 allude to Ps 91:13 ("You will tread on the lion and the adder, the young lion and the serpent you will trample under foot") in contexts that are eschatological:

MT Ps 91:13: "You will tread (תדרך) on the lion and the adder (פתן), the young lion and the serpent (תנין) you will trample (תרמס)."

LXX Ps 90:13: "You will tread on the asp and serpent (ἐπ᾽ ἀσπίδα καὶ βασιλίσκον ἐπιβήσῃ), and you will trample (καταπατήσεις) on the lion and dragon."

Lk 10:19: "I have given you authority to tread on snakes and scorpions (πατεῖν ἐπάνω ὄφεων καὶ σκορπίων), and over all the power of the enemy; and nothing will hurt you."

T. Levi 18:12: "And he will grant to his children authority to trample on (πατεῖν ἐπί) wicked spirits."

Because Q's Jesus fulfills the oracle of Isa 61:12, which foretells the advent of an anointed eschatological figure,[7] it would be fitting for him to be challenged with a scriptural text for Israel's king, and especially a text with

5. Cf. Gerhardsson, *Testing*, p. 59.
6. E.g., A. Caquot, "Le Psaume XCI," *Semitica* 8 (1958), pp. 21–37.
7. See pp. 104–7, 109–14.

eschatological content. Maybe, then, this is precisely what the devil does by quoting Ps 91:13 in Q 4:10–11.

But another possibility is even more intriguing. Some modern writers have thought that Psalm 91 was composed as an apotropaic prayer to ward off demons.[8] However one decides that issue, there is ample evidence that the psalm came to be used as such. *b. Šeb.* 15b gives to it the title "A song against evil occurrences,"[9] which the Epstein edition explains as "the psalm referring to evil spirits or demons" (cf. *y. Šabb.* 6:8b). Moreover, both ancient Jews and Christians used Psalm 91 as a talisman against evil spirits,[10] and the LXX, Peshitta, and targum all translate 91:6 so that it refers explicitly to demons.[11] No less importantly, Qumran's 11Q11 (11QapocrPs) is a collection of four apotropaic psalms, of which Psalm 91 is a member.[12] Clearly Psalm 91 was already read in pre-Christian times as a talisman to ward off evil.

What might this mean for one's understanding Q's temptation narrative? If hearers of Q thought of Psalm 91 as apotropaic and recognized that the devil is quoting from it, there would be great irony: Satan would be quoting from a text that was used to drive away evil spirits. One might even find humor here: the devil is so incompetent that he seeks help from a text that is his enemy.

Although this reading must unfortunately remain conjectural, one thing is clear: when the devil quotes, he does so imperfectly. In its entirety Ps 91:11–12 says, "For he will command his angels concerning you to guard you in all your ways. On their hands they will bear you up, so that you will not dash your foot against a stone." When the devil cites these lines, he leaves out "in all your ways" (Q 4:10–11). The deletion might have been noticed by hearers steeped in the Psalms. So one could, recalling that already in Gen 3:2 the serpent misquotes God, seek in the omission a hermeneutical clue. According to R. V. G. Tasker, "The omission in fact destroys the truth of the original, which does not encourage the faithful to tempt God by taking

---

8. See esp. Robert J. Burrelli, "A Study of Psalm 91 with Special Reference to the Theory That It Was Intended as a Protection against Demons and Magic" (Ph.D. diss., University of Cambridge, 1993), pp. 1–2. He refers to P. Haupt, A. A. Macintosh, W. O. E. Oesterley, Julius Wellhausen, and A. J. Wensinck.

9. שיר של פגעים. Cf. the appearance of הפגעוןים in 11Q11 5:2, which is followed in column 6 by Psalm 91.

10. See Pirim Hugger, *Jahwe meine Zuflucht: Gestalt und Theologie des 91. Psalms* (Münsterschwarzacher Studien 13; Münsterschwarzach: Vier-Türme, 1971), pp. 322–23, and the other sources cited by Burrelli, "Psalm 91," p. 8, n. 13. For early Christian interpretation, see R. Arbesmann, "The 'Daemonium Meridianum' and Greek and Latin Patristic Exegesis," *Traditio* 14 (1958), pp. 17–31.

11. LXX: "the demon of noonday"; Peshitta: "a spirit that devastates at midday"; Targum: "the band of demons that injure at midday."

12. É. Puech, "11QPsApª: un rituel d'exorcismes: Essai de reconstruction," *RevQ* 14 (1990), pp. 377–408; idem, "Les deux derniers psaumes davidiques du rituel d'exorcisme 11QPsApª IV 4–V 14," in *The Dead Sea Scrolls: Forty Years of Research* (ed. D. Dimant and U. Rappaport; STDJ 10; Leiden: Brill, 1992), pp. 64–89.

unnecessary risks, but assures him that God will keep him safe wherever his way may lead, provided he is obedient to the divine will."[13] Jesus does not, however, castigate the devil for misrepresenting Scripture, so maybe it is better to infer that the absence of "in all your ways" is instead simply an abbreviation that reflects application to a particular circumstance rather than to all of life.[14] Ancient authors often omitted from citations words not immediately pertinent.[15]

Q 9:57–58 // Ps 8:4–8. When Jesus instructs a prospective disciple that "Foxes have holes, and the birds of the air (τὰ πετεινὰ τοῦ οὐρανοῦ) have nests, but the Son of man (ὁ υἱὸς τοῦ ἀνθρώπου) has nowhere to lay his head,"[16] this is likely an intimation of Psalm 8, which is seemingly the only place in Jewish literature where "son of man" and "the birds of the air" are found together.[17] This psalm, perhaps an inner-biblical exegesis of Gen 1:26–28,[18] proclaims the honor and glory of mortals (v. 4, LXX: υἱὸς ἀνθρώπου), who have dominion over the beasts of the field and "the birds of the air" (v. 9, LXX: τὰ πετεινὰ τοῦ οὐρανοῦ). Jesus, however, declares that the Son of man is worse off than the birds and beasts, for he, unlike them, is without a home. So far from his head being crowned with glory and honor, Jesus finds no place to rest.

---

13. R. V. G. Tasker, *The Gospel according to St. Matthew* (TNTC; Grand Rapids: Eerdmans, 1973), p. 54.

14. Cf. M. Hasitschka, "Die Verwendung der Schrift in Mt 4,1–11," in Tuckett, ed., *The Scriptures in the Gospels*, p. 488.

15. Many examples of this appear in Christopher D. Stanley, *Paul and the Language of Scripture: Citation Technique in the Pauline Epistles and Contemporary Literature* (SNTSMS 69; Cambridge: Cambridge University Press, 1992). According to Schultz, *Search for Quotation*, p. 123, "The exact quotation is virtually non-existent in Egyptian literature. Orthographic changes, syntactical simplification, substitution of near synonyms, variations in word order, grammatical updating, necessary adjustments in person, number and verbal forms, as well as extensive paraphrasing and expansions frequently occur." Cf. his comments on p. 147 regarding the Jewish Apocrypha and Pseudepigrapha.

16. Mt 8:20 and Lk 9:58 are identical except that Matthew prefaces the words with λέγει αὐτῷ, Luke with εἶπεν αὐτῷ.

17. So Mahlon H. Smith, "No Place for a Son of Man," *Forum* 4/4 (1988), pp. 83–107. Commentators have most often missed this allusion, but see Poole, *Commentary*, vol. 3, p. 35 (the Son of man is here "the person mentioned who was to have all things put under his feet, Psal. viii. 6"); William Dodd, *Commentary*, vol. 3, ad Mt 8:18–20 (observing that the "son of man" has here the sense of weakness and frailty he has in Ps 8:5 and elsewhere; cf. Jansen, *Tetrateuchus*, p. 77); John Morrison, *An Exposition of the Book of Psalms, Explanatory, Critical, and Devotional* (London: Ebenezer Palmer, 1832), vol. 1, p. 87; A. Jones, "The Gospel of Jesus Christ according to St. Matthew," in *A Catholic Commentary on Holy Scripture* (ed. Dom Bernard Orchard et al.; Toronto/New York/Edinburgh: Thomas Nelson & Sons, 1953), p. 866 (he cites Ps 8:5 but does not use it in his exposition); and Kirk, *Composition*, pp. 341–42 (who suggests that Psalm 8 links Q 9:57–60 and 10:21–22). Christian commentators on Psalm 8 so rarely cite Mt 8:20 and Lk 9:58 because they are naturally put in mind rather of the *explicit* citations of Psalm 8 in the New Testament, especially Mt 21:16; 1 Cor 15:27; and Heb 2:6–8.

18. Cf. Brevard Childs, *Biblical Theology in Crisis* (Philadelphia: Westminster, 1970), pp. 151–55. Childs is far from the first to suggest this. Already *Midr. Tehillim*, ad loc., makes the connection.

The echo of a well-known scripture[19] in Jesus' aphorism moves one to reflection. How can Jesus speak as he does if Psalm 8 says that God has crowned the Son of man with δόξη and τιμῇ, given him dominion over creation, and put all things under his feet, including the beasts of the field and birds of the air? There must be irony here, although how exactly it should be explicated Q leaves to the hearer.

1 Cor 15:25–28; Eph 1:22; and Heb 2:5–9 cite Psalm 8 to confirm the present or future exaltation of Jesus. Q 9:57–58 is closer to another exegetical tradition, one that quotes or alludes to Psalm 8 in statements that disparage Adam, Israel, or humanity. In *t. Soṭah* 6:4–5 and *b. Sanh.* 38b, the angels contemptuously utter the words of Ps 8:5 after God creates Adam.[20] In *Pesiq R.* 25:4, the angels pronounce the same words when the Torah is given. So too in *Midr. Tehillim* on Ps 8:5 when the Shekinah enters the tent of meeting.[21]

Although these rabbinic texts express the evaluation of jealous or unhappy angels, 1QS 11:20–21 offers a cynical reapplication of Ps 8:5 from a specifically human point of view: "Who can comprehend your glory? What, indeed, is the son of man, among your marvelous works?[22] Born of a woman, how can he dwell before you, he whose kneading is from dust and whose corpse is food for maggots?" These words are like Q 9:57–58 in that "the son of man" prods remembrance of Psalm 8. They are also reminiscent of Q 9:57–58 in that the cynicism is not overturned by anything in the immediate context, so the sense of the intertext, Psalm 8, is undone.

Another pre-Christian text that inverts Psalm 8 appears in the Bible itself, in Job 7:17–18.[23] Here Job asks, "What is a human being that you

---

19. For the popularity of this psalm with early Christians see C. H. Dodd, *According to the Scriptures: The Sub-structure of New Testament Theology* (London: Fontana, 1965), pp. 32–34.

20. See Gary A. Anderson, "The Exaltation of Adam and the Fall of Satan," *Journal of Jewish Thought and Philosophy* 6 (1997), pp. 105–34. Although Anderson does not note the fact, the rabbinic tradition he traces is seemingly known to Tertullian, *Patientia* 5.5 (CCSL 1/1, p. 303).

21. The Peshitta puts Ps 8:5 on the lips of "foes," perhaps to be identified with rebellious angels.

22. Both "works" (מעשי) and "What... is the son of man" (מה...בן־אדם) recall Ps 8:3 (מעשי), 4 (מה...בן־אדם), and 6 (מעשי).

23. "These two verses are often regarded as a bitter parody of Ps viii." So Marvin H. Pope, *Job* (AB; Garden City, N.Y.: Doubleday, 1973), p. 62. "Parody" appears already in F. Delitzsch, *Biblical Commentary on the Book of Job* (Edinburgh: T. & T. Clark, 1872), vol. 1, p. 124; "bitter parody" in A. Maclaren, *The Psalms* (New York: A. C. Armstrong & Son, 1903), vol. 1, p. 73. Cf. A. F. Kirkpatrick, *The Book of Psalms (I–XLI)* (Cambridge: Cambridge University Press, 1892), pp. 39–40; and Paul E. Dion, "Formulaic Language in the Book of Job: International Background and Ironical Distortions," *SR* 16 (1987), pp. 190–91. Dion compares Kipling's ironic use of "What is Man that we should care for him" in chap. 1 of *The Jungle Book*, where Bagheera says this to Mowgli. Note also Kellett, *Quotation and Allusion*, pp. 48–49, who writes, "I know of no better example of the Swift-like quotation than Job's bitter travesty of the eighth Psalm."

make so much of him, that you set your mind on him, attend to him every morning...?" This is surely an allusion to the well-known psalm:

Ps 8:4   מה־אנוש כי־תזכרנו...תפקדנו
Job 7:17–18   מה־אנוש כי תגדלנו...ותפקדנו

The context in Job is unremitting pessimism:

> I loath my life; I would not live forever.
> Let me alone, for my days are a breath.
> What is a human being that you make so much of him,
> that you set your mind on him,
> attend to him every morning,
> test him every moment?
> Will you not look away from me for a while,
> let me alone until I swallow my spittle?
> If I sin, what do I do to you, you watcher of humanity?
> Have you made me your target? (Job 7:16–20)

According to Michael Fishbane,

> Whereas the psalmist exalts the human species to near-divine status, and regards this exaltation as a sign of divine favor, Job inverts the liturgical teaching and mocks it; for he implies that God's providence is less than beneficial for humankind.... Job has hooked his argument on the latent ambiguity in the question "What is man?," and transformed it from a remark which marvels how mere humankind could be so exalted by divinity into a sarcastic, contentious sneer.[24]

Something similar also appears in Ps 144:3: "O Lord, what is a human being that you regard him, or the son of man that you think of him?"

Ps 8:4   מה־אנוש כי־תזכרנו ובן־אדם כי   תפקדנו
Ps 144:3   מה־אדם   ותדעהו בן־אנוש   ותחשבהו

According to Mitchell Dahood, "With this variation on Ps viii 5 the psalmist turns from his contemplation of Yahweh's goodness to reflect upon the insignificance and the transitory character of the object of God's munificence."[25]

Although Q 9:57–58 agrees with 1 Cor 15:27; Heb 2:6–8; and other early Christian texts in identifying the figure of Ps 8:4 with Jesus,[26] the Say-

---

24. Fishbane, *Biblical Interpretation*, p. 285. He goes on to observe that Job's "exegetical revision" of Ps 8:5–7 is soon thereafter attacked by Eliphaz in Job 15:14.

25. Mitchell Dahood, *Psalms III: 101–150* (AB 17A; Garden City, N.Y.: Doubleday, 1970), p. 300. There may also be an echo of Ps 8:4 in Ecclus 18:7–8; so Patrick W. Skehan and Alexander A. Di Lella, *The Wisdom of Ben Sira: A New Translation with Notes* (AB 39; Garden City, N.Y.: Doubleday, 1987), p. 285.

26. This may be in part because the text was already messianic in Judaism. See Adela Yarbro Collins, "The Apocalyptic Son of Man Sayings," in *The Future of Early Christianity: Essays in*

ings Source goes another way when it fails to allude to Psalm 8 in order to exalt the Son of man. Jesus' self-deprecatory declaration in Q rather betokens humiliation and so is closer to Ps 144:3; Job 7:17–18; and 1QS 11:20–21. In other words, in asserting that the Son of man is less privileged than foxes and birds, Q 9:57–58 keeps company not with early Christian uses of Psalm 8 but with Jewish texts that allude to Ps 8:4 in order to communicate humanity's humble condition.

Q 13:34–35[27] **// Psalm 118:26.** This prophetic oracle ends with a tacit quotation from Psalm 118, a psalm that was quite popular in the early church[28] and which may already have been messianic in first-century Judaism:[29] "O Jerusalem, Jerusalem, who kills the prophets.... See, your house is forsaken. You will not see me until you say, 'Blessed is he who comes in the name of the Lord.' "[30]

Q 13:35	εὐλογημένος ὁ ἐρχόμενος ἐν ὀνόματι κυρίου
LXX Ps 117:26	εὐλογημένος ὁ ἐρχόμενος ἐν ὀνόματι κυρίου
MT Ps 118:26	ברוך הבא בשם יהוה[31]
Tg. 118:26	בריך דאתי בשום מימרא דיהוה

In its original context, Ps 118:26a is immediately followed by this: "We bless you from the house (LXX: οἴκου; MT: בית) of the Lord" (v. 26b). It is probably not coincidence that the prophecy of Q 13:35b is also joined to a statement about the "house" (οἶκος) of the Lord: "Behold, your house is forsaken" (Q 13:35a).[32] Psalm 118 speaks not only of worshipers blessing the one who comes in the name of the Lord but also of a blessing that comes from the Lord's house, from the temple. Surely this explains why Q's assertion about the forsaken house — which probably embraces both

---

Honor of Helmut Koester (ed. Birger A. Pearson; Minneapolis: Fortress, 1991), pp. 222–23. She argues that Dan 7:13 might itself be a deliberate allusion to Psalm 8 and related psalms in which בן־אדם was understood messianically. The targum has the definite בר־נשא for the MT's בן־אדם; see Francis J. Moloney, "The Reinterpretation of Psalm VIII and the Son of Man Debate," *NTS* 27 (1981), pp. 656–72.

27. On the placement of Q 13:34–35 after Q 11:51, see p. 85.

28. See Barnabas Lindars, *New Testament Apologetic* (London: SCM, 1961), pp. 43–44, 111–12, 169–74, 179–80, 184–86. Note Mk 11:9–10; 12:10; Acts 2:33; 4:11; 1 Pet 2:7; *1 Clem.* 48:2; *Did.* 12:1; *Acts Pet.* 24; *Barn.* 6:4; *T. Sol.* 23:4.

29. Joachim Jeremias, *The Eucharistic Words of Jesus* (London: SCM, 1966), pp. 256–60; J. Ross Wagner, "Psalm 118 in Luke-Acts: Tracing a Narrative Thread," in Evans and Sanders, eds., *Early Christian Interpretation*, pp. 157–61; E. Werner, " 'Hosanna' in the Gospels," *JBL* 65 (1946), pp. 97–122.

30. The cryptic reference is more often missed by the older commentators than by more recent exegetes, who regularly cite it, although note Jerome, *Comm. Mt* ad loc. (CCSL 77, p. 222); and Paschasius Radbertus, *Exp. Mt libri XII (IX–XII)* ad Mt 23:39 (CCCM 56B, ed. B. Paulus, p. 1145). Part of the reason is the inevitable canonical reading: the words recall for traditional ecclesiastical readers above all the entry of Jesus into Jerusalem, which Lk 13:35 is usually presumed to prophesy.

31. This is the Hebrew in 11QPsalms[a] frag. E i line 2.

32. Matthew adds ἔρημος. (Its omission in B L ff² sy⁵ sa bo^pt is probably assimilation to Luke. But many — including Westcott and Hort — have thought the word a later interpolation.)

Jerusalem and the temple — is accompanied by another that concerns the coming redemption. According to Q 13:34–35a, Jerusalem and its temple have fallen into sin and so are headed for disaster. It follows that the temple in the capital cannot be the source of any proper blessing. That is, those in the temple do not now bless the one who will someday come as the Son of man. And this in turn means that the words of Ps 118:26, if they be understood (as Q understands them) as prophetic, must refer to some time yet ahead: the time for the blessing of the one who comes in the name of the Lord is moved into the future. So Q 13:35 reflects a consistent interpretation of Ps 118:26. "Your house is forsaken" — a biblical phrase[33] — is the reason why there is presently no fulfillment of the prophetic psalm, why the exclamation "Blessed is he who comes in the name of the Lord" is yet to be heard.

In making the words of Ps 118:26 an acclamation of Jerusalemites, Q 13:34–35 agrees with the Christian accounts of the entry into Jerusalem, where the crowds greet him with, "Blessed is he who comes in the name of the Lord."[34] Does this coincidence reflect Jewish tradition? Is it a coincidence that, in the late *Midr. Ps* 118:26, the line from Psalm 118 is again uttered by "the men of Jerusalem" (at the time of the eschatological redemption, in agreement with Q 13:34–35 but not Mk 11:9–10 par.)?

Q 12:24 // Psalm 147:9 (?). Jesus says that the ravens (κόρακας)[35] "neither sow nor reap nor gather into barns...yet God feeds them" (ὁ θεὸς τρέφει αὐτούς).[36] This reminds one of two scriptures, the first being Job 38:41 ("Who provides the raven its prey, when its young ones cry to God, and wander about for lack of food?"), the second being the possible source of Job 38:41, namely, Ps 147:9, in which God "gives to the beasts their food, and to the young ravens which cry."[37]

---

33. On this phrase as an allusion to Jer 12:7, see pp. 126–28.

34. Mt 21:9; Mk 11:9–10; Lk 19:38; Jn 12:13.

35. So Luke. Mt 6:26 has "the birds of the air" (τὰ πετεινὰ τοῦ οὐρανοῦ), which is usually attributed to Matthean redaction; cf. R. J. Dillon, "Ravens, Lilies, and the Kingdom of God (Matthew 6:25–33/Luke 12:22–31)," *CBQ* 53 (1991), p. 610, who calls this view "the consensus." Contrast Siegfried Schulz, *Q: Spruchquelle der Evangelisten* (Zurich: Theologischer Verlag, 1972), p. 150, who thinks Matthew rather preserves Q.

36. So the IQP and Lk 12:24. Mt 6:26: καὶ ὁ πατὴρ ὑμῶν ὁ οὐράνιος τρέφει αὐτά.

37. Cf. Hugh of Saint Cher, *Comm. Mt* ad 5:12 (*Opera Omnia* 6, p. 26); Albertus Magnus, *Tert. part. Ps (CI-CL)* ad Ps 147:9 (*Opera Omnia*, ed. A. Borgnet, p. 522); Grotius, *Operum theologicarum*, vol. 2, pt. 1, p. 408 ("Nam circa corvorum pullos specialim Dei curam Iobus & Psalmgraphus praedicant"); also Maldonatus, *Commentarii*, vol. 1, p. 105; Andrew A. Bonar, *Christ and His Church in the Book of Psalms* (London: James Nisbet & Co., 1859), p. 448; Hühn, *Alttestamentlichen Citate*, p. 10; Dittmar, *Vetus Testamentum*, p. 17; Lagrange, *Saint Luc*, p. 362; Ernst Fuchs, *Studies of the Historical Jesus* (SBT; London: SCM, 1964), p. 107; Catchpole, *Quest for Q*, p. 37; William L. Holladay, *The Psalms through Three Thousand Years: Prayerbook of a Cloud of Witnesses* (Minneapolis: Fortress, 1993), p. 116.

Job 38:41

LXX τίς δὲ ἡτοίμασεν κόρακι βοράν;
     νεοσσοὶ γὰρ αὐτοῦ πρὸς κύριον κεκράγασιν
     πλανώμενοι τὰ σῖτα ζητοῦντες

MT   מִי יָכִין לָעֹרֵב צֵידוֹ
     כִּי־יְלָדוֹ אֶל־אֵל יְשַׁוֵּעוּ
     יִתְעוּ לִבְלִי־אֹכֶל

Targum מן יתקן לעורבא מזוניה
        ארום בנוי לאלהא יבעון
        תעיין מדליה מיכלא

Ps 147:9

LXX διδόντι τοῖς κτήνεσι τροφὴν αὐτῶν
     καὶ τοῖς νεοσσοῖς τῶν κοράκων τοῖς ἐπικαλουμένοις αὐτόν

MT   נוֹתֵן לִבְהֵמָה לַחְמָהּ
     לִבְנֵי עֹרֵב אֲשֶׁר יִקְרָאוּ

Targum יהיב לבעירא מזונה
        לבני עורבא דיקרן

Whereas Q's text has only "raven" in common with LXX Job 38:41, LXX Ps 146:9 has both τροφήν and κοράκων, while Q appears to have had τρέφει and κόρακας. So, although the proposition is scarcely beyond all doubt, it is natural to suppose that ancients familiar with the liturgy of the Psalms heard in Q 12:24 familiar language.

It is not clear, however, that a knowledge of Psalm 147:9 in any way enlarges the meaning or impact of Q 12:24. We may have here nothing more than a biblical idiom.[38] One might, however, speculate that an allusion to Ps 147:9, which is about God feeding *young* ravens, suggests that the image in Q is not of God supplying carrion but of God feeding youngsters in the nest. This at least occurred to Theophylact, for he says that Jesus mentions ravens because they do not feed their young, who instead get food when they open their mouths so that the wind under the guidance of providence can blow food to them.[39] That ravens neglect their young is also an opinion that appears in *b. Ketub.* 49b.

Q 13:27 // Ps 6:8. Mt 7:23 and Lk 13:27 resemble Ps 6:8 ("Depart from me, all you workers of evil"):

---

38. Cf. the apparent use of the language of Ps 147:9 in *b. B. Bat.* 8a.

39. Theophylact *apud* Aquinas, *Catena aurea* ad Lk 12:24–26. Cf. Jerome, *Tract. Ps* 146.9 (CCSL 78, ed. Germanus Morin, p. 333).

Lk 13:27   ἀπόστητε ἀπ' ἐμοῦ πάντες   ἐργάται   ἀδικίας
Mt 7:23   ἀποχωρεῖτε ἀπ' ἐμοῦ   οἱ ἐργαζόμενοι τὴν ἀνομίαν
LXX Ps 6:9 ἀπόστητε ἀπ' ἐμοῦ πάντες οἱ ἐργαζόμενοι τὴν ἀνομίαν
MT Ps 6:9   סורו ממני כל פעלי און
Tg. Ps 6:9 זורו מיני כל עבדי שקר

Given that the word statistics argue strongly for the Lukan character of
ἐργάται ἀδικίας,[40] Q probably had ἀποχωρεῖτε/ἀπόστητε[41] ἀπ' ἐμοῦ
(πάντες) οἱ ἐργαζόμενοι τὴν ἀνομίαν, "Away from me all those working
lawlessness."[42] This is an unmarked quotation of Ps 6:8.[43]

How does this affect interpretation? One might be content to observe
that "Away from me, etc." makes Jesus speak the language of Scripture and
so adds solemnity.[44] But it may be pertinent that, in the psalm, the speaker
is a sufferer who is vindicated by God. Did some hearers of Q recognize that
the psalmist's words are particularly appropriate coming from Jesus?[45]

Another question follows when Ps 6:8 is read in its entirety: "Away from
me, all you workers of evil, for the Lord has heard the sound of my weeping"
(κλαυθμοῦ). Is it just coincidence that Q's "Away from me all those working
lawlessness" (13:27) was immediately followed by a unit that featured and
probably began with a reference to weeping — "There people will weep
(κλαυθμός) and gnash their teeth" (13:28–29)?[46] Maybe a contributor to Q
was led to place Q 13:28–29 where it is because of its catchword connection
with the scriptural subtext of Q 13:27.

Q 13:28–29 // Ps 107:3 (?); Ps 112:10 (?). (i) Mt 8:11–12 refers to many
coming "from east and west" (ἀπὸ ἀνατολῶν καὶ δυσμῶν), Lk 13:28–29 to
people coming "from east and west and north and south" (ἀπὸ ἀνατολῶν
καὶ δυσμῶν καὶ ἀπὸ βορρᾶ καὶ νότου). We do not know which stood in

---

40. ἀδικία: Mt: 0; Mk: 0; Lk-Acts: 6. Luke uses ἐργάτης four times but never οἱ
ἐργαζόμενοι or ὁ ἐργαζόμενος. See Jeremias, *Sprache*, p. 232.
41. Matthew shows no fondness for either ἀποχωρέω (1x) or ἀφίστημι (0x). Luke-Acts
shows a fondness for both ἀποχωρέω (3x) and ἀφίστημι (10x). An obvious motive for either
author to have changed one word into the other does not appear, unless the explanation be
that Luke assimilates to the LXX.
42. The IQP reconstructs the Q text behind Mt 7:23 = Q 13:27 as follows: "And he will
say [[to you]], I do not know you . . . <<Away>> from me, evil<<doers>>."
43. Cf. Albertus Magnus, *En. sec. partem Evangelium Lucae (X–XXIV)* ad 13:27 (Opera
Omnia 23, ed. A. Borgnet, p. 316); Lagrange, *Saint Luc*, p. 390; John Martin Creed, *The
Gospel according to St. Luke* (London: Macmillan, 1930), p. 185; France, *Jesus and the Old
Testament*, p. 241; Fitzmyer, *Luke*, vol. 2, pp. 1025–26; Sand, *Matthäus*, p. 155; Tuckett, *Q*,
p. 423; Bovon, *Lukas*, vol. 2, p. 434.
44. Cf. 1 Macc 3:6 (πάντες οἱ ἐργάται τῆς ἀνομίας); 2 *Clem.* 4:5 (ὑπάγετε ἀπ' ἐμοῦ . . .
ἐργάται ἀνομίας).
45. Cf. Gundry, *Old Testament*, p. 76: it is "striking that in the context of Ps 6:9, it is the
sufferer vindicated by Yahweh who tells the workers of iniquity to depart. Did Jesus have this
in mind with regard to himself?"
46. For the argument that Q's unit began with "There people will weep," see Davies and
Allison, *Matthew*, vol. 2, pp. 25–26.

Q.[47] Whereas Luke, or a transmitter of Q[Lk], might have added "and north and south" in order to highlight the theme of universalism[48] or to gain an allusion to Ps 107:3 (see below), Matthew, in accordance with his habit of abbreviating, might have omitted the words as superfluous.

Because the status of Luke's "and north and south" remains in doubt, it is necessary to investigate the background both of Matthew's phrase and of Luke's fuller expression. To take the former first, it probably does not allude to a specific intertext. Nonetheless, those shaped by the Hebrew Bible will know that "east and west" are often associated with the return of Jews to the land promised to Abraham, as in Zech 8:7–8 ("Thus says the Lord of hosts: I will save my people from the east country and from the west country; and I will bring them to Jerusalem"); Bar 4:4 ("Behold, your sons are coming, whom you sent away; they are coming, gathered from east and west, at the word of the Holy One, rejoicing in the glory of God"); and 5:5 ("Arise, O Jerusalem, stand upon the height and look toward the east, and see your children gathered from west and east, at the word of the Holy One, rejoicing that God has remembered them"). Knowledge of texts such as these would encourage one to understand Q 13:28–29, not as a prophecy of the eschatological ingathering of Gentiles (the reading of most modern scholars), but as a promise of the return of dispersed Israel: in the future the scattered Israelites will stream in from the east, from Assyria and Babylon,[49] and from the west, from Egypt.[50] One may compare Isa 27:12–13 ("On that day the Lord will thresh from the channel of the Euphrates to the Wadi of Egypt, and you will be gathered one by one, O people of Israel. And on that day a great trumpet will be blown, and those who were lost in the land of Assyria and those who were driven out to the land of Egypt will come and worship the Lord on the holy mountain of Jerusalem"); Hos 11:11 ("They shall come trembling like birds from Egypt, and like doves from the land of Assyria"); and Zech 10:10 ("I will bring them home from the land of Egypt and gather them from Assyria").[51]

But what of Luke's longer expression, "from east and west and north

---

47. For a review of opinions and arguments, see M. Eugene Boring, "A Proposed Reconstruction of Q 13:28–29," in *Society of Biblical Literature 1989 Seminar Papers* (ed. David J. Lull; Atlanta: Scholars Press, 1995), pp. 1–22.

48. Cf. Acts 2:9–11. When all the world is in mind, "north and south and east and west" is more common than just "east and west." Recall the play upon Adam's name in *Sib. Or.* 3:24–26 and *2 En.* 30:13 (in Greek the four letter's of Adam's name are taken to represent the four cardinal directions). Note also Gen 28:14; 1 Kgs 7:25; Isa 43:5–6 (Grimm, *Weil Ich Dich Liebe*, pp. 192–96, argues that Mt 8:11–12 = Lk 13:28–29 depends upon these verses from Isaiah); *b. Šabb.* 118b.

49. Cf. Isa 46:11; Jer 49:28; *Sib. Or.* 5:113; *As. Mos.* 3:1, 13–14.

50. In 1 Kgs 4:30 and *Sib. Or.* 5:112–13 "Egypt" and "east" are counterparts. In the *Babylonian Talmud* "west" is used for Palestine (e.g., *b. Yeb.* 117a), but that is a late development and obviously represents a non-Palestinian perspective.

51. See further Allison, *Jesus Tradition in Q*, pp. 176–91.

and south"? If it stood in Q was it intended, as so many commentators have thought, to allude to Ps 107:2–3?[52]

Lk 13:29   ἀπὸ ἀνατολῶν καὶ δυσμῶν καὶ ἀπὸ βορρᾶ καὶ νότου
LXX Ps 106:3   ἀπὸ ἀνατολῶν καὶ δυσμῶν καὶ   βορρᾶ καὶ θαλάσσης
MT Ps 107:3   ממזרח וממערב מצפון ומים
Tg. Ps 107:3   ממדינחא וממערבא מציפונא ומן ימא סטר דרומא

The NRSV translates the line from the psalm with this: "from the east and from the west, from the north and from the south." Unhappily there is some doubt as to whether this is a correct translation. The MT and LXX both have "from the east and from the west, from the north and from overseas." The NRSV translators, it seems, inferred that the end of the MT (ומים) is corrupt. Their English presupposes a Hebrew text with ומימין ("and from the right," that is, "the south"). Are they to be followed? Although one always hesitates to emend without manuscript authority, the ומי of the Masoretic text seems redundant, for "from the sea" is naturally understood to signify "from the west" (from the Mediterranean), and "from the west" has already been used. It is accordingly possible that, through corruption, ומימין became ומים and that Ps 107:3 originally had "from the east and from the west, from the north and from the south." Indeed, perhaps a Hebrew or Greek text with this reading was known in the first century.

Another possibility is that ומים is original but referred not to the Mediterranean but to "the southern seas" (cf. the targum),[53] that is, the Gulf of Aqabah (cf. 2 Chr 8:17).[54] In any event the link between Lk 13:28–29 and Ps 107:3 remains attractive, and the implications for interpretation are significant, for Ps 107:1–3 plainly refers to Jewish pilgrims or immigrants coming to Palestine: those gathered from the four points of the compass are God's scattered people. So whoever catches an allusion in Lk 13:28–29 to Ps 107:3 will immediately think of Jewish exiles returning to their land.[55]

Even if one misses a specific allusion to Ps 107:3, the scripturally informed would likely still be led to think of an ingathering of the diaspora, for Ps 107:3 is not the only biblical text to envisage the scattered Jews returning from the four points of the compass. Isa 43:5–6 ("Do not fear, for I am with you; I will bring your offspring from the east, and from the west I will gather you; I will say to the north, 'Give them up,' and to the south, 'Do

---

52. Cf. Gill, *Commentary*, vol. 3, p. 298; Dittmar, *Vetus Testamentum*, p. 19; B. H. Branscomb, *Jesus and the Law of Moses* (New York: Richard R. Smith, 1930), p. 190; Shires, *Old Testament*, p. 147; Fitzmyer, *Luke*, vol. 2, p. 641. Albertus Magnus, *Comm. Ps (CI–CL)* ad loc. (Opera Omnia, ed. A. Borgnet, p. 111), recalls Mt 8:11 when commenting on Ps 107:2–3.

53. ימא סטר דרומא, "sea on the southern side."

54. So Dahood, *Psalms*, vol. 3, p. 81.

55. The MT, LXX, and targum refer to a past event, so the psalm is postexilic. Did the author of Q 13:28–29 construe the Hebrew of Ps 107:3 as a prophetic perfect, or do we rather have here a typological appropriation of Scripture — the eschatological return will be like the earlier return from exile?

not withhold; bring my sons from far away and my daughters from the end of the earth' ") and LXX Zech 2:10 (God will gather exiles "from the four winds of heaven") also envision this.

(ii) Q 13:28–29 ends with words that Matthew turned into a recurring refrain — "there people will weep and gnash their teeth" (ἐκεῖ ἔσται ὁ κλαυθμὸς καὶ ὁ βρυγμὸς τῶν ὀδόντων).[56] "Gnash" (βρύχω) + "tooth" (ὀδούς) — an expression of hatred — appears five times in the LXX.[57] Three of these translate the Hebrew expression חרק + על + [ב]שנים] with βρύχω + ἐπί + τοὺς ὀδόντας:[58]

> Job 16:9: "In his anger he [God] cast me [Job] down, he gnashed his teeth upon me (ἔβρυξαν ἐπ' ἐμὲ τοὺς ὀδόντας); the weapons of his robbers have fallen upon me."

> LXX Ps 34:16: "They tried me, they sneered at me contemptuously, they gnashed their teeth upon me (ἔβρυξαν ἐπ' ἐμὲ τοὺς ὀδόντας αὐτῶν)."

> LXX Ps 36:12: "The sinner will watch for the just and will gnash his teeth upon him (βρύξει ἐπ' αὐτὸν τοὺς ὀδόντας αὐτοῦ)."

Q is closer to two other texts:

> Ps 112:10: "The sinner will see [the exhaltation of the poor] and be angry, he will gnash his teeth (LXX: τοὺς ὀδόντας αὐτοῦ βρύξει) and be consumed. The desire of the wicked will perish."

> Lam 2:16: "All your enemies have opened their mouth against you; they have hissed and gnashed their teeth (ἔβρυξαν ὀδόντας) and said, 'We have swallowed her up. This is the day we have looked for; we have found it, we have seen it.' "

Of these two lines, Q 13:29 resembles LXX Ps 111:10 in particular. Both Q 13:29 and LXX Ps 111:10 depict sinners being judged,[59] both use a future tense (βρύξει), and both have the wicked gnash their teeth upon seeing (Q: ὄψησθε;[60] LXX Ps 111:10: ὄψεται) the good fortune of the just. It is possible, then, that Q 13:29 alludes to Ps 112:10.[61]

But caution is in order, for the use of βρυγμός ("gnashing") or βρύχω ("I gnash") with ὀδούς ("tooth") at some point probably became an eschatological topos:

---

56. Mt 8:12; 13:42, 50; 22:13; 24:51; 25:30.

57. βρυγμός is used in the LXX only in Prov 19:12 and Ecclus 51:3, in neither case in connection with "teeth."

58. The formula appears in the NT only in Acts 7:54. Cf. *Ps.-Clem. Hom.* 1.13; *Ep. Lugd.* 1.60. For rabbinic parallels, see Schlatter, *Matthäus*, pp. 279–80.

59. Cf. the eschatological interpretation in *Lev Rab.* 23:1.

60. Only Luke has the verb, but for the originality of Luke's version here, see Davies and Allison, *Matthew*, vol. 2, p. 26.

61. So Grotius, *Operum theologicarum*, vol. 2, pt. 1, p. 96 (on Mt 8:12); and Gundry, *Old Testament*, p. 77. Cf. Hesychius of Jerusalem, *Frag. Ps* ad loc. (PG 93.1329A); Albertus Magnus, *Comm. Ps (CI-CL)* ad loc. (Opera Omnia, ed. A. Borgnet, p. 186); and Gill, *Commentary*, vol. 3, p. 315.

Sib. Or. 2:305–6 (describing punishment in Gehenna): "They will all gnash their teeth (ἐπιβρύξουσι δ' ὀδοῦσιν), wasting away with thirst and raging violence."

Sib. Or. 8:104–105: "Everyone who looks will hear a mournful great bellowing from Hades and gnashing of teeth (βρυγμὸν ὀδόντων)."

Sib. Or. 8:231 (prophesying the judgment at resurrection): "A lament will rise from all and gnashing of teeth (βρυγμὸς ὀδόντων)"

Sib. Or. 8:350 (depicting eschatological disturbances): "All the souls of men will gnash their teeth (βρύξουσιν ὀδοῦσιν)."

Ps.-Hippolytus, *Consumm.* 45 (GCS 1/2, ed. H. Achelis, p. 308): "You will inherit with him (the devil) the darkness and the unquenchable fire and the sleepless worm and the gnashing of teeth (βρυγμὸν τῶν ὀδόντων)."

Already in Matthew the eschatological "gnashing of teeth" has become a refrain that may be independent of the originating intertext, so we cannot exclude this possibility for Q.

II. Synthesis

(i) Q cites or alludes to verses from three of the five books of Psalms, from Psalms 1–41, 90–106, and 107–50:

Ps 6:8 — Q 13:27 (allusion)
Psalm 8 — Q 9:57–58 (allusion)
Ps 91:12 — Q 4:10–11 (marked citation)
Ps 107:3 — Q 13:28–29 (allusion?)
Ps 112:10 — Q 13:28–29 (allusion?)
Ps 118:26 — Q 13:34–35 (unmarked quotation)
Ps 147:9 — Q 12:24 (allusion?)

Books II (Psalms 42–72) and III (Psalms 73–89) are not referred to. No psalm is used more than once, nor do any of the noncanonical psalms known from Qumran seem to be alluded to.

(ii) Four of the Q texts just listed occur within a narrow space:

Q 13:27 — Ps 6:8 (allusion)
Q 13:28–29 — Ps 107:3 (allusion?)
Q 13:28–29 — Ps 112:10 (allusion?)
Q 13:34–35 — Ps 118:26 (unmarked quotation)

This appears, however, to be nothing more than coincidence, for not only does a question mark hang over the allusions in Q 13:28–29, but in the Sayings Source, Q 13:34–35 probably belonged with the woes in chapter 11.[62]

---

62. See above, pp. 85–86.

(iii) At least three of Q's references to the Psalms likely reflect a knowledge of Jewish interpretive traditions. When Q 9:57–58 alludes to Ps 8:4–8 in order to abase rather than exalt its human speaker, it falls in line with the cynical uses of Psalm 8 in Ps 144:3; Job 7:17–18; 1QS 11:20–21; *t. Soṭ.* 6:4–5; *b. Sanh.* 38b; and elsewhere. The citation of Ps 118:26 in Q 13:34–35 agrees with *Midr. Rab.* 118:26 in putting the biblical line on the lips of Jerusalemites and in applying the verse to the eschatological redemption. And the use of the phrase "gnashing of teeth" to depict those who flunk the eschatological judgment appears also in *Sib. Or.* 2:305–6 and 8:104–5, which are often assigned to Jewish hands.

(iv) Over half of Q's possible references to the Psalms are in the service of eschatology. The acclamation from Ps 118:26 in Q 13:34–35 ("Blessed is the one who comes in the name of the Lord") will be uttered when the Son of man returns. The words of Ps 6:8, "Away from me you doers of evil," appropriated in Q 13:27, will be spoken to the unrighteous on the last day. And the possible allusions to Ps 107:3 and 112:10 in Q 13:28–29 belong to a prophecy about the ingathering of the diaspora and the final judgment. So we find in Q what we also find in Qumran's pesher on Psalm 37 (4QpPsᵃ),[63] in the Septuagint's Psalter,[64] in the Christian narratives of Jesus' passion,[65] and in the targum on the Psalms,[66] namely, an assumption that many of the Psalms feature eschatological prophecies.

---

63. According to Maurya P. Horgan, *Pesharim: Qumran Interpretations of Biblical Books* (CBQMS 8; Washington, D.C.: Catholic Biblical Association, 1979), p. 194, 4QpPsᵃ's "interpretation of Psalm 37 is mainly eschatological."

64. For a discussion of this issue, see esp. Joachim Schaper, *Eschatology in the Greek Psalter* (Tübingen: Mohr Siebeck, 1995).

65. On the Psalm in the canonical passion narratives, see Joel Marcus, "The Old Testament and the Death of Jesus: The Role of Scripture in the Gospel Passion Narratives," in *The Death of Jesus in Early Christianity* (ed. John T. Carroll and Joel B. Green; Peabody, Mass.: Hendrickson, 1995), pp. 206–12.

66. For some of the relevant texts, see Samson H. Levey, *The Messiah: An Aramaic Interpretation: The Messianic Exegesis of the Targum* (Cincinnati/New York/Los Angeles/Jerusalem: Hebrew Union College-Jewish Institute of Religion, 1974), pp. 105–24.

Chapter 8

Wisdom Literature

I. Texts

(Q 7:35.) There is no allusion to any specific text in Jesus' claim that Wisdom is justified by her "children" (τέκνων). Both Proverbs and Ecclesiasticus do, however, speak of Wisdom's "sons:"

Prov 8:32: Wisdom says, "My son (υἱέ, בנים), listen to me."

Ecclus 4:11: "Wisdom teaches her sons (υἱούς, בניה)."[1]

So here Q may borrow an idiom from the Wisdom literature.

Q 12:22–31 // Prov 6:6–11. Jesus here makes, in the words of Catchpole, an "appeal, typical of the wisdom tradition...to the natural world. The illustrations make contact with the situation of the hearers by referring to activities which are normal and necessary if the basics of human existence are to be produced.... Yet these activities are seen as expressions of that anxiety which the hearers are required to avoid! This involves a resounding clash with the wisdom tradition, which lavishly praises the worker and severely chides the non-worker."[2] In a footnote he cites a series of texts from Proverbs (6:6–8; 10:26; 12:24, 27; 13:4; 15:19; 18:9; 19:15, 24; 20:4; 26:13–16) and a couple from Ecclesiasticus (2:12; 7:15). But Catchpole overlooks that Q 12:22–31 seemingly relates itself to one of these texts in particular.

According to John N. Jones, Q 12:22–31 is meant to "echo and invert one particular passage of Solomonic wisdom, Prov 6:6–11," and he is not the only one to have discerned a parallel between the two texts.[3] Q encourages disciples not to be anxious about their lives, about what they will eat or

---

1. Albertus Magnus, *En. prim. part. Luc. (I–IX)* ad loc. (Opera Omnia 22, ed. A. Borgnet, p. 495), observes this parallel.

2. Catchpole, *Quest for Q*, p. 35.

3. John N. Jones, " 'Think of the Lilies' and Prov 6:6–11," *HTR* 88 (1995), pp. 175–77. Cf. Cyril of Alexandria apud Aquinas, *Catena aurea* ad Lk 12:24–26; Trapp, *Commentary*, vol. 3, p. 20; J. G. Williams, *Those Who Ponder Proverbs: Aphoristic Thinking and Biblical Literature* (Sheffield: JSOT Press, 1981), p. 50; John F. Healey, "Models of Behavior: Matt 6:26 (// Luke 12:24) and Prov 6:6–8," *JBL* 108 (1989), pp. 497–98; idem, *The Targum of Proverbs* (Aramaic Bible 15; Collegeville, Minn.: Michael Glazier, 1991), p. 21, n. 5. Maldonatus, *Commentarii*, vol. 1, p. 105; and Bovon, *Lukas*, vol. 2, p. 304, cite the text when considering Mt 6:26; and Scott, *Commentary*, vol. 3, ad loc., cites Mt 6:26 when commenting on Prov 6:6–11.

wear. As supporting evidence, Jesus refers to the ravens, who do not sow or reap or use storehouses[4] and yet are fed by God,[5] and to lilies, which neither toil nor spin but are beautifully arrayed. Prov 6:6–11 also appeals to nature, but to opposite effect: "Go the ant, O sluggard, consider its ways, and be wise.... It prepares its food in summer, and gathers its sustenance in harvest." The LXX adds a companion illustration: "Or go to the bee, and learn how diligent it is, and how earnestly it is engaged in its work, whose labors kings and private citizens use for health, and it is desired and respected by all; although weak in body, it is advanced by honoring wisdom."[6] So while in LXX Proverbs the natural world offers two parables promoting work, Q has two examples from the natural world of a divine benevolence supporting creatures that do not work for food and clothing. The industry of the ant and bee gains success; the ravens and lilies are providentially taken care of without working:

LXX Prov 6:6–11	*Q 12:22–31*
First illustration (6–8)	First illustration (24)
"Go to the ant... and see (ἰδών)."	"Look (ἐμβλέψατε) at the ravens."
It prepares its "food" (τροφήν)	They do not reap or harvest.
and makes abundant storage in the harvest.	"God feeds (τρέφει) them" (cf. the use of "food," τροφή, in v. 23).
Second illustration (8a–b)	Second illustration (27–28)
"Go to the bee and learn."	"Consider the lilies."
It works earnestly.	"They neither toil nor spin."
Its produce is used by kings, and the bee has respect.	Solomon was not arrayed like them.
Moral (9–11)	Moral (29–31)
Be diligent,	Seek the kingdom,
and poverty will flee from you.	and you need not worry about food or drink or clothing.

What does one make of these parallels? On the one hand, Q's failure elsewhere to engage Proverbs is against seeing the intertext here, as is the minimal number of verbal links. On the other hand, Q does elsewhere display similar witty reversals of scriptural texts.[7] Moreover, Prov 6:6–11 was traditionally thought to have been authored by Solomon (Prov 1:1), and he is mentioned in the middle of our passage (12:27).

---

4. Lk 12:24: "they have neither storehouses nor barn" (ἀποθήκη); Mt 6:26: "nor gather into barns" (ἀποθήκας).

5. On this line, see the discussion on pp. 164–66, where the possibility of an allusion to Ps 147:9 is raised.

6. On this addition, see Johann Cook, *The Septuagint of Proverbs: Jewish and/or Hellenistic Proverbs? Concerning the Hellenistic Colouring of LXX Proverbs* (VTSup 69; Leiden/New York/Cologne: Brill, 1997), pp. 164–68. He argues that LXX Prov 6:8a–c was composed by the Greek translator under the influence of Hellenistic sources (maybe Aristotle).

7. See pp. 192–97.

The more weighty, and some might think determinant, fact, however, is another. J. F. Healey[8] has observed that whereas there are good parallels to the notion that God provides for the birds and other creatures,[9] Mt 6:26 = Lk 12:24 is seemingly alone in its striking assertion that the animals do not harvest — with one exception. MT Prov 6:7 says that the ant has no קָצִין, that is, "chief" or "leader." But the LXX has, "without having any cultivated land" (ἐκείνῳ γὰρ γεωργίου μὴ ὑπάρχοντος), and the targum and Peshitta have, "it has no harvest" (חצדא). Clearly behind the versions is the reading קָצִיר = "harvest" (not קָצִין = "leader"), which is presumably under the influence of v. 8 ("and gathers its sustenance in harvest" [בקציר]). This then is the missing parallel to Q 12:24: in both places animals do not harvest.

What the ancients might have made of Prov 6:7 as it is rendered in the versions is difficult to see because "it has no harvest" does not well suit the context, which goes on to speak of the ant's industry. But the reading is nonetheless attested, and it stands some chance of lying behind Q's denial in 12:24. Furthermore, to an audience familiar with the variant reading for Prov 6:7, Jesus' statement might well have sent them to that verse, as it did Cyril of Alexandria, who wrote regarding Lk 12:24: "Whereas our Lord might have taken an example from those who have cared least about earthly things, such as Elijah, Moses, John, and the like, he made mention of the birds, following the Old Testament, which sends us to the bee and the ant, and others of the same kind, in whom the creator has implanted certain natural dispositions."[10] Should we not follow Cyril and suppose that Q 12:22–31 does indeed ironically turn Prov 6:6–11 upside down?

When one asks what might be Q's motivation for thus treating a passage of Scripture, the obvious answer would seem to lie in Q's eschatological outlook. To quote Catchpole again,

> Only one explanation seems ready to hand for such a clash. That is, the tradition belongs to a situation which is special in character and short in duration. It belongs to that period of time conditioned by the expectation of an imminent eschatological crisis. It applies to such persons as have abandoned self-sufficiency and independence for the sake of attachment to Jesus.[11]

Q 12:27 // Solomonic traditions: Ecclesiastes (?), Canticles (?). On the possible links between "lily" and Canticles and between "toil" and Ecclesiastes, see pp. 152–54.

---

8. Healey, "Models of Behavior."

9. E.g., Job 12:7–9; 38:41; Ps 104; 147:9; *Ps. Sol.* 5:9–10; *m. Qidd.* 4:14; *b. Šabb.* 33b (cf. SB 1, pp. 582–83).

10. Preserved in Aquinas, *Catena aurea* ad Lk 12:24–26.

According to J. Duncan M. Derrett, "Birds of the Air and Lilies of the Field," *DownR* 105 (1987), pp. 181–92, our passage is a "direct midrash" upon Psalm 104. I cannot see, however, that he gathers any evidence for this, and I myself have found none.

11. Catchpole, *Quest for Q*, p. 35.

II. Analysis

(i) The results of this chapter are meager. Q 7:35 uses an expression found in Prov 8:32 and Ecclus 4:11 (Wisdom's children), while Q 12:22–31 may allude ironically to Prov 6:6–11 and further remind one of the link between Solomon and lilies in Canticles and between Solomon and toil in Ecclesiastes.

(ii) Does the sparsity of references to Wisdom literature have implications for those theories of Q that have so stressed its Wisdom affinities? How is it that a document supposedly so beholden to the sapiential tradition never quotes it? Why is it that Q prefers to allude to other portions of Scripture? It is indeed true that Q's form as a collection of sayings has good parallels in the Wisdom literature, and also true that Q's scant allusions to that literature might show an awareness of four separate books — Proverbs, Ecclesiastes, Canticles, Ecclesiasticus. A sapiential influence is surely present. Nonetheless, maybe those who have so stressed Q's sapiential dimensions need to clarify why Q refers to Wisdom literature so much less than to the Pentateuch, the historical books, and the writing prophets.[12]

---

12. For the argument that Q has more of a prophetic than a sapiential background, see Sato, *Q und Prophetie;* idem, "Wisdom Statements in the Sphere of Prophecy," in *The Gospel behind the Gospels* (ed. Ronald A. Piper; NovTSup 75; Leiden: Brill, 1995), pp. 139–58.

Chapter 9

Extracanonical Texts

At least three passages in Q might, some have thought, use or allude to a book neither in the Tanak nor in the Apocrypha.

(i) Often proposed is a link between Q 11:2–4, the Lord's Prayer, and the old Aramaic prayer known as the Kaddish,[1] an early form of which was presumably close to the following:

> Exalted and hallowed be his great name
>> in the world which he created according to his will.
> May he cause his kingdom to rule
>> in your lifetime and in your days
>> and in the whole house of Israel, speedily and soon.
> Praised be his great name from eternity to eternity.
> And to this say: Amen.[2]

At some point in time the Kaddish became a well-known liturgical text. The problem for the student of the New Testament, however, is that the experts on Jewish liturgy have been unable to demonstrate that this prayer was known, much less well known, by the date of Q's composition, the mid-first century C.E. So while the obvious resemblances between the Kaddish and the Lord's Prayer raise the interesting possibility that Jewish hearers of Q 11:2–4 would have perceived it as a sort of revision of or even alternative to a prayer known to them from the synagogal liturgy, our ignorance regarding the genesis and spread of the Kaddish prohibits any confidence in the matter.

A few scholars have associated the Lord's Prayer with a second Jewish prayer, the Amidah, or Eighteen Benedictions,[3] whose widespread use in the first century is, in contrast to the Kaddish, often assumed,[4] even though

---

1. Cf. David de Sola Pool, *The Kaddish* (New York: Bloch, 1929), pp. 21–23; and Jeremias, *Theology*, p. 198.

2. See Ismar Elbogen, *Jewish Liturgy: A Comprehensive History* (Philadelphia: Jewish Publication Society, 1993), pp. 80–84 (he argues that it is "very ancient" and observes the parallels with the Lord's Prayer); and Lawrence A. Hoffman, *The Canonization of the Synagogue Service* (Notre Dame, Ind.: University of Notre Dame Press, 1979), pp. 56–65.

3. E.g., Gordon J. Bahr, "The Use of the Lord's Prayer in the Primitive Church," *JBL* 84 (1965), pp. 153–59.

4. But its precise forms and the relationship between the Palestinian and Babylonian recensions are matters for discussion. See Elbogen, *Jewish Liturgy*, pp. 24–37.

Josephus shows no knowledge of it. There are several parallels which, taken together, are intriguing:

- While early Christian tradition instructs believers to say the Lord's Prayer three times a day while standing, the rabbis offer the same instruction for the Eighteen Benedictions.[5]

- The Lord's Prayer resembles in content and length some of the abbreviations of the Amidah; for example, *b. Ber.* 29a preserves a short prayer with a simple address ("O Lord") that asks for forgiveness and nourishment and has an eschatological outlook: "What is meant by an abbreviated eighteen? Rab said: 'An abbreviated form of each blessing.' Samuel said: 'Give us discernment, O Lord, to know your ways, and circumcise our heart to fear you, and forgive us so that we may be redeemed, and keep us far from our sufferings, and fatten us in the pastures of your land, and gather our dispersions from the four corners of the earth, and let them who err from your prescriptions be punished, and lift up your hand against the wicked, and let the righteous rejoice in the building of your city and the establishment of the temple in the exalting of the horn of David your servant and the preparation of a light for the son of Jesse your Messiah. Before we call may you answer. Blessed are you, O Lord, who hears prayer.' "

- Tertullian's advice to add one's own petitions to the Lord's Prayer[6] recalls the rabbinic counsel to append personal prayers after completing the Eighteen Benedictions (*b. 'Abod. Zar.* 7b).

- The sixth benediction asks for forgiveness for transgressions and blesses God as the one who forgives, which may be compared with the supplication for forgiveness in Q 11:4. The ninth benediction prays that God might fill the world with produce, whereas Q 11:3 is a prayer for bread.

- The fourteenth benediction asks God to restore the fortunes of Jerusalem and the kingdom of the house of David, and the Lord's Prayer opens by petitioning God to bring the kingdom (Q 11:2).

- Some have detected parallels of rhythm and even rhyme between the Lord's Prayer and the Amidah.[7]

In view of these similarities, one cannot exclude the possibility that Jewish Christians who knew the Lord's Prayer would have construed it as either a substitute for the Eighteen Benedictions or as an outline of private prayer to be subjoined to the Amidah.[8]

---

5. *Did.* 8:3; *Apost. const.* 7.24 (ed. Funk, vol. 1, pp. 409–11); *m. Ber.* 4:1.

6. Tertullian, *Orat.* 10 (CSEL 20, ed. A Reifferscheid and G. Wissowa, p. 187).

7. W. D. Davies, *The Setting of the Sermon on the Mount* (Cambridge: Cambridge University Press, 1966), pp. 310–11; K. G. Kuhn, *Achtzehngebet und Vaterunser und der Reim* (WUNT 1; Tübingen: Mohr Siebeck, 1950), pp. 30–40.

8. For the Lord's Prayer as an outline see Isaac of Nineveh, *The Second Part* 14:36 (CSCO 554, ed. Sebastin Brock, p. 68). Matthew's "Pray then in this way" (οὕτως, 6:9) may reflect such an understanding. For the Amidah as an outline see *t. Ber.* 3:5; *m. Ber.* 4:4; *m. 'Aboth* 2:13; *Sifre* on Num 12:13; *Mek.* on Exod 15:25; and *b. Ber.* 29b.

(ii) According to Marc Philonenko, Q 11:49–51[9] does not just resemble *Jub.* 1:12 but actually alludes to it:[10]

> Q 11:49: "Therefore also the Wisdom of God said, *I will send* them prophets and apostles, and some of them they will *kill* and *persecute*."

> *Jub.* 1:12: "And *I will send* witnesses to them so that I may testify to them, but they will not listen and will *kill* the witnesses. They will *persecute* those too who study the Law diligently."[11]

The parallel is indeed striking, but the theme of God's sending messengers who are rejected is hardly confined to *Jubilees* and Q 11:49, as the following passages illustrate:

> 2 Chr 24:19: "Yet he (God) sent prophets among them to bring them back to the Lord; they testified against them, but they would not listen."

> Jer 7:24–26: "Yet they did not obey or incline their ear, but, in the stubbornness of their evil will, they walked about in their own counsels, and looked backward rather than forward. From the day that your ancestors came out of the land of Egypt until this day, I have persistently sent all my servants the prophets to them, day by day; yet they did not listen to me or pay attention, but they stiffened their necks. They did worse than their fathers did."

> Jer 25:4: "And the Lord persistently sent you all his servants the prophets, you have neither listened nor inclined your ears to hear."

> Jer 35:14–15: "But I myself have spoken to you persistently, and you have not obeyed me. I have sent to you all my servants the prophets, sending them persistently, saying, 'Turn now everyone of you from your evil way, and amend your doings, and do not go after other gods to serve them, and then you shall live in the land that I gave to you and your ancestors.' But you did not incline your ear or obey me."

> Tg. Jer 32:33: "They have turned their backs to my worship, and have not set the fear of me before their faces; although I have sent to them all my servants the prophets, rising up early and instructing them; but they do not wish to receive instruction."

Also comparable is 2 Chr 36:15–16: "The Lord, the God of their fathers, sent persistently to them by his messengers, because he had compassion on his people and on his dwelling place; but they kept mocking the messengers

---

9. In addition to what follows, see the discussion of 11:49–51 on pp. 149–52.

10. Marc Philonenko, "Les paroles de Jésus contre 'cette génération' et la tradition qoumrânienne," in *Geschichte — Tradition — Reflexion: Festschrift für Martin Hengel zum 70. Geburtstag, Band III: Frühes Christentum* (ed. Hubert Cancik, Hermann Lichtenberger, and Peter Schäfer; Tübingen: Mohr Siebeck, 1996), pp. 89–95.

11. The Hebrew has been partially preserved in 4Q216 2:12–13: ואשלחה אל[י]הם עדים [להעיד בהם ולא ישמעו ואת העדים יהרוגן] ואת מבקשי [ה]תורה ירדופן. This is the reconstruction of J. C. VanderKam and J. T. Milik, "The First Jubilees Manuscript from Qumran Cave 4: A Preliminary Edition," *JBL* 110 (1991), p. 251.

of God, despising his words, and scoffing at his prophets, until the wrath of the Lord against his people became so great that there was no remedy." The Chronicler goes on to recount the subsequent desolation of the temple, as does Q 13:35, and Matthew's addition of ἔρημος ("desolate") could indicate that he was reminded, when reading Q 11:49ff., of 2 Chr 36:15–21, where ἐρημώσεως appears (see Mt 23:38).[12]

What are the relationships between the texts just cited? Several observations allow us to sort the data. (*a*) A literary connection between 2 Chr 36:15–16 and the three similar verses from Jeremiah seems likely enough:

Jer 7:25	אשלח אליכם ... הנביאים ... השכם ושלח
Jer 25:4	ושלח יהוה אליכם ... הנבאים השכם ושלח
Jer 35:15	ואשלח אליכם ... הנבאים השכים ושלח
2 Chr 36:15	וישלח יהוה אלהי ... מלאכיו השכם ושלח

Given that the Chronicler goes on to refer to Jeremiah explicitly and to his prophecy about seventy years (2 Chr 36:21; cf. Jer 25:11–12; 29:10), the direction of borrowing is manifest. (*b*) If, as one presumes, 2 Chr 24:19 comes from the same author as 2 Chr 36:15–16, then it too surely depends upon Jeremiah. (*c*) *Jub.* 1:12 has probably been influenced by 2 Chr 24:19, for the theme of "witnesses" (עדים) in the former has its parallel in the latter ("they testified [יעידו] against them").[13] In addition, the theme of murder ("they will kill the witnesses") appears in 2 Chr 24:20–22. (*d*) Tg. Jer 32:33 is closely related to Tg. Jer 7:25–26; 25:4; and 35:14–15, which are of course rewritings of MT Jer 7:25–26; 25:4; and 35:14–15.[14] The relationships between the various texts may be depicted, then, thus:

Jer 7:25–26; 25:4; 35:14–15[15]

2 Chr 24:19; 2 Chr 36:15–16   Tg. Jer 7:25–26; 25:4; 32:33; 35:15

Jub. 1:12

---

12. But this is far from certain because other texts join ἔρημος and οἶκος; see, e.g., LXX Jer 22:5; Hag 1:9; Tob 14:4.

13. Cf. 2 Kgs 17:13, which gives to the prophets the tasking of "witnessing" (עוד).

14. Tg. Jer 7:25–26: "From that day that your fathers went forth from the land of Egypt to this day, so I have sent to you all my servants the prophets, every day, rising up early and sending them. But they did not heed my Memra nor incline their ear, but hardened their neck; they did worse than their fathers." Tg. Jer 25:4: "And the Lord sent to you all his servants, the prophets, rising up early and sending them; but you did not listen, nor incline your ear to listen." Tg. Jer 35:15: "And I sent to you all my servants the prophets, rising up early and sending them . . . but you did not incline your ear nor heed my Memra." Tg. Jer 32:33: "I sent to them all my servants the prophets, rising up early and instructing them; but they do not wish to receive instruction."

15. The relationship of these verses to each other and the determination of which might go back to an early form of Jeremiah and which might be due to later hands are issues beyond the scope of this work.

One need only complete the genealogy by observing that the verses in Jeremiah themselves may depend upon 2 Kgs 17:13–15.

What then of Q 11:49? Against Philonenko's proposal, the Q saying differs from *Jub.* 1:12 in being about "prophets" and others,[16] not "witnesses" (עֵדִים), so in this particular Q is closer to 2 Chr 24:19; 36:15–16; Jer 25:4; and Tg. Jer 32:33. Further, the evidence that R. H. Charles gathered in order to show that *Jubilees* may have influenced some early Christian writers is meager.[17] Most importantly of all, Philonenko has missed the fact that Q 11:49, like *Jub.* 1:12, depends directly upon 2 Chr 24:19. The clear evidence for this is reviewed on pp. 149–52 herein, to which the reader is referred. The resemblances between *Jub.* 1:12 and Q 11:49, then, are to be explained, not by positing the latter's dependence upon the former, but by observing that both use the same intertext, namely, 2 Chr 24:19.

(iii) The third text to be considered is Q 12:42–46. The servant who, in Jesus' parable, eats and drinks and beats others and is then cut in half has sometimes called to mind the court tale of *Ahiqar*, in which the wicked Nathan does these things (3:2; 4:15) and then is cut in half (8:38). R. H. Charles thought that "the language of Ahikar has colored one of our Lord's parables."[18] This is possible, in which case Q 12:46 might be reckoned an allusion. Standing in the way of this proposal, however, is J. M. Lindenberger's assertion that *Ahiqar* and Q 12:42–46 simply share a "proverbial convention" about the fate of untrustworthy stewards.[19]

There is not much to go on in judging between these two opinions, for Lindenberger does not support his contention by citing anything more than *Ahiqar* and the Synoptics. The prudent judgment accordingly may be that if Q's audience was familiar with the tale of *Ahiqar*, then Q 12:46 would have reminded them of it. But we unfortunately have no way to establish such familiarity.

●

---

16. Luke has "prophets and apostles" (προφήτας καὶ ἀποστόλους). Mt 23:34 has "prophets" (προφήτας), "wise" (σοφούς), and "scribes" (γραμματεῖς). Did Matthew turn Q's twin offices ("prophets and apostles") into an ecclesiastical (and yet thoroughly Jewish) triad (cf. Mt 23:8–10)? But then "prophets and apostles" is often assigned to Luke; so Jeremias, *Sprache*, p. 209. Maybe Q had "prophets and wise ones." If so, Matthew added a synonym for "wise ones" ("scribes"), while Luke preferred to name messengers of the old and new dispensations. But in a matter such as this we cannot pass beyond mere conjecture.

17. R. H. Charles, *The Book of Jubilees or the Little Genesis* (London: A. & C. Black, 1902), pp. lxxxiii–lxxxv.

18. R. H. Charles, *The Apocrypha and Pseudepigrapha of the Old Testament in English*, vol. 2, *Pseudepigrapha* (Oxford: Clarendon, 1913), p. 719. Cf. Keener, *Matthew*, p. 594. It may be relevant that, according to J. M. Lindenberger, in *The Old Testament Pseudepigrapha* (ed. James H. Charlesworth; Garden City, N.Y.: Doubleday, 1985), vol. 2, p. 484, n. 34, "There is some evidence that parallels between Ah[iqar], Aesop, and Joseph were observed in antiquity. One of the Syr. MSS of Ah[iqar] contains a collection of Aesop's fables attributed to 'Josephus.'" For the link between Q 12:42–46 and Josephus see pp. 87–92.

19. Lindenberger, in Charlesworth, ed., *Old Testament Pseudepigrapha*, vol. 2, p. 487.

The results of this brief chapter are negligible. It is possible but uncertain that Q 11:2–4 draws upon the Kaddish prayer or the Amidah, and Q 12:46 might allude to the tale of *Ahiqar*. Beyond these uncertainties, there do not appear to be any direct references to noncanonical books.[20] Q seems almost exclusively preoccupied with texts that appear in the canon. Since use of the Apocrypha is also nonexistent or minimal,[21] it is possible that most of the contributors to Q were already living with a collection of books that, for all practical purposes, was fairly close to what we know as the Tanak.

---

20. On the relationship between 4Q521 2 + 4 ii 12 (4QMessianic Apocalypse) and Q 7:22, see pp. 111–13.

21. On the parallel between Ecclus 4:11 and Q 7:35, see p. 172.

Chapter 10

Retrospect

Scripture in Q

I. Q'S Bible and Preferences

Q activates the following scriptural subtexts:

The Pentateuch

Scripture	Marked Quotation	Unmarked Quotation	Explicit Reference	Allusion
Gen 4:8–16			Q 11:49–51	
Gen 4:15, 24				Q 17:3–4(?)
Genesis 6–9			Q 17:26–27	
Gen 15:1				Q 6:23
Gen 13:10, 11; 19:17, 25, 28				Q 3:5(?)
Gen 19:1–29			Q 10:12 Q 17:28–29 (+ 31–32?)	
Gen 19:17, 26				Q 9:62
Genesis 39				Q 12:42–46
Exod 8:19				Q 11:20
Exod 12:11				Q 12:35–38
Exod 12:11, 34–36				Q 10:4(?)
Exodus 16				Q 11:3
Exod 20:12				Q 14:26
Exod 23:20	Q 7:27			
Exod 33:11–23				Q 10:21–22
Lev 19:2				Q 6:36
Lev 19:17				Q 6:37–38 Q 17:3–4
Lev 19:18				Q 6:27
Deut 1:35				Q 11:29–30
Deut 5:16				Q 14:26

Scripture	Marked Quotation	Unmarked Quotation	Explicit Reference	Allusion
Deut 6:13	Q 4:8			
Deut 6:16	Q 4:12			
Deut 8:3	Q 4:4			
Deut 21:20				Q 7:34
Deut 24:1–4				Q 16:18
Deut 33:9				Q 14:26(?)
Deut 34:1–4				Q 4:5–7

The Prophets

Scripture	Marked Quotation	Unmarked Quotation	Explicit Reference	Allusion
Former prophets				
1 Sam 25:6				Q 10:5(?)
1 Kgs 19:19–21				Q 9:57–62
2 Kgs 4:29				Q 10:4
Writing prophets				
Isa 6:6–9				Q 10:23–24(?)
Isa 14:13,15				Q 10:15
Isa 26:19				Q 7:22
Isa 29:18–19				Q 7:22
Isa 35:5–6				Q 7:22
Isa 42:18 (cf. v. 7)				Q 7:22
Isa 50:6, 8				Q 6:29–30
Isa 51:1–2				Q 3:8
Isa 51:8				Q 12:33–34(?)
Isa 54:9–10				Q 17:26–27
Isa 61:1–2				Q 6:20–23
				Q 7:22
Jer 12:7				Q 13:35
Ezek 17:22–24				Q 13:19
Ezek 31:2–18				Q 13:19
Amos 3:5				Q 12:6(?)
Jonah			Q 11:29–30	
Jonah 3			Q 11:32	
Mic 7:6		Q 12:51–53		
Hab 2:3				Q 12:45(?)
Mal 3:1	Q 7:27			
Mal 4:1				Q 3:17(?)

Writings

Scripture	Marked Quotation	Unmarked Quotation	Explicit Reference	Allusion
Ps 6:8		Q 13:27		
Psalm 8				Q 9:57–58
Ps 91:12	Q 4:9			
Ps 107:3				Q 13:28–29(?)
Ps 112:10				Q 13:28–29(?)
Ps 118:26		Q 13:34–35		
Ps 147:9				Q 12:24?
Prov 6:6–11				Q 12:22–31
Dan 4:10–33				Q 13:19
Dan 7:9–14				Q 12:8–9
				Q 12:40
				Q 17:24, 26, 30(?)
				Q 22:30
2 Chr 9:1–12			Q 11:31	
2 Chr 24:17–25			Q 11:49–51	

Q borrows from all three major divisions of the Tanak — the Pentateuch, the Prophets, and the Writings. Nonetheless, the Sayings Source favors particular portions of the Bible. If we leave aside the several likely allusions to the judgment scene in Dan 7:13–14, only the Pentateuch, the Psalms, and Isaiah — the first two of which are cited in a formal manner (4:4, 8, 10, 12; 7:27) — are referred to repeatedly. So while it might be anachronistic to speak of Q's canon within the canon, because Q may not have known any canon in our sense of the word,[1] its contributors either knew certain portions of the Tanak better than others or found certain portions more useful for their purposes. Perhaps both were true at the same time.

This result should not surprise, for what we find in Q we find elsewhere. Among early Christians, the three most popular portions of the Hebrew Bible were Isaiah, the Psalms, and the five books of Moses. To judge from the indices in the Loeb edition, this is so already in the apostolic fathers,[2] and the statistical charts of Stuhlhofer confirm the same thing for the entire period up to Eusebius.[3] Furthermore, the table entitled "Loci citati vel

---

1. See esp. John Barton, *Oracles of God: Perceptions of Ancient Prophecy in Israel after the Exile* (New York/Oxford: Oxford University Press, 1986).

2. Kirsopp Lake, *The Apostolic Fathers* (Cambridge, Mass./London: Harvard University Press/William Heinemann, 1952), vol. 2, pp. 391–93.

3. Stuhlhofer, *Gebrauch der Bibel von Jesus bis Euseb.* Cf. the index of biblical passages at the end of vol. 2 of Edgar Hennecke and Wilhelm Schneemelcher, *New Testament Apocrypha*, vol. 2, *Writings Related to the Apostles, Apocalypses, and Related Subjects* (ed. R. McL. Wilson; Cambridge/Louisville: James Clark & Co./Westminster/John Knox, 1992), pp. 753–54; also J. K. Elliott, *The Apocryphal New Testament: A Collection of Apocryphal Christian Literature in English Translation* (Oxford: Clarendon, 1993), p. 740.

allegati" in the 27th edition of the Nestle-Aland Greek New Testament contains approximately eighteen columns of entries for the Pentateuch, eight columns each for Isaiah and the Psalms, and no more than three for any other book.[4] So Q's fondness for the Pentateuch, the Psalms, and Isaiah is par for the early Christian course.

But it is also in line with what we know of Judaism. According to James C. VanderKam, among the Dead Sea Scrolls "the book of Psalms is present in the largest number of copies (36), with the next two being Deuteronomy (29) and Isaiah (21). Of the others, only Exodus (17), Genesis (15), and Leviticus (13) break into double figures."[5] As for the Pseudepigrapha, the index of scriptural references at the end of Sparks's *Apocryphal Old Testament* gives first place to Genesis, second place to Isaiah, third place to Exodus, fourth place to the Psalms, and fifth place to Deuteronomy.[6] The most frequently cited books in the Loeb edition of Philo are, in order: Genesis, Exodus, Deuteronomy, Leviticus, Psalms, 1 Samuel, Isaiah. The list of biblical passages at the end of Montefiore and Loewe's *Rabbinic Anthology* shows this order: the Psalms then Deuteronomy then Isaiah then Genesis then Exodus.[7] It is true that the index of scriptural citations at the end of Danby's *Mishnah* lists more entries for Proverbs than for Isaiah, but that result is skewed by the inordinate interest tractate *Aboth* has in Proverbs (nineteen out of the thirty-one of the Mishnah's quotations appear in *m. 'Aboth*).[8] Isaiah beats Proverbs in the indices to the Soncino editions of the *Babylonian Talmud* and *Midrash Rabbah,* and in both collections the most cited portion of Scripture is the Pentateuch followed by the Psalms and then Isaiah.[9]

The tendency in both Jewish and Christian literature from antiquity can be seen in Bradley H. McLean's index of *Citations and Allusions to Jewish Scripture in Jewish and Christian Writings through 180 C.E.*[10] Here too nothing comes close to being listed as often as the Psalms and Isaiah, except

---

4. Cf. the statistics in Gleason L. Archer and Gregory C. Chirichigno, *Old Testament Quotations in the New Testament* (Chicago: Moody, 1983), p. xvii.

5. James C. VanderKam, *The Dead Sea Scrolls Today* (Grand Rapids: Eerdmans, 1994), pp. 30–32. Cf. Lawrence H. Schiffmann, *Reclaiming the Dead Sea Scrolls: The History of Judaism, the Background of Christianity, the Lost Library of Qumran* (Philadelphia/Jerusalem: Jewish Publication Society, 1994), p. 163 (with slightly different counts).

6. H. F. D. Sparks, ed., *The Apocryphal Old Testament* (Oxford: Clarendon, 1984), pp. 967–69.

7. C. G. Montefiore and H. Loewe, *A Rabbinic Anthology* (New York: Schocken, 1974), pp. 746–52.

8. Herbert Danby, *The Mishnah* (Oxford: Oxford University Press, 1933), pp. 807–11.

9. *Babylonian Talmud: Index Volume* (ed. I. Epstein; London: Soncino, 1952), pp. 473–620; *Midrash Rabbah: Index Volume* (ed. Judah J. Slotki; London: Soncino, 1939), pp. 139–322.

10. McLean, *Citations and Allusions.* Within the Pentateuch, the ranking is this: Genesis, Exodus, Deuteronomy, Leviticus, Numbers.

for Genesis and Exodus; and the Pentateuch, if taken as a unit, soundly beats both.[11]

That the pattern emerging from investigation of Q matches the pattern exhibited by the scriptural indices of other ancient Jewish and Christian writings is perhaps some reason for thinking the present investigation to be on the right track, for one might expect the upshot of an uncontrolled search for verbal and thematic parallels between Q and the Tanak to be governed by random chance, in which case no pattern should emerge. The proposed subtexts, however, do not exhibit a haphazard distribution throughout the biblical corpus. They tend rather to come from the same sources that ancient Jews and Christians preferred to mine.

It is instructive to compare Q's use of the Bible with C. H. Dodd's conspectus of passages that the early Church favored for testimonies to its *kerygma*.[12] While the Psalms and Isaiah (but not the Pentateuch) dominate Dodd's study, Q makes use of only two of the sixteen psalms that were primary and secondary sources of testimonies (Psalms 8 and 118).[13] And of the sections from Isaiah that Dodd deemed to have been most popular,[14] less than half of Q's references to Isaiah come from them. Moreover, of the remainder of passages that Dodd characterized as primary or secondary sources of testimonies,[15] Q refers to only one (Mal 3:1–16: Q 7:27 quotes Mal 3:1) or two (Habakkuk 1–2 — if Q 12:45 alludes to Hab 2:3). So while there is nothing peculiar about Q's interest in Isaiah and the Psalms, its choice of particular texts within those collections, and its failure to use so many popular passages, is intriguing. Q seems to be largely independent of the apologetical currents Dodd mapped.

It accords with this result that Dodd had nothing to say about Chronicles. No portion of that book appears either in his "primary sources of testimonies" or in his "subordinate and supplementary sources."[16] Q, however, shows a knowledge of and maybe even preference for Chronicles over Kings. Q 11:49–51 refers to a story found in the Hebrew Bible only in 2 Chr 24:17–25, and Q 11:31 adverts to the story of Solomon and the queen of the

---

11. The same phenomenon seems to hold for Gnostic sources; see R. McL. Wilson, "The Gnostics and the Old Testament," in *Proceedings of the International Colloquium on Gnosticism, Stockholm August 20–25, 1973* (ed. Geo Widengren; Stockholm/Leiden: Almqvist & Wiksell/ Brill, 1973), pp. 164–68.

12. C. H. Dodd, *According to the Scriptures*, pp. 107–8.

13. Psalms 2; 8; 16; 22; 31; 34; 38; 41; 42; 43; 69; 88; 90; 110; 118; 132. Cf. the chart of NT quotations and allusions to the Psalms in LarsOlov Eriksson, *"Come, Children, Listen to Me!" Psalm 34 in the Hebrew Bible and in Early Christian Writings* (CBOT 32; Stockholm: Almqvist & Wiksell, 1991), p. 107.

14. Isa 6:1–9:7; 11:1–10; 28:16; 39:9–14; 40:1–11; 49:1–13; 50:4–11; 52:13–53:12; 58:6–10; 61.

15. Gen 12:3; 22:18; Deut 18:15, 18; 2 Sam 7:13–14; Jer 7:1–5; 31:10–34; Daniel 12; Hosea; Joel 2–3; Amos 9:11–12; Habakkuk 1–2; Zechariah 9–14; Mal 3:1–16.

16. C. H. Dodd, *According to the Scriptures*, pp. 107–8.

South with an expression (τὴν σοφίαν Σολομῶνος) that is from the version in LXX Chronicles, not the version in LXX Kings.

II. How Q Recalls Subtexts

Q recalls Scripture in several different ways:

(i) Explicit citations appear in Q 4:4 (Deut 8:3), 8 (Deut 6:13), 10–11 (Ps 91:11–12), 12 (Deut 6:16); and 7:27 (Exod 23:20; Mal 3:1). On each occasion γέγραπται, "it is written," is used:

4:4		γέγραπται	ὅτι
4: 8		γέγραπται	
4:10		γέγραπται γὰρ	ὅτι
4:12		γέγραπται	ὅτι
7:27	οὗτός ἐστιν περὶ οὗ	γέγραπται	

All of these formulas can be found in Jewish and other Christian texts.[17]

(ii) Q makes explicit reference to particular scriptural events or personalities in 10:12 (Sodom in Genesis 19), in 11:29–30, 32 (Jonah), in 11:31 (Solomon in 2 Chronicles 9), in 11:49–51 (Abel in Genesis 4 and Zechariah in 2 Chronicles 24), in 12:27 (Solomon's glory), in 17:26–27 (Noah and the flood), and in 17:28–29 (+ 31–32; Lot and Sodom). Over half of these involve the first half of Genesis, which indicates a special interest in protology.

(iii) Q's favorite manner of reference is to draw key words, phrases, themes, or images from well-known texts. Enough is borrowed so that the borrowing can be recognized: Q wants to be found out. This is the case in Q 3:8 (Isa 51:1–2); 6:20–23 (Isa 61:1–2), 23 (Gen 15:1), 27 (Lev 19:18), 29–30 (Isa 50:6, 8), 36 (Lev 19:2), 37 (Lev 19:17); 7:22 (Isa 26:29; 29:18–19; 35:5–6; 42:18; 61:1–2), 34 (Deut 21:20); 9:57–58 (Ps 8:5–9), 62 (Gen 19:17, 26); 10:4 (2 Kgs 4:29), 21–22 (Exod 33:11–23); 11:3 (Exodus 16), 20 (Exod 8:19), 29–30 (Deut 1:35); 12:8–9 (Dan 7:13–14), 22–31 (Prov 6:6–11), 35–38 (Exod 12:11), 40 (Dan 7:13–14), 42–46 (Genesis 39); 13:19 (Daniel 4; Ezekiel 17; 31); 14:26 (Exod 20:12 = Deut 5:16); 17:3–4 (Lev 19:17); and 22:28–30 (Dan 7:9–14). All of these are cases of oblique reference. Key words from a subtext are reproduced, and the reader catches an allusion because there are additional parallels of theme, imagery, circumstance, etc.

(iv) Q contains at least three embedded quotations, that is, texts that have been dug up and transplanted without acknowledgment. Q 12:51–53 is a loose citation of Mic 7:6 ("The son treats the father with contempt, the daughter rises up against her mother"), Q 13:35 quotes Ps 118:26 ("Blessed

---

17. Fitzmyer, *Semitic Background*, pp. 8–10.

is he who comes in the name of the Lord"), and Q 13:27 takes up a phrase
from Ps 6:8 ("Depart from me, all you workers of evil").

(v) In Q 9:57–62 are call stories that are told in such a way that they
recall a famous antecedent: the circumstances and telling of Jesus' call to
discipleship imitate 1 Kgs 19:19–21, where Elijah calls Elisha.

(vi) Q 6:27 and 14:26 use phrases whose word order and rhythm are
deliberately imitative:

Q 6:27	ἀγαπᾶτε τοὺς ἐχθροὺς ὑμῶν
Lev 19:18	ἀγαπήσεις τὸν πλησίον σου
Q 14:26	μισεῖ τὸν πατέρα ἑαυτοῦ καὶ τὴν μητέρα
Exod 20:12 = Deut 5:16	τίμα τὸν πατέρα σου καὶ τὴν μητέρα

(vii) In at least one case content alone suffices to recall a subtext. When
Jesus, in Q 16:18, prohibits divorce, the scripturally informed, as the ecclesiastical commentaries show us, cannot but ask about the relationship to
the one Pentateuchal passage that regulates divorce, Deut 24:1–4.

Unlike some other ancient texts, Q does not signal a quotation by in-
verting the original.[18] Nor are its borrowings ever signaled by solecisms,
grammatical inconcinnities created by the retention of an intertext's original
syntax.[19]

III. Heightening Authority and Attention

If it is true in general that one cannot speak the totally unfamiliar because
intelligibility requires recollection, it is also true in particular that in the
first-century world of Jewish Christianity, where anything new in religion
had to explain itself over against the old, it was close to inevitable that Q's
contributors anchored their speech in the familiar, authoritative Scriptures.
Anything else would not have spoken persuasively to a Jewish audience.
As Willey has written, "Not just anything can be said: new interpretations
tend to be circumscribed by what the tradition, interpreted according to the
community's exegetical norms, will yield. The indwelling of the authoritative
text in the audience necessitates the indwelling of the authoritative text in the
new interpretation."[20] It cannot surprise, then, that Q's Jesus speaks with
biblical idioms and with the reassuring voices of Moses, Isaiah, and the

---

18. This device appears to have been rediscovered by P. C. Beentjes, "Discovering a New
Path of Intertextuality: Inverted Quotations and their Dynamics," in *Literary Structure and
Rhetorical Strategies in the Hebrew Bible* (ed. L. J. de Regt, J. de Waard, and J. P. Fokkelman;
Assen: Van Gorcum, 1996), pp. 31–50.

19. On this, see Gregory K. Beale, "Solecisms in the Apocalypse as Signals for the Presence
of Old Testament Allusions: A Selective Analysis of Revelation 1–22," in Evans and Sanders,
eds., *Early Christian Interpretation*, pp. 421–46. Mt 2:19–21 also offers an example; see
Allison, *New Moses*, pp. 142–43.

20. Willey, *Remember the Former Things*, p. 70.

psalmists. Without a scriptural articulation, Q's audience would not have felt solidarity with Q's speaker.

Beyond its self-authenticating use of biblical language, Q refers to Scripture and borrows its language in order to incite hearers to become more active.[21] In any context the explicit soon becomes tedious. The allusion is a way of fighting tedium. Meaning is infolded not to obscure but to improve communication: allusions give the imagination more to do — "What is concealed spurs the reader into action"[22] — and so heighten attention. The implicit allows the pleasure of discovery, and hearers who are invited to fill gaps appreciate the authors who respect them enough not to shout.

A simple illustration of how all this works appears in the book of Wisdom. Chapter 10 summarizes the stories of great men from Adam to Moses — without once mentioning anyone's name. Adam is "the first-formed father" (10:1). Cain is "an unrighteous man" (10:3). Noah and Abraham and Lot and Jacob and Joseph are all called "a/the righteous man" (10:4, 5, 6, 9, 13). Moses is "a servant of the Lord" (10:15). Clearly the author of Wisdom intentionally avoided naming his subjects. And just as clearly he expected his audience to do this simple thing for themselves. Why? The silence draws us further into the book by asking us to make our own contribution. Perhaps also the absence of names is an enticement to turn the unnamed into types (cf. the types elsewhere in Wisdom). For this allusions are just what is needed. More would be less.

Matters are similar in Q, where Scripture is not the object of any great controversy, so that there is little occasion to cite the Bible formally and to do exegesis upon it. But Q does regularly allude to Scripture. And when it does, it does not steal but borrows openly, with the intention of being recognized. The language is not supposed to be vaguely familiar but precisely known. The scriptural phrases should be mnemonic triggers, set to create intertextual exchanges.

IV. Allusive Meaning

Such intertextual exchanges usually enlarge meaning. Consider the first section of Q, 3:7–7:35. It is only knowledge of the pertinent intertexts that allows one to see that John's call to repentance (Q 3:8–9) rejects a scripturally based tenet (cf. Isa 51:1–2), that Jesus' temptations in the wilderness

---

21. For what follows I have borrowed from Arthur Koestler, "Literature and the Law of Diminishing Returns," in *The Heel of Achilles: Essays 1968–1973* (New York: Random House, 1974), pp. 119–37.

22. Wolfgang Iser, "Interaction between Text and Reader," in *The Reader in the Text: Essays on Audience and Interpretation* (ed. Susan R. Suleiman and Inge Crosman; Princeton: Princeton University Press, 1980), p. 111.

are a typological replay of Israel's foundational religious experience in the Sinai (Q 4:1–13), that the Sermon on the Plain is partly a provocative rewriting of a central chapter in the Pentateuch (Leviticus 19), that Jesus' ministry fulfills eschatological oracles from Deutero-Isaiah (Q 6:20–23 and 7:18–23 draw upon Isaiah 61), and that the charge in Q 7:34 that Jesus is a glutton and drunkard is an indictment echoing Deut 21:18–22, where such a one is stoned and then hung up.

The same thing appears in Q's second section, Q 9:57–11:13. Q 9:57–58, where the homeless Son of man has less than the birds and the beasts, becomes ironic when it is read against Psalm 8, where the honored son of man has all things, including the birds and the beasts, under his feet. The call of Jesus in Q 9:57–62 is the more radical when read against Elijah's call of Elisha in 2 Kgs 19:19–21. The allusion to Gen 19:17 and 26 in Q(?) 9:62 is so appropriate because Lot's wife, according to tradition, remained tied to her past. One fully understands the claim of Q 10:22 only upon realizing that Jesus is here the rival of Moses, who knew and was known by God, who exclusively received the divine revelation in its fullness, and who handed down that revelation to others. And those who hear in Q 11:3 an allusion to the story of the manna will, when they pray the Lord's Prayer and ask for daily bread, be comforted by the textual memory of God supplying Israel bread in the wilderness.

The biblical language of Q 3:7–7:35 and 9:57–11:13 is not stereotypical or free-floating religious jargon. And so it is throughout Q, which rather encourages juxtapositions that create meaning.

Some of these juxtapositions produce typologies. The citations of Deuteronomy 6 and 8 in Q 4:1–13 make Jesus relive the events of the exodus, while Q 12:35–38, which exhorts disciples to let their loins be girded and their lamps lit (cf. Exod 12:11), does the same thing for his followers; and Q 7:27 (cf. Exod 23:20), where John the Baptist is the messenger who goes before to prepare the way, includes the Baptist in the same scheme. The language of both Q 10:22, where Jesus is the exclusive knower and revealer of God (cf. Exod 33:11–23), and of 11:20, where Jesus casts out demons by the finger of God (cf. Exod 8:19), makes him like Moses, which also furthers the typology. And in 6:27–45 (cf. Leviticus 19); 14:26 (cf. Exod 20:12 = Deut 5:16); 16:18 (cf. Deut 24:1–4); and 17:3–4 (cf. Lev 19:17), Jesus offers imperatives that serve as addenda to or revisions of the words of Moses.

Typology arises also from the naming of Sodom in 10:15 and the naming of Lot in 17:28–29 (and, if they are assigned to Q, the mention of Lot's wife in 17:32 and the allusion to her in 9:62): these texts liken Jesus' period to another when divine judgment fell from heaven. The same end is gained by the reference to Noah and the flood in 17:26–27 as well as by the various descriptions of "this generation" (7:31; 11:29–32, 50–51), which summon before the mind's eye the notorious generations of Noah and of Moses and their dismal fates. Thus protology mingles with and supplements the exodus typology, as it does so often in Jewish and Christian sources.[23]

Related to typology are the two occasions on which Q turns Scriptures into proof texts. It does this first in 7:22, where Jesus' ministry is characterized by prophecies from Isaiah — "the blind see," etc. The Sayings Source does this also in 7:27, where John the Baptist is identified with words that merge Exod 23:20 and Mal 3:1: John is the messenger who prepares the eschatological way. Q 7:22 and 27 together interpret the days of Jesus as the era of the fulfillment of eschatological expectations, which is also what the texts that create a typology do, for they assume the theologoumenon that the end is like the beginning: if Jesus' day recalls the days of Genesis, it follows that the end has come and that prophecies are being fulfilled. Likewise comparable is 12:51–53, which, by citing Mic 7:6, brings this prophecy of the latter days into the ministry of Jesus. The allusions to Dan 7:13–14 in Q 12:8–9, 40; and 22:30 also belong here, for they make Jesus the content of an eschatological oracle.

There are also less-loaded uses of Scripture. These include the occasions on which Q uses biblical language just because it is biblical, that is, without alluding to any particular subtext. In these instances — for instance, some of the biblical formulations listed on pp. 6–8 — we have deliberate archaizing: the Sayings Source is trying to sound like the Bible. It thereby quietly borrows authority for itself: that which sounds like the authoritative Scriptures is itself going to sound authoritative.

There are further occasions on which the Tanak supplies illustrative material. In Q 11:31, for example, the queen of the South serves as a warning for those who, unlike her, fail to heed wisdom, and in Q 11:32 the Ninevites who repented at the preaching of Jonah serve this purpose. In Q 12:27 Solomon becomes a foil to the wild lilies, whose splendor surpasses the dress of the great king.

It is interesting that Q takes most of its intertexts from well-known stories, not prophetic or sapiential discourses. The result is that the hearer sees pictures that are already stored in the memory. Q 11:14–52, Q's third major section, offers several examples. Q 11:20 retrieves the image of Moses competing with Pharaoh's magicians (Exod 8:19). Q 11:30 brings to the mind Jonah in the streets of Nineveh (so too 11:32). Q 11:31 conjures the dramatic scene of the queen of Sheba in the court of Solomon (2 Chronicles 9). And 11:49–51 calls forth the image we have of Cain and Abel on the field of slaughter (Gen 4:8–16), as well as that of the bloody stoning of Zechariah (2 Chr 24:20–22). For those who can associate its lines with their memories of traditional stories, in each of these instances Q pictorially illustrates itself in the mind's eye — a rhetorical plus and an aid to memory.

---

23. See Allison, *New Moses*, pp. 200–207; also R. Chernus, *Redemption and Chaos: A Study in the Symbolism of the Rabbinic Aggada* (Ann Arbor: University Microfilms, 1978).

V. Reversing Subtexts

In addition to constructing typologies, providing proof texts, and supplying imagery, illustrations, and authoritative language, there is a less obvious but nonetheless prominent way in which Q uses the Bible. Q often creates a contrast with subtexts or even inverts them. This creates striking incongruities that make the text louder and more memorable. Again it will be convenient to offer a list:

Q 3:8 warns one not to rely upon descent from Abraham, to whom God can raise up children from rocks, whereas the subtext, Isa 51:1–2, says, "Look to the rock from which you were hewn....Look to Abraham your father."

Q 6:27–45 contains several imperatives that reverse commandments in Leviticus 19.

Q 9:57–58 offers a cynical reapplication of Ps 8:5: Providence does not meet the basic needs of the Son of man.

Q 9:57–62 shows Jesus to be more stringent than Elijah, who according to 3 Βασ 19:19–21 and Josephus, *Ant.* 8.354, permitted his disciple Elisha to return home.

Q 10:4, in alluding to 2 Kgs 4:29, which commands the taking of a staff, prohibits taking a staff.

Q 10:4 prohibits itinerants from taking silver, bread bag, sandals, and staff, all of which Moses famously commanded the Israelites to take with them in their departure from Egypt (Exod 12:11, 34–36).

Q 10:21–22 transfers to Jesus attributes reserved by Scripture for Moses exclusively (Exodus 33; Num 12:6–8; Deut 34:10).

Q 11:31 recalls the famous story of Solomon and the queen of Sheba in order to draw an analogy that it breaks: a greater than Solomon is here.

Q 12:22–31, which teaches that one need not worry about food and clothing because God takes care of the beasts who do not work, stands in tension with the Wisdom tradition, above all Prov 6:6–11, where the lesson is that one should work like the beasts.

Q 12:27 recalls the unsurpassed glory of Solomon only in order to subordinate it to the common lilies of the field.

Q 13:19 transfers to the kingdom of God imagery that Ezekiel and Daniel associate with ungodly powers.

Q 14:26 commands one to hate father and mother, which cannot but make one think about the Decalogue, where honor of father and mother is commanded.

Q 16:18 prohibits divorce and inevitably provokes the informed to ask what this does to Deut 24:1–4.

Q 17:3–4, which demands that one forgive again and again, alludes to Lev
19:17, which exegetes sometimes understood to require making reproof
again and again (cf. the MT's הוכח תוכיח).

In all these cases Q uses Scripture neither to illustrate a point nor to
vindicate Jesus but to express something provocatively. There is a distance
or disparity between the sacred subtext and the word of Jesus, a disparity
or distance that often generates irony. The dictionaries say that irony is
created when the intended meaning of a sentence is the opposite of what
that sentence expresses. This is not quite what is going on in Q. The Sayings
Source instead offers intertextual irony: it is not that the text says one thing
and means another but that the subtext says one thing and the text another.
One might be tempted to espy in all this an incongruity, for whereas Q
16:17 denies any genuine contradiction between Jesus and the Law and the
Prophets,[24] does not the reversal of scriptural subtexts in fact abolish scriptural authority (cf. perhaps Q 16:16 — "the law and the prophets were until
John")?[25] Do we perhaps have here reason to surmise that Q 16:17 cannot

---

24. In Q 16:16–17 we read that "the law and the prophets" were "until John" (v. 16),
which is followed by the declaration that it is easier for heaven and earth to pass away "than
for one stroke of a letter in the law to be dropped" (v. 17). The function of the latter in its
present context is surely to prevent a misreading of the former: the law cannot be abandoned.
It also cuts off an antinomian reading of the next verse, 16:18, Jesus' denial of divorce. So the
text reinforces the implicit lesson of Q's intertextuality: Scripture is not being discarded. For
a survey of scholarship on the law in Q, see William R. G. Loader, *Jesus' Attitude towards
the Law*, pp. 390–431. His own conclusion, on p. 431, may be endorsed: "Q assumes the
Law's validity.... It is neither replaced nor surpassed nor modified, except by addition. Yet the
addition is such that the Law can remain (intact) in the background and does, through much
of Q. Jesus gives eschatological Torah, but it includes also pressing the demands of those who
have gone before, including John, but also Moses; for their demands remain valid." See further
Tuckett, *Q*, pp. 393–424.

25. In passing one wonders whether the phrase "the law and the prophets were until John"
tells us anything about how Q's Bible was conceptually divided. "The law and the prophets"
was a traditional expression that reflects a very old way of conceiving of Jewish Scripture; see
Steven Chapman, *The Law and the Prophets: A Study in Old Testament Canon Formation*
(FAT 27; Tübingen: Mohr Siebeck, 2000). It appears also in 2 Macc 15:9 ("encouraging them
from the law and the prophets"); 4 Macc 18:10 ("he taught you the law and the prophets"); Mt
7:12 (the golden rule is "the law and the prophets," cf. 5:17; 11:13; 22:40); Jn 1:45 ("we have
found him about whom Moses in the law and the prophets wrote"); Acts 13:15 ("reading the
law and the prophets"; cf. 24:14; 28:23); Rom 3:21 ("the righteousness of God" is "attested
by the law and the prophets"); and Ignatius, *Smyr.* 5.1 ("neither the prophecies nor the law
of Moses"). The expression reckons Scripture as a collection with two parts, the first made
up of the νόμος, the five books of Moses, the remainder of the prophets, οἱ προφῆται (cf. Lk
16:29, 31). It does not follow, however, that Q's contributors and audiences did not know
the common tripartite division of Scripture that appears to be referred to in several places,
such as the prologue of Ecclesiasticus ("many great teachings have been given to us through
the law and the prophets and the others that followed them"); Philo, *Vit. Con.* 25 ("laws
and oracles delivered through the mouth of prophets and psalms and the other books"); and
Josephus, *C. Ap.* 1.38–49 ("the books of Moses...the prophets subsequent to Moses...the
remaining four books"; "the prophets subsequent to Moses" are probably Joshua, Judges +
Ruth, 1–2 Samuel, 1–2 Kings, Chronicles, Ezra + Nehemiah, Esther, Job, Isaiah, Jeremiah +
Lamentations, Ezekiel, the minor prophets, Daniel; "the remaining four books" are presumably
Psalms, Canticles, Proverbs, Ecclesiastes). (Line 10 of 4Q397 14–21 has been reconstructed to

come from the same stage or editors as those texts that play themselves off against the Torah?

Such an inference would fail to recognize that many Jewish interpreters felt the independence and freedom not only to rewrite Scripture[26] but also to turn it upside down and even contradict it: the creative dynamic of tradition meant that assimilation involved dissimilation.[27] Thus Jewish authors often used "authoritative Torah-teaching as a didactic foil,"[28] even to say something quite different or antithetical to the sacred text. Indeed, "the Jewish device of twisting Scripture, of subjecting the earlier canon to radical reinterpretation by means of subtle reformulations, is now recognized as central to the Bible as a whole."[29] We have already seen how often the undoing of apparent human insignificance in Psalm 2 is itself ironically undone in several sources.[30] Similarly, Psalm 144, in rewriting Psalm 18, turns it from a thanksgiving into a complaint.[31] Job often takes traditional positive formulas and turns them into their opposites.[32] Thus, in 3:1–13, the man from the land of Uz depicts his own disintegration by reversing Genesis 1.[33]

Turning to the prophets, Joel 3:9–10 prophesies war ("Proclaim this among the nations: Prepare war, stir up the warriors. Let all the soldiers draw near, let them come up. Beat your plowshares into swords, and your pruning hooks into spears") in the language of a famous prophecy of peace

---

refer to "the book of Moses," "the words of the prophets," "David," and "the words of the days" [= Chronicles], but the text is very uncertain.) The Gospel of Luke at least divides the Bible both ways. If in 16:16 we read of "the law and the prophets" and in 16:29 and 31 of "Moses and the prophets," in Luke 24:44 we find the tripartite division: "the law of Moses and the prophets and the Psalms." So it would be unwise to insist that Q 16:16 implies a bipartite conception of Q's Bible.

26. Aside from the targums, which are often much more than translations, one may cite in illustration Deuteronomy, Chronicles, *Jubilees*, the Genesis Apocryphon, the Temple Scroll, the *Liber Antiquitatum Biblicarum*, the *Life of Adam and Eve*, and Josephus's *Jewish Antiquities*.

27. It suffices here to recall the works of Fishbane and the literary study of Herman Meyer, *Poetics of Quotation*.

28. Michael Fishbane, "Torah and Tradition," in *Tradition and Theology in the Old Testament* (ed. Douglas A. Knight; Philadelphia: Fortress, 1977), p. 277. The entire article (pp. 275–300) is instructive in showing how later Jewish tradition often controverts earlier Jewish tradition, including Scripture.

29. David G. Roskies, *Against the Apocalypse: Responses to Catastrophe in Modern Jewish Culture* (Cambridge, Mass./London: Harvard University Press, 1984), p. 19. One should not forget that the Jewish phenomenon is part of a wider phenomenon; see, e.g., Genette, *Palimpsests*, pp. 33–35, on "the parodic distortion of proverbs," which he suggests is "as old and popular as the proverb itself."

30. See pp. 160–63 above.

31. Eberhard Baumann, "Struktur-Untersuchungen im Psalter II," *ZAW* 62 (1950), pp. 148–51.

32. Paul E. Dion, "Formulaic Language in the Book of Job: International Background and Ironical Distortions," *SR* 16 (1987), pp. 187–93; Tryggve N. D. Mettinger, "Intertextuality: Allusion and Vertical Context Systems in Some Job Passages," in *Of Prophets' Visions and the Wisdom of Sages* (ed. Heather A. McKay and David J. A. Clines; JSOTSS 162; Sheffield: JSOT Press, 1993), pp. 257–80.

33. Michael Fishbane, "Jer 4:23–26 and Job 3:1–13: A Recovered Use of the Creation Pattern," *VT* 21 (1971), pp. 151–62.

(Isa 2:4 = Mic 4:3: "They will beat their swords into plowshares, and their spears into pruning hooks; nation will not lift up sword against nation, neither will they learn war any more"). Joel makes similar rhetorical moves elsewhere, as when he transfers prophetic threats against Babylon (Isa 13:6) and Egypt (Ezek 30:2) into warnings against Jerusalem (Joel 1:15) and when the prophecy that the wilderness will be turned into Eden (Isa 51:3; Ezek 36:35) becomes a prophecy that Eden will be turned into a wilderness (Joel 2:3).[34] Jonah seems to revise the narrow understanding of divine grace within Joel 2:1–17 — unless it is Joel 2:1–17 that is narrowing the more universal understanding of Jonah.[35] In Isa 19:19–25, the language of Exod 3:7–9 and 8:16–24 is metamorphosized, as Michael Fishbane points out:

> Now it is the Egyptians who have oppressors (לחצים) and who cry (יצעקו) to YHWH; and now, remarkably, an altar to YHWH will be built *in* Egypt as a sign (אות) that he will send them (stem: שלח) a deliverer to save them (והצילם). Through these acts of deliverance, moreover, YHWH will be known (stem: ידע) to the Egyptians, who will sacrifice to him (stem: זבח). Though YHWH will plague (ונגף) the Egyptians, he will in the end respond to their prayers (stem: עתר) and heal them.... Egypt, the first oppressor, will one day have its share in an exodus-type event; indeed, teaches the prophet, the true new exodus will be nothing less than the redemption of the original enemy in a manner typologically similar to the foundational redemption of YHWH's chosen people.[36]

Deutero-Isaiah revises Genesis in declaring that God creates darkness (45:7; contrast Gen 1:2) and that God needs no rest (40:28; contrast Gen 2:2–3).[37] Deutero-Isaiah also rewrites Lamentations by transforming its laments into promises of restoration from exile.[38] Dan 12:4 — which foretells that, at the end (קץ), "Many will be running back and forth (ישטטו), and knowledge will increase" — takes up Amos 8:12 — at the end (קיץ, v. 2) "they will run back and forth (ישוטטו), seeking the word of the Lord but will not find it" — and so turns prophetic pessimism into words of hope.[39] Examples of the seeming subversion of Scripture also appear outside of the Bible. 1QpHab 7:2 goes against the plain sense of Hab 2:2 ("Write the

---

34. Hans Walter Wolff, *Joel and Amos: A Commentary on the Books of the Prophets Joel and Amos* (Hermeneia; Philadelphia: Fortress, 1977), p. 11.

35. Thomas B. Dozeman, "Inner-Biblical Interpretation of Yahweh's Gracious and Compassionate Character," *JBL* 108 (1989), pp. 207–23.

36. Fishbane, *Biblical Interpretation*, pp. 367–68.

37. A. Kapelrud, "The Date of the Priestly Code (P)," *ASTI* 3 (1964), pp. 58–64; Sommer, *A Prophet Reads Scripture*, pp. 142–45.

38. T. Linafelt, "Surviving Lamentations," *HBT* 17 (1995), pp. 45–61; Willey, *Remember the Former Things*, pp. 48–50. For the argument that Deutero-Isaiah undoes negative texts in Jeremiah, see Sommer, *A Prophet Reads Scripture*, pp. 32–72.

39. For possible examples of Jeremiah using Psalms ironically, see Holladay, *Psalms*, pp. 41–45. But see also the criticism of Jerome F. D. Creach, "Like a Tree Planted by the Temple Stream: The Portrait of the Righteous in Psalm 1:3," *CBQ* 61 (1999), pp. 34–46.

vision; make it plain on tablets") when it says, "The fulfillment of the end-time he did not make known to him" (the prophet Habakkuk).[40] 4Q393 modifies Neh 9:16–25, so that whereas the latter "asserts that God did not abandon his people despite their disobedience, but enabled them to dispossess kingdoms and peoples and take possession of their houses and fields, 4Q393 frg. 3 complains that God has forsaken his people. Consequently, the very things which Nehemiah 9:22–25 announces that God gave to the Israelites are the things for which 4Q393 petitions."[41] *Asc. Isa* 3:8–9 makes this observation: "Moses said, 'There is no one who can see the Lord and live.' But Isaiah has said, 'I have seen the Lord, and behold I am alive.' " According to R. Jeremiah, in *b. B. Meṣ.* 59b, it is written in the Torah, "After the majority one must incline," whereas the text here cited, Exod 23:2, in fact says, "After the majority you will not incline." R. Ishmael, in *b. Giṭ.* 56b, teaches: "You [God] heard the blaspheming and insults of that wicked man and kept silent. 'Who is like you, O Lord, among the mighty' (באלים, Exod 15:11)? [Read rather,] 'Who is like you among the mute' (באלמים)?" Even the targumim sometimes engage in what has been called "converse translation," making the Bible say the opposite of what it says.[42] In Tg. Onq. on Gen 4:14, for instance, Cain's remark that he will be hidden from God's face (so MT) becomes, "It is impossible to hide from before you." And in the targum on Mal 2:16, the MT's statement that God hates divorce is turned into, "But if you hate her, divorce her."

Early Christian literature also contains examples of the reversal of scriptural subtexts, and many of these are often ironic. Mt 2:6 inserts οὐδαμῶς, "not at all," into its quotation of Mic 5:2, so that Micah remarks upon Bethlehem's insignificance whereas Matthew — who elsewhere affirms the continuing authority of the Law and the Prophets (5:17–20) — outright denies it. In Rom 10:6–8, Paul transmutes the exhortation to do the law in Deut 30:11–14 ("It is not in heaven.... Neither is it beyond the sea.... No, the word is very near to you; it is in your mouth and in your heart for you to observe it") into a statement about his law-free gospel. A less obvious but still striking example occurs in Revelation, if one looks at the book in its entirety. The Apocalypse throughout "draws extensively on the temple chapters of Ezekiel 40–48, while denying the existence of the very thing these chapters are about," namely, a new temple (see Rev 21:22).[43]

---

40. W. H. Brownlee, *The Midrash Pesher of Habakkuk* (SBLMS 24; Missoula, Mont.: Scholars Press, 1979), p. 109.

41. Daniel K. Falk, "Biblical Adaptation in 4Q392 *Works of God* and 4Q393 *Communal Confession*," in *The Provo International Conference on the Dead Sea Scrolls: Technological Innovations, New Texts, and Reformulated Issues* (ed. Donald W. Parry and Eugene Ulrich; STDJ 30; Leiden/Boston/Cologne: Brill, 1999), p. 144.

42. Michael L. Klein, "Converse Translation: A Targumic Technique," *Biblica* 57 (1976), pp. 515–37.

43. Moyise, *Old Testament in the Book of Revelation*, p. 114.

Returning now to Q, I should like to suggest, in view of the texts just reviewed, that its intertextual irony is not an example of Christian antinomianism but an illustration of the interpretive freedom of Jewish rhetoric. On this view of things, Q's irony retains its full force precisely because the authoritative subtexts remain authoritative — just as Q 16:17 demands. In Q the Tanak is not a ghost. It lives as ever. Q's Jesus may be bringing out of his treasure some new things, but one must still remember the things of old, which remain imperatives. Q is not about eradication but transformation. The issue accordingly is not the authority of the Bible but how it is to be understood and reapplied in the new situation wrought by Jesus.

Is there perhaps an analogy here with 11QTemple? The Temple Scroll often alters the Pentateuchal legislation, and the author cannot have been trying to hide this, for surely the Torah was too well known to his audience for him to get away with such deceit. So we must conclude that in the Temple Scroll, "the reader confronts the text as a *new* Torah, even while perceiving the biblical base around which the sources and innovations were integrated. One may confidently surmise that this was the very hope and intent of the author."[44] In like manner, Q's sayings are perceived as new precisely when one sees the old that is in them, the old that they do not abolish but supplement and transform. We may think that sometimes the supplement is more radical than Q 16:17 should tolerate, but the tension is neither unique to Q nor uniquely Christian.

Perhaps instead of interpreting Q's irony from the standpoint of Christian anxiety about the law, we would do better to liken Q's Jesus to Harold Bloom's characterization of the "strong poet."[45] According to Bloom, the poet who wishes to do more than imitate authoritative predecessors must "distort," "antithetically complete," "repeat," "convert," "purge," and gain "priority" over them. All of this appears in Q. Q 7:27 distorts Scripture when it conflates Exod 23:20 with Mal 3:1 and so turns the verse from Exodus into what the verse from Malachi alone is, namely, a prophetic oracle. Q 10:21–22 antithetically completes Scripture when it lifts attributes that the Pentateuch associates exclusively with Moses as revealer and transforms them exclusively to Jesus as revealer. Q 4:1–13 repeats Scripture when it quotes from Deuteronomy in its typological replay of the exodus. Q 7:22, with its several allusions to Isaiah, converts Scripture to its own cause when it in effect turns the prophet into a Christian, someone who testifies on behalf of Jesus. Q 17:3–4 purges Scripture when it eliminates the exegetical possibility that Lev 19:17 enjoins repeated rebukes. And Q in its entirety gains priority over its authoritative predecessor by interpreting the Tanak as a collection of oracles awaiting fulfillment — for which is greater, the words of prophetic hope or the record of their realization in history?

---

44. Fishbane, "Mikra at Qumran," p. 351.
45. Harold Bloom, *The Anxiety of Influence* (New York: Oxford University Press, 1973).

VI. Intertextual Density

Some ancient writings are so intertextually dense that almost every single word or phrase has a biblical antecedent. We saw this when examining 4Q521 2 + 4 ii 12 (4QMessianic Apocalypse),[46] and several other Qumranic compositions are, like the prayer of Tom Sawyer's mother, "built from the ground up of solid scriptural quotations, welded together with a thin mortar of originality." Portions of Revelation are also glutted with Scripture. Although various counts differ, it is indicative that Henry Barclay Swete, drawing upon the tables of Westcott and Hort, could state that of Revelation's 404 verses, 278 contain references to the Bible.[47] Consider a specific scene, Rev 1:12–17:[48]

and turning I saw seven gold lampstands:	καὶ ἐπιστρέψας εἶδον ἑπτὰ λυχνίας
Zech 4:2	ἑπτὰ λύχνοι
and in the midst of the lampstands:	καὶ ἐν μέσῳ τῶν λυχνιῶν
Zech 4:2	λύχνοι
one like a son of man:	ὅμοιον υἱὸν ἀνθρώπου
Dan 7:13	ὡς υἱὸς ἀνθρώπου
clothed with a long robe:	ἐνδεδυμένον ποδήρη
Ezek 9:11	ἐνδεδυκὼς τὸν ποδήρη
girded around his chest:	περιεζωσμένον πρὸς τοῖς μαστοῖς
Dan 10:5	περιεζωσμένη
with a golden sash:	ζώνην χρυσᾶν
Dan 10:5	ἐν χρυσίῳ
his head and his hair:	ἡ δὲ κεφαλὴ αὐτοῦ καὶ αἱ τρίχες
Dan 7:9	θρὶξ τῆς κεφαλῆς αὐτοῦ
were white as white wool:	λευκαὶ ὡς ἔριον
Dan 7:9	ὡσεὶ ἔριον καθαρόν
white as snow:	λευκὸν ὡς χιὼν
Dan 7:9	ὡσεὶ χιὼν λευκόν
his eyes were like a flame of fire:	οἱ ὀφθαλμοὶ αὐτοῦ ὡς φλὸξ πυρός
Dan 10:6	λαμπάδες πυρός
his feet were like burnished bronze:	καὶ οἱ πόδες αὐτοῦ ὅμοιοι χαλκολιβάνῳ
Dan 10:6	καὶ οἱ πόδες ὡσεὶ χαλκὸς ἐξαστράπτων
refined as in a furnace:	ὡς ἐν καμίνῳ πεπυρωμένης
Dan 3:6	κάμινον τοῦ πυρός
and his voice:	καὶ ἡ φωνὴ αὐτοῦ
Dan 10:6	καὶ ἡ φωνή

---

46. See above, pp. 111–12. Holladay, *Psalms*, pp. 106–8, counts twenty-nine reminiscences of Scripture in 1QH 5:5–19.

47. Swete, *The Apocalypse of St. John* (London: Macmillan, 1911), p. cxl.

48. For what follows I draw upon Moyise, *Old Testament in the Book of Revelation*, p. 44.

was like the sound of many waters: Ezek 1:24	ὡς φωνὴ ὑδάτων πολλῶν ὡς φωνὴν ὕδατος πολλοῦ
and from his mouth: Isa 49:2	καὶ ἐκ τοῦ στόματος αὐτοῦ στόμα μου
came a sharp, two-edged sword: Isa 49:2	ῥομφαία δίστομος ὀξεῖα ἐκπορευομένη μάχαιραν ὀξεῖαν
and his face was like the sun: Judg 5:31	καὶ ἡ ὄψις αὐτοῦ ὡς ὁ ἥλιος ὡς ἔξοδος ἡλίου
shining with full force: Judg 5:31	φαίνει ἐν τῇ δυνάμει αὐτοῦ ἐν δυνάμει αὐτοῦ

This is a mosaic. How exactly it is supposed to function is unclear. Given the repeated use of Daniel 7 and 10, the informed hearer might recall some of those texts, but the biblical language is so fulsome, the parallels come so thick and fast and are so dispersed throughout the Tanak, that one wonders whether the amplitude is not self-defeating profligacy. To multiply allusions overmuch is perhaps to destroy them. One is reminded of what Boswell said about modern warfare: "There is so much doing every where that we cannot tell what is doing any where."

This appraisal may, however, overlook that Revelation was presumably intended to be heard not once but on multiple occasions. Moreover, the recognition that most of John's language is drawn from scriptural descriptions of God, angels, or Daniel's one like a son of man[49] does aid with interpretation, for it lends to Jesus the same aura of sanctity and mystery that surrounds those figures. The intention and effect would be radically different if Revelation had drawn its adjectives for Jesus from descriptions of Cain, Goliath, and the devil.

Whatever one makes of Revelation, the problem of how to interpret a dense ensemble of quotations does not face the interpreter of Q. The Sayings Source is far from being as intertextually thin as the Elephantine papyri, but it is certainly thinner than 4QMessianic Apocalypse and Revelation: it is not a cento. In its approximately 230 verses, Q makes about fifty references to Scripture (quotations, explicit references, allusions). Many verses and even some larger units (e.g., Q 14:16–23 and 19:12–27) lack specific subtexts. This happily makes interpretation easier. Q, unlike Rev 1:12–17, nowhere overwhelms us with its allusions, even if they are rather plentiful in Q 4:1–13, in the Sermon on the Plain, and in 11:49–51 + 34–35. Q's allusive phrases are more often than not spaced, that is, embedded within phrases that do not allude. This creates a sort of intertextual rhythm: the allusions are periodic, not constant. The result may not be as conspicuous as when Plato sticks in bits from Homer that do not fit Attic prose, but Q's ability

---

49. A. T. Hanson, *The Living Utterances of God* (London: Darton, Longman & Todd, 1983), p. 168.

to write sentences that do not recall subtexts makes the sentences that do recall them look all the more deliberate.

VII. Running Subtexts

Deutero-Isaiah returns several times to Psalm 98.[50] 4Q521 is a sort of ensemble of phrases from Psalm 146.[51] *Ps. Sol.* 11 and Ecclesiasticus 36 both contain many allusions to Deutero-Isaiah.[52] Mk 15:25–39 cites or alludes to Psalm 22 five times.[53] John 6 goes back consistently to Psalm 78 and Isaiah 55.[54] Revelation 13 returns again and again to Daniel 3 and 7,[55] Revelation 18 mines Ezekiel 26–28 repeatedly,[56] and Revelation 20–22 seems to follow the order of Ezekiel 37–48.[57] Such examples of allusive clusters or protracted allusions are common. In like fashion, Q contains a few short sections in which the same part of Scripture is drawn upon several times. The first example is in Q 4:1–13, the story of Jesus' temptation. This, as we have observed, is a haggadic legend largely built upon texts from Deuteronomy 6 and 8. This can be seen from the parallels:

The temptation of Jesus	*The story of Israel*
Jesus is "led" in the wilderness, 4:1	Israel is "led" in the wilderness, Deut 8:2
Jesus is in the wilderness for forty days and there tempted, 4:2	Israel is in the wilderness for forty years and there tempted, Deut 8:2, 4
Jesus is tempted by hunger, 4:2–3	Israel is tempted by hunger, Deut 8:3
Jesus is God's "son," 4:3, 9	Israel's is God's "son," Deut 8:5
"A person does not live by bread alone," 4:4	"A person does not live by bread alone," Deut 8:3

---

50. Cf., e.g., Isa 42:10 with Ps 98:1 (cf. also Ps 96:1), 7 (cf. also Ps 96:11); Isa 52:10 with Ps 98:1–2; Isa 55:12 with Ps 98:8.

51. See above, pp. 111–12.

52. On the former, see Joachim Schüpphaus, *Die Psalmen Salomos: Ein Zeugnis jerusalemer Theologie und Frömmigkeit in der Mitte des vorchristlichen Jahrhunderts* (ALGHJ 7; Leiden: Brill, 1977), pp. 55–56. On Ecclesiasticus 36 and Isaiah, note Schultz, *Search for Quotation*, pp. 157–59.

53. Cf. Mk 15:24 with Ps 22:18; Mk 15:29 with Ps 22:7; Mk 15:30 with Ps 22:8; Mk 15:31 with Ps 22:8; Mk 15:34 with Ps 22:1.

54. Diana M. Swancutt, "Hungers Assuaged by the Bread from Heaven: 'Eating Jesus' as Isaian Call to Belief: The Confluence of Isaiah 55 and Psalm 78(77) in John 6.22–71," in Craig A. Evans and James A. Sanders, eds., *Early Christian Interpretation of the Scriptures of Israel: Investigations and Proposals* (JSNTSS 148; Sheffield: Sheffield Academic Press, 1997), pp. 218–51.

55. Gregory K. Beale, *The Use of Daniel in Jewish Apocalyptic Literature and in the Revelation of St. John* (Lanham, Md.: University Press of America, 1984).

56. Moyise, *Old Testament*, pp. 73–74.

57. A. Vanhoye, "L'utilisation du livre d'Ezéchiel dans l'Apocalpyse," *Bib* 43 (1962), pp. 436–76.

The temptation of Jesus	*Deuteronomy*
"Worship the Lord your God, and serve only him," 4:8	"Fear the Lord your God, and serve only him," Deut 6:13
"You will not tempt the Lord your God," 4:12	"You will not tempt the Lord your God," Deut 6:16

Q 4:1–13 does not simply quote from Deuteronomy 6 and 8: it draws upon Deuteronomic subtexts again and again.

The second unit that returns to the same subtext is Q 6:27–45, which offers a rewriting of Leviticus 19. Not only do the three themes that dominate this section of Q — vengeance, love, judging others — come from Leviticus 19, but there is a series of provocative inversions that amount not to exegesis but to transformation. If, for example, Lev 19:2 enjoins Israel to be holy because the Lord God is holy, Q 6:36 asks hearers to be merciful because the heavenly Father is merciful. And if Lev 19:18 requires love of neighbor and prohibits revenge against "any of your people," Q 6:27 demands love of enemies and seemingly prohibits revenge against anybody. And if LXX Lev 19:17 says, "You will judge your neighbor," Q 6:37 says, "Judge not." Clearly much of the force of the Sermon on the Plain depends upon the reader's knowing Leviticus 19 and perceiving that Q's Jesus is repeatedly using it as a foil.

The last few woes in Q 11 offer another example of a running subtext, this being the latter half of 2 Chronicles 19:

Q 11:49: "I will send them prophets."
  2 Chr 24:19: "He sent prophets among them."

Q 11:49: "Some they will kill."
  2 Chr 24:20–22: the stoning of Zechariah

Q 11:50, 51: "required of this generation"
  2 Chr 24:22: "May the Lord see and avenge!"

Q 11:51: "the blood of Zechariah"
  2 Chr 24:25: "the blood of (Zechariah) the son of the priest Jehoiada"

Q 11:51: "Zechariah, who perished between the altar and the house"
  2 Chr 24:21: "stoned him to death in the court of the house of the Lord"

Q 13:34: "stoning those sent to you"
  2 Chr 24:21: "stoned him to death"

Q 13:34–35: "Your house is forsaken."
  2 Chr 24:18, 21: "the house of the Lord"

Given these several parallels, is it only coincidence that Q 11:47 uses the expression "your fathers" (πατέρες ὑμῶν: only here in Q) while 2 Chr 24:18 and 24 use "their fathers" (LXX: πατέρων αὐτῶν), or that whereas Q 11 delivers woes against Jewish leaders (Pharisees and probably scribes: 11:39,

42, 43, 46), the criminals in 2 Chr 24:17ff. are "the officials of Judah" (v. 17; cf. v. 23)?

There is a fourth section of Q where the intertexts may have helped shaped the narrative, although this is far from certain. Q 7:27 cites Mal 3:1 as a prophecy of John the Baptist's ministry and thereby identifies him with the eschatological Elijah (cf. Mal 4:5). There closely follows, in Q 9:57–62, the use of 1 Kgs 19:19–21, the story of Elijah calling Elisha. And very shortly after that, in the missionary discourse, there is an allusion to 2 Kgs 4:29, where Elisha sends a disciple to perform a miracle (Q 10:4). So there is a concentration of implicit references to passages concerning Elijah and Elisha. This might well be coincidence, but we may also wonder whether the underlying subtexts might have been partially responsible for the near association of these units.

The question of running subtexts is perhaps of some value for questions having to do with the compositional history of a couple of units. It would seem, for example, that the consistent use of Deuteronomy in Q 4:1–13 is likely to be the work of a single creative author. Q's temptation story probably does not have a complex tradition history.[58] One might similarly urge, although this would contradict most current analyses, that both Q 11:49–51 + 13:34–35 and the central core of the Sermon on the Plain were created at once, the former as a rewriting of 2 Chronicles 24, the latter as a dialogue with Leviticus 19. This possibility for Q 6 is bolstered by the structural symmetries of the section, which do not look like the product of a long evolutionary history.[59] But the point will not be pressed here, in part because of the possibility that contributors to Q piled new allusions to a subtext on top of already existing allusions to that subtext. Matthew, for instance, recognized the Mosaic background of Q 10:21–22 and added more Mosaic material to it.[60]

VIII. The Jewish Exegetical Background

Q does not in any straightforward sense offer exegesis of the Bible, but it does presuppose exegesis. Time and time again Q perceives the Tanak not directly but through the eyes of Jewish exegetical tradition. This is only what one would anticipate. The following offers an overview:

Q 3:8 seems to presuppose the association, found in rabbinic texts, between זכות, "merit," and rocks or mountains.

---

58. See further my article, "Behind the Temptations of Jesus: Q 4:1–13 and Mark 1:12–13," in *Authenticating the Deeds of Jesus* (ed. Bruce Chilton and Craig A. Evans; NTTS 28/2; Leiden: Brill, 1999), pp. 195–213.

59. Allison, *Jesus Tradition in Q*, pp. 79–95.

60. See also the discussion of Matthew's redaction of Q 6:29–30 on pp. 107–8. There it is argued that he elaborated upon an already-existing allusion to Isa 50:6.

Q 4:1–13, like so many other Jewish texts, turns the story of the exodus into a type.

Q 6:20–23, in its allusive use of Isaiah 61, has parallels in 11QMelchizedek and elsewhere.

Q 6:23, like Tg. Neof. 1 and Tg. Ps-J. on Gen 15:1, turns God's pledge of great reward to Abraham into an eschatological promise.

Q 6:27–45 creatively engages Leviticus 19 in a way reminiscent of the *Testament of Gad* and *Pseudo-Phocylides*.

Q 7:18–23, in putting together phrases from Isaiah, reminds one of 4Q521 2 + 4 ii 12 (4QMessianic Apocalypse).

Q 7:27 combines Exod 23:20 and Mal 3:1, as does *Exod Rab.* 32:9.

Q 9:57–58 uses Ps 8:5–9 in an ironic fashion, which is something found in several Jewish sources, beginning with Job 7:17–18.

Q 9:57–62 gains force from the exegesis of 1 Kgs 19:19–21 found in Josephus and LXX: whereas Elijah lets Elisha say farewell, Jesus does not let his disciple return home to say goodbye; and 9:62 alludes to Gen 19:17 and 26 in a way that reflects the interpretive tradition that Lot's wife looked back because she was too attached to her past (Philo, *Leg. all.* 3.213; etc.).

Q 10:12, following both biblical prophets and many later sources, refers to inhospitable Sodom in a warning of eschatological destruction.

Q 10:15, in borrowing the language of Isa 14:13, 15, belongs to a tradition that applies that Isaianic text to the opponents of the righteous.

Q 10:21–22 presupposes the far-flung exegetical tradition of interpreting Exod 33:11–23 in the light of Num 12:1–8 and Deut 34:10–12.

Q 11:20, where Jesus, in apparent contrast to other exorcists, casts out demons by the finger of God, recalls the traditions about the opponents of Moses, who were in league with the devil and were no match for the finger of God.

Q 11:29 transfers language associated with the generations of Noah and Moses to its own contemporary generation, as does Ps 78:8; and the verdict, found in the rabbis, that those two generations were particularly corrupt is presupposed, as also in Q 11:29–30.

Q 11:32 agrees with the extracanonical tradition that the Ninevites were more inclined to repentance than Israel.

Q 11:49–51 probably presupposes legends about the blood of Abel and Zechariah as well as the tradition that Cain was stoned.

Q 13:34–35 turns Ps 118:26 into an eschatological refrain, as it is in rabbinic literature.

Q 12:8–9 agrees with the parables of *1 Enoch* and *4 Ezra* in seeing in Dan 7:13–14 a prophecy of an individual eschatological deliverer.

Q 12:22–31 appears to depend upon the tradition, found in the LXX, targum, and Peshitta, that the ants have no harvest.

Q 12:35–38 seems to assume the old belief, associated often with the targums on Exod 12:42 and 15:18, that the Messiah will come on Passover night; and the typological transformation of Exod 12:42 already has a precedent in Isa 52:11–12.

Q 12:42–46 picks up on a part of the Joseph story that ancients, as opposed to moderns, much stressed, namely, his promotion from servant to overseer, and it reflects the tradition that makes Joseph an illustration of faithful service that gains eschatological reward (cf. the *Testament of Joseph*).

Q 12:51–53 presupposes the conventional application of Mic 7:6 to the messianic woes.

Q 13:19 uses the language common to Daniel 4 and Ezekiel 17; 31 with reference to God's eschatological planting, an application well attested in Judaism.

Q 16:18 opposes divorce, to which there is a parallel in Mal 2:16.

Q 17:3–4, in its use of Lev 19:17, stands particularly close to *T. Gad* 6, and it seems to set itself against the interpretation, known from the rabbis, that understands הוכח תוכיח/ἐλέγμῷ ἐλέγξεις to counsel repeated rebuke.

Q 17:26–27, in correlating the end with Noah's flood, is using a traditional eschatological type.

Q 17:28–29 (+ 31–32), like Q 10:12, assumes that the story of Lot leaving Sodom is a lesson for the end time, as it is so often elsewhere; and 17:31–32 (whose place in Q is uncertain) presupposes the tradition that Lot's wife looked back because she was too attached to Sodom.

Q 22:28–30 reminds one of *Tan.* B Leviticus 7, which finds in the thrones (plural) of Dan 7:9 places of honors for the great ones of Israel.

In sum, Q sees many of its subtexts through conventional Jewish exegesis.

In addition to showing knowledge of exegetical traditions attached to particular texts, Q also appears to have used a technique that the rabbis later included in the seven rules of Hillel, namely, גזירה שוה, analogy of expression — a rule that encourages one to bring together texts that share a word or expression. There are three or (if one counts Q 10:4–5 as an allusion to Exod 12:11, 34–36 as well as to 2 Kgs 4:29) four places in Q where more than one subtext is drawn upon and where the subtexts are joined by catchword:

Q 7:27, quoting a combination of Exod 23:20 and Mal 3:1

Exod 23:20: "I am going to send a messenger… before you… on your way"

MT: הנה אנכי שלח
מלאך
לפניך…בדרך

LXX: ἰδοὺ ἐγὼ ἀποστέλλω
τὸν ἄγγελόν μου
πρὸ προσώπου σου…τῇ ὁδῷ

Mal 3:1: "I am sending my messenger…. the way before me"

MT: הנני שלח
מלאכי
דרך לפני

LXX: ἰδοὺ ἐγὼ ἐξαποστέλλω
τὸν ἄγγελόν μου
ὁδόν πρὸ προσώπου μου

Q 9:57–62, alluding to Gen 19:12–26 and 1 Kgs 19:19–21

Gen 19:17, 26: "behind"
MT: אחרי
LXX: ὀπίσω

1 Kgs 19:20, 21, 22: "behind"
MT: אחרי
LXX: ὀπίσω

Q 10:4–5, alluding to Exod 12:11, 34–36 (?) and 2 Kgs 4:29

Exod 12:11: "loins girded"
MT: מתניכם חגרים
LXX: αἱ ὀσφύες ὑμῶν περιεζωσμέναι

2 Kgs 4:29: "Gird up your loins"
MT: חגר מתניך
LXX: ζῶσαι τὴν ὀσφύν

Exod 12:11: "your staffs in your hands"
MT: מקלכם בידכם
LXX: αἱ βακτηρίαι ἐν ταῖς χερσὶν ὑμῶν

2 Kgs 4:29: "my staff in your hand"
MT: משענתי בידך
LXX: τὴν βακτηρίαν μου ἐν τῇ χειρί

Q 11:49–51 + 13:34–51, referring to Gen 4:8–16; 2 Chr 24:17–25; Jer 12:7; Ps 118:26

2 Chr 24:18, 21: "the house of the Lord"
MT: בית יהוה
LXX: οἴκου κυρίου

Ps 118:26: "the house of the Lord"[61]
MT: בית יהוה
LXX: οἴκου κυρίου

2 Chr 24:20: "forsaken"
MT: עזבתם…יעזב
LXX: ἐγκατελίπετε…ἐγκαταλείψει

Jer 12:7: "forsaken"
MT: עזבתי
LXX: ἐγκαταλέλοιπα

2 Chr 24:25: "bloods"
MT: דמי
LXX: αἵμασιν

Gen 4:10: "blood(s)"
MT: דמי
LXX: αἵματος

Unfortunately one cannot, in these cases, eliminate coincidence because Q is nowhere explicit about its exegetical procedures and because any two random texts often share some vocabulary. Nonetheless, since in the forego-

---

61. Cf. Mk 11:17, which brings together Isa 56:7 and Jer 7:11, presumably because they both use the word "house."

ing cases from Q the proposed catchwords are also key words in the relevant Q texts, one suspects that coincidence is not an adequate explanation.

IX. The Stages of Q

The use of a particular unit of Scripture across a document can be an argument in favor of that document's compositional unity. Jonathan Campbell has recently contended that CD 1–8 + 19–20, which makes repeated use of Exodus 31–35; Leviticus 26; Deuteronomy 27–32; Isaiah 28; 51; 59; and Hos 5:10–12, "can be viewed as a unified document when its employment of Scripture is taken as the main criterion for establishing its credentials as a well-constructed text."[62] Surely Revelation's compositional unity is reinforced by the seer's characteristic allusions to definite parts of Isaiah, Ezekiel, and Daniel throughout.[63] And the *Apocryphon of John* shows itself to be the work of a single author in that it develops in consistent dialogue with the early chapters of Genesis.[64]

Q contains nothing truly comparable. There are three references to the story of Lot (Q 9:62; 10:12; 17:28–29 [+ 31–32?]), four if one follows Kloppenborg in seeing in Q 3:5 an allusion to Gen 13:10, 11; 19:17, 25, 28. There are also at least three references to Dan 7:9–14 (Q 12:8–9; 12:40; 22:30), but to judge from Mark, M, L, and John, allusions to these verses were a feature of several, or most, strands of the Jesus tradition. For the rest, Q does not regularly return to a single verse or particular section of Scripture. This result is consistent with what most modern scholarship already accepts, namely, that Q was not created at once but was produced in stages: it is a composite document made up primarily of units that originally circulated in isolation, a document that grew as several hands contributed to it.

Is there any other way in which Q's intertextuality impinges upon some of the hypothetical stages reconstructed by modern scholars? According to Kloppenborg, Scripture is less forcibly present in his reconstruction of Q's first stage (Q^1) than in his reconstruction of its second and third stages (Q^2 and Q^3).[65] C. M. Tuckett, on the other hand, has asserted that "scripture

---

62. Campbell, *Scripture in the Damascus Document*, p. 198.

63. Beale, *The Use of Daniel*; Fekkes, *Prophetic Traditions*; Vanhoye, "L'utililsation du livre d'Ezéchiel dans l'Apocalypse."

64. Søsren Giversen, "The Apocryphon of John and Genesis," *ST* 17 (1963), pp. 60–76.

65. John S. Kloppenborg, "Literary Convention, Self-Evidence, and the Social History of the Q People," *Semeia* 55 (1992), p. 84 (neither "Israel's epic history nor the Torah figures importantly as a redemptive medium for this layer of Q. The rhetoric of the Sayings Gospel does not proceed from the premise of the self-evident truth of the Torah"; he goes on to speak of "those who were geographically or socially distant from the redemptive media of the Temple or Torah, or those who had come to perceive those media as inefficacious"); idem, introduction to *Conflict and Invention: Literary, Rhetorical, and Social Studies on the Sayings Gospel Q* (ed. John Kloppenborg; Valley Forge, Pa.: Trinity Press International, 1995), p. 9. Cf. Wendy Cotter, " 'Yes, I Tell You, and More than a Prophet,' " in ibid., pp. 135–36.

is far more fundamental in Q than first impressions might imply; and such influence pervades the Q material across any alleged boundaries between different possible strata."[66] Who is correct?

If one compares the chart on the following pages with Kloppenborg's stages, it can hardly be said that his Q1 — Q 6:20–49; 9:57–60 (61–62?); 10:2–11, 16; 11:2–4, 9–13; 12:2–7, 11–12, 22b-34; 13:24; 14:26–27, 34–35; 17:33 — shows little interest in Scripture. The following list displays the likely scriptural intertexts for Kloppenborg's Q[1]:[67]

Q 6:20–23	allusive use of Isa 61:1–2
Q 6:23	allusion to Gen 15:1
Q 6:27	allusion to Lev 19:18
Q 6:29–30	allusion to Isa 50:6, 8
Q 6:36	allusion to Lev 19:2
Q 6:37	allusion to Lev 19:17
Q 9:57–62	allusions to Genesis 19; 1 Kgs 19:19–21; Psalm 8
Q 10:4	allusion to 2 Kgs 4:29
Q 11:3	allusion to Exodus 16
Q 12:22–31	allusion to Prov 6:6–11
Q 12:27	reference and allusions to traditions about Solomon
Q 14:26	allusion to Exod 20:12 = Deut 5:16

Although there are no formal quotations, allusions to Scripture are regular, particularly in the largest segment, the Sermon on the Plain. Maybe, then, Tuckett's evaluation is more prudent. Maybe we cannot find any hypothetical stratum of Q not pervaded by Scripture.

This is not to say, however, that Q's intertextuality is ubiquitous. Allusions may commence, continue through, and conclude Q, but there are nonetheless, as stated above, verses bereft of intertexts. These include the story of the healing of the centurion's son or servant (Q 7:1–10), two long narrative parables (Q 14:16–23, invitations to a banquet; 19:12–27, parable of the pounds), and a number of short proverbs or aphorisms: 6:38, 39, 40, 43, 44, 45; 11:17, 21–22, 33, 34; 12:2, 7a; 13:30; 14:11, 34–35; 17:37; 19:26. The absence of Scripture from these last verses is no surprise: it is in the nature of many concise proverbs to be secular wisdom unattached to a literary text. It also does not startle that a couple of parables might be free-standing compositions, for other parables in Jewish and Christian sources are free of scriptural subtexts. It is not so easy, however, to explain the absence of a specific scriptural background to Q 7:1–10. Everywhere else Q associates Jesus' miracles with the Bible (Q 4:1–13; 7:19–23; 11:20), and Q 7:1–10 could easily have been manipulated to recall Elisha's miracle in

---

66. Tuckett, "Scripture in Q," p. 26.
67. Omitted from this list are allusions marked by a question mark on pp. 182–84.

Q Text	Pentateuch	Isaiah	Psalms	Other
3:5	Gen 13:10, 11; 19:17, 25, 28 (allusion?)			
3:8		Isa 51:1–2 (allusion)		
3:17				Mal 4:1 (allusion?)
4:4	Deut 8:3 (marked quotation)			
4:5–7	Deut 34:1–4 (allusion)			
4:8	Deut 6:16 (marked quotation)			
4:9			Ps 91:12 (marked quotation)	
4:12	Deut 6:13 (marked quotation)			
6:20–23		Isa 61:1–2 (allusion)		
6:23	Gen 15:1 (allusion)			
6:27	Lev 19:18 (allusion)			
6:29–30		Isa 50:6, 8 (allusion)		
6:36	Lev 19:2 (allusion)			
6:37	Lev 19:17 (allusion)			
7:22		Isa 26:19; 29:18–19; 35:5–6; 42:18; 61:1–2 (allusions)		
7:27	Exod 23:20 (marked quotation)			Mal 3:1 (marked quotation)
7:34	Deut 21:20 (allusion)			
9:57–62				1 Kgs 19:19–21 (allusion)
9:57–58			Psalm 8 (allusion)	
9:62(?)	Gen 19:17, 26 (allusion)			
10:4	Exod 12:11, 34–36 (allusion?)			2 Kgs 4:29 (allusion)

Q Text	Pentateuch	Isaiah	Psalms	Other
10:5				1 Sam 25:6 (allusion?)
10:12	Genesis 19 (explicit reference)			
10:15		Isa 14:13, 15 (allusion)		
10:21–22	Exod 33:11–23 (allusion)			
10:23–24		Isa 6:9–10 (allusion?)		
11:3	Exodus 16 (allusion)			
11:20	Exod 8:19 (allusion)			
11:29–30	Deut 1:35 (allusion)			Jonah (explicit reference)
11:31				2 Chr 9:1–12 (explicit reference)
11:32				Jonah 3 (explicit reference)
11:49–51	Gen 4:8–16 (explicit reference)			2 Chr 24:17–25 (explicit reference)
13:34–35			Ps 118:26 (unmarked quotation)	Jer 12:7 (allusion)
12:6				Amos 3:5 (allusion?)
12:8–9				Dan 7:13–14 (allusion)
12:22–31				Prov 6:6–11 (allusion)
12:24			Ps 147:9 (allusion?)	
12:27				explicit reference to Solomon's glory– 1 Kings 1–11; 2 Chronicles; Ecclesiastes(?); Canticles(?)
12:33–34		Isa 51:8 (allusion?)		
12:35–38	Exod 12:11 (allusion)			

Q Text	Pentateuch	Isaiah	Psalms	Other
12:40				Dan 7:13–14 (allusion)
12:42–46	Genesis 39 (allusion)			
12:45				Hab 2:3 (allusion?)
12:46				Ahiqar (allusion?)
12:51–53				Mic 7:6 (unmarked quotation)
13:19				Ezekiel 17; 31 (allusion); Daniel 4 (allusion)
13:27			Ps 6:8 (unmarked quotation)	
13:28–29			Ps 107:3 (allusion?); 112:10 (allusion?)	
14:26	Exod 20:12 = Deut 5:16 (allusion); Deut 33:9 (allusion?)			
16:18	Deut 24:1–4 (allusion)			
17:3–4	Lev 19:17 (allusion); Gen 4:15, 24 (allusion?)			
17:24, 26, 30 (?)				Dan 7:9–14 (allusions?)
17:26–27	Genesis 6–9 (explicit reference)	Isa 54:9–10 (allusion)		
17:28–29 (+31–32)	Genesis 19 (explicit reference)			
22:28–30				Dan 7:9–14 (allusion)

2 Kgs 5:1–14. But whatever one makes of Q 7:1–10, neither the absence nor presence of subtexts much helps us with the question of Q's evolution.

In this connection it should be added that attempts to reconstruct Q's history through appeal to its agreements and disagreements with the LXX are dubious.[68] Not only are there serious questions about how far our MT

---

68. Contrast Siegfried Schulz, *Q*, p. 49.

and LXX are accurate reflections of texts available in the first century, but the LXX and MT largely agree in the intertexts that Q refers to, so in most cases one can hardly claim that concurrence with the LXX means much of anything. Further, Q's references to Scripture are mostly allusive, which means that there was no interest in reproducing the precise wording of its precursor texts. So disagreement with the LXX hardly means anything more than agreement with it. And, finally, we have no way of determining whether or not a Greek translator or editor of Q occasionally assimilated this quotation or that allusion to the LXX. But if such assimilation did take place, Septuagintal influence on a unit would, obviously, indicate neither the creation of that unit in Greek nor the creation of its scriptural reference at a secondary stage.

X. Rewriting the Tanak

Q does not argue about Scripture, nor does it argue much from Scripture. Q is also neither exegesis nor midrash, if those expressions imply consistently starting from the Bible or consciously trying to illumine the Bible.

But if Q is sparing in its clear statements about Scripture, implicitly it speaks volumes, for every new text rewrites the old ones it relates itself to. Just as in physics, where it is, we are told, impossible for the observer not to influence the thing observed, so it is with literature: every receptor text, when it pulls subtexts to itself, alters future reading of them.[69] The new colors the old as much as the old colors the new. Thus it is that Q inevitably persuades believing hearers to understand the Hebrew Bible in a certain way. When, for example, Q establishes a parallel between the inhabitants of Sodom and the hearers of Jesus, between the eschatological future and the biblical past, we end up, so to speak, not only remembering the future but also reimagining the past, for, as so many of the ecclesiastical commentaries show us, Christian readers of Genesis now typically recall words of Jesus (Lk 9:61: βλέπων εἰς τὰ ὀπίσω) when they come to chapter 19 and the story of Lot's wife, who looked at the things behind. The texts in the Jesus tradition that allude to Genesis 19 become themselves alluded to when Genesis 19 is read: text and subtext exchange roles.

This example from Luke and Genesis is only one instance of what happens to the Bible again and again to those who read it through the eyes of Q. It is not just Genesis 19 but all of the Tanak that gets transformed. By relating himself so regularly to the Law, the Prophets, and the Writings, Q's Jesus makes them his own. He lays claim to be the true heir of the scriptural estate. Further, just as the sundry voices of Scripture, when conceived of as a single authoritative book, contribute to Q's unity, so does Q make a unity

---

69. This insight is famously associated with T. S. Eliot, "Tradition and Individual Talent," in *Selected Essays* (new ed.; San Diego/New York/London: HBJ, 1950), pp. 3–11.

out of the diverse biblical voices by turning them all into servants of Jesus. Q's contributors and readers look down the well of Scripture and naturally see the reflection of their own religion, which means the face of Jesus. Thus the Sayings Source writes a new Bible as it reconfigures the Tanak into a collection of oracles that foreshadow, prophesy, and illustrate the words and deeds of the Son of man. The intertextual Jesus draws all biblical texts to himself.

Chapter 11

The Allusive Jesus

I. Jesus and the Scriptures

Most of the Jewish literature that has survived from the period between the Maccabees and the destruction of the second temple is, in one way or another, in constant dialogue with the Tanak. The same is true of primitive Christian literature, including the earliest written deposits of the Jesus tradition known to us, Q and Mark. One might, then, employ the criterion of dissimilarity to contend that the literary Jesus, who so regularly refers to Scripture, cannot be identified with the historical Jesus of Nazareth, for the former's references to the Bible do not distinguish him from characteristic emphases of Judaism and the Church, both of which were intertextual factories. Gerd Theissen has written,

> We must remember that where the Christian sources attribute clearly identifiable scriptural quotations or allusions to biblical traditions to Jesus, it is by no means certain that these go back to him. For the biblical scriptures depict a perception and interpretation of reality which was common to all Jews (and Christians). After Easter the story and message of Jesus were interpreted and continued to be told in the light of scripture.[1]

The criterion of dissimilarity, however, is an unwieldy and perilous tool, and it has promised results that it cannot deliver, as Theissen himself has well argued.[2] In the present case, moreover, it seems more plausible that if most of Palestinian Judaism was an intertextual Judaism, we might expect a Palestinian teacher such as Jesus to be an intertextual teacher. What Jewish teachers do we know of who did not feel constrained to relate their words continually to the Tanak?

The primitive Church's interest in the Bible, so far from weakening the inference from Judaism's fixation on Scripture, fortifies it, for if, as the sources lead us to believe, and as a critical sifting of them confirms, many of the first Christian disciples preoccupied themselves with the First Testament, what

---

1. Gerd Theissen and Annette Merz, *The Historical Jesus: A Comprehensive Guide* (Minneapolis: Fortress, 1998), p. 357.
2. Gerd Theissen and Dagmar Winter, *Die Kriterienfrage in der Jesusforschung: Vom Differenzkriterium zum Plausibilitätskriterium* (NTOA 34; Freiburg/Göttingen: Universitätsverlag/Vandenhoeck & Ruprecht, 1997).

reason do we have for imagining that such preoccupation emerged only after Easter? If, as it seems, early leaders of the Church turned immediately to biblical texts to interpret the passion and resurrection of Jesus,[3] surely it was only because some of them were already accustomed to using such texts to make sense of things.

But this is a big generalization, and it can only become fully persuasive through a careful examination of each individual unit in the Jesus tradition, canonical and noncanonical. Such an examination cannot be undertaken within the present volume, which confines itself to the Sayings Source. One may nonetheless observe that many of the Q sayings that allusively refer to the Scriptures or recast them are taken by many competent scholars to belong to the original tradition. Consider the following seven examples, all of which John Dominic Crossan has attributed to Jesus:[4]

Q 6:20–21, the first three beatitudes, draw upon the prophetic oracle in Isa 61:1–2.

Q 9:58 informs a would-be follower, in language that ironically alludes to Psalm 8, that while foxes have holes and birds of the air have nests, the Son of man has nowhere to lay his head.

Q 9:62, the call to put hand to the plow and not look at the things behind, alludes to both the call of Elisha in 1 Kings 19 and to the fatal error of Lot's wife in Genesis 19.

Q 11:20, Jesus' declaration that he casts out demons by the finger of God, depends upon Exod 8:19 and traditions about the contest between Moses and the magicians of Egypt.

Q 12:27 asks one to consider the lilies, how they grow yet neither toil nor spin, and how even Solomon in all his glory was not arrayed like one of these.

Q 12:51–53 appends to the declaration that Jesus has come not to bring peace but a sword a paraphrase of Mic 7:6: "For the son treats the father with contempt, the daughter rises up against her mother, the daughter-in-law against her mother-in-law."

Q 14:26 enjoins disciples to hate their own father and mother, an imperative that inevitably invites comparison with the fifth of the Ten Commandments, which requires love of father and mother.

A few might wish to contend that Crossan has not been skeptical enough, that some of these sayings do not in fact go back to Jesus. Rudolf Bultmann rejected the authenticity of Q 9:58, and the Jesus Seminar has printed Lk

---

3. Cf. 1 Cor 15:3–4: κατὰ τὰς γραφάς, "according to the scriptures." See further Donald Juel, *Messianic Exegesis: Christological Interpretation of the Old Testament in Early Christianity* (Philadelphia: Fortress, 1988).

4. John Dominic Crossan, *The Historical Jesus: The Life of a Mediterranean Jewish Peasant* (San Francisco: HarperCollins, 1991).

(Q) 9:62 in black, Lk (Q) 12:51–53 in gray. (The other five, however, come in red or, in one case, pink.)[5] Some others might want to urge, especially in the case of Q 6:20–23, that the scriptural language is secondary.[6] Certainly elsewhere, as in Q's story of Jesus' temptation, the biblical references come from the Church, not Jesus. Still others might query whether each of the proposed allusions has been sufficiently established.

To all this one can only respond that most of the units just cited are regularly reckoned to Jesus; that, unlike Matthew's formula quotations and the biblical citations added to 1QS,[7] most of the relevant scriptural language cannot be stripped off without destroying everything;[8] and that, in the seven cases cited, the present volume makes the case for the proposed allusions, all of which have been espied by others. So the way is cleared to entertain the possibility that the intertextual Jesus of Q is not a misleading representative of the historical Jesus. Indeed, those persuaded that many more than seven of Q's allusive units derive from Jesus will necessarily believe that the consciously intertextual nature of Q corresponds to the consciously intertextual nature of Jesus' speech, that he "evidently knew the Old Testament well"[9] and presupposed an audience able to catch allusions to it.

Of late much work has been done on the intertextuality of both the First and Second Testaments. We have learned about the numerous allusions to Scripture in, for example, Deutero-Isaiah, Matthew, and Paul. What needs to be remembered is that such intertextuality was at home in oral performances: Deutero-Isaiah, Matthew, and the Epistles of Paul were, like all other writings in antiquity, intended to be read aloud. This means that their scriptural allusions were designed to be perceived by ears, not eyes. This matters so much because Jesus' teaching was, from every indication, oral. We have no evidence that he ever wrote anything. Indeed, we do not know what sort of education he might have had, nor even know for sure whether he could read, although this may be the best guess.[10] But our ignorance in

---

5. Bultmann, *History of the Synoptic Tradition*, p. 28; Robert W. Funk, Roy W. Hoover, and the Jesus Seminar, *The Five Gospels: The Search for the Authentic Words of Jesus* (New York: Macmillan, 1993).

6. See above, pp. 104–7.

7. 1QS contains explicit citations missing from 4QS^b and 4QS^d; see Sarianna Metso, "The Use of Old Testament Quotation in the Qumran Community Rule," in *Qumran between the Old and New Testaments* (ed. Frederick H. Cryer and Thomas L. Thompson; JSOTSS 290/Copenhagen International Seminar 6; Sheffield: Sheffield Academic Press, 1998), pp. 217–31.

8. The exception is Q 6:20–21. See pp. 104–7. On the originality of the allusion in Q 12:51–53 as opposed to the variant in *Gos. Thom.* 16, see Allison, "Q 12:51–53 and Mark 9:11–13 and the Messianic Woes," p. 295, n. 32.

9. C. K. Barrett, *Jesus and the Gospel Tradition* (Philadelphia: Fortress, 1968), p. 41.

10. See Meier, *A Marginal Jew*, vol. 1, pp. 268–78. On p. 276 Meier writes: "If we take into account that Jesus' adult life became fiercely focused on the Jewish religion, that he is presented by almost all the Gospel traditions as engaging in learned disputes over Scripture and halaka with students of the Law, that he was accorded the respectful — but at that time vague — title of rabbi or teacher, that more than one Gospel tradition presents him preaching

these particulars is no argument against Jesus' ability to allude. Even if he did not write anything, and even if he could not read at all, the evidence is that he and his hearers, whether formally educated or not, had heard Scripture recited often enough that large portions of it were quite familiar to them, sufficiently so that oblique and sometimes even subtle references to it could be appreciated. Q may not presuppose the sort of intertextual expertise on display in the Dead Sea Scrolls,[11] but it also does not presuppose the sort of religious ignorance people have so often associated with peasants of the Middle Ages. Q's Jesus rather takes for granted an oral literacy in the Scriptures.

II. The Eschatological, Mosaic Jesus

Q, in accord with its declaration that the kingdom of God has arrived and/or come near (10:9, 11; 11:20), reads the Scriptures from an eschatological perspective. It construes John the Baptist as the historical realization of the prophecy in Mal 3:1 (Q 7:27). It interprets Jesus as the fulfillment of oracles in the book of Isaiah, especially Isa 61:1–2 (Q 6:20–21; 7:22). It characterizes the present with the eschatological language of Mic 7:6: now is the time not of peace but of the sword, of the eschatological tribulation, when children rise up against their parents (Q 12:52–53). Q also borrows the language of Dan 7:13–14 in forecasting Jesus' imminent return (Q 12:8–9; 12:40; 22:30).

Q's eschatological perspective is congruent with the outlook of the historical Jesus, a millenarian prophet who longed for the fulfillment of Jewish eschatological expectations and so necessarily looked for the fulfillment of the scriptural texts that grounded those expectations.[12] Apart from the issue of which, if any, of the Q texts cited in the previous paragraph might be assigned in whole or in part to Jesus himself, their collective conviction that the present is the time of eschatology entering history faithfully represents the worldview of Jesus.

This fact should come as no surprise. Quite a few sources show us that certain religious Jews readily interpreted their own experiences with the aid of an eschatological scheme.[13] Even Josephus, who seems so distant from

---

or teaching in the synagogues . . . and that, even apart from formal disputes, his teaching was strongly imbued with the outlook and language of the sacred texts of Israel, it is reasonable to suppose that Jesus' religious formation in his family was intense and profound, and included instruction in reading biblical Hebrew."

11. Cf. what Josephus has to say about the Essenes in *Bell.* 2.136 ("They display an extraordinary interest in the writings of the ancients"), 159 (some "are versed from their early years in holy books").

12. Dale C. Allison Jr., *Jesus of Nazareth: Millenarian Prophet* (Minneapolis: Fortress, 1999).

13. For some examples, see Dale C. Allison Jr., *The End of the Ages Has Come: An Early Interpretation of the Death and Resurrection of Jesus* (Philadelphia: Fortress, 1985), pp. 6–14, 101–6. See also now the provocative work of Michael O. Wise, *The First Messiah: Investigating the Savior before Jesus* (San Francisco: HarperSanFrancisco, 1999).

all apocalyptic expectation, "understood the prophecies in Numbers 23–24 and in Daniel (2 and 7–10) to be predictions referring to Josephus's own lifetime, partly the catastrophe in the year 70 CE and partly the approaching eschatological redemption of the Jewish people."[14] That Jesus similarly thought of scriptural prophecies as fulfilled in his own day is only to be expected of one whose outlook was so thoroughly eschatological.

One particular dimension of Q's eschatology merits further remark. Chapter 2 sets forth the evidence that, in the Sayings Source, Jesus is like Moses, rewrites parts of the Torah, and experiences a new exodus. One can ask to what extent the typology created by these themes is a secondary imposition upon the tradition and to what extent it may reflect the self-conception of the historical Jesus. On the one hand, the appearance of the new exodus and new Moses motifs throughout the Jesus tradition as well as in Acts and Paul shows us that these themes go back to an early time in the Church, and certainly some of the things that go back so far do so because they were already there on the other side of Easter — opposition to divorce, for example, and the emphasis upon loving one's neighbor. On the other hand, we know from the temptation story, which surely does not preserve words of Jesus, that the new exodus theme could be added at a secondary stage. We must give the creativity of the post-Easter tradents its due.

In sorting through this problem, one needs to ask whether any of the pertinent Q material has a decent chance of going back to Jesus. The answer is that some of it does. Despite the skepticism of the Jesus Seminar, the Lord's Prayer, with its request for daily bread that alludes to the tale of the manna (Q 11:3), probably comes from Jesus.[15] So too Q 11:20, where Jesus alludes to Exod 8:19 in claiming that he casts out demons by the finger of God. Here the speaker is indicating "that he places himself alongside Moses and Aaron, genuine messengers from God who were empowered by him to perform symbolic miracles connection with Israel's liberation from slavery."[16] Also pertinent are the sayings in Q 6:27ff. that revise Leviticus 19 as well as Q 14:26, which daringly inverts the commandment to honor father and mother: in these two places — where so many have not doubted that we hear a pre-Easter voice — Jesus seemingly sets his words over against Moses. And then there is Q 11:29–30, where Jesus' generation is spoken of with language characteristic of the generation of Moses ("This generation is an evil generation"; cf. Deut 1:35). This may reflect the idiom and perspective of Jesus.[17]

---

14. Per Bilde, "Josephus and Jewish Apocalypticism," in *Understanding Josephus: Seven Perspectives* (ed. Steve Mason; JSPSS 32; Sheffield: Sheffield Academic Press, 1998), p. 54.

15. Cf. Meier, *A Marginal Jew*, vol. 2, p. 294.

16. Ibid., p. 411.

17. Cf. Martin Hengel, "Kerygma oder Geschichte? Zur Problematik einer falschen Alternative in der Synoptikerforschung aufgezeigt an Hand einiger neuer Monographien," *ThQ* 101 (1971), p. 334.

Taken together, these several units strongly suggest that the eschatological Jesus, like Deutero-Isaiah long before him, conceived of the coming of
the kingdom in his own day as a sort of new exodus. One might even speculate, as did Ben F. Meyer, that Jesus, who surely conceived of himself as an
eschatological prophet (cf. Q 7:22), found the fulfillment of Deut 18:15, 18
(God will raise up a prophet like Moses) in his own ministry.[18] To this one
could find a parallel in Dositheus, who appears to have been "an early first
century A.D. eschatological figure among the Samaritans, who applied the
'Prophet like Moses' passage of Dt. 18 to himself. As the Prophet, he was,
in all likelihood a miracle-worker and the author of new texts and/or interpretations of biblical law."[19] But however that particular issue is judged,
the main point stands — and it is strengthened by other sources besides Q.
Matthew's tradition, for example, preserves two parallel units (Mt 5:21–
22, 27–28) in which "You have heard that it was said to those of old" (by
Moses at Sinai) is the foil for "But I [Jesus] say to you." I have elsewhere
argued that these two units rest upon words of Jesus,[20] and in them we have
the same phenomenon as in Q 6:27ff. and Q 14:26: Jesus recalls Moses
only in order to daringly go his own and different way. If Jesus really did
speak these words, he must have been consciously relating himself in some
profound way to the lawgiver.

Again, those of us who strongly suspect that behind the various versions
of the two feedings of multitudes[21] lies a meal with a large crowd in a
deserted place, a meal that was, in a way reminiscent of the Jewish sign
prophets in Josephus,[22] intended to be an eschatological symbol, an antici-
pation of the messianic feast, will probably feel that Jesus, like most of those
sign prophets, was recalling memories of the exodus.[23] Commentators from
patristic times on have certainly been put in mind of the manna in the wilder-

---

18. Ben F. Meyer, "Appointed Deed, Appointed Doer: Jesus and the Scriptures," in Chilton
and Evans, eds., *Activities of Jesus*, p. 171. Contrast Teeple, *Mosaic Eschatological Prophet*,
pp. 115–18. The term "scripture prophet," used by Michael Wise, *The First Messiah*, is
appropriate for Jesus.

19. Stanley Jerome Isser, *The Dositheans: A Samaritan Sect in Late Antiquity* (SJLA 17;
Leiden: Brill, 1976), p. 163.

20. Allison, *Jesus of Nazareth*, pp. 185–87. Cf. Luz, *Matthew*, vol. 1, pp. 276–79, 281,
291.

21. Mt 14:13–21; 15:32–39; Mk 6:30–44; 8:1–10; Lk 9:10–17; Jn 6:1–15.

22. See Josephus, *Ant.* 18.85–87 (the Samaritan who claimed he would recover the sacred
vessels that Moses had deposited); *Ant.* 20.97–99 (Theudas, who tried to part the Jordan
in imitation of Moses' successor, Joshua), 167–68 (unnamed "impostors and deceivers" who
called upon people to follow them into the desert and who promised to show "unmistakable
marvels and signs that would be wrought in harmony with God's design"; cf. *Bell.* 2.258–60),
188 (an unnamed "imposter" "who had promised them salvation and rest from troubles if they
chose to follow him into the wilderness"); *Bell.* 2.261–63 (= *Ant.* 20.169–72: the would-be
ruler from Egypt who led his followers from the desert to the Mount of Olives; cf. Acts 21:38).

23. Allison, *New Moses*, pp. 73–84; P. W. Barnett, "The Jewish Sign Prophets — A.D. 40–
70: Their Intention and Origin," *NTS* 27 (1981), pp. 679–97. But for caution in this matter, see
Rebecca Gray, *Prophetic Figures in Late Second Temple Jewish Palestine: The Evidence from
Josephus* (New York/Oxford: Oxford University Press, 1993), pp. 112–44. She is confident of

ness,[24] and John's probably independent account not only relates that the crowd regarded Jesus as "the (Mosaic?) prophet" (6:14) but further draws several parallels and contrasts between Jesus and Moses (6:25ff.). Maybe John here has it right.

And then there is the Last Supper. In both Mk 14:24 and Mt 26:28, where the Last Supper is a Passover meal, Jesus speaks of "my blood of the covenant" (τὸ αἷμά μου τῆς διαθήκης). Similarly, in Lk 22:20 and 1 Cor 11:25 he uses the expression "the new covenant in my blood" (Lk: ἡ καινὴ διαθήκη ἐν τῷ αἵματί μου; Paul: ἡ καινὴ διαθήκη ἐστὶν ἐν τῷ ἐμῷ αἵματι). Both phrases function partly as allusions to Exod 24:8: "Moses took the blood and dashed it on the people and said, 'See the blood of the covenant (MT: דַּם־הַבְּרִית; LXX: τὸ αἷμα τῆς διαθήκης) that the Lord has made with you in accordance with all these words.' " As John Lightfoot commented,

> Moses sprinkled all the people with blood, and said, "This is the blood of the covenant which God hath made with you:" and thus that old covenant or testimony was confirmed. In like manner, Christ having published all the articles of the new covenant, he takes the cup of wine, and gives them to drink, and saith, "This is the new testament in my blood:" and thus the new covenant is established.[25]

Matthew clearly divined the allusion and enlarged it,[26] and the perception that the Lord's Supper should be connected with the exodus appears in John 6, where allusions to the Last Supper (e.g., 6:53–58) stand beside references to the miracle of the manna. There is also 1 Cor 10:1–5, where the Eucharist is likened to the supernatural food Israel ate in the wilderness. So we have here a very old tradition. How old? If one can think that "my blood of the covenant" or "the new covenant in my blood" represents something Jesus said,[27] one would have additional evidence that he himself drew a significant

---

a connection with Moses and the exodus only for Theudas and the Egyptian: about the others we are, Gray thinks, insufficiently informed to draw such a conclusion.

24. E.g., Cyril of Alexandria, *Comm. Lk* 48 (citing Ps 78:24; CSCO Scriptores Syri 70, ed. J.-B. Chabot, p. 159); Eusebius, *Dem. ev.* 3.2 (92b-c) (GCS 23, ed. I. A. Heikel, p. 98).

25. John Lightfoot, *Commentary*, vol. 2, p. 353. Cf. Maldonatus, *Commentarii*, vol. 1, p. 406; Bengel, *Gnomon*, ad loc.; Gundry, *Old Testament*, pp. 57–58. "Blood of the covenant" also appears in Zech 9:11, but (*a*) Zech 9:11 may itself be an allusion to Exod 24:8 (cf. the targum on Zech 9:11: "You also, for whom a covenant was made by blood, I have delivered you from bondage to the Egyptians"); (*b*) Exod 24:8 is the only place in the Tanak where blood-sprinkling for cleansing is connected with a meal, as in the Gospels; (*c*) the Peshitta as well as Tg. Ps.-J. and Tg. Onq. on Exod 24:8 use a demonstrative, which agrees with the NT's τοῦτο; and (*d*) the Greek of Mk 14:24 = Mt 26:28 (τὸ αἷμά μου τῆς διαθήκης) is closer to LXX Exod 24:8 (τὸ αἷμα τῆς διαθήκης) than to LXX Zech 9:11 (ἐν αἵματι διαθήκης).

26. Details in Allison, *New Moses*, pp. 256–61.

27. I cannot here discuss the tradition history of the Lord's Supper or the question of a Semitic equivalent for "my blood of the covenant" or the origin of the tradition. Suffice it to say that one sympathizes with Strauss, *Jesus*, p. 634, who in view of Paul's testimony found it hard to doubt that the words of institution rest upon words of Jesus; and further that, despite the doubts of many, who have regarded an allusion to Exod 24:8 as secondary, a good case

analogy between himself and Moses and/or between his own time, that of the latter days, and the redemption from Egypt.

III. The Ironic Jesus

If Q's allusive, eschatological, Mosaic Jesus is not a misleading representative of the historical Jesus of Nazareth, what about that other prominent feature of Q's intertextuality, namely, the way it inverts subtexts to startle and generate irony? Here too Q seems to put us in touch with the originating tradition. Consider the following six passages or verses:

Q 6:27–45, which contains several imperatives that reverse commandments of Leviticus 19

Q 9:58, which offers a cynical reapplication of Ps 8:5

Q 12:22–31, which, against the spirit of Prov 6:6–11 and other Wisdom texts, encourages believers not to worry because God takes care of animals that do not work

Q 13:19, which describes the kingdom of God with imagery that Ezekiel and Daniel associate with ungodly powers

Q 14:26, which commands one not to honor father and mother but to hate father and mother

Q 16:18, which prohibits divorce despite the provision for it in Deut 24:1–4

In all these places Scripture is not appealed to as a supporting authority but is instead turned upside down and used as a foil for saying something different. This provocative use of the Tanak, as we have seen, has good parallels in Jewish tradition, especially in Deutero-Isaiah. So it cannot be classified as antinomian rhetoric, nor can we apply the criterion of dissimilarity and forthwith attribute the relevant units to the historical Jesus. There are, however, other means by which to argue that the historical Jesus was the ironically allusive Jesus.

One way is to decide, one by one, which of the sayings cited might in fact be plausibly attributed to Jesus. I forego that exercise here and content myself with an appeal to the Jesus Seminar, which many of us think is not optimistic enough about tracing synoptic sayings to Jesus. Its voting resulted in coloring eight of the verses in Q 6:27–41 and six of the verses in Q 12:22–31 red or pink, and it also prints Q 9:58; 13:19; and 14:26 in pink. Only 16:18, Jesus' prohibition of divorce, is not in red or pink. It gets gray — surely an idiosyncratic judgment. Few have doubted that the prohibition of divorce goes back to Jesus.

---

can be made for its belonging to the original tradition. See Rudolf Pesch, *Das Abendmahl und Jesu Todesverständnis* (QD 80; Freiburg/Basel/Vienna: Herder, 1978).

A second way to confirm that Jesus liked to allude to biblical subtexts in a daring manner would be to observe that such a use of Scripture is not just a feature of Q. Mt 5:21–22 cites Exod 20:13 = Deut 5:17, the prohibition of murder, not in order to agree or disagree with it but in order to transcend it. Similarly, Mt 5:27–28 quotes Exod 20:14 = Deut 5:18, the command not to commit adultery, and then goes beyond it to demand more. In both of these places, whose authenticity can be reasonably maintained,[28] Scripture is not the last word but the first word only: Moses is not enough. Another intriguing passage for comparison is Mk 12:35–37, which has Jesus set Ps 110:1 against itself. If David (the author of the psalm according to the superscription) calls the Messiah "lord," how can the Messiah be his son? The question "represents a puzzling piece of christology that is at home neither in first-century Judaism, nor in first-century Christianity, nor in the flow of Mark's story."[29] This is at least some reason to ask whether Mk 12:35–37 preserves a memory.[30] Whatever one's judgment on that matter, Q is not the only source in which Jesus quotes the Tanak neither to illumine a point nor to support an argument but rather to provocatively transcend it.[31] We have here a teaching method that belongs to more than one strand of the Jesus tradition.

A third way of coming to the conclusion that Jesus himself, and not just the tradition about him, undid subtexts builds upon the fact that such a rhetorical strategy fits with what we otherwise know of him. Robert Funk has rightly remarked that Jesus'

> stories are laced with surprise. As with all good jokes and stories, one cannot anticipate the outcome. His listeners did not anticipate that everyone would be invited to the dinner party. They did not expect those hired last to be paid the same as those hired in the morning. They didn't believe things would turn out well for the shrewd manager. In other words, Jesus detypifies, he defamiliarizes common perceptions. He says the unexpected. He confounds by contradicting what everybody already knows.[32]

---

28. See n. 20 on p. 218.

29. Joel Marcus, *The Way of the Lord: Christological Exegesis of the Old Testament in the Gospel of Mark* (Louisville: Westminster/John Knox, 1992), p. 140.

30. See further the survey of opinion and evaluation of arguments pro and con in Davies and Allison, *Matthew*, vol. 3, pp. 250–51.

31. See further the interesting article of John A. T. Robinson, "Did Jesus Have a Distinctive Use of Scripture?" in *Christological Perspectives: Essays in Honor of Harvey K. McArthur* (ed. Robert F. Berkey and Sarah A. Edwards; New York: Pilgrim, 1982), pp. 49–57. In this Robinson urges that Jesus sometimes used Scripture not to add an aura of authority or confirm a point or to offer exegesis but to turn it into a challenge — "using the Bible to pose rather than to prove" (p. 54).

32. Robert W. Funk, *Honest to Jesus: Jesus for a New Millennium* (San Francisco: Harper-SanFrancisco, 1996), pp. 153–54. Also relevant is Jesus' use of the aphorism, which so often makes its point by contradiction. See Crossan, *In Fragments*, esp. his discussion of proverb and aphorism on pp. 3–36.

Surely few would disagree with what Funk says here, and his words apply equally well to Q 6:27–45; 9:58; 12:22–31; 13:19; 14:26; and 16:18 once their subtexts are exposed. In these places Jesus defamiliarizes common perceptions, says the unexpected, and contradicts what everyone knows. So once again we are encouraged to believe that Jesus liked referring to a text in order to say something not in that text. He appears to have been akin to Aristophanes, who quoted from Euripides precisely in order to give his predecessor's famous words a new twist and make them mean what they did not mean before, or maybe even a bit like so many contemporary journalists who habitually construct headlines out of familiar expressions. The allusive Jesus reformulated and in some cases we might say even deformed tradition in order to convey his urgent message. It was and remains an effective and memorable strategy. One understands why the tradition has people asking themselves, "What is this? A new teaching" (Mk 1:27), and even why some of Jesus' followers came to believe that something greater than the intertext is here.

Appendix

Doubtful Allusions

In addition to allusions that may be regarded as probable or uncertain (the latter are marked throughout this book with a question mark), there are others that, despite having exegetical sponsorship, seem unlikely.[1] This appendix examines a number of them, some because they appear in more than one commentary, others because they would be potentially meaningful if established, still others because it is instructive to see why certain proposals do not persuade.

I. The Pentateuch

Q 7:24 // Exodus 14–15. Jesus asks the crowd regarding John, "What did you go out into the wilderness to see? A reed (κάλαμον) shaken (σαλευό-μενον) by the wind (ἀνέμου)?" Commentators regularly think of the shaken reed as standing for an everyday sight that would hardly attract a crowd. Gerd Theissen has suggested that it may instead allude to Herod, who opposed John the Baptist, exhibited inconstant character (cf. "shaking"), lived in luxury (cf. Q 7:25), and used the reed on his coins as a symbol of his reign.[2]

But there is yet a third possibility. "What did you go out into the wilderness to behold?" echoes Mt 24:15: "If they say to you, Behold, he is in the wilderness, do not go out." This verse has to do with false prophets and false messiahs, and it reminds us of certain prophetic pretenders discussed by Josephus, such as the so-called Egyptian, who thought of himself as destined to rule and led his followers on a new exodus trek through the desert (*Bell.* 2.261–63). One may ask whether Q 7:24 has anything to do with such people, for the reference in the next verse to royal attire (Q 7:25) would be consistent with a messianic connotation, and the reed could be an exodus motif. If κάλαμος is a collective (as in LXX Job 40:16 and elsewhere), the image of reeds blown by the wind might be designed to recall Exodus 14–15, where God sends forth a strong wind to drive back the Sea of Reeds.

---

1. Cf. the threefold classification of proposed allusions in Benjamin D. Sommer, "New Light on the Composition of Jeremiah," *CBQ* 61 (1999), pp. 646–66.

2. Gerd Theissen, *The Gospels in Context: The Social and Political History in the Synoptic Tradition* (Minneapolis: Fortress, 1991), pp. 26–42.

Jesus would then be asking, "Did you go out into the wilderness to see a man repeat the wonders of the exodus?" Certainly people at a later time did just that (Josephus, *Ant.* 20.97–99). This interpretation, however, has to my knowledge never been defended at length by any commentator,[3] and it can be nothing more than a bare possibility.[4]

Q 10:7 // Lev 19:13; Deut 24:14–15. If Jesus tells the disciples that "the laborer (ἐργάτης) deserves his wages (μισθοῦ),"[5] the holiness code says that "you will not keep for yourself the wages (μισθός) of a laborer (μισθωτοῦ) until morning" (Lev 19:13). Deuteronomy says similarly, "You will not withhold the wages (μισθόν) of the poor and needy (πένητος καὶ ἐνδεοῦς)…. You will pay them their wages (μισθόν) daily before sunset, because they are poor and their livelihood depends on them" (24:14–15). Commentators occasionally cite the Pentateuchal texts when looking at Lk 10:7 or Mt 10:10,[6] and we have seen already that Q shows a special interest in Leviticus 19.[7] But both Lev 19:3 and Deut 24:14–15 focus upon payment before sundown, a circumstance that plays no role in the Q text. Also, only one word is shared with the LXX, μισθός.

(Q 10:25–28 // Deut 6:5; Lev 19:18). The agreements between Lk 10:25–28 and Mt 22:34–40 against Mk 12:28–34 are numerous and not obviously explicable in terms of independent editing and/or textual corruption.[8] So some have argued that Q may have contained a version of the commandment to love that brought together Deut 6:5 and Lev 19:18.[9] Others, however, have thought that Matthew and Luke used a different version of Mark from the one that we possess, or that Matthew and Luke could have known our pericope as it stood in Mark and also have known it through oral tradition.[10] In favor of the latter possibility, the double commandment to love was presumably well known in and treasured by the early Church,[11] and one guesses that the pronouncement story in which Jesus delivered that commandment circulated widely, and in slightly different forms. In any case the

---

3. But I raised the possibility in Davies and Allison, *Matthew*, vol. 2, p. 247.

4. See further J. Ian H. McDonald, "Questioning and Discernment in Gospel Discourse: Communicative Strategy in Matthew 11:2–19," in *Authenticating the Words of Jesus* (ed. Bruce Chilton and Craig A. Evans; NTTS 28/1; Leiden/Boston/Cologne: Brill, 1999), pp. 350–52. His conclusion is that "a messianic interpretation of 'a man clothed in soft raiment' lacks cogency."

5. So Lk 10:7. Mt 10:10 has τροφῆς, "food," but this is redactional; see Allison, *Jesus Tradition in Q*, p. 107.

6. E.g., Hodgson, "On the Gattung of Q," p. 80.

7. See above, pp. 29–38.

8. But see Gnilka, *Matthäusevangelium*, vol. 2, pp. 157–58; and Neirynck, "The Minor Agreements," pp. 61–64.

9. See, e.g., Tuckett, *Q*, pp. 416–18.

10. That Lk 10:25-8 draws upon tradition independent of Mark is widely held; see the commentaries. For signs of non-Markan tradition, see Jeremias, *Sprache*, p. 190. At the same time, dependence upon Mark is clear; cf. Lk 20:39 with Mk 12:28, 32, and Lk 20:40 with Mk 12:34.

11. See 1 Jn 4:21; *Did.* 1:2; Polycarp, *Ep.* 3.3; Justin, *Dial.* 93 (PTS 47, ed. M. Marcovich, p. 231); Sextus, *Sent.* 106a-b; Tertullian, *Adv. Marc.* 5.8 (PL 2.490B); etc.

accord between Lk 10:25–28 and Mt 22:34–40 is insufficient to let us speak here confidently of Q, so their intertextuality is beyond the bounds of this investigation.

Q 13:34 // Deut 32:11.[12] According to Richard Horsley, Q 13:34 contains "a reference to a significant piece of the prophetic repertoire in Israelite tradition," namely,

> the image of the hen gathering her brood under her wing (*nossia* = the "children" of the city, i.e., the Israelite villages ostensibly gathered around and under the protection of the capital city). This alludes to the prophetic Song of Moses in Deuteronomy 32, in which God is "like an eagle that stirs up its nest [translated in the LXX with *nossia*], that hovers over its young, as it spreads its wings" (Deut 32:11).[13]

Horsley is only one of many to have recalled the parallel. It is indeed more often than not noted in the commentaries on Mt 23:37 and Lk 13:34, including already those of Apollinarius of Laodicea, Cyril of Alexandria, and Bede.[14] But there is a problem with finding in Q 13:34 an allusion to Deut 32:11. The image of a bird taking nestlings under wing is found often in the Tanak and in later Jewish literature, and there is no evidence that Deut 32:11 is being referred to in most of the relevant texts.[15] Given this, it is understandable that most commentators, including already Apollinarius and Cyril, cite more than one scriptural parallel to Jesus' words about a hen gathering her brood under her wings (the two fathers refer to LXX Ps 35:8), and further that some who cite parallels to Mt 23:37 = Lk 13:34 even overlook Deut 32:11 entirely.[16] It seems safest, then, to conclude that Q 13:34 does not allude to Deut 32:11 in particular but rather uses a common biblical image of God's care.[17] This was the conclusion of Chrysostom: "Everywhere in the prophets is this same image of the wings, and in the song of Moses and the Psalms, indicating his [God's] great protection and care."[18] Q 13:34 borrows the language not of one biblical text but of several.

Q 12:28 // Gen 3:21. The God who clothes "the grass in the field" (ἀγρῷ τὸν χόρτον) will all the more clothe Jesus' followers. The idea of God cloth-

---

12. On the placement of Q 13:34–35 between Q 11:51 and 52, see p. 85.

13. Richard A. Horsley, "Israelite Traditions in Q," in Horsley and Draper, *Whoever Hears You Hears Me*, p. 121. Cf. p. 282.

14. Apollinarius of Laodicea, *Comm. Mt* frag. 121 (TU 61, ed. J. Reuss, p. 41); Cyril of Alexandria, *Comm. Mt* frag. 263 (TU 61, ed. J. Reuss, p. 243; this text is closely related to that of Apollinarius); Bede, *Luc. exp.* ad Lk 13:34 (CCSL 120, ed. D. Hurst, p. 274). Cf. Albertus Magnus, *Super Mt cap. XV–XXVIII* ad loc. (Opera Omnia 21/2, ed. B. Schmidt, p. 558); Hühn, *Alttestamentlichen Citate*, p. 28; Marshall, *Luke*, p. 575; Sand, *Matthäus*, p. 475.

15. See, e.g., Ruth 2:12; Ps 17:8; 36:7; 57:1; 61:4; 63:7; 91:4; Isa 31:5; *4 Ezra* 1:30 (probably an allusion to Mt 23:37); *2 Bar.* 41:4. The rabbinic expression "to come under the wings of the Shekinah" is also a parallel.

16. E.g., Gnilka, *Matthäusevangelium*, vol. 2, p. 303, cites Isa 31:5 and Ps 36:8.

17. So too Luz, *Matthäus*, vol. 3, p. 381, on Mt 23:37.

18. Chrysostom, *Hom. Mt* 74.3 (PG 58.681). Cf. Paschasius Radbertus, *Exp. Mt libri XII (IX–XII)* ad 23:37 (CCCM 56B, ed. B. Paulus, p. 1143).

ing human beings appears in Gen 3:21: "And the Lord God made garments of skins for the man and for his wife, and clothed them." One is tempted to see in Q 12:28 an allusion to this verse for several reasons. (*a*) Gen 3:21 was well known, the object of much speculation.[19] (*b*) Q 12:28 refers to "the grass of the field" (ἐν ἀγρῷ τὸν χόρτον). The expression appears twice in the LXX creation narrative, in 2:5 (χόρτον ἀγροῦ) and 3:18 (χόρτον τοῦ ἀγροῦ). So it might send hearers back to Genesis.[20] (*c*) The theme of Q 12:22–31 is God's providence over creation (*creatio continua*), which might also revive memories of Genesis. (*d*) So too might the theme of having to work (cf. Gen 3:17–19).[21] (*e*) Gen 3:21 is about God clothing a man and a woman, and the Q passage has in view both men and women; for in the words of Ulrich Luz, "Why does Jesus say that birds do not do the work of men [sow and reap], and that lilies do not do the work of women [toil and spin]? This makes sense only if it is applied to men and women who have left their ordinary work for the sake of the kingdom of God."[22] (*f*) If Matthew changed Q's "ravens" to "birds of the air" (τὰ πετεινὰ τοῦ οὐρανοῦ), he might have been motivated by a desire to recall Genesis, for while the phrase occurs approximately fifty times in the LXX, it is particularly characteristic of the creation narrative (Gen 1:26, 28, 30; 2:19, 20).

Despite these points, it may be wise to doubt that Q 12:28 alludes to Gen 3:21. (*a*) The expression "grass of the field" is not confined to the creation story. It also appears in 4 Βασ 19:26 (χόρτος ἀγροῦ) and Jer 12:4 (ὁ χόρτος τοῦ ἀγροῦ). (*b*) Q and LXX Genesis use different verbs for "clothe" (Mt: ἀμφιέννυμι; //Lk: ἀμφιάζω; LXX Gen: ἐνδύω). (*c*) The proposed allusion suffers the further disadvantage that ancient and modern commentators on Matthew 6 or Luke 12 mention Genesis 3 very rarely.[23] In view of these facts, and because in such matters it is better to err on the side of caution than of enthusiasm, there is insufficient cause to suppose that Q 12:28 should direct an audience to Genesis.

Even if Q 12:28 does not allude to any particular text, it does have a definite biblical background. Often in the Bible grass is a simile or metaphor for the brevity and frailty of human life.[24] In Q, however, this is not so. For Jesus, the brave show of the flora which is here today and gone tomorrow

---

19. See Kugel, *Traditions*, pp. 132–36, and the literature cited there.

20. Philo, *Leg. all.* 1.21, 24; *Opif.* 194; and Theophylus, *Autol.* 2.19 (SC 20, ed. G. Bardy and J. Sender, p. 146), use "grass of the field" in creation contexts.

21. Cf. Jerome, *Comm. Mt* ad 6:25 (CCSL 77, p. 40); Geoffrey Babion (?), *Comm. Mt* ad Mt 6:25 (PG 162.1312B); Trapp, *Commentary*, vol. 5, p. 110. Sometimes it is suggested that the call to live like the ravens is based in eschatology: since the end corresponds to the beginning, and since in the beginning Adam and Eve did not have to toil for food, the kingdom of God means the recovery of paradisiacal conditions.

22. Luz, *Matthew*, 1:408.

23. But note Hans Dieter Betz, *Sermon on the Mount*, pp. 479–80; and Olsthoorn, *Jewish Background*, p. 52.

24. E.g., Ps 37:2; 90:5–6; 102:11; 103:15–16; Isa 37:27; 40:6–7; cf. Job 14:1–2.

into the oven[25] does not express the fleeting, transitory nature of life but instead shows that the God who lavishes infinite pains on the grass and flowers, brief though their appearance be, can be counted on all the more to take care of those who seek the kingdom.[26] This novel twisting of an old motif augments the irony of Q 12:22–31, for we have seen in an earlier chapter that our text appears to be an unexpected reversal of Prov 6:6–11. Moreover, rabbinic literature contrasts the carefree life of animals with the distressing burdens of humanity[27] — in stark contrast to Q 12:22–31, where God's providential care for animals extends to human beings, who need not be anxious. So the Q passage seems to be intentionally provocative. It reverses the old lesson drawn from the short-lived grass, it inverts Prov 6:6–11, and its inference from the seemingly carefree life of the beasts is the opposite of that drawn by the Mishnah.[28]

II. Isaiah

Q 3:17 // Isa 66:24. According to Marius Reiser, the concluding phrase of Q 3:17 ("will burn with [or: in] unquenchable fire," κατακαύσει πυρὶ ἀσβέστῳ) is "an allusion to Isa. 66:24."[29] The latter, which is perhaps the more memorable for being the very last verse in all of Isaiah, reads: "And they will go out and look at the dead bodies of the people who have rebelled against me; for their worm will not die, their fire will not be quenched (LXX: τὸ πῦρ αὐτῶν οὐ σβεσθήσεται),[30] and they will be an abhorrence to all flesh." Although it is doubtful that the idea of unquenchable eschatological fire entered Judaism via this verse (see below), surely Isa 66:24 was influential in spreading that idea. Further, some texts do clearly allude to Isa 66:24 (which was to become one of Christianity's most important proof texts for

---

25. The language and imagery are familiar; cf. Mal 4:1 ("the day is coming, burning like an oven [κλίβανος], when all the arrogant and all evildoers will be stubble; that day that comes shall burn them up"); Ecclus 10:10 ("the king of today [σήμερον] will die tomorrow [αὔριον]"); 1 Macc 2:63 ("Today [σήμερον] they will be exalted, but tomorrow [αὔριον] they will not be found").

26. Cf. Manson, *Sayings*, p. 113.

27. *m. Qidd.* 4:14: "R. Simeon b. Eleazar says, 'Have you ever seen a wild animal or a bird practicing a craft? Yet they have their sustenance without care and were they not created for nothing else but to serve me? But I was created to serve my maker. How much more then ought I have to have sustenance without care? But I have wrought evil and forfeited my [right to] sustenance [without care].'" Variants in SB 1, pp. 436–37.

28. Some have also thought the appeal to ravens might have been surprising; see Olsthoorn, *Jewish Background*, p. 35, who notes that their greediness was proverbial, that they destroyed cornfields, that they were superstitiously feared, and that they were unclean.

29. Reiser, *Jesus and Judgment*, p. 180. Cf. Eusebius, *Comm. Isa* 2.51 (GCS Eusebius 9, ed. J. Ziegler, pp. 379–80; 410–11); Bruno Astensius, *Comm. Mt* 1.6 (PL 165.88A); Albertus Magnus, *En. prim. part. Luc. (I–IX)* ad loc. (Opera Omnia 22, ed. A. Borgnet, p. 286); Lapide, *Commentary*, vol. 1, p. 122.

30. MT: אשם לא תכבה; Targum: וראשתהון לא תטפי.

the everlasting nature of hell; cf. Augustine, *Civ. Dei* 21.9). Mk 9:48 ("their worm never dies, and the fire is never quenched") is an example:

Mk 9:48   ὁ   σκώληξ αὐτῶν οὐ τελευτᾷ
                           καὶ τὸ πῦρ   οὐ σβέννυται
LXX Isa 66:24   ὁ γὰρ σκώληξ αὐτῶν οὐ τελευτήσει
                           καὶ τὸ πῦρ αὐτῶν οὐ σβεσθήσεται

Additional examples are supplied by *LAB* 63:4 ("a fiery worm will" enter Doeg the Syrian, and he will dwell in "inextinguishable fire forever"); *Vision of Ezra* 34 ("he saw in a dark place the worm that does not die [*vermem immortalen*]"); and *b. Pesaḥ*. 54a ("the fire [אור] that the Holy One, blessed be he, created on the second day of the week will never be extinguished [אין לו כבייה לעולם]"; this prefaces a citation of Isa 66:24).[31] On the other hand, Isa 34:9–10 ("her land will become burning pitch. Night and day it will not be quenched" [LXX: οὐ σβεσθήσεται]) and Jer 7:20 ("it will burn and not be quenched" [LXX: καυθήσεται καὶ οὐ σβεσθήσεται]) already speak of divine judgment as a burning that will not go out, so Isa 66:24 is not the only Scripture passage that a hearer of Q 3:17 might recall. Moreover, there are additional texts which show us that the threat of unquenchable fire did not always have its moorings in a particular intertext. *Sib. Or.* 2:253 ("the blazing river and the unquenchable flame," φλογὸς ἀσβέστου); Ignatius, *Eph.* 16.2 ("Such a one will go in his foulness to the unquenchable fire," εἰς τὸ πῦρ τὸ ἄσβεστον); and Justin Martyr, *Dial.* 120.5 ("he will send others to the condemnation of the unquenchable fire," ἀσβέστου πυρός)[32] appear to be examples of such.[33] In addition, the words and images of Q 3:17 are different from those of Isa 66:24: Q says nothing of bodies or onlookers or worms. So there is probably not enough here to verify a relationship between Isa 66:24 and Q 3:17.

Q 6:22 // Isa 51:7. Although reconstruction of the precise form of Q 6:22 escapes us, the fourth beatitude in both Matthew and Luke blesses those who are reproached (ὀνειδίσωσιν) and spoken against. One might ascertain here dependence upon Isa 51:7: "Do not fear the reproach of others, and do not be dismayed when they revile you" (MT: אל־תיראו חרפת אנוש ומגדפתם אל־תחתו; LXX: μὴ φοβεῖσθε ὀνειδισμὸν ἀνθρώπων καὶ τῷ φαυλισμῷ αὐτῶν μὴ ἡττᾶσθε).[34] The theme is similar, and Q's ὀνειδίσωσιν matches

31. See also *2 Clem.* 7:6; 17:5; Justin, *1 Apol.* 52.8 (PTS 38, ed. M. Marcovich, p. 105); *Dial.* 44.3; 130.2; 140.3 (PTS 47, ed. M. Marcovich, pp. 17–18, 295, 311–12).

32. PTS 47, ed. M. Marcovich, p. 278.

33. Cf. *Ps.-Clem. Rec.* 3.26 (GCS 51, ed. B. Rehm, p. 116); *Ps.-Clem. Hom.* 3.6 (GCS 42, ed. B. Rehm, p. 59); Pap. Paris Suppl. gr. 574, 3070.

34. So Gundry, *Old Testament*, pp. 71–72. Christian commentators on Isaiah sometimes note the parallel; see, e.g., Cyril of Alexandria, *Comm. Isa* ad loc. (PG 70.1119C); Jerome, *Comm. Isa* 14.51.7–8 (CCSL 73A, ed. M. Adriaen and F. Glorie, p. 563); and Butler, *The Bible-Work*, vol. 8, p. 268.

LXX Isaiah's ὀνειδισμόν.There is, however, only one verbal overlap — unless Luke's οἱ ἄνθρωποι ("whenever people hate you") is judged to be from Q (LXX Isa 51:7 has ὀνειδισμὸν ἀνθρώπων,"reproach of people").[35] Beyond that, surely Luke's "cast out your name as evil" (ἐκβάλωσιν τὸ ὄνομα ὑμῶν ὡς πονηρόν) is a Semitism from Q, and it corresponds neither to the Hebrew text nor the targum on Isa 51:7: the idiom is not associated with that verse.[36] So one can have no confidence that Q 6:22 is designed to remind one of Isaiah's imperatives in the face of reproach and reviling.

Q 10:21 // Isa 29:14. "I thank you Father, lord of heaven and earth, for you hid (ἔκρυψας) these things from the wise (σοφῶν) and learned (συνετῶν), and disclosed them to babes. Yes, Father, for such seemed well pleasing to you." The three words in parentheses also appear in Isa 29:14, which in the LXX reads, "I will destroy the wisdom (σοφίαν) of the wise (σοφῶν), and I will hide (κρύψω) the discernment (σύνεσιν) of the discerning (συνετῶν)." There is also an overlap of theme between the two verses: in both the wise and discerning are rejected. So maybe Q 10:21 could be a reapplication of Isa 29:14, a verse referred to in Mt 15:8–9; Mk 7:6–7; and 1 Cor 1:19.[37]

The observations just made, however, lay but a weak groundwork on which to base much of anything. The theme of Isa 29:14 is common enough. According to Josephus, *Ant.* 2.222, God has shown that human intelligence (σύνεσιν) is worth nothing, and in 11Q5 18:3–5 we read that wisdom speaks to the simple and gives insight to those without understanding. Already the Hebrew Bible shows a strong tendency to use "wise" and "discerning" and related words in a pejorative manner: it is recognized that those who profess to be devoted to wisdom often are not.[38] Further, σοφός and συνετός, like σοφία and σύνεσις, are a natural pair,[39] so their joint appearance does not direct us to a particular intertext.[40] Sometimes common vocabulary is nothing more than coincidence. Who would want to suggest

---

35. Note also that as Q has "on account of the Son of man," the targum on Isa 51:7 refers to the reproaches of "the sons of men" (בני אנשא).

36. Matthew Black, *An Aramaic Approach to the Gospels and Acts* (3d ed.; Oxford: Clarendon, 1967), pp. 135–36. But the IQP does not assign the phrase to Q.

37. Grimm, *Jesus und das Danielbuch, Band I*, pp. 67–68. Cf. Hodgson, "On the Gattung of Q," p. 81.

38. E.g., Job 5:13; Isa 5:21; Jer 8:8; 9:23–24; 49:7; Obad 8; Bar 3:23; Ecclus 37:16–21. Cf. 1QH 11(3):14–15; Josephus, *Bell.* 6.313.

39. E.g., Prov 16:21; Dan 2:21; *Ps. Sol.* 17:42; Col 1:9; Josephus, *Ant.* 11.57–58; *2 Bar.* 46:5; *T. Zeb.* 6:1; etc.

40. One could strengthen the case for an allusion to Isa 29:14 if one could, with James M. Robinson, "Kerygma and History," in James M. Robinson and Helmut Koester, *Trajectories through Early Christianity* (Philadelphia: Fortress, 1971), p. 42; and Peter Richardson, "The Thunderbolt in Q and the Wise Man in Corinth," in *From Jesus to Paul: Studies in Honor of F. W. Beare* (ed. Peter Richardson and J. C. Hurd; Waterloo, Canada: Wilfred Laurier, 1984), pp. 91–111, believe that in 1 Corinthians 1–4 Paul draws upon the tradition behind Q 10:21–22, for there he cites Isa 29:14 (see v. 19). But the evidence is inconclusive; see C. M. Tuckett, "1 Corinthians and Q," *JBL* 102 (1983), pp. 618–19.

that the several words common to Q 10:21–22 and LXX 2 Chr 2:11–14 mean anything?

> And Hiram said, "Blessed be the Lord (κύριος) God of Israel, who made heaven (οὐρανόν) and earth (γῆν), who gave to David the king a wise (σοφόν) son (υἱόν), and one endowed with knowledge (σύνεσιν) and understanding, who will build a house for the Lord (κυρίῳ), and a house for his kingdom. And now I have sent to you a wise (σοφόν) and understanding (σύνεσιν) man who belonged to Hiram my father (πατέρα) (his mother was of the daughters of Dan and his father [πατήρ] was a Tyrian), skilled to work in gold…and to understand every device, whatsoever you will give him to do with your wise ones (σοφῶν) and the wise ones (σοφῶν) of my lord (κυρίου) David your father (πατρός)." (2 Chr 2:12–14)

Texts can share several words without one being dependent on the other. To cite another example, *Jos. Asen.* 12:3–5, like Q 10:21–22, contains the key words "heaven" (οὐρανόν), "earth" (γῆν), "lord" (κύριε), "confess" (ἐξομολογήσομαι), "reveal" (ἀποκαλύψω), and "before you" (ἐνώπιον σου), but this means next to nothing. Chance must be given its due.[41]

Q 10:23–24 // Isa 52:15. According to Grimm, Q 10:23–24 alludes to Isa 52:15: "Kings will shut their mouths because of him; for that which had not been told them they will see, and that which they had not heard they shall contemplate."[42] Whereas in Q the kings did not see and hear what others now see and hear, in Isaiah the kings will see and hear what they formerly had not been told or did not contemplate. There is further similar vocabulary:

	"many"	"kings"	"see"	"hear"
Q	πολλοί	βασιλεῖς	ἰδεῖν/βλέπετε	ἀκοῦσαι/ύετε
LXX Isaiah	πολλά	βασιλεῖς	ὄψονται	ἀκηκόασιν

Isaiah's lines are about foreign kings, whereas Q's kings, being yoked with "prophets,"[43] must be Jewish kings. This is why Grimm reconstructs an original — a Semitic original he attributes to Jesus — without "prophets." This allows him to establish thematic coherence between the two texts. His reasons for such a reconstruction, however, are not compelling, and in any case Q itself, which is our concern, had, according to the IQP, "prophets and

---

41. Adrian Leske, "Matthew," in *The International Bible Commentary: A Catholic and Ecumenical Commentary for the Twenty-First Century* (ed. W. R. Farmer; Collegeville, Minn.: Liturgical Press, 1998), p. 1292, thinks that Matthew's equivalent of Q 10:21–22 alludes to Isa 63:16 ("For you are our father, though Abraham does not know us and Israel does not acknowledge us, you, O Lord, are our father"). But coincidence is also the explanation for this parallel, which otherwise does not, to my knowledge, appear in the commentaries.

42. Grimm, *Weil Ich Dich Liebe*, pp. 112–24. Cf. his "Selige Augenzeugen," *ThZ* 26 (1970), pp. 172–83.

43. "Prophets and kings" may be without parallel, but Q 11:29–32 places Jonah and Solomon side by side.

kings." And since it is artificial to associate a prophecy about pagan kings with Q 10:23–24, and since there are equally close parallels elsewhere,[44] one can have no confidence in Grimm's proposed allusion. At the same time, since Grimm is nonetheless not alone in being reminded of Isa 52:15 when reading Mt 13:16–17 and Lk 10:23–24,[45] others may wish to leave open the bare possibility that Q 10:23–24 alludes to that verse.

Q 12:4–7 // Isa 51:7–8. Grimm has claimed that the consoling unit that begins and ends with "fear not" (v. 4, μὴ φοβεῖσθε; v. 7: μὴ φοβεῖσθε) is related to Isa 51:7–8: "Listen to me, you who know righteousness, you people who have my teaching in your hearts; do not fear (LXX: μὴ φοβεῖσθε; MT: אל־תיראו) the reproach of others, and do not be dismayed when they revile you. For the moth will eat them up like a garment, and the worm will eat them like wool; but my deliverance will be forever, and my salvation to all generations."[46] Grimm observes that both texts have the plural, μὴ φοβεῖσθε, and that they enjoin one not to fear individuals whose earthly power does not pass beyond death. But these observations are vitiated by others. (*a*) "Fear not" is so common in Jewish tradition that it does not readily help mark an allusion.[47] (*b*) Isa 51:7–8, which is not much cited or alluded to in old Jewish or Christian literature, contains nothing related to Gehenna (Q 12:5), sparrows (Q 12:6–7), or hairs (Q 12:7).

Q 14:16–24 // Isa 35:3, 5–6; 61:1–2. The parable of the wedding feast in Mt 22:1–10 has a parallel in Lk 14:15–24, so many have supposed that both rest upon a parable in Q.[48] Given this, one may take notice of Grimm's contention that Luke's version shows dependence upon Isaiah. In Lk 14:17 a servant (δοῦλον) is sent (ἀπέστειλεν) to announce a new time, and Grimm thinks this elicits Isa 61:1–2, where the anointed prophet, who can be identified with the suffering servant of Deutero-Isaiah, is sent (LXX: ἀπέσταλκεν) to announce the in-breaking of a new era. Further, in Lk 14:21, the householder, whose invitations have hitherto been refused, sends out his servant to bring in "the poor and maimed and blind and lame" (τοὺς πτωχοὺς καὶ ἀναπείρους καὶ τυφλοὺς καὶ χωλούς), and these last are the objects of special attention in Isa 35:3 ("Strengthen the weak hands, and make firm the feeble knees"), 5–6 ("Then the eyes of the blind [τυφλῶν] will be opened . . . the lame [χωλός] will leap like a deer"); and 61:1–2 ("to preach good news to the poor [πτωχοῖς]").

Grimm's proposal invites attention if only because Q elsewhere alludes

---

44. For targumic parallels, see Martin McNamara, *The New Testament and the Palestinian Targum to the Pentateuch* (AnBib 27; Rome: Pontifical Biblical Institute, 1966), pp. 240–45.

45. See, e.g., Marshall, *Luke*, p. 439; and Otto Betz, "Jesus and Isaiah 53," in *Jesus and the Suffering Servant: Isaiah 53 and Christian Origins* (ed. William H. Bellinger Jr. and William R. Farmer; Harrisburg, Pa.: Trinity Press International, 1998), p. 81.

46. Grimm, *Weil Ich Dich Liebe*, pp. 157–59.

47. μὴ φοβηθῆτε: LXX: 15; NT: 2. μὴ φοβεῖσθε: LXX: 18; NT: 9.

48. See the survey of opinion in Kloppenborg, *Q Parallels*, p. 166.

to Isa 35:5–6 and 61:1–2,[49] but it is beset with two insuperable difficulties. The first is that although Matthew and Luke clearly preserve variants of the same parable, one can have no confidence that it stood in Q. One can always postulate heavy editing on the part of Matthew and Luke to explain their wide divergence, but the fact remains that relatively few words are shared. The longest common phrase is εἰς τὰς ὁδούς (Mt 22:10 = Lk 14:23). One understands why Luz for one does not assign the parable to Q.[50] Second, even if one dissents from Luz and allocates Mt 22:1–10 = Lk 14:15–24 to Q, the vast differences in wording between the two accounts make it all but impossible to reconstruct Q at this point. The IQP conveys the uncertainty of the whole matter by printing the entirety of what it conjectures for Q 14:16–22 in brackets. In such a case as this, although the exegete may be willing, the textual basis is too weak.

III. Jeremiah, Ezekiel, Minor Prophets, Daniel

Q 10:21–22 // Dan 2:19–23. Werner Grimm, who finds in Q 10:21 ("I thank you Father, lord of heaven and earth, for you hid these things from the sages and learned and revealed them to babes. Yes, Father, for such seemed fitting to you") an allusion to Isa 29:14,[51] also reckons the Q text to be a reworking of Dan 2:19–23.[52] Here Daniel blesses and thanks the God of heaven, who has revealed to him the mystery (of the interpretation of Nebuchadnezzar's dream), the God of wisdom and understanding who gives wisdom to the wise and knowledge to those who have understanding, who reveals deep and hidden things. Theodotion's version shares five key words with Q 10:21–22:

Q 10:21–22	οὐρανοῦ	σοφῶν	συνετῶν	ἀπεκάλυφας	ἀπεκάλυφας
Theod. Dan 2:19–23	οὐρανοῦ	σοφία	σύνεσις	ἀπεκαλύφθη	ἀπόκρυφα
		σοφίαν	σύνεσιν	ἀποκαλύπτει	
		σοφοῖς			

Grimm contends that Q 10:21 turns Dan 2:19–23 upside down: Jesus bestows divine revelation upon those denied a divine revelation in Daniel. Given that other texts in Q rewrite scriptural texts in surprising ways,[53] the suggestion is inviting.

The difficulty, however, is that the several possible pointers to an allusion are insufficiently specific. For σοφία/σοφός and σύνεσις/συνετός

49. See pp. 104–7, 109–14.
50. Luz, *Matthäus*, vol. 3, pp. 232–33. Cf. Davies and Allison, *Matthew*, vol. 3, p. 194.
51. See the discussion on pp. 229–30, where this proposal is rejected.
52. Grimm, *Jesus und das Danielbuch, Band I*, pp. 1–69.
53. See above, pp. 192–97.

are a customary twosome,[54] and both words are joined with κρύπτω and ἀποκαλύπτω in contexts that do not depend upon Daniel 2.[55] Furthermore, there are good thematic parallels to Q 10:21, including the famous Jeremiah 31, which make the knowledge of God an eschatological gift.[56] Q 10:21 then is unlikely to allude to Daniel 2 in particular.

Q 11:42 // Mic 6:8. Regarding the language of the woe in Q 11:42, Luke's version condemns those who forsake "justice" (κρίσιν) and the "love of God" (ἀγάπην τοῦ θεοῦ). The Matthean parallel, 23:23, denounces those who abandon justice, mercy, and faith. Matthew's triad might be under the influence of Mic 6:8, where the LXX enjoins doing justice, loving mercy, and walking with God:

Matthew	justice	mercy	faith
	κρίσιν	ἔλεος	πίστιν
Micah	justice	to love mercy	to walk with the Lord God
LXX	κρίμα	ἀγαπᾶν ἔλεον	τοῦ πορεύεσθαι μετὰ κυρίου θεοῦ
MT	משפט	אהבת חסד	לכת עם־אלהיך
Targum	דין דקשוט	מרחם גמילות חסדא	להלכא בדחלתא דאלהך[57]

The parallels, at first glance, are intriguing. Unfortunately, it is impossible to say whether or not Matthew or Luke is here closer to Q.[58] Moreover, similar strings of virtues appear elsewhere:[59]

Hos 2:19	righteousness	justice	mercy	compassion
LXX	δικαιοσύνη	κρίματι	ἐλέει	οἰκτιρμοῖς
MT	צדק	משפט	חסד	רחמים
Targum	קשטא	דינא	חסדא	רחמי
Zech 7:9	just judgments	mercy	compassion	
LXX	κρίμα δίκαιον	ἔλεος	οἰκτιρμόν	
MT	משפט אמה	חסד	רחמים	
Targum	דין דקשוט דיני	חסדא	רחמי	

Moreover, LXX Exod 34:6–7 characterizes the deity as "compassionate" (οἰκτίρμων) and "merciful" (ἐλεήμων), and as one who does "justice" (δικαιοσύνην) and shows "mercy" (ἔλεος). So Q 11:42 probably does not allude to any particular text but rather reproduces a biblical topos.

---

54. See, e.g., Prov 16:21; Theod. Dan 2:21; 5:14; Bar 3:23; Ecclus 15:3; *Ps. Sol.* 17:42; 1 Cor 1:19; Col 1:9; Josephus, *Ant.* 11.57–58; *2 Bar.* 46:5; *T. Zeb.* 6:1; etc.

55. E.g., Ecclus 1:6 and Eph 1:17.

56. On this, see esp. Knowles, *Jeremiah*, pp. 213–14.

57. The targum adds "You will be modest" (הוי צניע) between "to love acts of kindness" and "walking in the fear of the Lord."

58. But one suspects Luke is, for κρίσις (Mt: 12; Mk: 0; Lk: 4) is a Matthean favorite, whereas ἀγάπη (Mt: 1; Mk: 0; Lk: 1) is not typically Lukan.

59. In addition to what follows, see Fishbane, *Biblical Interpretation*, pp. 335–50.

Q 17:37 // Hab 1:8. On the suggested connection between "Wherever the corpse is, there the eagles will be gathered together" and Hab 1:8, see p. 243.

IV. Samuel, Kings, Chronicles

Q 4:1–13 // 1 Kgs 10:1–13. Kim Paffenroth has noticed several parallels between the story of Jesus' temptation and Solomon's encounter with the queen of Sheba.[60] Both accounts tell of a hero being tested by an adversary with difficult questions or challenges, with the upshot that, in the end, the adversary, being bested, departs. Paffenroth further notes that πειράζω appears in both accounts (3 Βασ 10:1; Q 4:2, 12) and that, in some Jewish sources, the queen of Sheba, who walks onto the Q stage in 11:31, becomes equated with the Lilith, the female demon who becomes the bride of Satan in later Jewish folklore.[61] But all of this is very far from establishing an allusion. The commentators on Matthew 4 and Luke 4 have not been put in mind of the queen of Sheba, nor are there any key phrases that belong uniquely to the Q passage and 1 Kings 10; and the scriptural background of Jesus' temptation is supplied by the story of Israel's wandering in the wilderness, as the citations from Deuteronomy establish.[62] Paffenroth's parallel suffers the further disadvantage that although the queen of Sheba is a "sorceress" (γόης) in *T. Sol.* 19:3, this is not exactly the same as calling her a demon, so the date of her gaining demonic status is uncertain. In any case, Q 11:31, where her function is the same as that of the repenting Ninevites who will rise on the last day and condemn "this generation," presents her as a wholly sympathetic figure. The facts, then, discredit the notion that Q 4:1–13 was designed to recall 1 Kgs 10:1–13.

Q 7:1–10 // 1 Kgs 17:1–16; 2 Kgs 5:1–14. (i) 1 Kgs 17:1–16, where Elijah speaks with authority and provides food for a foreigner, is, according to Tom Brodie, one "component" of Lk 7:1–10, where Jesus heals a centurion's son or servant.[63] If one were to accept Brodie's argument, then Q 7:1–10 might have been designed to direct informed memories to 1 Kgs 17:1–16. The problem with supposing this, however, is that the similarities between the two texts are tenuous, as Brodie's own chart reveals:

1 Kgs 17:8–9a: the word comes to Elijah and sends him to Sarepta
Lk 7:1: when he had completed his words...he went to Capernaum

---

60. Kim Paffenroth, "The Testing of the Sage: 1 Kings 10:1–13 and Q 4:1–13 (Lk 4:1–13)," *ExpT* 107 (1996), pp. 142–43.
61. See, e.g., Tg. Job 1:15: "Lilith, the Queen of Sheba and of Margod."
62. See above, pp. 25–29.
63. Tom Brodie, "Not Q but Elijah: The Saving of the Centurion's Servant (Luke 7:1–10) as an Internalization of the Saving of the Widow and Her Child (1 Kgs 17:1–16)," *IBS* 14 (1992), pp. 54–71.

1 Kgs 17:9b: a foreign widow, whose child is about to die, will care for Israel's
  prophet
Lk 7:2, 5: a foreign officer, whose servant is about to die, loves the
  Jewish people

1 Kgs 17:10b-11, 13: requests for sustenance
Lk 7:3–4, 6a: requests for life

1 Kgs 17:18: the widow recalls her sins
Lk 7:6b–7: the officer expresses unworthiness

1 Kgs 17:14: solemn pronouncement (about God): the Lord's word assures life
Lk 7:9: solemn pronouncement (about response to God): the soldier's
  great faith

1 Kgs 17:15–16: the prophetic word fulfilled: the food lasts; the widow and
  child live
Lk 7:10: Jesus' word fulfilled: the servant is well

These analogies are not impressive, and their number is even fewer if one
assigns the double delegation of Lk 7:3–6 to Lukan redaction (a debated
issue).[64] Further, despite the common uses of πορεύομαι, εἰσ[έρχομαι], and
ποιέω,[65] the proposed parallels share no significant wording. That is, no
particular word or phrase in Q 7:1–10 serves as a trigger for reminiscence
of Elijah and 1 Kgs 17:1–16. This explains why there appears to be no
precedent for Brodie's hypothesis in the commentaries.

Brodie's case only gets off the ground in the first place because 1 Kgs
17:17–24, which is the pericope that follows 1 Kgs 17:1–16, is indeed reminiscent of the pericope that follows Lk 7:1–10, namely, Lk 7:11–17: both
recount the resurrection of a widow's son. The latter passage, however, has
no Matthean parallel, and it has hardly ever been assigned to Q.[66] On the
usual reconstructions of Q, nothing in the immediate context of Q 7:1–10
prods one to recall the Elijah cycle. In sum, then, there is no allusion to
1 Kgs 17:1–16 in Q 7:1–10.

(ii) David Friedrich Strauss, in proposing a mythological genesis for the
story of the healing of the centurion's son or servant, claimed that the synoptic incident is a "reflection" of 2 Kgs 5:1–14, Elisha's healing of Naaman's
leprosy.[67] Others have also drawn the parallel,[68] and there is no denying a

---

64. See Robert A. J. Gagnon, "Statistical Analysis and the Case of the Double Delegation
in Luke 7:3–7a," *CBQ* 55 (1993), pp. 709–31; idem, "Luke's Motives for Redaction in the
Account of the Double Delegation in Luke 7:1–10," *NovT* 36 (1994), pp. 122–45; idem, "The
Shape of Matthew's Q Text of the Centurion at Capernaum: Did It Mention Delegations?"
NTS 40 (1994), pp. 133–42; idem, *Jesus and the Capernaum Official: Tracing the History of
a Story* (forthcoming).
65. πορεύομαι: 3 Βασ 17:3, 5, 9, 10, 11, 15; Q 7:6 (?), 8. εἰσ[έρχομαι]: 3 Βασ 17:10, 12,
13; Q 7:1, 2, 6, 8. ποιέω: 3 Βασ 17:5, 12, 13, 15; Q 7:8.
66. Brodie himself calls into question the Q hypothesis, so this is for him no stumbling
block.
67. Strauss, *Jesus*, p. 471.
68. E.g., L. C. Crockett, "Luke 4:25–27 and Jewish-Gentile Relations in Luke-Acts," *JBL*

certain correspondence. In both instances, for example, a Jewish prophet heals a pagan from a distance, in the one case a centurion's son or slave, in the other a Syrian army commander; and both times it is not the ill individual who requests the healing but another (in 2 Kings the Syrian king writes a letter on Naaman's behalf). We cannot doubt, moreover, that the legends of Elisha influenced other stories in the synoptic tradition (see above on Q 9:59–62[69] and recall the resemblances between 2 Kgs 4:42–44, which immediately precedes 2 Kgs 5:1–14, and the feeding miracles). Nevertheless, Q 7:1–10 and 2 Kgs 5:1–4 share no suggestive vocabulary, the differences between the two stories are considerable,[70] and Q 7:1–10 is closer in many respects to some other tales of long-distance healing.[71] It is unlikely, then, that Q 7:1–10 was crafted as an allusion to 2 Kgs 5:1–14.

Q 12:7 // 1 Sam 14:45; 2 Sam 14:11; 1 Kgs 1:52. Jesus affirms that all "the hairs of your head are all counted." Most commentators, who wrongly think that this saying is about God's parental care, cite for comparison 1 Sam 14:45 ("As the Lord lives, not one hair of his head shall fall to the ground; for he has worked with God today"); 2 Sam 14:11 ("As the Lord lives, not one hair of your son shall fall to the ground"); and 1 Kgs 1:52 ("If he proves to be a worthy man, not one of his hairs shall fall to the ground; but if wickedness is found in him, he shall die") as well as a couple of verses from the New Testament[72] and *b. B. Bat.* 16a.[73] But in all of these sayings mention is made of a single hair falling to the ground or perishing. The Q saying, on the other hand, is not about one hair but about all the hairs (plural) of one's head, and nothing is said about those hairs falling or perishing,

---

88 (1969), p. 182; D. A. S. Ravens, "The Setting of Luke's Account of the Anointing: Luke 7.2–8.3," *NTS* 34 (1988), pp. 286–87.

69. Pp. 142–45.

70. In commenting on Lk 7:1–10 and 2 Kings 5, Gagnon, "Luke's Motives," p. 128, n. 16, writes: "To be sure, we hear of various 'sendings' in the Naaman episode but at no time does the one requesting the healing ever send any intermediaries to the healer. Naaman is indeed a respected officer but his reputation arises from his pagan military exploits, not from benefactions to the Jews. Naaman's bringing of great treasures to Elisha, unlike the centurion's synagogue-building activity, is a *quid pro quo* act. The role played by the Jewish girl in the Naaman episode bears little resemblance to that of the Jewish elders in the centurion pericope (the former commends the Jewish healer, the latter commends the Gentile suppliant). Naaman is humbled by Elisha's insistence that he baptize himself in the tiny Jordan River and be healed at a distance; the centurion amazes Jesus with his humility and his faith for a distance healing. Naaman converts following the demonstration of the power of Elisha's God; the centurion's faith precedes Jesus' demonstration of power."

71. See Uwe Wegner, *Der Hauptmann von Kafarnaum (Mt 7,28a; 8,5–10.13 par Lk 7,1–10): Ein Beitrag zur Q-Forschung* (WUNT 2/14; Tübingen: Mohr Siebeck, 1985), pp. 344–61, discussing, in addition to 2 Kings 5, Mk 7:24–30; Lk 17:12–19; *b. Ber.* 34b; *b. B. Qam.* 50a; the Epidauros inscription in Dittenberger, *SIG* 3:318; and Philostratus, *VA* 3.38.

72. Lk 21:18: "But not a hair of your head will perish." Acts 27:34: "None of you will lose a hair from your heads."

73. "I have created many hairs in man, and for every hair I have created a separate groove, so that two should not suck from the same groove, for if two were to suck from the same groove they would impair the sight of a man. I do not confuse one groove with another." See Keener, *Matthew*, p. 327.

only that they are numbered. Moreover, the Hebrew Bible passages cited promise deliverance from physical evil, but in Q 12:7 the disciples do not escape danger but are rather killed. Certainly the point about the sparrow is not that it will not fall to the ground[74] but rather that when it does, the event will somehow be within God's will. How, then, can Q 12:7 have the same import as a proverb that promises rescue from trouble?

Q 12:7 recalls not 1 Sam 14:45 and its parallels but those texts, such as Ps 40:12,[75] where hairs, stars, grass, raindrops, and the sands of the sea are expressions of innumerableness.[76] The point is not God's providential care but the contrast between human ignorance and divine omniscience,[77] which is here a strategy for dealing with the problem of evil (as in Job and some of the apocalyptic literature). There is no intertextual relationship with any of the verses so often cited.

Q 12:8–9 // 1 Sam 2:30. One occasionally runs across the suggestion that Q 12:8–9 is a rewriting of 1 Sam 2:30:[78]

a	those who honor me
b	I (God) will honor
c	those who despise me
d	shall be treated with contempt

There is no doubt that the structural parallel is striking. But there are several units from early Christian literature that feature correlations between human activity in the apodosis and future divine activity in the protasis. Three examples:

Mt 6:14–15

a	if you forgive sins
b	God will forgive you
c	if you do not forgive sins
d	God will not forgive you

Mk 4:24–25

a	to the one who has
b	will more be given
c	to the one who has not
d	what that one has will be taken away

---

74. Only Matthew refers to falling to the earth, but in this he is probably closer to Q; see Davies and Allison, *Matthew*, vol. 2, p. 208 (conjecturing as original: "and one of them will not fall without God"); and Jeremias, *Sprache*; pp. 212–13.

75. "Evils have encompassed me without number; my iniquities have overtaken me, until I cannot see; they are more than the hairs of my head, and my heart fails me."

76. Full documentation in Allison, *Jesus Tradition in Q*, pp. 168–75. Cf. Zeller, *Mahnsprüche*, p. 100.

77. ἠρίθμηνται is, as the commentators have always recognized, a divine passive: "are numbered [by God]."

78. See, e.g., Gundry, *Old Testament*, pp. 77–78.

Rev 22:18–19
  a   to the one who adds to the prophecies of the book
  b   God will add its plagues
  c   to the one who takes away from the prophecies of the book
  d   God will take away that person's share in the tree of life

These are members of what Ernst Käsemann called "sentences of holy law,"[79] and unless one is prepared to urge that all of them depend upon 1 Sam 2:30, it is difficult to see why Q 12:8–9 should be any different.

V. Psalms

Q 4:10–11 // Ps 2:8. The occasional suggestion that Q 4:5–7 — the promise that the devil can give Jesus "all the kingdoms of the world" — adverts ironically to Ps 2:8 ("Ask of me, and I will make the nations your heritage, and the ends of the earth your possession") fails to persuade.[80] The verbal links are minimal, there are no other allusions in the temptation narrative to Psalm 2, which otherwise plays no role in Q, and the promise of universal sovereignty appears elsewhere in the Hebrew Bible, so it is not uniquely associated with Ps 2:8 in particular (see, e.g., Dan 7:14). As argued in chapter 3, a more likely background for Q 4:5–7 is Moses' vision in Deuteronomy 32 of all the land and the traditions that grew up around that vision.[81]

Q 12:42 // Ps 104:27. In Mt 24:45 the question, "Who then is the faithful and wise servant whom the lord put over his household to give them food at the proper time?" is a clear allusion to LXX Ps 103:27 (cf. 144:15),[82] as so many commentators recognize:[83]

Lk 12:42	διδόναι ἐν καιρῷ τὸ σιτομέτριον
Mt 24:45	δοῦναι αὐτοῖς τὴν τροφὴν ἐν καιρῷ
LXX Ps 103:27	δοῦναι τὴν τροφὴν αὐτοῖς εὔκαιρον[84]

In three respects Matthew is closer than Luke to the line from the Psalm — (a) in having the second aorist infinitive "to give" (δοῦναι), (b) in using τὴν τροφήν ("food") rather than τὸ σιτομέτριον ("ration"), and (c) in employing the dative plural personal pronoun αὐτοῖς ("to them"). Since, however,

---

79. Ernst Käsemann, "Sentences of Holy Law in the New Testament," in *New Testament Questions of Today* (Philadelphia: Fortress, 1969), pp. 66–81. See further Klaus Berger, "Zu den sogenannten Sätzen heiligen Rechts," *NTS* 17 (1970), pp. 10–40.

80. Catchpole, *Quest for Q*, p. 230, speaks of "the hint of Ps 2:8 in Q 4:6/Matt 4:9, picking up the echo of Ps 2:7 in Q 3:22." Both "hint" and "echo" are too generous, especially as we do not know that Mt 3:17 = Lk 3:22 stood in Q (see Mk 1:11).

81. See further above, pp. 27–28.

82. Cf. the echo in 4QPs[f] 9:10: בעתה [ותתן] פריה: "will give its fruit in its season."

83. Note, e.g., Albertus Magnus, *Super Mt cap. XV–XXVIII* ad loc. (Opera Omnia 21/2, ed. B. Schmidt, p. 117); Schlatter, *Matthäus*, p. 717; Gundry, *Old Testament*, p. 89.

84. MT: לתת אכלם בעתו. Targum: למיהן מזונהון בזימניה.

Luke's σιτομέτριον is a New Testament *hapax legomenon* and so not obviously Lukan, and since τροφή[85] is Matthean redaction in 3:4 diff. Mk 1:6 and 10:10 diff. Lk 10:7, it seems prudent to assign the scriptural language in Mt 24:45 not to Q but to Matthew.

Q 15:4–5 // Ps 119:176. Mt 18:12–14 asks, "If one has a hundred sheep (πρόβατα) and one of them has gone astray (πλανηθῇ), does he not leave the ninety-nine and go in search (ζητεῖ) of the one that went astray (πλανώμενον)?" Lk 15:4 similarly asks, "Which one of you, having a hundred sheep (πρόβατα), and one of them has gone astray (ἀπολέσας), does not leave the ninety-nine in the wilderness and go after the one which is lost (ἀπολωλός), until he finds it?" Commentators of both Matthew and Luke are sometimes reminded of Ps 119:176: "I have gone astray like a lost sheep; seek out your servant, for I do not forget your commandments."[86] The LXX version shares certain key words with both Matthew and Luke

LXX Ps 118:176	ἐπλανήθην	πρόβατον	ἀπολωλός	ζήτησον
Mt 18:12–13	πλανηθῇ	πρόβατα		ζητεῖ
	πλανώμενον			
	πεπλανημένοις			
Lk 15:4–6		πρόβατα	ἀπολέσας	
			ἀπολωλός	

Matthew himself, however, may have introduced both πλανέω and ζητέω;[87] and "lost" (ἀπόλλυμι) + "sheep" (πρόβατον), which also appears in Jer 50:6 ("My people have become lost sheep"; LXX 27:6: πρόβατα ἀπολωλότα ἐγενήθη ὁ λαός), is surely not enough to constitute an allusion (cf. Mt 10:6; 15:24). Furthermore, Matthew was perhaps reminded not of Ps 119:176 but of the verse just cited, Jer 50:6. In this last the shepherds have led the sheep astray "on the mountains (ἐπὶ τὰ ὄρη); from mountain (ὄρους) to hill they have gone astray (ἀπεπλάνησαν)," whereas in Mt 18:12–13 the ninety-nine are left "on the mountains" (ἐπὶ τὰ ὄρη),[88] and πλάνεω ("go astray") appears three times: πλανηθῇ, πλανώμενον, πεπλανημένοις.

VI. Wisdom Literature

Q 6:45 // Prov 12:14. John Kloppenborg's synopsis of Q cites LXX Prov 12:14 ("From the fruits [καρπῶν] of his mouth [στόματος] will the soul of a man [ἀνδρός] be filled with good [ἀγαθῶν], and the reward of his lips will be given him") as a parallel to Q 6:43–45: "There is no sound tree

---

85. Mt: 4; Mk: 0; Lk: 1.
86. E.ḡ., Albertus Magnus, *Super Mt cap. XV–XXVIII* ad loc (Opera Omnia 21/1, ed. B. Schmidt, p. 480); and Shires, *Old Testament*, p. 147.
87. See Davies and Allison, *Matthew*, vol. 2, pp. 773–74.
88. Luke has "in the desert," ἐν τῇ ἐρήμῳ.

that bears bad fruit (καρπόν), nor again an unsound tree that bears good fruit (καρπόν). For by its fruit (καρποῦ) the tree is known. . . . The good person (ἀγαθὸς ἄνθρωπος) from the good (ἀγαθοῦ) treasure brings forth good things (ἀγαθά), but the evil one from the evil (treasure) brings forth evil. For from an abundance of the heart the mouth (στόμα) speaks."[89] There is a coincidence of theme as well as some sharing of words:

| Q 6:45 | καρπόν/οῦ | στόμα | ἄνθρωπος | ἀγαθοῦ/ά |
| LXX Prov 12:14 | καρπῶν | στόματος | ἀνδρός | ἀγαθοῦ/ά |

But nothing about Prov 12:14 is particularly memorable,[90] and the metaphorical use of "fruit" for speech is found in too many other texts besides these for one to find here a deliberate allusion as opposed to a biblical topos.[91] It is understandable that there is no tradition in the commentaries of citing Prov 12:14 to illustrate Mt 12:35 = Lk 6:45 or of citing Mt 12:35 = Lk 6:45 to illustrate Prov 12:14.[92]

Q 7:32 // Ecclus 3:4. Modern commentators on Mt 11:17 = Lk 7:32 ("We fluted to you and you did not dance, we wailed and you did not mourn") often cite Ecclus 7:34 ("Do not avoid those who weep, but mourn with those who mourn"), a verse that Paul may allude to in Rom 12:15 ("Rejoice with those who rejoice, weep with those who weep").[93] But Q 7:32 is no more a direct allusion to this than it is to Eccles 3:4 ("a time to mourn, and a time to dance"). A better guess is that both Q and Sirach are drawing upon a Greek proverb. We find the following in Herodotus 1.141:

> The Ionians and Aeolians immediately after the Persian conquest of Lydia sent representatives to Cyrus at Sardis, to try to obtain from him the same terms as they had under Croesus, their former master. Cyrus replied to their request by the story of the fluteplayer who saw some fish in the sea and played his flute to them in the hope that they would come ashore. When they refused to do so, he took a net, netted a large catch, and hauled them in. Seeing the fish jumping about, he said to them: "It is too late to dance now: you might have danced to my music, but you would not."

With this one may compare Aesop, *Fab.* 27 (ed. Halm, p. 13): A fisherman, upon bringing his catch to shore, says to the fish: "O you most wicked creatures! When I was playing the flute [to attract you], you did not dance; but now, when I cease [and have you in the net], you do it."

---

89. Kloppenborg, *Q Parallels*, p. 43.

90. Bradley H. McLean, *Citations and Allusions to Jewish Scripture in Jewish and Christian Writings through 180 C.E.* (Lewiston, N.Y./Queenston/Lampeter: Edwin Mellen, 1992), has no entry for this verse.

91. Note Prov 13:2; 18:20; Isa 57:18; Ecclus 27:6; Mt 12:33; Heb 13:15; Jas 3:10–12.

92. Albertus Magnus, *Super Mt cap. I–XIV* ad 12:35 (Opera Omnia 21/1, ed. B. Schmidt, p. 384), instead cites Prov 15:2 and 18:4.

93. Cf. Gnilka, *Matthäusevangelium*, vol. 1, p. 423.

Q 11:3 // Prov 30:8. For Robert Gundry, the petition for bread in the Lord's Prayer, understood as a request for required daily sustenance, is directly related to Prov 30:8, "Feed me the food that I need:"[94]

Q 11:3 τὸν ἄρτον ἡμῶν τὸν ἐπιούσιον δίδου ἡμῖν σήμερον
"Give us each day our daily bread."

LXX Prov 30:8 σύνταξον δέ μοι τὰ δέοντα καὶ τὰ αὐτάρκη
"Appoint for me the things needful and sufficient."

MT Prov 30:8 הטריפני לחם חקי
"Feed me the food that I need."

Tg. Prov 30:8 זונני לחמא מסתי
"Feed me the food that I need."

Rick Byargeon, agreeing with Gundry, observes that Prov 30:8 belongs to a prayer and further that the prayer asks for God's name not to be profaned (cf. Q 11:2); so, according to Byargeon, the Lord's Prayer depends directly upon Prov 30:7–9.[95] We have seen, however, that Exodus 16 provides a convincing background for Q 11:3, where ἐπιούσιος probably means "for the coming day," not "bread needful for existence."[96] Moreover, beyond the single word "bread" in the MT (לחם) and the targum (לחמא), there are no verbal links between the two texts: the relevant clause in LXX Prov 30:8 shares not a single word with Q 11:3.[97]

Q 11:9–13 // Wisdom traditions. The extravagance of the promise in these verses is underlined by repetition:

ask (αἰτεῖτε)	→	and it will be given (δοθήσεται) you
seek (ζητεῖτε)	→	and you will find (εὑρήσετε)
knock (κρούετε)	→	and it will be opened (ἀνοιγήσεται) to you

The language is repeated in the triadic justification that follows:

everyone who asks (αἰτῶν)	→	receives (λαμβάνει)
the one seeking (ζητῶν)	→	finds (εὑρίσκει)
to the one knocking (κρούοντι)	→	it will be opened (ἀνοιγήσεται)

---

94. Gundry, *Old Testament*, p. 75. Cf. Gill, *Commentary*, vol. 3, p. 592; Charles Bridge, *An Exposition of the Book of Proverbs* (New York: Robert Carter & Brothers, 1831), p. 508; France, *Jesus and the Old Testament*, pp. 244–45. Sometimes the parallel is noted only to be dismissed; so, e.g., W. J. Deane, S. T. Taylor-Taswell, and W. F. Adeney, *Proverbs* (Pulpit Commentary; New York/London: Funk & Wagnalls, n.d.), p. 573.

95. Rick W. Byargeon, "Echoes of Wisdom in the Lord's Prayer (Matt 6:9–13)," *JETS* 41 (1998), pp. 353–65. Cf. already Scott, *Holy Bible*, vol. 3, ad Prov 30:7–9: "There is a remarkable coincidence between this prayer and several clauses of the Lord's Prayer."

96. See Davies and Allison, *Matthew*, vol. 1, pp. 607–9.

97. התן and δῶς (cf. Q's δίδου) do, however, occur in the earlier part of Prov 30:8: "Give me neither wealth nor poverty."

Although Q 11:9–13 does not allude to any particular text, the language has reminded many of certain Wisdom texts:

Prov 1:28: "They will seek (LXX: ζητήσουσιν) me diligently but will not find (LXX: εὑρήσουσιν) me."[98]

Prov 8:17: "I [wisdom] love those who love me, and those who seek (LXX: ζητοῦντες) me diligently find (LXX: εὑρήσουσιν) me."

Wisd 6:12: Wisdom "is found (εὑρίσκεται) by those who seek (ζητούντων) her."

It is far from obvious, however, that Q 11:9–13 has anything to do with seeking and finding wisdom. Commentators on Matthew and Luke have rather consistently taken the passage in its Matthean and Lukan contexts to be about prayer; and in Q our text immediately followed the Lord's Prayer. Q 11:9–13 accordingly invites the same reading as Mt 7:7–11 and Lk 11:9–13 (cf. also Jn 16:23–24). So while the comparable Wisdom texts make the language of Q 11:9–13 familiar, they do nothing more. In fact, someone steeped in the Scriptures might just as well think of 2 Sam 21:1 or Ps 27:7–8. In the former we read that David "sought (LXX: ἐζήτησεν) the face of the Lord," which means he prayed, and the same idiom is used in the same way in the latter (LXX: ἐζήτησεν, ζητήσω). Even closer is Jer 29(36):12–13: "Then when you call upon me and come and pray to me, I will hear you. When you search (LXX: ἐκζητήσατε) for me, you will find (LXX: εὑρήσετε) me, if you seek (LXX: ζητήσετε) me with all your heart, I will let you find me, says the Lord." Clearly the language of seeking and finding belonged as much to prayer as to wisdom. When one adds that other texts use "ask" and "give" or "knock" and "open" with reference to human petition and divine response, it would seem that Q 11:9–12 is the conventional language of prayer, found in the Bible and elsewhere.[99]

Q 11:42 // Eccles 7:18. The occasionally noticed parallel between Eccles 7:18 ("It is good that you should take hold of the one, without letting go of the other") and the end of Q 11:42 ("these things you should have done without neglecting the others")[100] is of little consequence. The parallel is stronger in English than in Greek, where there is only one insignificant verbal link (Q: ταῦτα; Ecclesiastes: τούτῳ — τούτου).

Q 12:24 // Job 38:41. For the argument that Q 12:24 may use Ps 147:9 but not Job 38:41, see pp. 164–65.

---

98. Cf. Eccles 7:23–29, which is likewise about seeking and not finding.

99. For αἰτέω of prayer, see LXX 1 Βασ 1:17, 27; 2 Chr 1:11–12; Ps 21:4; and Philo, *Migr. Abr.* 121 — all with δίδωμι. For knocking, see *b. Meg.* 12b ("he knocked at the gates of mercy and they were opened to him"). Grimm, *Weil Ich Dich Liebe*, pp. 152–54, calls attention to Isa 55:6 ("Seek the Lord while he may be found") and 65:1 ("I was ready to be sought by those who did not ask for me; I was ready to be found by those who did not seek me").

100. See, e.g., Gnilka, *Matthäusevangelium*, vol. 2, p. 289.

Q 17:4 // Prov 24:16. Theodor Zahn wondered whether Lk 17:4, which refers to someone sinning seven times a day, might not have in view Prov 24:16 ("for though they [the righteous] fall seven [LXX: ἑπτάκι] times, they will rise again"); and Bengel observed that "many" thought this.[101] But Bengel went on to reject the proposed allusion. The verbal overlap is minimal ("seven"), and Prov 24:16 was probably never known well enough to be recalled without additional markers.

Q 17:37 // Job 9:26; 15:23; 39:27–30. The enigmatic prophecy "Wherever the corpse is, there the eagles will be gathered together" has been illustrated with several texts:

Job 9:26: "like an eagle swooping on the prey"

LXX Job 15:23: "He [the tyrant] is cut down as food for vultures (γυψίν), and he knows in himself that he will remain a carcass (πτῶμα), and the dark day will terrify him."

Job 39:27–30: "Is it at your command that the eagle mounts up and makes his nest on high? . . . and where the slain are, there is he."[102]

Hab 1:8: "They fly like an eagle swift to devour."

The closest of these is Job 39:30. One can hardly speak, however, of a deliberate allusion to that verse. Not only is the overlap in vocabulary minimal (ἀετοί/ός), but it is unclear how a knowledge of Job 39:30 might illuminate the enigmatic Q 17:37. Beyond that, the closest parallels to Q 17:37 appear not in the Bible but outside it: Cornutus, *Nat. deorum* 21 ("the birds [vultures] . . . gather together wherever there are [ὅπου ποτ' ἄ...ῇ] many corpses [πτώματα] slain in war"); Aelianus, *Hist. anim.* 2.46; Lucian, *Navig.* 1; Seneca, *Ep.* 95.43 ("voltur est, cadaver expectat"); Martial 6.62.4 ("cuius vulturis hoc erit cadaver"); Lucan 6.550–51. Q 17:37 contains a secular proverb, not a biblical allusion. Both the form ("where . . . there") and the content of Q 17:37 were conventional in the Greco-Roman world.[103]

---

101. Zahn, *Lukas*, p. 592, n. 30; Bengel, *Gnomon*, ad loc. Cf. Paschasius Radbertus, *Exp. Mt libri XII (V–VIII)* ad Mt 18:21–22 (CCCM 56A, ed. B. Paulus, p. 898); Albertus Magnus, *Super Mt cap. XV–XXVIII* ad Mt 18:21–22 (Opera Omnia 21/1, ed. B. Schmidt, p. 485).

102. So MT. The LXX changes the beginning of this to: "At your command the eagle mounts up, and the vulture (γύψ) lodges sitting on its brood." The alteration makes it unclear whether the final clause refers to eagle or vulture.

103. A. Ehrhardt, *The Framework of the New Testament Stories* (Manchester: University of Manchester Press, 1964), pp. 53–58.

Modern Works Cited

Achtemeier, Paul J., "*Omne verbum sonat:* The New Testament and the Oral Environment of Late Western Antiquity," *JBL* 109 (1990), pp. 3–27.

———, *1 Peter: A Commentary on First Peter* (Hermeneia; Minneapolis: Fortress, 1996).

Ainsworth, Henry, *Annotations on the Pentateuch*, vol. 1 (Edinburgh: Blackie & Sons, 1843).

Alford, Henry, *The Greek Testament*, vol. 1, *The Four Gospels* (Chicago: Moody, 1958).

Allison, Dale C., Jr., "Anticipating the Passion: The Literary Reach of Matthew 26:47–27:56," *CBQ* 56 (1994), pp. 701–14.

———, "Behind the Temptations of Jesus: Q 4:1–13 and Mark 1:12–13," in *Authenticating the Deeds of Jesus* (ed. Bruce Chilton and Craig A. Evans; NTTS 28/2; Leiden: Brill, 1999), pp. 195–213.

———, *The End of the Ages Has Come: An Early Interpretation of the Death and Resurrection of Jesus* (Philadelphia: Fortress, 1985).

———, *Jesus of Nazareth: Millenarian Prophet* (Minneapolis: Fortress, 1999).

———, *The Jesus Tradition in Q* (Harrisburg, Pa.: Trinity Press International, 1997).

———, "Mark 12:28–31 and the Decalogue," in *The Gospels and the Scriptures of Israel* (ed. Craig A. Evans and W. R. Stegner; JSNTSS 104/Studies in Scripture in Early Judaism and Christianity 3; Sheffield: JSOT Press, 1994), pp. 270–78.

———, *The New Moses: A Matthean Typology* (Minneapolis: Fortress, 1993).

———, "Q 12:51–53 and Mk 9:11–13 and the Messianic Woes," in *Authenticating the Words of Jesus* (ed. B. Chilton and C. A. Evans; NTTS 28/1; Leiden: Brill, 1999), pp. 289–310.

Alter, Robert, *The World of Biblical Literature* (New York: HarperCollins, 1992).

Anderson, Bernard W., "Exodus Typology in Second Isaiah," in *Israel's Prophetic Heritage: Essays in Honor of James Muilenburg* (ed. Bernard W. Anderson and Walter Harrelson; New York: Harper & Row, 1962), pp. 177–95.

Anderson, Gary A., "The Exaltation of Adam and the Fall of Satan," *Journal of Jewish Thought and Philosophy* 6 (1997), pp. 105–34.

Anderson, Sherwood, "The Egg," in *Certain Things Last: The Selected Short Stories of Sherwood Anderson* (ed. Charles E. Modlin; New York: Four Walls Eight Windows, 1992), pp. 26–38.

Andrews, Lancelot, *The Private Devotions of Lancelot Andrews* (New York: Meridian, 1961).

Arbesmann, R., "The 'Daemonium Meridianum' and Greek and Latin Patristic Exegesis," *Traditio* 14 (1958), pp. 17–31.

Archer, Gleason L., and Gregory C. Chirichigno, *Old Testament Quotations in the New Testament* (Chicago: Moody, 1983).

Bahr, Gordon J., "The Use of the Lord's Prayer in the Primitive Church," *JBL* 84 (1965), pp. 153–59.

Bailey, Kenneth E., "Informal Controlled Oral Tradition and the Synoptic Gospels," *Asian JT* 5 (1991), pp. 35–54.

Barnett, P. W., "The Jewish Sign Prophets — A.D. 40–70: Their Intention and Origin," *NTS* 27 (1981), pp. 679–97.

Barrett, C. K., *Jesus and the Gospel Tradition* (Philadelphia: Fortress, 1968).

Barton, John, *Oracles of God: Perceptions of Ancient Prophecy in Israel after the Exile* (New York/Oxford: Oxford University Press, 1986).

Bauckham, Richard, "The Parable of the Vine: Rediscovering a Lost Parable of Jesus," *NTS* 33 (1987), pp. 84–101.

———, "Synoptic Parousia Parables and the Apocalypse," *NTS* 23 (1977), pp. 162–76.

Baumann, Eberhard, "Struktur-Untersuchungen im Psalter II," *ZAW* 62 (1950), pp. 115–52.

Beale, Gregory K., "Solecisms in the Apocalypse as Signals for the Presence of Old Testament Allusions: A Selective Analysis of Revelation 1–22," in *Early Christian Interpretation of the Scriptures of Israel: Investigations and Proposals* (ed. Craig A. Evans and James A. Sanders; JSNTSS 148; Sheffield: Sheffield Academic Press, 1997), pp. 421–46.

———, *The Use of Daniel in Jewish Apocalyptic Literature and in the Revelation of St. John* (Lanham, Md.: University Press of America, 1984).

Beasley-Murray, G. R., *Jesus and the Kingdom of God* (Grand Rapids: Eerdmans, 1986).

Beckwith, Roger, *The Old Testament Canon of the New Testament* (Grand Rapids: Eerdmans, 1985).

Beentjes, P. C., "Discovering a New Path of Intertextuality: Inverted Quotations and Their Dynamics," in *Literary Structure and Rhetorical Strategies in the Hebrew Bible* (ed. L. J. de Regt, J. de Waard, and J. P. Fokkelman; Assen: Van Gorcum, 1996), pp. 31–50.

Bengel, J. A., *Gnomon of the New Testament*, vol. 1 (Philadelphia: Perkinpine & Higgins, 1864).

Ben-Porat, Ziva, "The Poetics of Literary Allusion," *PTL: A Journal for Descriptive Poetics and Theory of Literature* 1 (1976), pp. 105–28.

Berger, Klaus, "Zu den sogenannten Sätzen heiligen Rechts," *NTS* 17 (1970), pp. 10–40.

Bernays, Jacob, *Über das phokylideische Gedicht: Ein Beitrag zur hellenistischen Litteratur* (Berlin: Hertz, 1856).

Betz, Hans Dieter, *The Sermon on the Mount: A Commentary on the Sermon on the Mount, Including the Sermon on the Plain (Matthew 5:3–7:27 and Luke 6:20–49)* (Hermeneia; Minneapolis: Fortress, 1995).

Betz, Otto, "Jesus and Isaiah 53," in *Jesus and the Suffering Servant: Isaiah 53 and Christian Origins* (ed. William H. Bellinger Jr. and William R. Farmer; Harrisburg, Pa.: Trinity Press International, 1998), pp. 70–87.

Beza, Theodore, *Annotationes maiores in Novum Testamentum* (n.p.: Henri Estienne, 1594).

Bilde, Per, "Josephus and Jewish Apocalypticism," in *Understanding Josephus: Seven Perspectives* (ed. Steve Mason; JSPSS 32; Sheffield: Sheffield Academic Press, 1998), pp. 35–61.

Black, Matthew, *An Aramaic Approach to the Gospels and Acts* (3d ed.; Oxford: Clarendon, 1967).

Blank, Sheldon, "The Death of Zechariah in Rabbinic Literature," *HUCA* 13 (1938), pp. 327–46.

Bloom, Harold, *The Anxiety of Influence* (New York: Oxford University Press, 1973).

Bloomfield, S. T., *Recensio Synoptica: Annotationis Sacrae* (London: C. & J. Rivington, 1826).

Bock, Darrell L., *Luke*, vol. 2, *9:51–24:53* (Grand Rapids: Baker, 1996).

Bockmuehl, Markus, " 'Let the Dead Bury Their Dead' (Matt. 8:22/Luke 9:60): Jesus and the Halakah," *JTS* 49 (1998), pp. 553–81.

Boismard, Marie-Émile, *Moses or Jesus: An Essay in Johannine Christology* (Louvain/Minneapolis: Peeters/Fortress, 1993).

Bolin, Thomas M., *Freedom beyond Forgiveness: The Book of Jonah Re-Examined* (JSOTSS 236; Copenhagen International Seminar 3; Sheffield: Sheffield Academic Press, 1997).

Bonar, Andrew A., *Christ and His Church in the Book of Psalms* (London: James Nisbet & Co., 1859).

Booth, Wayne C., *Critical Understanding: The Powers and Limits of Pluralism* (Chicago: University of Chicago Press, 1979).

Borg, Marcus, *Conflict, Holiness, and Politics in the Teaching of Jesus* (Lewistown, N.Y.: Edwin Mellen, 1984).

Boring, M. Eugene, "A Proposed Reconstruction of Q 13:28–29," in *Society of Biblical Literature 1989 Seminar Papers* (ed. David J. Lull; Atlanta: Scholars Press, 1995), pp. 1–22.

Bosold, Iris, *Pazifismus und prophetische Provokation: Das Grußverbot Lk 10,4b und sein historischer Kontext* (SBS 90; Stuttgart: Katholisches Bibelwerk, 1978).

Bovon, François, *Das Evangelium nach Lukas* (2 vols.; EKKNT 3; Zurich and Düsseldorf/Neukirchen-Vluyn: Benziger/Neukirchener, 1989, 1996).

Boyarin, Daniel, *Intertextuality and the Reading of Midrash* (Bloomington: Indiana University Press, 1990).

Branscomb, B. H., *Jesus and the Law of Moses* (New York: Richard R. Smith, 1930).

Brawley, Robert L., *Text to Text Pours Forth Speech: Voices of Scripture in Luke-Acts* (Bloomington/Indianapolis: Indiana University Press, 1995).

Brehm, H. Alan, "Vindicating the Rejected One: Stephen's Speech as a Critique of the Jewish Leaders," in *Early Christian Interpretation of the Scriptures of Israel: Investigations and Proposals* (ed. Craig A. Evans and James A. Sanders; JSNTSS 148; Sheffield: Sheffield Academic Press, 1997), pp. 266–99.

Bridge, Charles, *An Exposition of the Book of Proverbs* (New York: Robert Carter & Brothers, 1831).

Brin, Gershon, "Divorce at Qumran," in *Legal Texts and Issues: Proceedings of the Second Meeting of the International Organization for Qumran Studies, Cambridge 1995* (ed. Moshe Bernstein, Florentino García Martínez, and John Kampen; STDS 23; Leiden/New York/Cologne: Brill, 1997), pp. 231–49.

Brodie, Tom, "Not Q but Elijah: The Saving of the Centurion's Servant (Luke 7:1–10) as an Internalization of the Saving of the Widow and Her Child (1 Kgs 17:1–16)," *IBS* 14 (1992), pp. 54–71.

Brooke, George J., "The Deuteronomic Character of 4Q 252," in *Pursuing the Text: Studies in Honour of Ben Zion Wacholder on the Occasion of His Seventieth Birthday* (ed. John C. Reeves and John Kampen; JSNTSS 184; Sheffield: Sheffield Academic Press, 1994), pp. 121–35.

Brown, Raymond E., *The Gospel according to John* (2 vols.; AB 29; Garden City, N.Y.: Doubleday, 1966).

———, "The Pater Noster as an Eschatological Prayer," in *New Testament Essays* (Garden City, N.Y.: Doubleday, 1968), pp. 275–320.

Brownlee, W. H., *The Midrash Pesher of Habakkuk* (SBLMS 24; Missoula, Mont.: Scholars Press, 1979).

Bucer, Martin, *In sacra quatuor evangelia* (Strasbourg: Roberti Stephani, 1553).

Buchan, John, *Greenmantle* (Oxford/New York: Oxford University Press, 1993).

Buchanan, George Wesley, *The Gospel of Matthew* (2 vols.; Mellen Biblical Commentary; Lewiston, N.Y.: Edwin Mellen, 1996).

Büchner, D. L., "Micah 7:6 in the Ancient Old Testament Versions," *Journal of Northwest Semitic Languages* 19 (1993), pp. 159–68.

Bultmann, Rudolf, *The History of the Synoptic Tradition* (rev. ed.; New York: Harper & Row, 1976).

Burrelli, Robert J., "A Study of Psalm 91 with Special Reference to the Theory That It Was Intended as a Protection against Demons and Magic" (Ph.D. diss., University of Cambridge, 1993).

Burrows, Millar, *The Dead Sea Scrolls of St. Mark's Monastery* (2 vols.; New Haven: ASOR, 1950–51).

Butler, J. Glentworth, *The Bible-Work. The Old Testament*, vol. 7, *1 Kings XII–XXII, 2 Kings, 2 Chronicles X–XXXVI, Ezra, Nehemiah, Esther, Isaiah, Four Chapters, Jeremiah, Eighteen Chapters* (New York: Butler Bible-Work, 1894).

———, *The Bible-Work. The Old Testament*, vol. 8, *Isaiah, Jeremiah, Lamentations* (New York: Butler Bible-Work, 1894).

Byargeon, Rick W. "Echoes of Wisdom in the Lord's Prayer (Matt 6:9–13)," *JETS* 41 (1998), pp. 353–65.

Caird, George B., *The Revelation of St. John the Divine* (BNTC; 2d. ed.; London: A. & C. Black, 1984).

Calmet, Augustin, *Commentarium literale in omnes ac singulos tum Veteris cum Novi Testamenti libros* (7 vols.; n.p.: Augustae Vindelicorum & Graecii, 1734–35).

Calvin, John, *A Harmony of the Gospels Matthew, Mark, and Luke* (3 vols.; ed. David W. Torrance and T. F. Torrance; Grand Rapids: Eerdmans, 1972).

Campbell, Jonathan G., *The Use of Scripture in the Damascus Document 1–8, 19–20* (BZAW 228; Berlin/New York: de Gruyter, 1995).

Caquot, A., "Le Psaume XCI," *Semitica* 8 (1958), pp. 21–37.

Caragounis, Chrys C., *The Son of Man: Vision and Interpretation* (WUNT 2/38; Tübingen: Mohr Siebeck, 1986).

Carlston, Charles E., and D. Norlan, "Once More — Statistics and Q," *HTR* 64 (1971), pp. 59–78.

Carmignac, Jean, *Recherches sur le "Notre Père"* (Paris: Letouzey & Ané, 1969).

Carson, D. A., and H. G. M. Williamson, eds., *It Is Written: Scripture Citing Scripture* (Cambridge: Cambridge University Press, 1988).

Casale, Cesare Marcheselli, " 'Andate e annunciate a Giovanni ciò che udite e vedet' (Mt. 11,4; Lc. 7,22)," in *Testimonium Christi: Scritti in onore di Jacques Dupont* (Brescia: Paideia, 1985), pp. 257–88.

Casey, Maurice, *Son of Man : The Interpretation and Influence of Daniel 7* (London: SPCK, 1979).

Catchpole, David R., *The Quest for Q* (Edinburgh: T. & T. Clark, 1993).

Chapman, Steven, *The Law and the Prophets: A Study in Old Testament Canon Formation* (FAT 27; Tübingen: Mohr Siebeck, 2000).

Charles, R. H., ed., *The Apocrypha and Pseudepigrapha of the Old Testament in English*, vol. 2, *Pseudepigrapha* (Oxford: Clarendon, 1913).

———, *The Book of Jubilees or the Little Genesis* (London: A. & C. Black, 1902).

Charlesworth, James H., ed., *The Old Testament Pseudepigrapha* (2 vols.; Garden City, N.Y.: Doubleday, 1983, 1985).

Chernus, R., *Redemption and Chaos: A Study in the Symbolism of the Rabbinic Aggada* (Ann Arbor: University Microfilms, 1978).

Childs, Brevard, *Biblical Theology in Crisis* (Philadelphia: Westminster, 1970).

Ciampa, Roy E., *The Presence and Function of Scripture in Galatians 1 and 2* (WUNT 2/102; Tubingen: Mohr Siebeck, 1998).

Collins, Adela Yarbro, "The Apocalyptic Son of Man Sayings," in *The Future of Early Christianity: Essays in Honor of Helmut Koester* (ed. Birger A. Pearson; Minneapolis: Fortress, 1991), pp. 220–28.

———, "The 'Son of Man' Tradition and the Book of Revelation," in *The Messiah: Developments in Earliest Judaism and Christianity* (ed. J. H. Charlesworth; Minneapolis: Fortress, 1992), pp. 560–61.

Collins, John J., *Daniel: A Commentary on the Book of Daniel* (Hermeneia; Minneapolis: Fortress, 1993).

———, "The Works of the Messiah," *DSD* 1 (1993), pp. 1–15.

A Commentary upon the Holy Bible from Henry & Scott; with Numerous Observations and Notes from Other Writers (London: The Religious Tract Society, n.d.).

Cook, F. C., *The Holy Bible*, vol. 3, *II Kings-Esther* (New York: Charles Scribner's Sons, 1886).

Cook, Johann, *The Septuagint of Proverbs: Jewish and/or Hellenistic Proverbs? Concerning the Hellenistic Colouring of LXX Proverbs* (VTSup 69; Leiden/New York/Cologne: Brill, 1997).

Cotter, Wendy, " 'Yes, I Tell You, and More than a Prophet,' " in *Conflict and Invention: Literary, Rhetorical, and Social Studies on the Sayings Gospel Q* (ed. John S. Kloppenborg; Valley Forge, Pa.: Trinity Press International, 1995), pp. 135–50.

Creach, Jerome F. D., "Like a Tree Planted by the Temple Stream: The Portrait of the Righteous in Psalm 1:3," *CBQ* 61 (1999), pp. 34–46.

Creed, John Martin, *The Gospel according to St. Luke* (London: Macmillan, 1930).

Crenshaw, James L., "Education in Ancient Israel," *JBL* 104 (1985), pp. 601–15.

———, *Education in Ancient Israel* (New York: Doubleday, 1998).

Crockett, L. C., "Luke 4:25–27 and Jewish-Gentile Relations in Luke-Acts," *JBL* 88 (1969), pp. 177–83.

Crossan, John Dominic, *In Fragments: The Aphorisms of Jesus* (San Francisco: Harper & Row, 1983).

———, *In Parables: The Challenge of the Historical Jesus* (New York: Harper & Row, 1973).

———, *The Historical Jesus: The Life of a Mediterranean Jewish Peasant* (San Francisco: HarperCollins, 1991).

Cullmann, Oscar, *The Christology of the New Testament* (rev. ed.; Philadelphia: Westminster, 1965).

Culpepper, R. Alan, "Luke," in *The New Interpreter's Bible* (Nashville: Abingdon, 1995), vol. 9, pp. 1–490.

Cyster, R. F., "The Lord's Prayer and the Exodus Tradition," *Theology* 64 (1961), pp. 377–81.

Dabeck, P., " 'Siehe, es erscheinen Moses und Elias' (Mt 17,3)," *Bib* 23 (1947), pp. 175–89.

Dahl, Nils Alstrup, *Jesus in the Memory of the Early Church* (Minneapolis: Augsburg, 1976).

Dahood, Mitchell, *Psalms*, vol. 3, *101–150* (AB 17a; Garden City, N.Y.: Doubleday, 1970).

Danby, Herbert, *The Mishnah* (Oxford: Oxford University Press, 1933), pp. 807–11.

Daube, David, "Concessions to Sinfulness in Jewish Law," *JJS* 10 (1959), pp. 1–13.

Davies, W. D., "Paul and the New Exodus," in *The Quest for Context and Meaning: Studies in Biblical Intertextuality in Honor of James A. Sanders* (ed. Craig A. Evans and Shemaryahu Talmon; Leiden/New York/Cologne, 1997), pp. 443–63.

———, *The Setting of the Sermon on the Mount* (Cambridge: Cambridge University Press, 1966).

Davies, W. D., and Dale C. Allison Jr., *A Critical and Exegetical Commentary on the Gospel according to St. Matthew* (3 vols.; ICC; Edinburgh: T. & T. Clark, 1988, 1991, 1997).

Day, John, "The Dependence of Isaiah 26:13–27:11 on Hosea 13:4–14:10 and Its Relevance to Some Theories of the Redaction of the 'Isaiah Apocalypse,' " in *Writing and Reading the Scroll of Isaiah: Studies of an Interpretive Tradition* (ed. Craig C. Broyles and Craig A. Evans; VTSup 70,1; Leiden/New York/Cologne: Brill, 1997), vol. 1, pp. 357–68.

Deane, W. J., S. T. Taylor-Taswell, and W. F. Adeney, *Proverbs* (Pulpit Commentary; New York/London: Funk & Wagnalls, n.d.).

de Jonge, Henk Jan, "The Sayings on Confessing and Denying Jesus in Q 12:8–9 and Mark 8:38," in *Sayings of Jesus: Canonical and Non-Canonical: Essays in Honour of Tjitze Baarda* (ed. William L. Petersen, Johan S. Vos, and Henk J. de Jonge; NovTSup 89; Leiden/New York/Cologne: Brill, 1997), pp. 106–21.

Delitzsch, F., *Biblical Commentary on the Book of Job*, vol. 1 (Edinburgh: T. & T. Clark, 1872).

Derrett, J. D. M., *The Ascetic Discourse: An Explanation of the Sermon on the Mount* (Eilsbrunn: Ko'amar, 1989).

———, "Birds of the Air and Lilies of the Field," *DownR* 105 (1987), pp. 181–92.

Deterding, Paul E., "Exodus Motifs in First Peter," *Concordia Journal* 7 (1981), pp. 58–65.

Dillon, R. J., "Ravens, Lilies, and the Kingdom of God (Matthew 6:25–33/Luke 12:22–31)," *CBQ* 53 (1991), pp. 605–27.

Dimant, Devorah, "Qumran Sectarian Literature," in *Jewish Writings of the Second Temple Period: Apocrypha, Pseudepigrapha, Qumran Sectarian Writings, Philo, Josephus* (ed. Michael E. Stone; CRINT 2; Assen/Philadelphia: Van Gorcum/Fortress, 1984), pp. 483–550.

———, "Use and Interpretation of Mikra in the Apocrypha and Pseudepigrapha," in *Mikra: Text, Translation, Reading, and Interpretation of the Hebrew Bible in Ancient Judaism and Early Christianity* (ed. Martin Jan Mulder; CRINT 2/1; Assen/Maastricht/Philadelphia: Van Gorcum/Fortress, 1988), pp. 379–419.

Dindorf, G., *Epiphanii Episcopi Constantiae Opera* (Leipzig: Weigel, 1859–1862), vol. 4.

Dion, Paul E., "Formulaic Language in the Book of Job: International Background and Ironical Distortions," *SR* 16 (1987), pp. 187–93.

Dittmar, Wilhelm, *Vetus Testamentum in Novo: Die alttestamentlichen Parallelen des Neuen Testaments im Wortlaut der Urtexte und der Septuaginta* (Göttingen: Vandenhoeck & Ruprecht, 1903).

Dodd, C. H., *According to the Scriptures: The Sub-structure of New Testament Theology* (London: Fontana, 1965).

———, *Historical Tradition in the Fourth Gospel* (Cambridge: Cambridge University Press, 1963).

———, *The Parables of the Kingdom* (rev. ed.; New York: Charles Scribner's Sons, 1961).

Dodd, William, *A Commentary on the Books of the Old and New Testament*, vol. 3 (London: R. Davies, 1770).

Doddridge, Philip, *The Family Expositor; or, a Paraphrase and Version of the New Testament* (Amherst, Mass.: J. S. & C. Adams & L. Boltwood, 1836).

Doeve, J. W., *Jewish Hermeneutics in the Synoptic Gospels and Acts* (Assen: Van Gorcum, 1954).

Donaldson, Terrence L., *Jesus on the Mountain: A Study in Matthean Theology* (JSNTSS 8; Sheffield: JSOT Press, 1985).

Downing, F. Gerald, "A bas les aristos. The Relevance of Higher Literature for the Understanding of the Earliest Christian Writings," *NovT* 30 (1988), pp. 212–30.

———, "Word-Processing in the Ancient World: The Social Production and Performance of Q," *JSNT* 64 (1996), pp. 29–48.

Dozeman, Thomas B., "Inner-Biblical Interpretation of Yahweh's Gracious and Compassionate Character," *JBL* 108 (1989), pp. 207–23.

Dunn, James D. G., "John the Baptist's Use of Scripture," in *The Gospels and the Scriptures of Israel* (ed. Craig A. Evans and W. Richard Stegner; JSNTSS 104; Sheffield: Sheffield Academic Press, 1994), pp. 42–54.

Ebner, Martin, *Jesus — ein Weisheitslehrer? Synoptische Weishheitslogien im Traditionsprozess* (HBS 15; Freiburg: Herder, 1998).

Eco, Umberto, "Between Author and Text," in *Interpretation and Overinterpretation* (ed. Stefan Collini; Cambridge: Cambridge University Press, 1992), pp. 67–88.

————, *The Limits of Interpretation* (Bloomington/Indianapolis: Indiana University Press, 1990).

Ehrhardt, A., *The Framework of the New Testament Stories* (Manchester: University of Manchester Press, 1964).

Elbogen, Ismar, *Jewish Liturgy: A Comprehensive History* (Philadelphia: Jewish Publication Society, 1993).

Eliot, T. S., "Tradition and Individual Talent," in *Selected Essays* (new ed.; San Diego/New York/London: HBJ, 1950), pp. 3–11.

Elliott, J. K., *The Apocryphal New Testament: A Collection of Apocryphal Christian Literature in English Translation* (Oxford: Clarendon, 1993).

Eriksson, LarsOlov, *"Come, Children, Listen to Me!" Psalm 34 in the Hebrew Bible and in Early Christian Writings* (CBOT 32; Stockholm: Almqvist & Wiksell, 1991).

Evans, C. F., *Saint Luke* (TPINTC; London/Philadelphia: SCM/Trinity Press International, 1990).

Evans, Craig A., *To See and Not Perceive: Isaiah 6.9–10 in Early Jewish and Christian Interpretation* (JSNTSup 64; Sheffield: JSOT Press, 1989).

————. "The Twelve Thrones of Israel: Scripture and Politics in Luke 22:24–30," in *Jesus in Context: Temple, Purity, and Restoration* (Bruce Chilton and Craig A. Evans; AGAJU 39; Leiden/New York/Cologne: Brill, 1997), pp. 455–79.

Evans, Craig A., and James A. Sanders, eds., *Paul and the Scriptures of Israel* (JSNTSS 83; Sheffield: JSOT Press, 1993).

Falk, Daniel K., "Biblical Adaptation in 4Q392 *Works of God* and 4Q393 *Communal Confession*," in *The Provo International Conference on the Dead Sea Scrolls: Technological Innovations, New Texts, and Reformulated Issues* (ed. Donald W. Parry and Eugene Ulrich; STDJ 30; Leiden/Boston/Cologne: Brill, 1999), pp. 126–46.

Farrar, F. W., *The First Book of Kings* (New York: A. C. Armstrong & Son, 1893).

Farrer, Austin, *The Triple Victory: Christ's Temptation according to St. Matthew* (Cambridge, Mass.: Cowley, 1990).

Fekkes, Jan, III, *Isaiah and Prophetic Traditions in the Book of Revelation: Visionary Antecedents and Their Development* (JSNTSS 93; Sheffield: JSOT Press, 1992).

Feldman, Louis H., *Josephus's Interpretation of the Bible* (Berkeley: University of California Press, 1998).

Fenton, J. C., *Saint Matthew* (Baltimore: Penguin, 1963).

Feuillet, A., "Les sources du livre de Jonas," *RB* 54 (1947), pp. 161–86.

Fields, Weston W., *Sodom and Gomorrah: History and Motif in Biblical Narrative* (JSOTSS 231; Sheffield: Sheffield Academic Press, 1997).

Findlay, J. A., "Luke," in *The Abingdon Bible Commentary* (ed. Frederick Carl Eiselen, Edwin Lewis, and David G. Downey; New York/Cincinnati/Chicago: Abingdon, 1929), pp. 1022–59.

Fishbane, Michael, *Biblical Interpretation in Ancient Israel* (Oxford: Clarendon, 1985).

————, "The Hebrew Bible and Exegetical Tradition," in *Intertextuality in Ugarit and Israel* (ed. Johannes C. de Moor; OS 40; Leiden/Boston/Cologne: Brill, 1998), pp. 15–30.

————, "Jer 4:23–26 and Job 3:1–13: A Recovered Use of the Creation Pattern," *VT* 21 (1971), pp. 151–62.

————, *Text and Texture: Close Readings of Selected Biblical Texts* (New York: Schocken, 1979).

————, "Torah and Tradition," in *Tradition and Theology in the Old Testament* (ed. Douglas A. Knight; Philadelphia: Fortress, 1977), pp. 275–300.

————, "Use, Authority, and Interpretation of Mikra at Qumran," in *Mikra: Text, Translation, Reading, and Interpretation of the Hebrew Bible in Ancient Judaism and Early Christianity* (ed. Martin Jan Mulder; CRINT 2/1; Assen/ Maastricht/Philadelphia: Van Gorcum/Fortress, 1988), pp. 339–77.

Fitzmyer, Joseph A., "Crucifixion in Ancient Palestine, Qumran Literature, and the New Testament," *CBQ* 40 (1978), pp. 493–513.

————, *Essays on the Semitic Background of the New Testament* (Missoula, Mont.: Scholars Press, 1974).

————, *The Gospel according to Luke* (2 vols.; AB 28; Garden City, N.Y.: Doubleday, 1981, 1985).

————, "The Priority of Mark and the 'Q' Source in Luke," in *To Advance the Gospel: New Testament Studies* (New York: Crossroad, 1981), pp. 3–40.

Fleddermann, Harry T., "The Demands of Discipleship: Matt 8,19–22 par. Luke 9,57–62," in *The Four Gospels 1992: Festschrift Frans Neirynck* (ed. F. Van Segbroeck et al.; BETL 100; Louvain: Louvain University Press, 1992), vol. 1, pp. 541–61.

Fletcher-Louis, Crispin H. T. *Luke-Acts: Angels, Christology, and Soteriology* (WUNT 2/94; Tübingen: Mohr Siebeck, 1996).

Flusser, David, "Blessed Are the Poor in Spirit . . . ," *IEJ* 10 (1960), pp. 1–13.

————. "Hillel and Jesus: Two Ways of Self-Awareness," in *Hillel and Jesus: Comparisons of Two Major Religious Leaders* (ed. James H. Charlesworth and Loren L. Johns; Minneapolis: Fortress, 1997), pp. 71–107.

France, R. T., *Jesus and the Old Testament: His Application of Old Testament Passages to Himself and His Mission* (London: Tyndale, 1971).

Frankemölle, Hubert, "Jesus als deuterojesajanischer Freudenbote? Zur Rezeption von Jes 52,7 und 61,1 im Neuen Testament, durch Jesus und in den Targumim," in *Jüdische Wurzeln christlicher Theologie* (BBB 116; Bodenheim: Philo, 1998), pp. 131–60.

————, "Die Makarismen (Mt 5,1–2; Lk 6,20–23): Motive und Umfang der redaktionellen Komposition," *BZ* 15 (1971), pp. 52–75.

Fuchs, Ernst, *Studies of the Historical Jesus* (SBT; London: SCM, 1964).

Fuller, R. H., *The Foundations of New Testament Christology* (London: Collins, 1969).

Funk, Robert W., *Honest to Jesus: Jesus for a New Millennium* (San Francisco: HarperSanFrancisco, 1996), pp. 153–54.

————, *Jesus as Precursor* (SBLSS 2; Philadelphia/Missoula, Mont.: Fortress/ Scholars Press, 1975).

Funk, Robert W., Roy W. Hoover, and the Jesus Seminar, *The Five Gospels: The Search for the Authentic Words of Jesus* (New York: Macmillan, 1993).

Gaechter, Paul, *Das Matthäus Evangelium: Ein Kommentar* (Innsbruck/Vienna/ Munich: Trolia, 1963).

Gagnon, Robert A. J., *Jesus and the Capernaum Official: Tracing the History of a Story* (forthcoming).

———. "Luke's Motives for Redaction in the Account of the Double Delegation in Luke 7:1–10," *NovT* 36 (1994), pp. 122–45.

———, "The Shape of Matthew's Q Text of the Centurion at Capernaum: Did It Mention Delegations?" *NTS* 40 (1994), pp. 133–42.

———, "Statistical Analysis and the Case of the Double Delegation in Luke 7:3–7a," *CBQ* 55 (1993), pp. 709–31.

Gamble, Harry Y., *Books and Readers in the Early Church: A History of Early Christian Texts* (New Haven/London: Yale University Press, 1995).

Genette, Gérard, *Palimpsests: Literature in the Second Degree* (Lincoln/London: University of Nebraska Press, 1997).

Gerhardsson, Birger, *Memory and Manuscript: Oral Tradition and Written Transmission in Rabbinic Judaism and Early Christianity* (Lund/Copenhagen: Gleerup/Ejnar Munksgaard, 1961).

———, *The Testing of God's Son (Matt 4:1–11 & Par.)* (CB,NT 2/1; Lund: Gleerup, 1966).

Gfrörer, August Friedrich, *Das Jahrhundert des Heils* (Stuttgart: C. Schweizerbart, 1838).

Gieschen, Charles A., *Angelomorphic Christology: Antecedents and Early Evidence* (AGJU 42; Leiden/Boston/Cologne: Brill, 1998).

Gill, John, *Gill's Commentary*, 6 vols. (Grand Rapids: Baker, 1980).

Giversen, Søsren, "The Apocryphon of John and Genesis," *ST* 17 (1963), pp. 60–76.

Glasson, T. Francis, *Moses in the Fourth Gospel* (SBT 40; London: SCM, 1963).

Glenthøj, Johannes Bartholdy, *Cain and Abel in Syriac and Greek Writers (4th–6th Centuries)* (CSCO 567 Subsidia 95; Louvain: Peeters, 1997).

Gnilka, Joachim, *Das Matthäusevangelium* (2 vols.; HTKNT I/1, 2; Freiburg: Herder, 1986, 1988).

Goldman, Shalom, *The Wiles of Women/The Wiles of Men: Joseph and Potiphar's Wife in Ancient Near Eastern, Jewish, and Islamic Folklore* (Albany: SUNY Press, 1995).

Goulder, M. D., *Luke — A New Paradigm* (2 vols.; JSNTSS 20; Sheffield: JSOT, 1989).

Graham, William A., *Beyond the Written Word: Oral Aspects of Scripture in the History of Religion* (Cambridge: Cambridge University Press, 1987).

Gray, John, *I and II Kings* (2d rev. ed.; Philadelphia: Westminster, 1970).

Gray, Rebecca, *Prophetic Figures in Late Second Temple Jewish Palestine: The Evidence from Josephus* (New York/Oxford: Oxford University Press, 1993).

Grech, P., "The 'Testimonia' and Modern Hermeneutics," *NTS* 19 (1973), pp. 318–24.

Green, Joel B., *The Gospel of Luke* (NIGTC; Grand Rapids/Cambridge, U.K.: Eerdmans, 1997).

Greenberg, Moshe, *Ezekiel 21–37* (AB 22A; New York: Doubleday, 1997).

Grelot, Pierre, *Jésus de Nazareth, Christ et Seigneur* (LD 167; Paris: Cerf, 1997).

———, "La quatrième demande du 'Pater' et son arrière-plan sémitique," *NTS* 25 (1975), pp. 299–314.

Grimm, Werner, *Jesus und das Danielbuch, Band I: Jesu Einspruch Gegen das Offenbarungssystem Daniels (Mt 11,25–27; Lk 17,20–21)* (ANTJ 6/1; Frankfurt am Main/Bern/New York: Peter Lang, 1984).

——, "Selige Augenzeugen," *ThZ* 26 (1970), pp. 172–83.

——, *Weil Ich Dich Liebe: Die Verkündigung Jesu und Deuterojesaja* (ANTJ; Bern/Frankfurt am Main: Herbert Lang/Peter Lang, 1976).

Grinfield, Edward William, *Scholia Hellenistica in Novum Testamentum,* vol. 1 (London: Gulielmus Pickering, 1848).

Grol, Harm W. M. van, "Exegesis of the Exile — Exegesis of Scripture?" in *Intertextuality in Ugarit and Israel* (ed. Johannes C. de Moor; OS 40; Leiden/Boston/Cologne: Brill, 1998), pp. 49–61.

Grotius, Hugo, *Operum theologicarum* (2 vols.; Amsterdam: Joannis Blaev, 1679).

Guelich, R., "The Matthean Beatitudes: 'Entrance Requirements' or Eschatological Beatitudes?" *JBL* 95 (1976), pp. 415–34.

Gundry, Robert H., *Matthew: A Commentary on His Literary and Theological Art* (Grand Rapids: Eerdmans, 1982).

——, *The Use of the Old Testament in St. Matthew's Gospel, with Special Reference to the Messianic Hope* (NovTSup 18; Leiden: Brill, 1967).

Gunn, David M., "Deutero-Isaiah and the Flood," *JBL* 94 (1975), pp. 493–508.

Gutbrod, W., "νόμος," *TDNT* 4 (1967), pp. 1036–91.

Haag, H., "בֵּן," *TDOT* 2 (1975), pp. 147–59.

Hagner, Donald A., *Matthew 1–13,* 2 vols. (WBC 33A; Dallas: Word, 1993).

Hanson, A. T., *The Living Utterances of God* (London: Darton, Longman & Todd, 1983).

Harnack, Adolf, *Bible Reading in the Early Church* (New York/London: G. P. Putnam's Sons/William & Norgate, 1912).

Harrington, Daniel J., *The Gospel of Matthew* (Sacra Pagina 1; Collegeville, Minn.: Michael Glazier, 1991).

Harris, William V., *Ancient Literacy* (Cambridge, Mass./London: Harvard University Press, 1989).

Hartman, Lars, "Reading Luke 17,20–37," in *The Four Gospels 1992: Festschrift Frans Neirynck* (ed. F. Van Segbroeck et al.; BETL 100; Louvain: Louvain University Press/Peeters), vol. 2, pp. 1661–75.

Hasitschka, M., "Die Verwendung der Schrift in Mt 4,1–11," in *The Scriptures in the Gospels* (ed. C. M. Tuckett; BETL 131; Louvain: Louvain University Press/Peeters, 1997), pp. 487–90.

Hassan, Ihab H., "The Problem of Influence in Literary History: Notes towards a Definition," in *Influx: Essays on Literary Influence* (ed. Ronald Primeau; Port Washington, N.Y./London: Kennikat, 1977), pp. 20–41.

Hatina, T. R., "Intertextuality and Historical Criticism in New Testament Studies: Is There a Relationship?" *BibInt* 7 (1999), pp. 28–43.

Hays, Richard B., "The Conversion of the Imagination: Scripture and Eschatology in 1 Corinthians," *NTS* 45 (1999), pp. 391–412.

——, *Echoes of Scripture in the Letters of Paul* (New Haven: Yale University Press, 1989).

Healey, John F., "Models of Behavior: Matt 6:26 (// Luke 12:24) and Prov 6:6–8," *JBL* 108 (1989), pp. 497–98.

————, *The Targum of Proverbs* (Aramaic Bible 15; Collegeville, Minn.: Michael Glazier, 1991).

Hebel, Udo, J., *Intertextuality, Allusion, and Quotation: An International Bibliography of Critical Studies* (New York: Greenwood, 1989).

Heil, Christoph, ed., *Q 12:8–12: Confessing or Denying, Speaking against the Holy Spirit, Hearings before Synagogues* (Documenta Q; Louvain: Peeters, 1997).

————, *Q 22:28, 30: You Will Judge the Twelve Tribes of Israel* (Documenta Q; Louvain: Peeters, 1998).

Hengel, Martin, *The Charismatic Leader and His Followers* (New York: Crossroad, 1981).

————, *Judaism and Hellenism: Studies in Their Encounter in Palestine during the Early Hellenistic Period*, vol. 1 (Philadelphia: Fortress, 1974).

————, "Kerygma oder Geschichte? Zur Problematik einer falschen Alternative in der Synoptikerforschung aufgezeigt an Hand einiger neuer Monographien," *ThQ* 101 (1971), pp. 323–36.

————, *The Son of God* (Philadelphia: Fortress, 1976).

Hennecke, Edgar, and Wilhelm Schneemelcher, *New Testament Apocrypha* (2 vols., ed. R. McL. Wilson; Cambridge/Louisville: James Clark & Co.; Westminster/John Knox, 1992).

Henry, Matthew, *Commentary on the Whole Bible*, vol. 1, *Genesis to Deuteronomy* (New York/London/Edinburgh: Fleming H. Revell, n.d.).

Hiers, Richard H., *The Kingdom of God in the Synoptic Tradition* (Gainesville: University of Florida Press, 1970).

Hill, David, *The Gospel of Matthew* (NCB; London: Oliphants, 1977).

Hirsch, E. D., *Cultural Literacy* (Boston: Houghton Mifflin, 1987).

Hodgson, R., "On the Gattung of Q: A Dialogue with James M. Robinson," *Bib* 66 (1985), pp. 73–95.

Hoffman, Lawrence A., *The Canonization of the Synagogue Service* (Notre Dame, Ind.: University of Notre Dame Press, 1979).

Hoffmann, Paul, *Studien zur Theologie der Logienquelle* (3d ed.; NTAbh 8; Münster: Aschendorff, 1982).

Holladay, William L., *The Psalms through Three Thousand Years: Prayerbook of a Cloud of Witnesses* (Minneapolis: Fortress, 1993).

————, "Was Trito-Isaiah Deutero-Isaiah After All?" in *Writing and Reading the Scroll of Isaiah: Studies of an Interpretive Tradition* (ed. Craig C. Broyles and Craig A. Evans; VTSup 70,1; Leiden/New York/Cologne: Brill, 1997), vol. 1, pp. 193–218.

Hollander, H. W., *Joseph as an Ethical Model in the Testaments of the Twelve Patriarchs* (SVTP 6; Leiden: Brill, 1981).

Holm-Nielsen, Svend, *Hodayot: Psalms from Qumran* (Acta Theologica Danica 2; Aarhus, Denmark: Universitetsforlaget, 1960).

Horgan, Maurya P., *Pesharim: Qumran Interpretations of Biblical Books* (CBQMS 8; Washington, D.C.: Catholic Biblical Association of America, 1979).

Horsley, Richard A., *Jesus and the Spiral of Violence: Popular Jewish Resistance in Roman Palestine* (San Francisco: Harper & Row, 1987).

————, "Q and Jesus: Assumptions, Approaches, and Analyses," *Semeia* 55 (1992), pp. 175–209.

Horsley, Richard A., and Jonathan A. Draper, *Whoever Hears You Hears Me: Prophets, Performance, and Tradition in Q* (Harrisburg, Pa.: Trinity Press International, 1999).

Houk, C. B., "ΠΕΙΡΑΣΜΟΣ, The Lord's Prayer, and the Massah Tradition," *SJT* 19 (1966), pp. 216–25.

Hübner, Hans, *Vetus Testamentum in Novo*, vol. 2, *Corpus Paulinum* (Göttingen: Vandenhoeck & Ruprecht, 1997).

Hugger, Pirim, *Jahwe meine Zuflucht: Gestalt und Theologie des 91. Psalms* (Münster-schwarzacher Studien 13; Münsterschwarzach: Vier-Türme, 1971).

Hühn, Eugen, *Die messianischen Weissagungen des israelitisch-jüdischen Volkes bis zu den Targumim, II. Teil: Die alttestamentlichen Citate und Reminiscenzen im Neuen Testamente* (Tübingen: Mohr Siebeck, 1900).

Isser, Stanley Jerome, *The Dositheans: A Samaritan Sect in Late Antiquity* (SJLA 17; Leiden: Brill, 1976).

Jacobs, Melancthon W., *Notes on the Gospels, Critical and Explanatory* (New York: Robert Carter & Brothers, 1872).

Jacobson, Arland D., "The Literary Unity of Q," *JBL* 101 (1982), pp. 365–89.

Jacobson, Howard, *A Commentary on Pseudo-Philo's Liber Antiquitatum Biblicarum, with Latin Text and English Translation* (2 vols.; AGJU 31; Leiden/New York/Cologne: Brill, 1996).

Jansen, Cornelius, *Tetrateuchus sive Commentarius in sancta Jesu Christi Euangelia* (Brussels: Francisci t'Serstevens, 1776).

Jensen, Joseph, "Helel Ben Shahar (Isaiah 14:12–15) in Bible and Tradition," in *Writing and Reading the Scroll of Isaiah: Studies of an Interpretive Tradition* (ed. Craig C. Broyles and Craig A. Evans; VTSup 70,1; Leiden/New York/Cologne: Brill, 1997), vol. 1, pp. 339–56.

Jeremias, Joachim, *The Eucharistic Words of Jesus* (London: SCM, 1966).

———, *New Testament Theology: The Proclamation of Jesus* (New York: Charles Scribner's Sons, 1971).

———, *The Parables of Jesus* (2d rev. ed.; New York: Charles Scribner's Sons, 1972).

———, *The Prayers of Jesus* (SBT 2/6; London: SCM, 1967).

———, *Die Sprache des Lukasevangeliums: Redaktion und Tradition im Nicht-Markusstoff des dritten Evangeliums* (MeyerK; Göttingen: Vandenhoeck & Ruprecht, 1980).

———, "Ἰερεμίας," *TDNT* 3 (1965), pp. 218–21.

———, "λίθος," *TDNT* 4 (1967), pp. 268–80.

———, "παῖς θεοῦ," *TDNT* 5 (1967), pp. 700–17.

Johnson, Luke Timothy, *The Gospel of Luke* (Sacra Pagina 3; Collegeville, Minn.: Michael Glazier, 1991).

———, "The Use of Leviticus 19 in the Letter of James," *JBL* 101 (1982), pp. 391–401.

Jones, A., "The Gospel of Jesus Christ according to St. Matthew," in *A Catholic Commentary on Holy Scripture* (ed. Dom Bernard Orchard et al.; Toronto/New York/Edinburgh: Thomas Nelson & Sons, 1953), pp. 851–904.

Jones, D. C., "A Note on the LXX of Malachi 2.16," *JBL* 109 (1990), pp. 683–85.

Jones, John N., " 'Think of the Lilies' and Prov 6:6–11," *HTR* 88 (1995), pp. 175–77.

Joseph, Gerald, "The American Triumph of the Egg: Anderson's 'The Egg' and Fitzgerald's *The Great Gatsby*," *Criticism* 7 (1965), pp. 131–40.

Juel, Donald, *Messianic Exegesis: Christological Interpretation of the Old Testament in Early Christianity* (Philadelphia: Fortress, 1988).

Kapelrud, A., "The Date of the Priestly Code (P)," *ASTI* 3 (1964), pp. 58–64.

Käsemann, Ernst, *New Testament Questions of Today* (Philadelphia: Fortress, 1969).

Kee, Howard Clark, "Jesus: A Glutton and Drunkard," in *Authenticating the Words of Jesus* (ed. B. Chilton and C. A. Evans; NTTS 28/1; Leiden: Brill, 1999), pp. 311–32.

Keener, Craig S., *Commentary on the Gospel of Matthew* (Grand Rapids/Cambridge, U.K.: Eerdmans, 1999).

Keesmaat, Sylvia C., "Exodus and the Intertextual Transformation of Tradition in Romans 8.14–30," *JSNT* 54 (1994), pp. 29–56.

———, *Paul and His Story: (Re)Interpreting the Exodus Tradition* (JSNTSup 181; Sheffield: Sheffield Academic Press, 1999).

Kelber, Werner H., "Jesus and Tradition: Words in Time, Words in Space," *Semeia* 65 (1995), pp. 139–67.

———, "Modalities of Communication, Cognition, and Physiology of Perception: Orality, Rhetoric, Scribality," *Semeia* 65 (1995), pp. 193–215.

Kellett, E. E., *Literary Quotation and Allusion* (Port Washington, N.Y./London: Kennikat, 1933).

Kiesow, Klaus, *Exodustexte im Jesajabuch* (OBO 24; Freiburg/Göttingen: Éditions Universitaires/Vandenhoeck & Ruprecht, 1979).

Kimball, Charles A., *Jesus' Exposition of the Old Testament in Luke's Gospel* (JSNTSup 94; Sheffield: JSOT Press, 1994).

Kirk, Alan, *The Composition of the Sayings Source: Genre, Synchrony, and Wisdom Redaction in Q* (NovTSup 91; Leiden/Boston/Cologne: Brill, 1998).

Kirkpatrick, A. F., *The Book of Psalms (I–XLI)* (Cambridge: Cambridge University Press, 1892).

Klein, Michael, "Associative and Complementary Translation in the Targumim," *Eretz-Israel* 16 (1982), pp. 134*-40*.

———, "Converse Translation: A Targumic Technique," *Biblica* 57 (1976), pp. 515–37.

Kloppenborg, John S., "City and Wasteland: Narrative World and the Beginning of the Sayings Gospel," *Semeia* 52 (1990), pp. 145–60.

———, ed., *Conflict and Invention: Literary, Rhetorical, and Social Studies on the Sayings Gospel Q* (Valley Forge, Pa.: Trinity Press International, 1996).

———, *The Formation of Q: Trajectories in Ancient Christian Wisdom Collections* (Studies in Antiquity and Christianity; Philadelphia: Fortress, 1987).

———, Introduction to *Conflict and Invention: Literary, Rhetorical and Social Studies on the Sayings Gospel Q* (ed. John Kloppenborg; Valley Forge, Pa.: Trinity Press International, 1995), pp. 1–21.

———, "Literary Convention, Self-Evidence, and the Social History of the Q People," *Semeia* 55 (1992), pp. 77–102.

———, *Q Parallels: Synopsis, Critical Notes, and Concordance* (Sonoma, Calif.: Polebridge, 1988).

————, "The Transformation of Moral Exhortation in *Didache* 1–5," in *The Didache in Context: Essays on Its Text, History, and Transmission* (ed. Clayton N. Jefford; NovTSupp 77; Leiden/New York/Cologne: Brill, 1995), pp. 88–109.

Kloppenborg, John S., and Leif E. Vaage, eds., *Early Christianity, Q, and Jesus* (Atlanta: Scholars Press, 1992) = *Semeia* 55.

Knowles, Michael, *Jeremiah in Matthew's Gospel: The Rejected-Prophet Motif in Matthean Redaction* (JSNTSS 68; Sheffield: JSOT Press, 1993).

Koenig, J., "L'herméneutique analogique du Judaïsme antique d'après les témoins textuelles d'Isaïe," *VTSupp* 33 (1982), pp. 1–103, 199–291.

Koestler, Arthur, *The Heel of Achilles: Essays 1968–1973* (New York: Random House, 1974).

Kollmann, B., "Lk 12.35–38 — ein Gleichnis der Logienquelle," *ZNW* 81 (1990), pp. 254–61.

Kosch, Daniel, *Die eschatologische Tora des Menschensohnes: Untersuchungen zur Rezeption der Stellung Jesu zur Tora in Q* (NTOA 12; Göttingen: Vandenhoeck & Ruprecht, 1989).

Kraft, Robert A., "Scripture and Canon in Jewish Apocrypha and Pseudepigrapha," in *Hebrew Bible/Old Testament: The History of Its Interpretation*, vol. 1, *From the Beginnings to the Middle Ages (until 1300). Part 1, Antiquity* (ed. Magne Saebø; Göttingen: Vandenhoeck & Ruprecht, 1996), pp. 199–216.

Kratz, R., "λίθος, ου, ὁ," *EDNT* 2 (1991), pp. 352–53.

Kristeva, Julia, "Word, Dialogue, and Novel," in *Desire in Language: A Semiotic Approach to Literature and Art* (ed. Léon S. Roudiez; New York: Columbia University Press, 1980), pp. 64–91.

Kugel, James L., "On Hidden Hatred and Open Reproach: Early Exegesis of Leviticus 19:17," *HTR* 80 (1987), pp. 43–62.

————, *Traditions of the Bible: A Guide to the Bible As It Was at the Start of the Common Era* (Cambridge, Mass./London: Harvard University Press, 1998).

Kuhn, K. G., *Achtzehngebet und Vaterunser und der Reim* (WUNT 1; Tübingen: Mohr Siebeck, 1950).

Lagrange, M.-J., *Évangile selon Saint Luc* (EB; Paris: J. Gabalda, 1927).

Lake, Kirsopp, *The Apostolic Fathers* (2 vols.; Cambridge, Mass./London: Harvard University Press/William Heinemann, 1952).

Lange, John Peter, *Commentary on the Holy Scriptures: Kings*, vol. 6 (Grand Rapids: Zondervan, n.d.).

Lapide, Cornelius à, *The Great Commentary of Cornelius à Lapide* (6 vols.; 2d ed.; London: John Hodges, 1874–87).

Leske, Adrian, "Matthew," in *The International Bible Commentary: A Catholic and Ecumenical Commentary for the Twenty-First Century* (ed. W. R. Farmer; Collegeville, Minn.: Liturgical Press, 1998), pp. 1253–1330.

Levenson, John R., *Theology of the Program of Restoration of Ezekiel 40–48* (HSM 10; Missoula, Mont.: Scholars Press, 1976).

Levertoff, P., "Matthew," in *A New Catholic Commentary on Holy Scripture* (ed. C. Gore, H. C. Goudge, and Al Guillame; London: Macmillan, 1928).

Levey, Samson H., *The Messiah: An Aramaic Interpretation: The Messianic Exegesis of the Targum* (Cincinnati/New York/Los Angeles/Jerusalem: Hebrew Union College-Jewish Institute of Religion, 1974).

Lewis, C. S., *The Literary Impact of the Authorized Version* (FBBS 4; Philadelphia: Fortress, 1963).

Lightfoot, John, *A Commentary on the New Testament from the Talmud and Hebraica* (4 vols.; Oxford: Oxford University Press, 1859).

Linafelt, T., "Surviving Lamentations," *HBT* 17 (1995), pp. 45–61.

Lindars, Barnabas, "Discourse and Tradition: The Use of the Sayings of Jesus in the Discourses of the Fourth Gospel," *JSNT* 13 (1981), pp. 83–101.

———, "The Image of Moses in the Synoptic Gospels," *Theology* 58 (1955), pp. 129–32.

———, *Jesus Son of Man* (Grand Rapids: Eerdmans, 1983).

———, *New Testament Apologetic* (London: SCM, 1961).

Loader, J. A., *A Tale of Two Cities: Sodom and Gomorrah in the Old Testament, Early Jewish and Early Christian Traditions* (Contributions to Biblical Exegesis and Theology 1; Kampen: J. H. Kok, 1990).

Loader, William R. G., *Jesus' Attitude towards the Law: A Study of the Gospels* (WUNT 2/97; Tübingen: Mohr Siebeck, 1997).

Löning, Karl, "Die Füchse, die Vögel und der Menschensohn (Mt 8,19f par Lk 9,57f)," in *Vom Urchristentum zu Jesus: Für Joachim Gnilka* (ed. Hubert Frankemölle and Karl Kertelge; Freiburg: Herder, 1989), pp. 82–102.

Lövestam, Evald, *Jesus and 'This Generation': A New Testament Study* (ConB 25; Stockholm: Almqvist & Wiksell, 1995).

Lührmann, Dieter, "Noah und Lot (Lk 17 26–29) — ein Nachtrag," *ZNW* 63 (1972), pp. 130–32.

Luther, Martin, *Luther's Commentary on Genesis*, vol. 1 (Grand Rapids: Zondervan, 1958).

———, *Martin Luthers Evangelien-Auslegung, Dritter Teil. Markus- und Lukasevangelium (Mark. 1–13; Luk. 3–21)* (ed. E. Mülhaupt; Göttingen: Vandenhoeck & Ruprecht, 1961).

Luz, Ulrich, *Das Evangelium nach Matthäus* (3 vols.; EKKNT 1; Zurich/Neukirchen-Vluyn: Benziger/Neukirchener, 1985, 1990, 1997). ET: *Matthew 1–7: A Commentary* (Minneapolis: Augsburg, 1989).

Maclaren, A., *The Psalms*, vol. 1 (New York: A. C. Armstrong & Son, 1903).

Magonet, Jonathan, *Form and Meaning: Studies in Literary Techniques in the Book of Jonah* (Bible and Literature Series; Sheffield: Almond, 1983).

Maier, Phil Johann, "Early Jewish Biblical Interpretation in the Qumran Literature," in *Hebrew Bible/Old Testament: The History of Its Interpretation*, vol. 1, *From the Beginnings to the Middle Ages (until 1300). Part 1, Antiquity* (ed. Magne Saebø; Göttingen: Vandenhoeck & Ruprecht, 1996), pp. 108–29.

Maldonatus, Juan, *Commentarii in Quatuor Evangelistas* (2 vols.; London/Paris: Moguntiae, 1853–54).

Mann, Jacob, *The Bible as Read and Preached in the Old Synagogue*, 2 vols. (Cincinnati: Jewish Publication Society, 1940).

Manson, T. W., *The Sayings of Jesus* (London: SCM, 1949).

———, *The Teaching of Jesus: Studies in Its Form and Content* (2d ed.; Cambridge: Cambridge University Press, 1935).

Manson, William, *Jesus the Messiah: The Synoptic Tradition of the Revelation of God in Christ: With Special Reference to Form-Criticism* (London: Hodder & Stoughton Ltd., 1943).

Marcus, Joel, *Mark 1–8: A New Translation with Introduction and Commentary* (AB 27A; Garden City, N.Y.: Doubleday, 2000).

———, "The Old Testament and the Death of Jesus: The Role of Scripture in the Gospel Passion Narratives," in *The Death of Jesus in Early Christianity* (ed. John T. Carroll and Joel B. Green; Peabody, Mass.: Hendrickson, 1995), pp. 205–33.

———, *The Way of the Lord: Christological Exegesis of the Old Testament in the Gospel of Mark* (Louisville: Westminster/John Knox, 1992).

Marmorstein, A. *The Doctrine of Merits in Old Rabbinical Literature* (New York: Ktav, 1968).

Marshall, I. H., *Commentary on Luke* (NIGTC; Grand Rapids: Eerdmans, 1978).

Martínez, F. García, "Man and Woman: Halakhah Based upon Eden in the Dead Sea Scrolls," in *Paradise Interpreted: Representations of Biblical Paradise in Judaism and Christianity* (ed. Gerard P. Luttikhuizen; Leiden/Boston/Cologne: Brill, 1999), pp. 95–115.

März, Claus-Peter, "Das Gleichnis vom Dieb. Überlegungen zur Verbindung von Lk 12,39 par Mt 24,43 und 1 Thess 5,2.4," in *The Four Gospels 1992: Festschrift Frans Neirynck* (ed. Van Segbroeck et al.; BETL 100; Louvain: Louvain University Press, 1992), vol. 1, pp. 633–48.

———, *"…lasst eure Lampen brennen!" Studien zur Q-Vorlage von Lk 12,35–14,24* (ETS 20; Leipzig: St. Benno, 1991).

McConville, J. G., "Ezra-Nehemiah and the Fulfillment of Prophecy," *VT* 36 (1986), pp. 205–24.

McDonald, J. Ian H., "Questioning and Discernment in Gospel Discourse: Communicative Strategy in Matthew 11:2–19," in *Authenticating the Words of Jesus* (ed. Bruce Chilton and Craig A. Evans; NTTS 28/1; Leiden/Boston/Cologne: Brill, 1999), pp. 333–62.

McDonald, Lee M., *The Formation of the Christian Biblical Canon* (rev. ed.; Peabody, Mass.: Hendrickson, 1995).

McLean, Bradley H., *Citations and Allusions to Jewish Scripture in Jewish and Christian Writings through 180 C.E.* (Lewiston, N.Y./Queenston/Lampeter: Edwin Mellen, 1992).

McNamara, Martin, *The New Testament and the Palestinian Targum to the Pentateuch* (AnBib 27; Rome: Pontifical Biblical Institute, 1966).

Meadors, Edward P., "The 'Messianic' Implications of the Q Material," *JBL* 118 (1999), pp. 253–77.

Meeks, Wayne A., *The Prophet-King: Moses Traditions and the Johannine Christology* (NovTSup 14; Leiden: Brill, 1967).

Meier, John P., "John the Baptist in Matthew's Gospel," *JBL* 99 (1980), pp. 383–405.

———, *A Marginal Jew: Rethinking the Historical Jesus* (2 vols.; ABRL; New York: Doubleday, 1994).

Menahem, R., "A Jewish Commentary on the New Testament: A Sample Verse," *Immanuel* 21 (1987), pp. 43–54.

Menken, M. J. J., "The References to Jeremiah in the Gospel according to Matthew (Mt. 2.17; 16.14; 27.9)," *ETL* 60 (1984), pp. 5–24.

Metso, Sarianna, "The Use of Old Testament Quotation in the Qumran Community Rule," in *Qumran between the Old and New Testaments* (ed. Frederick H. Cryer and Thomas L. Thompson; JSOTSS 290/Copenhagen International Seminar 6; Sheffield: Sheffield Academic Press, 1998), pp. 217–31.

Mettinger, Tryggve N. D., "Intertextuality: Allusion and Vertical Context Systems in Some Job Passages," in *Of Prophets' Visions and the Wisdom of Sages* (ed. Heather A. McKay and David J. A. Clines; JSOTSS 162; Sheffield: JSOT Press, 1993), pp. 257–80.

Meyer, Ben F., "Appointed Deed, Appointed Doer: Jesus and the Scriptures," in *Authenticating the Activities of Jesus* (ed. B. Chilton and C. A. Evans; NTTS 28/2; Leiden: Brill), pp. 155–76.

Meyer, Herman, *The Poetics of Quotation in the European Novel* (Princeton: Princeton University Press, 1968).

Michaelis, W., "πήρα," *TDNT* 6 (1968), pp. 119–21.

Miler, Jean, *Les Citations d'Accomplissement dans l'Évangile de Matthieu: Quand Dieu se rend présent en toute humanité* (AnBib 140; Rome: Pontifical Biblical Institute, 1999).

Moessner, D. P., *The Lord of the Banquet: The Literary and Theological Significance of the Lukan Travel Narrative* (Minneapolis: Fortress, 1989).

Moloney, Francis J., "The Reinterpretation of Psalm VIII and the Son of Man Debate," *NTS* 27 (1981), pp. 656–72.

Montefiore, C. G., and H. Loewe, *A Rabbinic Anthology* (New York: Schocken, 1974).

Morgan, Thaïs E., "Is There an Intertext in This Text? Literary and Interdisciplinary Approaches to Intertextuality," *American Journal of Semiotics* 3/4 (1985), pp. 1–40.

Morgen, M., "Lc 17,20–37 et Lc 21,8–11.20.20–24: Arrièe-fond scripturaire," in *The Scriptures in the Gospels* (ed. C. M. Tuckett; BETL 131; Louvain: Louvain University Press/Peeters, 1997), pp. 307–26.

Morrison, John, *An Exposition of the Book of Psalms, Explanatory, Critical, and Devotional,* vol. 1 (London: Ebenezer Palmer, 1832).

Moyise, Steve, *The Old Testament in the Book of Revelation* (JSNTSS 115; Sheffield: Sheffield Academic Press, 1995).

Müller, Mogens, *Der Ausdruck 'Menschensohn' in den Evangelien* (Acta Theologica Danica 17; Leiden: Brill, 1984).

Naveh, Joseph, and Shaul Shaked, *Magic Spells and Formulae: Aramaic Incantations of Late Antiquity* (Jerusalem: Magnes, 1993).

Neirynck, Frans, "The Minor Agreements and Q," in *The Gospel behind the Gospels: Current Studies in Q* (ed. Ronald A. Piper; NovTSup 75; Leiden/New York/Cologne: Brill, 1995), pp. 49–72.

———, "Q 6,20b-21; 7,22 and Isaiah 61," in *The Scriptures in the Gospels* (ed. C. M. Tuckett; BETL 131; Louvain: Louvain University Press/Peeters, 1997), pp. 27–64.

New, David S., *Old Testament Quotations in the Synoptic Gospels, and the Two-Document Hypothesis* (SCS 37; Atlanta: Scholars Press, 1993).

Newman, Judith H., "Lot in Sodom: The Post-Mortem of a City and the Afterlife of a Biblical Text," in *The Function of Scripture in Early Jewish and Christian Tradition* (JSNTSS 154; Sheffield: Sheffield Academic Press, 1998), pp. 34–44.

Nickelsburg, George W. E., Jr., *Resurrection, Immortality, and Eternal Life in Intertestamental Judaism* (HTS 26; Cambridge, Mass.: Harvard University Press, 1972).

Niditch, Susan, *Oral World and Written Word: Ancient Israelite Literature* (Louisville: Westminster/John Knox, 1996).

Niebuhr, Karl-Wilhelm, "4Q 521,2 II — Ein eschatologischer Psalm," in *Mogilany 1995: Papers on the Dead Sea Scrolls Offered in Memory of Aleksy Klawek* (ed. Z. J. Kapera; Qumranica Mogilanensia 15; Kraków: Enigma, 1998), pp. 151–68.

———, *Gesetz und Paränese: Katechismusartige Weisungsreihen in der frühjüdischen Literatur* (WUNT 2/28; Tübingen: Mohr Siebeck, 1987).

Nitzan, Bilhah, "The Laws of Reproof in 4QBerakhot (4Q286–290) in Light of Their Parallels in the Damascus Covenant and Other Texts from Qumran," in *Legal Texts and Issues: Proceedings of the Second Meeting of the International Organization for Qumran Studies, Cambridge 1995* (ed. Moshe Bernstein, Florentino García Martínez, and John Kampen; STDS 23; Leiden/New York/Cologne: Brill, 1997), pp. 149–65.

Norden, E., *Die Antike Kunstprosa*, vol. 1 (Stuttgart: Teubner, 1958).

O'Day, Gail R., "Jeremiah 9:22–23 and 1 Corinthians 1:26–31: A Study in Intertextuality," *JBL* 109 (1990), pp. 259–67.

Öhler, Markus, *Elia im Neuen Testament: Untersuchungen zur Bedeutung des alttestamentlichen Propheten im frühen Christentum* (BZNW 88; Berlin/New York: de Gruyter, 1997).

———, "The Expectation of Elijah and the Presence of the Kingdom of God," *JBL* 118 (1999), pp. 461–76.

Olsthoorn, M. F., *The Jewish Background and the Synoptic Setting of Mt 6,25–33 and Lk 12,22–31* (Studium Biblicum Franciscanium Analecta 10; Jerusalem: Franciscan, 1975).

Ong, Walter J., *Orality and Literacy: The Technology of the Word* (London: Methuen, 1982).

Osiander, Lucas, *Sacrorum Bibliorum*, vol. 3 (Tübingen: Georgium, 1592).

Osiek, Carolyn, "The Oral World of Early Christianity in Rome," in *Judaism and Christianity in First-Century Rome* (ed. Karl P. Donfried and Peter Richardson; Grand Rapids/Cambridge, U.K.: Eerdmans, 1998), pp. 151–72.

Oswalt, John N., *The Book of Isaiah: Chapters 40–66* (Grand Rapids/Cambridge, U.K.: Eerdmans, 1998).

Paffenroth, Kim, "The Testing of the Sage: 1 Kings 10:1–13 and Q 4:1–13 (Lk 4:1–13)," *ExpT* 107 (1996), pp. 142–43.

Paulien, Jon, *Decoding Revelation's Trumpets: Literary Allusions and the Interpretation of Revelation 8:7–12* (Andrews University Seminary Doctoral Dissertation Series 11; Berrien Springs, Mich.: Andrews University Press, 1987).

Pearce, Zachary, *A Commentary on the Four Evangelists and the Acts of the Apostles*, vol. 1 (London: E. Cox, 1777).

Pearson, John, *Critici sacri*, vol. 6 (Amsterdam: Balthasaris Christophi Wustii, 1698).

Peels, H. G. L., *The Vengeance of God: The Meaning of the Root NQM and the Function of the NQM-Texts in the Context of Divine Revelation in the Old Testament* (OTS 31; Leiden/New York/Cologne: Brill, 1995).

Penner, Todd C., "Inner-Biblical Interpretation, New Testament," in *Dictionary of Biblical Interpretation A-J* (ed. John H. Hayes; Nashville: Abingdon, 1999), pp. 540–43.

Perri, Carmela, "On Alluding," *Poetics* 7 (1978), pp. 289–307.

Perrin, Norman, *Jesus and the Language of the Kingdom* (Philadelphia: Fortress, 1976).

———, *Rediscovering the Teaching of Jesus* (New York: Harper & Row, 1976).

Pesch, Rudolf, *Das Abendmahl und Jesu Todesverständnis* (QD 80; Freiburg/Basel/ Vienna: Herder, 1978).

———, *Jesu Ureigene Taten? Ein Beitrag zur Wunderfrage* (QD 52; Freiburg/Basel/ Vienna: Herder, 1970).

———, *Das Markusevangelium* (2 vols.; 2d ed.; HTKNT 2; Freiburg/Basel/Vienna: Herder, 1977).

———, "Über die Autorität Jesu: Eine Rückfrage anhand des Bekenner- und Verleugnerspruchs Lk 12,8f par.," in *Die Kirche des Anfangs* (ed. Rudolf Schnackenburg, Josef Ernst, and Joachim Wanke; Freiburg: Herder, 1978), pp. 25–55.

Pesch, W., "Zur Exegese von Mt 6:19–21 and Lk 12,33–34," *Bib* 41 (1960), pp. 356–78.

Philonenko, Marc, "Les paroles de Jésus contre 'cette génération' et la tradition qoumrânienne," in *Geschichte — Tradition — Reflexion: Festschrift für Martin Hengel zum 70. Geburtstag, Band III: Frühes Christentum* (ed. Hubert Cancik, Hermann Lichtenberger, and Peter Schäfer; Tübingen: Mohr Siebeck, 1996), pp. 89–95.

Pietersma, A., *The Apocryphon of Jannes and Jambres the Magicians* (RGRW 119; Leiden/New York/Cologne: Brill, 1994).

Plummer, Alfred, *A Critical and Exegetical Commentary on the Gospel according to S. Luke* (ICC; Edinburgh: T. & T. Clark, 1922).

Pokorný, P., *The Genesis of Christology* (Edinburgh: T. & T. Clark, 1987).

Poole, Matthew, *A Commentary on the Holy Bible*, 3 vols. (McLean, Va.: Mac-Donald Publishing Co., 1962).

Pope, Marvin H., *Job* (AB; Garden City, N.Y.: Doubleday, 1973).

Primeau, Ronald, ed., *Influx: Essays on Literary Influence* (Port Washington, N.Y./London: Kennikat, 1977).

Puech, É., "Les deux derniers psaumes davidiques du rituel d'exorcisme 11QPsAp[a] IV 4–V 14," in *The Dead Sea Scrolls: Forty Years of Research* (ed. D. Dimant and U. Rappaport; STDJ 10; Leiden: Brill, 1992), pp. 64–89.

———, "11QPsAp[a]: un rituel d'exorcismes: Essai de reconstruction," *RevQ* 14 (1990), pp. 377–408.

Rabinowitz, Peter J., " 'What's Hecuba to Us?' The Audience's Experience of Literary Borrowing," in *The Reader in the Text: Essays on Audience and Interpretation* (ed. Susan R. Suleiman and Inge Crosman; Princeton: Princeton University Press, 1980), pp. 241–63.

Ravens, D. A. S., "The Setting of Luke's Account of the Anointing: Luke 7.2–8.3," *NTS* 34 (1988), pp. 282–92.

Rawlinson, A. E. J., *The New Testament Doctrine of the Christ* (London: Longmans, Green, 1926).

Reiser, Marius, *Jesus and Judgment: The Eschatological Proclamation in Its Jewish Context* (Minneapolis: Fortress, 1997).

Richardson, Peter, "The Thunderbolt in Q and the Wise Man in Corinth," in *From Jesus to Paul: Studies in Honor of F. W. Beare* (ed. Peter Richardson and J. C. Hurd; Waterloo, Canada: Wilfred Laurier, 1984), pp. 91–111.

Riffaterre, Michael, *Semiotics of Poetry* (Bloomington: Indiana University Press, 1978).

Robinson, James M., "Kerygma and History," in James M. Robinson and Helmut Koester, *Trajectories through Early Christianity* (Philadelphia: Fortress, 1971), pp. 20–70.

Robinson, John A. T., "Did Jesus Have a Distinctive Use of Scripture?" in *Christological Perspectives: Essays in Honor of Harvey K. McArthur* (ed. Robert F. Berkey and Sarah A. Edwards; New York: Pilgrim, 1982), pp. 49–57.

Roskies, David G., *Against the Apocalypse: Responses to Catastrophe in Modern Jewish Culture* (Cambridge, Mass./London: Harvard University Press, 1984).

Rosner, Brian S., *Paul, Scripture, and Ethics: A Study of 1 Corinthians 5–7* (AGAJU 22; Leiden/New York/Cologne: Brill, 1994).

Ross, J. M., "Which Zachariah?" *IBS* 9 (1987), pp. 70–73.

Rudolph, W., *Jona* (Tübingen: Mohr Siebeck, 1970).

Rüger, H. P., " 'Mit welchem Mass ihr messt, wird euch gemessen werden,' " *ZNW* 60 (1969), pp. 174–82.

Russell, D. S., *The Method and Message of Jewish Apocalyptic 200 BC–AD 100* (Philadelphia: Westminster, 1976).

Sabbe, M., "Can Mt 11,25–27 and Lc 10,22 Be Called a Johannine Logion?" in *LOGIA: Les Paroles du Jésus — The Sayings of Jesus. Mémorial Joseph Coppens* (ed. Joël Delobel; BETL 59; Louvain: Peeters/Louvain University Press, 1982), pp. 363–71.

Safrai, S., "Education and the Study of the Torah," in *The Jewish People in the First Century: Historical Geography, Political History, Social, Cultural, and Religious Life and Institutions* (ed. S. Safrai and M. Stern in cooperation with D. Flusser and W. C. van Unnik; Assen/Philadelphia: Van Gorcum/Fortress, 1976), vol. 2, pp. 945–70.

Sahlin, Harald, "The New Exodus of Salvation according to St. Paul," in *The Root of the Vine* (ed. A. Fridrichsen et al.; New York: Philosophical Library, 1953), pp. 81–95.

Sand, Alexander, *Das Evangelium nach Matthäus* (RNT; Regensburg: Friedrich Pustet, 1986).

Sanders, E. P., *Judaism: Practice and Belief 63 BCE–66 CE* (London/Philadelphia: SCM/Trinity Press International, 1992).

Sanders, James A., "From Isaiah 61 to Luke 4," in *Christianity, Judaism, and Other Greco-Roman Cults: Studies for Morton Smith at Sixty, Part One: New Testament* (ed. Jacob Neusner; SJLA 12; Leiden: Brill, 1975), pp. 75–106.

Sandmel, Samuel, "Parallelomania," *JBL* 81 (1962), pp. 1–13.

Sato, Migaku, *Q und Prophetie: Studien zur Gattungs- und Traditionsgeschichte der Quelle Q* (WUNT 2.29; Tübingen: Mohr Siebeck, 1988).

———, "Wisdom Statements in the Sphere of Prophecy," in *The Gospel behind the Gospels* (ed. Ronald A. Piper; NovTSup 75; Leiden: Brill, 1995), pp. 139–58.

Sawyer, John, *The Fifth Gospel: Isaiah in the History of Christianity* (Cambridge: Cambridge University Press, 1996).

Schaper, Joachim, *Eschatology in the Greek Psalter* (Tübingen: Mohr Siebeck, 1995).

Schiffmann, Lawrence H., *Reclaiming the Dead Sea Scrolls: The History of Judaism, the Background of Christianity, the Lost Library of Qumran* (Philadelphia/Jerusalem: Jewish Publication Society, 1994).

Schlatter, Adolf, *Der Evangelist Matthäus: Seine Sprache, sein Ziel, seine Selbständigkeit* (Stuttgart: Calwer, 1948).

———. *Das Evangelium des Lukas aus seinen Quellen erklärt* (2d ed.; Stuttgart: Calwer, 1960).

Schlosser, Jacques, "Les jours de Noé et Lot: A propos de Luc, XVII, 26–30," *RB* 80 (1973), pp. 13–36.

———, "L'utilisation des Écritures dans la source Q," in *L'Évangile exploré: Mélanges offerts à Simon Légasse* (ed. Alain Marchadour; LD 166; Paris: Cerf, 1996), pp. 123–46.

Schmid, Erasmus, *Opus sacrum posthumum* (Nuremberg: Michaelis Endteri, 1658).

Schnabel, Eckhard J., *Law and Wisdom from Ben Sira to Paul: A Tradition Historical Enquiry into the Relation of Law, Wisdom, and Ethics* (WUNT 2/16; Tübingen: Mohr Siebeck, 1985).

Schultz, Richard L., *The Search for Quotation: Verbal Parallels in the Prophets* (JSOTSup 180; Sheffield: Sheffield Academic Press, 1999).

Schulz, Anselm, *Nachfolgen und Nachahmen: Studien über das Verhältnis der neutestamentlichen Jüngerschaft zur urchristlichen Vorbildethik* (SANT 6; Munich: Kösel, 1962).

Schulz, Siegfried, *Q: Spruchquelle der Evangelisten* (Zurich: Theologischer Verlag, 1972).

Schüpphaus, Joachim, *Die Psalmen Salomos: Ein Zeugnis jerusalemer Theologie und Frömmigkeit in der Mitte des vorchristlichen Jahrhunderts* (ALGHJ 7; Leiden: Brill, 1977).

Schürmann, Heinz, *Das Lukasevangelium* (HTKNT 3/1, 2; Freiburg/Basel/Vienna: Herder, 1969, 1994).

Schutter, William L., *Hermeneutic and Composition in 1 Peter* (WUNT 2/30; Tübingen: Mohr Siebeck, 1989).

Schwemmer, Anna Maria, *Studien zu den frühjüdischen Prophetenlegenden* Vitae Prophetarum (2 vols.; TSAJ 50; Tübingen: Mohr Siebeck, 1996).

Scott, Thomas, *The Holy Bible* (Boston: Crocker & Brewster, 1844).

Shires, M., *Finding the Old Testament in the New* (Philadelphia: Westminster, 1974).

Siegert, Folker, "Early Jewish Interpretation in a Hellenistic Style," in *Hebrew Bible/Old Testament: The History of Its Interpretation*, vol. 1, *From the Beginnings to the Middle Ages (until 1300). Part 1, Antiquity* (ed. Magne Saebø; Göttingen: Vandenhoeck & Ruprecht, 1996), pp. 130–98.

Silberman, Lou H., "The Queen of Sheba in Jewish Tradition," in *Solomon and Sheba* (ed. James B. Pritchard; London: Phaidon, 1974), pp. 65–84.

Skehan, Patrick W., and Alexander A. Di Lella, *The Wisdom of Ben Sira: A New Translation with Notes* (AB 39; Garden City, N.Y.: Doubleday, 1987).

Smith, B. T. D., *The Parables of the Synoptic Gospels: A Critical Study* (Cambridge: Cambridge University Press, 1937).

Smith, Mahlon H., "No Place for a Son of Man," *Forum* 4/4 (1988), pp. 83–107.

Sola Pool, David de, *The Kaddish* (New York: Bloch, 1929).

Sommer, Benjamin D., "New Light on the Composition of Jeremiah," *CBQ* 61 (1999), pp. 646–66.

———, *A Prophet Reads Scripture: Allusion in Isaiah 40–66* (Contraversions: Jews and Other Differences; Stanford: Stanford University Press, 1999).

Sparks, H. F. D., ed., *The Apocryphal Old Testament* (Oxford: Clarendon, 1984).

Stanley, Christopher D., *Paul and the Language of Scripture: Citation Technique in the Pauline Epistles and Contemporary Literature* (SNTSMS 69; Cambridge: Cambridge University Press, 1992).

Steck, Otto H., *Israel und das gewaltsame Geschick der Propheten* (WMANT 23; Neukirchen-Vluyn: Neukirchener, 1967).

Stegner, William Richard, "The Use of Scripture in Two Narratives of Early Jewish Christianity (Matthew 4.1–11; Mark 9.2–8)," in *Early Christian Interpretation of the Scriptures of Israel* (ed. Craig A. Evans and James A. Sanders; JSNTSS 148; Sheffield: Sheffield Academic Press, 1997), pp. 98–120.

Steiner, Richard C., "Incomplete Circumcision in Egypt and Edom: Jeremiah (9:24–25) in the Light of Josephus and Jonckheere," *JBL* 118 (1999), pp. 497–505.

Strauss, David Friedrich, *The Life of Jesus Critically Examined* (Philadelphia: Fortress, 1972).

Strobel, A., *Untersuchungen zum eschatologischen Verzögerungsproblem auf Grund der spätjüdisch-urhristlichen Geschichte von Habakuk 2,2f.* (NovTSup 2; Leiden: Brill, 1961).

Stuhlhofer, Franz, *Der Gebrauch der Bibel von Jesus bis Euseb: Eine statistische Untersuchung zur Kanonsgeschichte* (TVG Monographien und Studienbücher; Wuppertal: R. Brockhaus, 1988).

Stuhlmueller, C., *Creative Redemption in Deutero-Isaiah* (AnBib 43; Rome: Biblical Institute, 1970).

Suleiman, Susan R., and Inge Crosman, eds., *The Reader in the Text: Essays on Audience and Interpretation* (Princeton: Princeton University Press, 1980).

Swancutt, Diana M., "Hungers Assuaged by the Bread from Heaven: 'Eating Jesus' as Isaian Call to Belief: The Confluence of Isaiah 55 and Psalm 78(77) in John 6.22–71," in *Early Christian Interpretation of the Scriptures of Israel: Investigations and Proposals* (ed. Craig A. Evans and James A. Sanders; JSNTSS 148; Sheffield: Sheffield Academic Press, 1997), pp. 218–51.

Sweeney, Marvin A., "The Book of Isaiah as Prophetic Torah," in *New Visions of Isaiah* (ed. Roy F. Melugin and Marvin A. Sweeney; JSOTSS 214; Sheffield: Sheffield Academic Press, 1996), pp. 50–67.

Swete, Henry Barclay, *The Apocalypse of St. John* (London: Macmillan, 1911).

Sysling, Harry, *Tehiyyat Ha-Metim: The Resurrection of the Dead in the Palestinian Targums of the Pentateuch and Parallel Traditions in Classical Rabbinic Literature* (TSAJ 57; Tübingen: Mohr Siebeck, 1996).

Talbert, Charles H., "Beginning to Study 'How Gospels Begin,' " *Semeia* 52 (1991), pp. 185–92.

———, *Literary Patterns, Theological Themes, and the Genre of Luke-Acts* (SBLMS 20; Missoula, Mont.: Scholars Press, 1974).

Talmon, Shemaryahu, ed., *Jewish Civilization in the Hellenistic-Roman Period* (Philadelphia: Trinity Press International, 1991).

Tàrrech, A. Puig, "Lc 10,18: La visió de la Caiguda de Satanàs," *Revista Catalana de Teologia* 3 (1978), pp. 217–43.

Tasker, R. V. G., *The Gospel according to St. Matthew* (TNTC; Grand Rapids: Eerdmans, 1973).

Taylor, Joan E., *The Immerser: John the Baptist within Second Temple Judaism* (Grand Rapids/Cambridge, U.K.: Eerdmans, 1997).

Teeple, Howard M., *The Mosaic Eschatological Prophet* (JBLMS 10; Philadelphia: Society of Biblical Literature, 1957).

Theissen, Gerd, *The Gospels in Context: Social and Political History in the Synoptic Tradition* (Minneapolis: Fortress, 1991).

Theissen, Gerd, and Annette Merz, *The Historical Jesus: A Comprehensive Guide* (Minneapolis: Fortress, 1998).

Theissen, Gerd, and Dagmar Winter, *Die Kriterienfrage in der Jesusforschung: Vom Differenzkriterium zum Plausibilitätskriterium* (NTOA 34; Freiburg/Göttingen: Universtitätsverlag/Vandenhoeck & Ruprecht, 1997).

Thompson, Michael, *Clothed with Christ: The Example and Teaching of Jesus in Romans 12.1–15.13* (JSNTSS 59; Sheffield: JSOT Press, 1991).

Trapp, John, *A Commentary on the Old and New Testaments* (5 vols.; 2d ed.; ed. W. Webster; London: Richard D. Dickinson, 1865).

Trench, Richard Chenevix, *Notes on the Parables of Our Lord* (8th ed.; New York: D. Appleton & Co., 1856).

———, *Studies in the Gospels* (2d ed.; London: Macmillan, 1867).

Trumbower, Jeffrey A., "The Role of Malachi in the Career of John the Baptist," in *The Gospels and the Scriptures of Israel* (ed. Craig A. Evans and W. Richard Stegner; JSNTSS 104; Sheffield: Sheffield Academic Press, 1994), pp. 28–41.

Tuckett, Christopher M., "1 Corinthians and Q," *JBL* 102 (1983), pp. 607–19.

———, *Q and the History of Early Christianity: Studies on Q* (Edinburgh: T. & T. Clark, 1996).

———, "Scripture in Q," in *The Scriptures in the Gospels* (ed. C. M. Tuckett; BETL 131; Louvain: Louvain University Press/Peeters, 1997), pp. 3–26.

———, "The Temptation Narrative in Q," in *The Four Gospels 1992: Festschrift Frans Neirynck* (ed. F. Van Segbroeck et al.; BETL 100; Louvain: Louvain University Press/Peeters), vol. 1, pp. 479–507.

Uchelen, N. A. van, "The Targumic Versions of Deuteronomy 33:15: Some Remarks on the Origin of a Traditional Exegesis," *JJS* 31 (1980), pp. 199–209.

Uro, R., "John the Baptist and the Jesus Movement," in *The Gospel behind the Gospels: Current Studies in Q* (ed. Ronald A. Piper; NovTSup 75; Leiden/New York/Cologne, 1995), pp. 231–57.

———, *Sheep among the Wolves: A Study on the Mission Instructions of Q* (Annales Academiae Scientiarum Fennicae Dissertationes Humanarum Litterarum 47; Helsinki: Suomalainen Tiedeakatemia, 1987).

van der Horst, Pieter W., " 'The Finger of God': Miscellaneous Notes on Luke 11:20 and Its *Umwelt*," in *Sayings of Jesus: Canonical and Non-Canonical: Essays in Honour of Tjitze Baarda* (ed. William L. Petersen, Johan S. Vos, and Henk J. de Jonge; NovTSup 89; Leiden/New York/Cologne: Brill, 1997), pp. 89–103.

————, *The Sentences of Pseudo-Phocylides* (SVTP 4; Leiden: Brill, 1978).

VanderKam, J. C., *The Dead Sea Scrolls Today* (Grand Rapids: Eerdmans, 1994).

VanderKam, J. C., and J. T. Milik, "The First Jubilees Manuscript from Qumran Cave 4: A Preliminary Edition," *JBL* 110 (1991), pp. 243–70.

Vanhoye, A., "L'utilisation du livre d'Ezéchiel dans l'Apocalpyse," *Bib* 43 (1962), pp. 436–76.

Vassiliadis, Petros, ΛΟΓΟΙ ΙΗΣΟΥ: *Studies in Q* (Atlanta: Scholars Press, 1999).

Vermes, Geza, *Jesus the Jew* (London: Fontana, 1972).

Wagner, J. Ross, "Psalm 118 in Luke-Acts: Tracing a Narrative Thread," in *Early Christian Interpretation of the Scriptures of Israel: Investigations and Proposals* (ed. Craig A. Evans and James A. Sanders; JSNTSS 148; Sheffield: Sheffield Academic Press, 1997), pp. 154–78.

Wailes, Stephen L., *Medieval Allegories of Jesus' Parables* (Berkeley: University of California Press, 1987).

Ward, R. B., "Partiality in the Assembly: James 2:2–4," *HTR* 62 (1969), pp. 87–97.

Wasserman, Earl R., "The Limits of Allusion in *The Rape of the Lock*," *Journal of English and Germanic Philology* 65 (1966), pp. 425–44.

Weder, Hans, *Die Gleichnisse Jesu als Metaphern: Traditions- und redaktionsgeschichtliche Analysen und Interpretationen* (FRLANT 120; Göttingen: Vandenhoeck & Ruprecht, 1984).

Wegner, U., *Der Hauptmann von Kafarnaum (Mt 7,28a; 8,5–10.13 par Lk 7,1–10): Ein Beitrag zur Q-Forschung* (WUNT 2/14; Tübingen: Mohr Siebeck, 1985).

Weiss, Johannes, *Jesus' Proclamation of the Kingdom of God* (ed. Richard H. Hiers and D. Larrimore Holland; Philadelphia: Fortress, 1971).

Wellhausen, Julius, *Das Evangelium Matthaei* (Berlin: Reimer, 1904).

Werner, E., " 'Hosanna' in the Gospels," *JBL* 65 (1946), pp. 97–122.

Wesley, John, *Explanatory Notes upon the New Testament* (New York: T. Mason and G. Lane, 1839).

West, Michael D., "Sherwood Anderson's Triumph: 'The Egg,' " *American Quarterly* 20 (1968), pp. 675–93.

Wettstein, Johann Jakob, *Novum Testamentum Graecum* (2 vols.; Amsterdam: Ex officina Dommeriana, 1751–52).

Wiefel, Wolfgang, *Das Evangelium nach Lukas* (THKNT 3; Berlin: Evangelische Verlagsanstalt, 1988).

————, *Das Evangelium nach Matthäus* (THKNT 1; Berlin: Evangelische Verlagsanstalt, 1988).

Wilkens, W., "Die Versuchung Jesu nach Matthäus," *NTS* 28 (1982), pp. 479–89.

Willey, Patricia Tull, *Remember the Former Things: The Recollection of Previous Texts in Second Isaiah* (SBLDS 161; Atlanta: Scholars Press, 1997).

Williams, J. G., *Those Who Ponder Proverbs: Aphoristic Thinking and Biblical Literature* (Sheffield: JSOT Press, 1981).

Wilson, R. McL., "The Gnostics and the Old Testament," in *Proceedings of the International Colloquium on Gnosticism, Stockholm August 20–25, 1973* (ed.

Geo Widengren; Stockholm/Leiden: Almqvist & Wiksell/Brill, 1973), pp. 164–68.

Wise, Michael O., *The First Messiah: Investigating the Savior before Jesus* (San Francisco: HarperSanFrancisco, 1999).

Wolff, Hans Walter, *Joel and Amos: A Commentary on the Books of the Prophets Joel and Amos* (Hermeneia; Philadelphia: Fortress, 1977).

Wolff, Peter, *Die frühe nachösterliche Verkündigung des Reiches Gottes* (FRLANT 171; Göttingen: Vandenhoeck & Ruprecht, 1999).

Wolzogen, Johann Ludwig, *Commentarius in Evangelium Lucae* (Opera Omnia; Amsterdam: n.p., 1656).

Young, Frances M., *Biblical Exegesis and the Formation of Christian Culture* (Cambridge: Cambridge University Press, 1997).

Zahn, Theodor, *Das Evangelium des Lukas ausgelegt* (4th ed.; Leipzig/Erlangen: A. Deichert, 1930).

———, *Das Evangelium des Matthäus* (Wuppertal: R. Brockhaus, 1984).

Zehnle, R. F., *Peter's Pentecost Discourse* (SBLMS 15; Nashville: Abingdon, 1971).

Zeller, Dieter, *Die weisheitlichen Mahnsprüche bei den Synoptikern* (FB 17; Würzburg: Echter, 1977).

———, *Kommentar zur Logienquelle* (SKKNT 21; Stuttgart: Katholisches Bibelwerk, 1984).

Zimmermann, Johannes, *Messianische Texte aus Qumran: Königliche, priesterliche und prophetische Messiasvorstellungen in den Schriftfunden von Qumran* (WUNT 104; Tübingen: Mohr Siebeck, 1998).

Zwingli, Ulrich, *Annotationes in Evangelium Matthaei* (ed. M. Schuler and J. Schulthess; Opera 6/1; Zurich: F. Schulthess, 1836).

Index of Names

Achelis, H., 115n.64, 170
Achtemeier, Paul J., 17n.55, 61n.173
Adeney, W. F., 241n.94
Adriaen, M., 104n.18, 126n.21, 132n.51, 136n.59, 228n.34
Aelfric, 54n.148
Aelianus, 243
Aesop, 180n.18, 240
Ainsworth, Henry, 54, 66n.193, 81n.30
Akiba, 37n.48, 38, 139
Albertus Magnus, 3, 30n.29, 39n.62, 47n.102, 52, 54n.141, 58n.158, 59n.165, 64n.183, 66n.193, 75n.3, 77n.10, 80, 87n.61, 101n.5, 108, 114n.54, 127n.23, 132n.51, 134n.56, 138n.71, 142n.2, 144n.8, 153n.55, 154n.58, 164n.37, 166n.43, 168n.52, 169n.61, 172n.1n.14, 227n.29, 238n.83, 239n.86, 240n.92, 243n.101
Albright, W. F., 127n.23
Allen, W. C., 127n.23
Alford, Henry, 64n.184, 66n.193, 92n.89
Allison, Dale C., Jr., 9n.28, 27n.14, 28n.15, 39n.47, 38n.57, 41n.73, 42n.83, 44n.88, 54n.144, 56n.154, 63n.182, 70n.202, 71n.208, 72n.209,n.212, 85n.1, 109n.37, 122, 151n.41, 166n.46, 167n.51, 169n.60, 188n.19, 191n.23, 202n.59, 215n.8, 216n.12,n.13, 218n.8, 219n.26, 221n.30, 224n.3,n.5, 232n.50, 237n.74,n.76, 239n.87, 241n.96
Allison, Kristine, x
Alter, Robert, 81n.33
Ambrose, 42, 93n.91, 146n.19
Anderson, Bernard W., 70n.205
Anderson, Gary, 101n.20
Anderson, Sherwood, 5
Andrews, Lancelot, 52

Apollinarius of Laodicea, 108n.353, 109n.36, 225
Apuleius, 54n.148
Aquinas, Thomas 82n.34, 96n.107, 134n.56, 146n.19, 165n.13, 172n.3, 174n.10
Arbesmann, R., 159n.10
Archer, Gleason L., 185n.4
Argyle, A. W., 127n.23
Aristotle, 173n.6
Artapanus, 54n.147, 89n.73, 90
Athanasius, 80, 97n.112
Augustine, 15, 31n.32, 80n.27, 97n.112, 115n.61, 228

Bahr, Gordon, J., 176n.3
Bailey, Kenneth E., 15n.44
Bardy, G., 226n.20
Bar-Hebraeus, 26n.9, 146n.19
Barnett, P. W., 218n.23
Barrett, C. K., 215n.9
Bartelink, G. J. M., 80n.30, 97n.112
Barton, John, 184n.1
Basil the Great, 65n.193
Bauckham, Richard, 137n.65
Baumann, Eberhard, 194n.31
Beale, Gregory K., 188n.19, 200n.55, 206n.63
Beare, F. W., 127n.23
Beasley-Murray, G. R., 134n.53, 138n.72
Beckwith, Roger, 84n.44
Bede, 48n.110, 53n.141, 65n.193, 80, 82n.34, 225
Beentjes, P. C., 188n.18
Bellinger, William H., Jr., 231n.45
Bengel, J. A., 39n.62, 92n.89, 94n.97, 144n.8, 219n.25, 243
Ben-Porat, Ziva, 21n.76
Berger, Klaus, 238n.79
Berkey, Robert F., 221n.31

271

Jansen, Joseph, 115n.64
Jastrow, M., 49n.121, 102n.11, 117
Jefferson, Thomas, 11
Jefford, Clayton N., 71n.208
Jeremias, Joachim, 40n.69, 52, 53n.136,
    54n.145, 78, 95n.102, 101, 121n.84,
    127n.26, 129n.30, 131n.43, 134,
    145n.15, 152n.47, 163n.29, 166n.40,
    176n.1, 180n.16, 224n.10, 237n.74
Jerome, 50n.123, 53, 60, 64n.188,
    84n.44, 104n.18, 109n.36, 115n.63,
    126, 136n.59, 151, 163n.30, 165, 39,
    195n.39, 218n.19, 226n.19, 228n.34
John the Persian, 50n.123
Johns, Loren, 54n.141
Johnson, Ben, 19
Johnson, Luke Timothy, 35, 142n.2
Jones, A., 160n.17
Jones, D. C., 65n.191
Jones, John N., 172
Joseph, Gerald, 5n.19
Josephus, 15, 16n.45, 47n.104,n.105,
    54n.147, 56n.152, 75n.2, 77n.13,
    79, 81n.32, 82, 83n.39, 84n.44, 87,
    88, 89n.73, 90, 93n.94, 95n.104,
    96n.107, 97, 102n.9, 120, 124n.7,
    125n.16, 137n.68, 143, 148, 149,
    151, 152n.45, 153, 155, 177,
    180n.18, 192, 193n.25, 194n.26,
    203, 216, 217, 218, 223, 224, 229,
    233n.54
Juel, Donald, 214n.3
Justin Martyr, 3, 42n.84, 47n.104,
    108n.35, 109n.36, 110n.39, 116n.67,
    120, 130n.36, 136n.153, 224n.11,
    228

Kampen, John, 32n.34, 65n.192,
    82n.35, 83n.35
Kapelrud, A., 195n.37
Kapera, Z. J., 32n.34
Käsemann, Ernst, 238
Kee, Howard Clark, 40n.69, 86n.54,
    138
Keener, Craig, 26n.7, 52n.130, 114n.54,
    180n.18, 236n.73

Keesmaat, Sylvia, 18n.59, 28n.18,
    71n.208
Kelber, Werner, 17n.55
Kellett, E. E., 18n.60, 161n.23
Kertelge, Karl, 78n.16
Kiesow, Klaus, 70n.205
Kimball, Charles A., 26n.7
King, Martin Luther, Jr., 1, 2, 4, 12, 17,
    19, 21
Kipling, Rudyard, 161n.23
Kirk, Alan, 9n.25, 95n.101, 160n.17
Kirkpatrick, A. F., 161n.23
Klein, Michael, 39n.63, 196n.42
Kloppenborg, John S., 9n.25, 29n.24,
    36n.46, 57n.156, 59n.163, 72, 74n.1,
    75, 76, 78, 95n.101, 97n.109, 100,
    122, 124n.11, 131n.43, 143n.7,
    144n.8, 206, 207, 231n.48, 239,
    240n.89
Knowles, Michael, 126n.19,
    127n.23,n.26, 233n.56
Koenig, J., 39n.63
Koester, Helmut, 229n.40
Koestler, Arthur, 189n.21
Koetschau, 115n.61, 129
Kollmann, B., 59
Kosch, Daniel, 3n.7
Kraft, Robert A., 2n.4
Kratz, R., 101n.5
Kristeva, Julia, 19n.66
Kugel, James L., 32n.34, 35n.443,
    37n.49, 40n.66, 67n.196, 68, 86n.52,
    226n.19
Kuhn, K. G., 177n.7

Lagrange, M.-J., 64n.184, 90n.76,
    101n.5, 127n.23, 134n.56, 164n.37,
    166n.43
Lake, Kirsopp, 184n.2
Lange, John Peter, 144n.8
Lapide, Cornelius à, 52, 66n.193,
    92n.89, 101n.5, 109n.39, 127n.23,
    153, 227n.29
Lemarié, J., 92n.89
Leroy-Molinghen, A., 46n.97, 50n.123
Leske, Adrian, 230n.41
Levenson, John R., 27n.14

Index of Scripture